Models for Effective Writing

J. KARL NICHOLAS

JAMES R. NICHOLL

Western Carolina University

ALLYN AND BACON

Boston London Toronto Sydney Tokyo Singapore

Editor in Chief, Humanities: Joseph Opiela
Editorial Assistant: Brenda Conaway
Production Administrator: Rowena Dores
Editorial-Production Service: York Production Services
Cover Administrator: Linda Dickinson
Manufacturing Buyer: Louise Richardson
Composition Buyer: Linda Cox

Library of Congress Cataloging-in-Publication Data

Models for effective writing / [edited by] J. Karl Nicholas, James R.
Nicholl.
   p.   cm.
  Includes index.
  ISBN 0-205-14001-7
  1. College readers. 2 English language—rhetoric. I. Nicholas,
J. Karl (James Karl). II. Nicholl, James R.
PE1417.M43 1994
808'.0427—dc20   93–11808
                                                                      CIP

 This textbook is printed on recycled, acid-free paper.

Credits

Pages 4: From *A Sand County Almanac: And Sketches Here and There* by Aldo
Leopold. Copyright © 1949, 1977 by Oxford University Press, Inc. Reprinted by
permission.

Page 42: Excerpt from "A Worn Path" in *A Curtain of Green and other Stories,*
copyright 1941 and renewed 1969 by Eudora Welty. Reprinted by permission of
Harcourt Brace Jovanovich, Inc.

*Credits continued on page 407, which constitutes an extension of the copyright
page.*

Printed in the United States of America
10 9 8 7 6 5 4 3 2 1   98 97 96 95 94 93

Contents

11 *Definition* 273

PART THREE: Persuasive Writing 299

12 *Argumentation Techniques* 305

Induction, Deduction, Refutation, Emotional Appeals

Topical Table of Contents

VIEWPOINTS ON LEISURE

VIEWPOINTS ON NATURE AND ECOLOGY

VIEWPOINTS ON WOMEN

VIEWPOINTS ON WORK

Preface

Models for Effective Writing was developed to help students increase their ability to read moderately difficult prose and to write effectively. When those skills are joined with critical, informed thinking, students will be able to use their enhanced communication skills to make valuable contributions to society on several levels. At the same time, they can derive personal satisfaction from success in business, science, education, and other professional fields.

The opening chapter of *Models for Effective Writing*, "The Reading Process," provides practical hints for improving reading comprehension, including a sample essay and suggestions for how best to read, understand, and remember the sorts of reading material that make up the body of the book. Chapter 2, "The Writing Process," descibes the time-honored tradition of using models to teach effective writing and explains the components of the writing process.

The book's main body has three parts, based on a writer's intended purpose: (1) Narrative-Descriptive Writing, (2) Expository Writing (explanatory), and (3) Persuasive Writing (argumentative). A further division results in ten chapters, each devoted to an important technique or rhetorial strategy for organizing and presenting written ideas.

Each chapter opens with a clear introductory explanation of its subject technique. Next comes a narrative example of a student applying that technique in conjunction with the writing process, resulting in a sample essay which illustrates that technique in clear form. Then follows a section comprised of student-written paragraphs and essays, to show that apprentice writers can master each technique; these samples will help boost the morale of fainthearted or previously unsuccessful student writers. Each chapter continues with a series of professionally written models of varying lengths, from short, single paragraphs to full-length essays, all chosen to illustrate various effective uses of the subject technique. The writing models are normally arranged within their respective section in order of increasing difficulty, and each selection is followed by discussion questions intended to help readers notice both content and form. Answers to these questions, along with additional teaching aids, such as sample vocabulary examinations and suggested writing topics, are provided in a separate *Instructor's Manual*, available upon request from the publisher.

The book closes with three other features: (1) an Appendix containing "A Short Guide to Material and Formal Fallacies"; (2) a Glossary providing concise definitions of writing terms used in the book (normally the names of these terms are printed in bold italic print on their first use in this text, like this: ***audience***); (3) an Index of Titles and Authors.

The writing models were chosen (1) to demonstrate the appropriate technique or writing strategy, (2) to be in a style worthy of study, and (3) especially in the case of professional writing, to have subject matter more timeless than timely. Refusing to try to catch and ride the next brief wave of topicality, we decided rather to be eclectic, even a bit old-fashioned, in our choices. Consequently, the selections should prove interesting to students of varying ages and backgrounds, especially for those who can become interested in well-wrought prose that often contains important ideas and provokes critical thought about both its style and content. Included are selections by representatives of diverse cultural groups, by female and male writers, and on a wide variety of subjects. An alternate Topical Table of Contents allows interested instructors and students to pick from that variety with more ease.

In preparing this book, we have especially benefited from the support, encouragement, and wisdom of Joseph Opiela, humanities editor-in-chief at Allyn & Bacon. Special thanks also go to his assistant, Brenda Conaway, along with Rowena Dores and Barbara Tsantinis. We are also grateful for the careful attention given to *Models for Effective Writing* in its development stages by the following reviewers: Margaret Franson, Valparaiso University; Loris Galford, McNeese State University; Charles Hill, Gadsden State Community College; Peggy Jolly, University of Alabama; Gloria John, Catonsville Community College; Kathy Mincey, Morehead State University; David Stooke, Marshall University. In the book's final stages we appreciated the careful, thoughtful copyediting and production work provided by Tamra Winters of York Production Services. The professionalism of all these people has been invaluable, though we certainly acknowledge our responsibility for any weak spots in this book, only asking that its users inform us of any detected.

Here at home, we are blessed always by the help of Mrs. Nancy Robinson Norgaard, the best of all possible English department secretaries. Further thanks go to our colleagues, William Paulk and Rick Boyer, for use of their previously published work. Finally, a few words are due our students, especially those whose writing serves here as models. Many of you are remembered, more are forgotten, but most of you learned to read and write better as we worked out ideas for this book together. Because of those experiences, *Models for Effective Writing* is a better book than it might have been, and we are better teachers. Thank you for everything.

J. K. N.
J. R. N.

1

The Reading Process

The reading selections in this book are included for two reasons. First, they serve as models for the writing patterns that you will be expected to learn to recognize in others' writing, and then to imitate in your own writing. We will discuss this relationship of your reading to your writing in the next chapter. But for the time being we will deal with the second purpose that the selections serve—namely, as reading assignments.

The need for the second purpose may not be readily apparent to you. You are reading this sentence, so you know how to read. In fact, you learned how to a long time ago. But there is more at stake here than polishing an acquired skill—a great deal more, in fact, if you expect to get full value from your education and to apply that education effectively in your professional as well as your private life.

Reading, Understanding, and Remembering

All of us have had the experience of trying to remember something that we read recently, and of being unsuccessful. Perhaps it was a newspaper description of a fatal pile-up on an Interstate highway or a magazine review of a new movie now showing at a nearby theater. We begin to share the information with someone, only to hesitate, before having to admit, "Well, I can't remember exactly. I think it said something like. . . ."

Such lapses are common. We can't be expected to remember everything that we've read, and generally we don't need to. Some-

1

times, however, we find ourselves in the position of *needing* to remember material: perhaps for a class we're taking, or for a job that we're expected to perform. At such times remembering may indeed be crucial, and if lapses of memory occur, then we are apt to regret not reading more carefully. *Careful* reading is the answer. We are going to give you some tips on how to read carefully, so that you can do two things:

1. understand what you have read, and
2. remember what you have read.

You must agree, however, that you are not likely to remember something you don't understand. Consequently, reading comprehension is the first and most important thing you must learn to do.

Keep Your Brain Engaged

The first step toward achieving a clear understanding of your reading is to keep your mind focused on the material you are trying to read. Perhaps this fact seems too obvious to be worth mentioning. Nevertheless, a wandering mind is the prime cause of comprehension failure. Like all human beings, you have an uncanny mind that can do more than one thing at a time. It can recognize and call the words on a printed page and at the same time flutter among a host of other distracting thoughts—the weekend trip home, the concert next Saturday, the conversation in the cafeteria yesterday, and what's for supper, anyway?

Distractions like these are harmless when they interrupt your casual reading, but you need to take steps to avoid them when you do serious reading, such as for work or school. Reading aloud is sometimes useful, but most minds can wander even then. For your important reading, we recommend making yourself—in body and mind—more alert. For example, you might try sitting in a chair at a desk or table instead of stretching out on a sofa or bed. That will help keep your body from getting too relaxed.

Now what about your mind? To keep your mind focused on your important reading, we suggest reading while holding a pencil in your hand. If you simply move the pencil's eraser below each line as you read it, at a speed that is just a little too fast for your mind to follow comfortably, then your mind will have to race a bit to keep pace. That bit of racing usually spells the difference between a mind that stays engaged in reading and one that tends to wander.

Do Something With It

Once you've managed to engage your mind by sitting up and by running your pencil along each line as you read it, you can take the next step toward improved comprehension. To achieve that, you need to do something with your reading.

Even people who read strictly for pleasure frequently feel that they need something more than just the experience of reading good books. For instance, they may form reading circles or book clubs, often at public libraries, to meet and talk over what they have read. Discussing their reading with other people helps those readers to understand better what they read privately. Similarly, any discussions that you have in your classes can have the same effect, allowing you a chance to question classmates about unclear passages or to compare responses to an especially thought-provoking paragraph or two. The very act of discussing what you have read will make the material more uniquely your own, as that sort of dialogue helps you to assimilate the new ideas contained in your reading into your ever-growing information system by examining, digesting, and filing for future use.

Mark It Up

In order to participate more profitably and enthusiastically in classroom discussions of reading assignments, you'll find it helpful to do some additional things with those selections beforehand. For example, the pencil used as a pacer also comes in handy as a means for doing something privately with your reading: You can use that pencil to mark the text as you read.

The most helpful thing you can do toward achieving an understanding of any piece of writing is to determine as soon as possible the writer's **thesis**; that is, the work's overall idea or point. Until you make that discovery, you will have to proceed tentatively, feeling your way. After you have determined the writer's thesis, you can read on with confidence, anticipating some things that the writer will include. The title of the piece is usually a good clue to the writer's main idea, but titles have to be fairly short and, consequently, do not always provide enough information to get the job done. If you read carefully the opening paragraph (or the first two or three paragraphs in longer essays), you will often find the writer's thesis. Underline it with your pencil, or highlight it with a marker. Read a bit further to determine whether this statement has been qualified or narrowed in some way. If it has, mark that qualification also. Let's look at a sample essay now to see exactly how this might be done.

Thinking Like a Mountain

ALDO LEOPOLD

A deep chesty bawl echoes from rimrock   1
to rimrock, rools down the mountain, and
fades into the far blackness of the night. It is
an outburst of wild defiant sorrow, and of
contempt for all the adversities of the world.

Every living thing (and perhaps many a   2
dead one as well) pays heed to that call. To
the deer it is a reminder of the way of all
flesh, to the pine a forecast of midnight scuf-
fles and of blood upon the snow, to the coyote a promise of gleanings to come, to the
cowman a threat of red ink at the bank, to
the hunter a challenge of fang against bullet.
Yet behind these obvious and immediate
hopes and fears there lies a deeper meaning,
known only to the mountain itself. <u>Only the</u>   *What does*
<u>mountain has lived long enough to listen</u>   *this mean?*
<u>objectively to the howl of a wolf.</u>

Those unable to decipher the hidden   3
meaning know nevertheless that it is there,
for it is felt in all wolf country, and distinguishes that country from all other land. It
tingles in the spine of all who hear wolves
by night, or who scan their tracks by day.

Even without sight or sound of wolf, it is implicit in a hundred small events: the midnight whinny of a pack horse, the rattle of rolling rocks, the bound of a fleeing deer, the way shadows lie under the spruces. Only the ineducable tyro can fail to sense the presence or absence of wolves, or the fact that mountains have a secret opinion about them.

unteachable beginner

What is that secret?

My own conviction on this score dates from the day I saw a wolf die. We were eating lunch on a high rimrock, at the foot of which a turbulent river elbowed its way. We saw what we thought was a doe fording the torrent, her breast awash in white water. When she climbed the bank toward us and shook out hcr tail, we realized our error: it was a wolf. A half-dozen others, evidently grown pups, sprang from the willows and all joined in a welcoming mêlée of wagging tails and playful maulings. What was literally a pile of wolves writhed and tumbled in the center of an open flat at the foot of our rimrock.

4

free-for-all

Personal account

In those days we had never heard of passing up a chance to kill a wolf. In a second we were pumping lead into the pack, but with more excitement than accuracy: how to aim a steep downhill shot is always confusing. When our rifles were empty, the old wolf was down, and a pup was dragging a leg into impassable slide-rocks.

5

We reached the old wolf in time to watch a fierce green fire dying in her eyes. I realized then, and have known ever since, that there was something new to me in those eyes› something known only to her and to the mountain. I was young then, and full of trigger-itch: I thought that because fewer wolves meant more deer, that

6

Aha!

no wolves would mean hunters' paradise.
But after seeing the green fire die, I sensed
that neither the wolf nor the mountain
agreed with such a view.

* * *

root out,
exterminate

Since then I have lived to see state after   7
state (extirpate) its wolves. I have watched
the face of many a newly wolfless mountain, and seen the south-facing slopes
wrinkle with a maze of new deer trails. I
have seen every edible bush and seedling   *disuse*
browsed, first to anaemic (desuetude), and
then to death. I have seen every edible tree
(defoliated) to the height of a saddlehorn.
Such a mountain looks as if someone had
given God a new pruning shears, and
forbidden Him all other exercise. In the end
the starved bones of the hoped-for deer herd,
dead of its own too-much, bleach with the
bones of the dead sage, or molder under the
high-lined junipers.

The effect of eliminating wolves.
The deer kill the mountain.

made leafless

I now suspect that just as a deer herd   8
lives in mortal fear of its wolves, so does a
mountain live in mortal fear of its deer. And
perhaps with better cause, for while a buck
pulled down by wolves can be replaced in
two or three years, a range pulled down by
too many deer may fail of replacement in as
many decades.

A mountain
takes longer
to recover
than a deer
herd does.

So also with cows. The cowman who
cleans his range of wolves does not realize
that he is taking over the wolf's job of
trimming the herd to fit the range. He has
not learned to think like a mountain. Hence
we have dustbowls, and rivers washing the
future into the sea.

Wolves
perform a
service for
the cattle-
men that
isn't readily
understood.

* * *

We all strive for safety, prosperity,   10
comfort, long life, and dullness. The deer
strives with his supple legs, the cowman
with trap and poison, the statesman with
pen, the most of us with machines, votes,

and dollars, but it all comes to the same thing: peace in our time. A measure of success in this is all well enough, and perhaps is a (requisite) to objective thinking, but too much safety seems to yield only danger in the long run. Perhaps this is behind Thoreau's (dictum) in wildness is the salvation of the world. Perhaps this is the hidden meaning in the howl of the wolf, long known among mountains, but seldom perceived among men.

necessity (margin note)

saying (margin note)

The mountain knows this! But do we? (margin note)

As mentioned earlier, an essay's title will usually furnish a general idea of the subject matter to follow. That is certainly true of this essay. Although at the outset it is not clear what Leopold means by thinking like a mountain, we nonetheless are prepared for the explanation that will emerge in the ensuing paragraphs. In other words, Leopold's title has provided us with an expectation that will focus our reading.

The essay's first paragraph does not serve to explain the title; instead, it introduces a wolf howling on the rimrock. Your initial response is probably to wonder what sort of connection might exist between the howling of a wolf and thinking like a mountain. You can register your puzzlement by placing a question mark in the margin alongside this paragraph. Surely the next paragraph will bring us back to the mountain and its thoughts.

In the second paragraph Leopold lists those for whom the wolf's howl holds a special meaning: the deer, the pine tree, the coyote, the cattleman, the hunter, and—lastly—the mountain. You underscore the last sentence in that paragraph because you sense that it holds a special significance: "Only the mountain has lived long enough to listen objectively to the howl of a wolf." Even as you underscore it, you may realize that this sentence is not the final explanation; it is only a reminder of a promise unfulfilled. Eventually, you will know what it means to think like a mountain, but not yet. You write in the margin: "What does this mean?"

In the next paragraph, Leopold continues to tantalize us. He concludes his further remarks about wolves with this sentence, which you also feel is important enough to underscore: "Only the ineducable tyro can fail to sense the presence or absence of wolves, or the fact that mountains have a secret opinion about them." You wonder: "What is that secret?" so you write that question in the margin. By now you have entered into a dialogue with the author.

The next three paragraphs contain a personal narrative, an account of how Leopold as a young man had participated in the shooting of a mother wolf and her cubs. He gave the reasons that prompted him then: "fewer wolves meant more deer . . . no wolves would mean hunters' paradise." You mark these reasons, as well as his somewhat startling conclusion: "I sensed that neither the wolf nor the mountain agreed with such a view." In the margin, you respond "Aha!" because now you have a fairly clear indication of what it means to "think like a mountain." Surely the decision to create a surplus of deer by killing wolves will prove as harmful to the mountain, in the long run, as it does to the wolves in the short run.

Your suspicions are confirmed in the next three paragraphs. You'd noted earlier that these paragraphs had been visually set off from the rest of the essay by a line of asterisks preceding and following them. Surely there was something special about those paragraphs. Now you see very clearly the reason for that special status. Having led us to speculate about the relationship that exists among the wolves, the deer, and the mountain, Leopold spells out that relationship for us. You mark these paragraphs as important by placing a vertical line in the margin beside each of them and by summarizing each paragraph's contents beside it in this manner: Para. 7: "The effects of eliminating wolves: the deer kill the mountain." Para. 8: "A mountain takes longer to recover than a deer herd does." Para. 9: "Wolves perform a service for the cattlemen that isn't readily understood." These brief summary statements are useful not just because they constitute a dialogue with the author, but because in composing these responses you've registered your own understanding of the essay's thesis. It has now become part of your information system.

In the concluding paragraph you underscore the quotation from Thoreau, "In wildness is the salvation of the world," which turns out to be the secret known by the mountain. You note appropriately, "The mountain knows this! But do we?" You also put a question mark in the margin to remind yourself of the paradoxical "too much safety seems to yield only danger in the long run."

While you have your pencil in hand, you will also be wise to circle any words whose meanings you are unsure of. Often, you need not go immediately to your dictionary to look them up, since you can form a pretty good idea of a word's meaning just from the sentence in which it appears. In this case you go ahead and mark several words, just to be safe: *ineducable, tyro, mêlée, extirpate, desuetude, defoliated, requisite,* and *dictum.* Later, when you've finished the reading assignment, you can look up the definitions and determine how close your guesses were. You may even wish to jot down synonyms or brief definitions in the margin.

When you've completed marking up the essay, it might look something like the sample "Thinking Like a Mountain" on pages 4–7 (but of course you will quickly develop your own marking system).

Outline It

If you're the kind of person who prefers not to mark up a book, or are reading materials that belong to others, such as library periodicals and books, there's an alternative method that you may use. You can devote a page in a notebook to each reading assignment, jotting down the thesis once you have discovered it, along with any additional observations that you wish to make. Some students find that one easy way to record these items is to create an outline in the form of a *branching diagram.*

When you discover the thesis of your reading assignment, state it in your own words in the middle of a sheet of paper. Draw a circle or box around your statement of the thesis, and then write the supporting information on spokes radiating from that central thesis statement. For instance, once you determined the thesis for "Thinking Like a Mountain," you might have stated it in your own words this way: "Killing wolves upsets a delicate balance in nature." This would serve as the central statement lodged within the circle, and radiating from it surely would be the two immediate effects arising from this claim, namely: *deer multiply as a result* and *cattle outgrow the range.* Below these statements you might wish to add other pieces of information gleaned from your reading. You might wish to include additional spokes. One spoke might focus on the author's early participation in the slaughter of wolves; another might deal with Leopold's concluding remarks about the riskiness of tampering with nature's balance and his allusion to Thoreau's notion that in wildness is the salvation of the world—an idea worth remembering.

Along with the outline you could also include questions or observations, as well as vocabulary items that you decided to look up. The resulting diagram might look something like Figure 1.1.

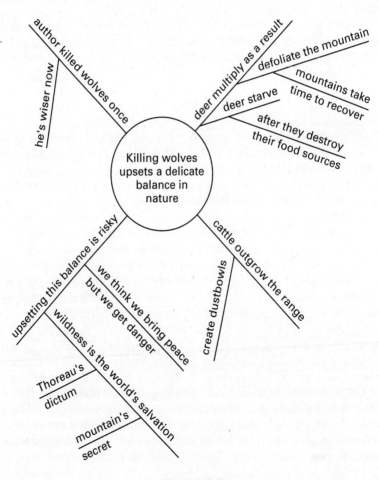

FIGURE 1.1

Whether you mark up the text and its margins or elect instead to outline your readings in a notebook, there is one final piece of advice that you'll find most useful. Try to discover, if you can, something about the writer. If you can find out any biographical data, such as the writer's age, education, occupation, political views, reputation, or affiliations, you may be able to use that information to set up some expectations about the way the piece develops, in much the same way that you set up some expectations based on the essay's title or thesis statement.

Regular readers of editorial pages will know ahead of time, for instance, that Marianne Means typically voices opinions of the political left, in comparison to Mike Royko, who shares many of her views but is much more likely to be ironic or otherwise humorous, while George Will almost always represents a conservative point of view in a scholarly and deliberate style.

So that you can have some biographical facts at your disposal as a way of preparing yourself for your reading in this book, we have provided a biographical headnote for each essay-length selection by a professional writer. It's a good idea to study that information before you begin the reading assignment, marking whatever facts seem to you most pertinent, and returning to the headnote after you have finished reading to make other marks as needed. Here is a headnote suitable for "Thinking Like a Mountain."

Aldo Leopold (1886–1948) was one of America's first ecologists. Educated at Yale, he joined the U.S. Forest Service in 1909 and worked in Arizona and New Mexico. There he developed his "land ethic," which ran counter to the thinking of his day. Rejecting the notion that the environment was something that belonged to humankind, Leopold believed that it was instead a community to which humankind belonged. In a series of essays during the 1920s, '30s, and '40s, Leopold expounded his "ecological consciousness." His philosophy is best summarized in Sand County Almanac *(1949), from which this essay is taken.*

Certain facts contained in the headnote would have had a direct bearing on your understanding of the essay to follow: Leopold was one of America's first ecologists and his notion of a "land ethic" ran counter to the thinking of his day. Armed with these two facts, you would have been much better prepared to formulate your expectations of what it means to think like a mountain.

Finally, you will also notice that we have included two sets of questions at the conclusion of each professional essay. These are labeled "Discussion: Content" and "Discussion: Form." As the word *discussion* suggests, these questions are intended to stimulate classroom discussions of the selections by examining their content or meaning and their organization and rhetorical form. Let's look now at the content questions associated with "Thinking Like a Mountain." We will return to this essay in the next chapter by examining the accompanying questions of form with respect to its organization and rhetorical tactics.

DISCUSSION: CONTENT

1. What particular problem concerns Leopold in this essay? Where does he state that problem in its clearest terms?
2. What broader ramifications or effects does the particular problem discussed here have? To what extent does Leopold allude to them? How does Leopold's *paradox* (see Glossary) in paragraph 10, that "too much safety serves to yield only danger in the long run," apply to aspects of life other than in wilderness settings? What examples confirming his statement come to mind in your own personal, school, and community life?
3. What does it mean to think like a mountain? What use is Leopold making of this notion? How does this notion have a broader application to human life in places other than the mountains, such as in our cities or along our waterways?

Since these questions are intended to generate classroom discussion, there will, of course, be a temptation to postpone answering them until you arrive in class. Resist that temptation. Go ahead and answer these questions as you complete your reading and marking of the selection. You surely have noticed that the practice of marginal markings or outlines that we have recommended has already done much to provide you with answers for the content questions anyway. A glance at the outline provides immediate answers for content questions 1 and 2.

In response to the first question, you note that the particular problem Leopold is concerned about is the effects of too many deer on the environment, specifically on a mountain. He shows that devastation in paragraph 7. The second question, which deals with broader ramifications or effects of the problem, is dealt with in paragraph 10. There Leopold refers to the grave dangers resulting from any disruption of the delicate balance of nature. Killing wolves is just one such disruption. The truth of the paradoxical claim that "too much safety serves to yield only danger" is borne out all too often: taking only easy courses will get you good grades but an inferior education; avoiding risks in other areas—from physical fitness, to civic affairs, to your love life—will all too frequently result in less than happy results. As the body builders tell us: "No pain, no gain."

Finally, the third question will require a bit more searching. You noted in your marginal markings, as well as in your diagram, that the mountain's secret is contained in Thoreau's statement: "In wildness is the salvation of the world." That statement makes a good deal of sense once you've read carefully the explanation Leopold provided in the starred section of the essay, and especially in paragraph 8, where he says that a mountain fears the deer as much as the deer fear wolves. People easily see the immediate effects of wolves—dead deer, dead cattle. However, they do not see the remote effects of too many deer—dead mountains—because they do not think like mountains. Beyond the wilderness setting, the importance of thinking like a mountain prevails. We welcome new industries to our communities without reflecting on the possibility that these industries may pollute our drinking water. We grumble over the expense of emission control devices on late model cars and often remove them so that gas mileage will improve, without stopping to consider the effect that such devices—or their absence—will have on the quality of the air we breathe.

So there you have it. Stay alert and use a pencil as you complete your reading assignments. Study the biographical head-notes and locate the thesis statement. Doing those two things will allow you to set up some expectations that your reading will more than likely fulfill. You will be reading with a purpose. Then mark the important passages that tend to confirm your expectations by supporting the thesis statement. Note any questions that the reading poses for you, and mark unfamiliar vocabulary words. Alternatively, you might prepare a branching diagram. When you finish reading, look up the unfamiliar words in a dictionary and then attend to the content questions, most of which will prove easy enough to answer if you read the assignment carefully and mark the text.

As you read and mark the assigned essays of this book, you will be improving your reading skills. Just as important, you will be adding to your mental reservoir of information, storing ideas for future use in your classes, in your conversations, and in papers that you will eventually write, for this class or for others.

As you read, you will also be adding to your storehouse of words, idioms, organizational devices, and stylistic tactics, and that brings us back to the first purpose of reading mentioned at the beginning of this chapter: your reading—whatever it may be—inevitably provides you with models for your writing. The next chapter deals with the process of writing and the ways in which the models contained in this book can assist you in successfully going through the stages of that process.

2

The Writing Process

By this point in your education you have probably figured out that few human activities are more important than the uniquely human form of expression that we call "writing." Indeed, the use of writing distinguishes humans from all other creatures, and educated humans from uneducated ones. Writing is especially important as the means for all lasting human communication; our beliefs, histories, laws, contracts, deeds, and wills all find permanent form in writing. As we interact with one another, we use writing to describe, to narrate, to explain, and to persuade.

Because writing is so important, people began to ponder its various elements centuries ago, striving to learn how and why writing works. Consequently, there developed various fields of study devoted to writing, each with its own designation. Most of us know, for instance, that grammar is one of those fields and that grammarians study such pieces of writing as words and sentences. The focus of this book, however, is not on any such narrow field; rather, it is on the study of writing in the broadest sense—on what the Greeks and Romans called ***rhetoric.***

Those two cultures, and most of their European successors over the following centuries, valued and honored effective speech and writing. When it became clear that a person's ability as an orator and as a writer could be improved through training, professional teachers of rhetoric (called rhetoricians) began to hold classes. Just as you will do when using this book, Greek and Roman pupils studied numerous examples (or models) of writing and speaking. They thereby learned the most effective and appropriate techniques to adapt for conveying their own ideas to specific reading and listening audiences. We will not concern ourselves with speech in this book, although several examples of writing that we've included were originally speeches. Rather, we've provided models of effective writing.

You understand, of course, that the models in this book are unique; other people wrote them for purposes and audiences and times that are different from yours. However, just as you can learn how to score better on the court or field by imitating the successful scoring moves of a more accomplished athlete, so also you can learn how to write more effectively by imitating the successful approaches of other writers. Furthermore, you probably understand that just as success in athletics, music, computer programming, or any other field does not come automatically or without practice and effort, so writing success also requires study and hard work. No piece of writing in this book sprang instantly and perfectly into being. If you could see this chapter as we first pieced it together—with its marginal notes, insertions, and scratched-out sentences—you would readily share our belief that no writer creates a perfect piece of writing on the first attempt, or even sometimes on the second or third.

That declaration about the difficulty of writing leads to this one: Writing is a process. Sometimes it begins with an assignment from a supervisor, teacher, or other authority figure; sometimes it comes from the heart or the mind (maybe as a sympathy note or as a letter of complaint). In any case, faced with the task, you begin the process. Inevitably, that process involves three basic related phases: *pre-writing, writing the first draft,* and *revising.*

Varieties of Pre-writing

During the prewriting phase of the writing process, you'll need to summon up all the resources that you have and bring them to bear on your chosen or assigned subject. At this time you may profitably consult actual models (such as the ones in this book) of the sort of writing that you plan to do. For example, if you need to write a movie review or want to pass on your recipe for a tasty dish, it would be helpful to examine a few reviews of other movies or to consult a cookbook to see what sorts of approaches others have used. You'll consider possible strategies you might want to employ, think about how best to reach your probable reading audience, and tinker with organizational schemes. You'll jot down useful illustrations, write yourself notes, and even make outlines. In other words, you will immerse yourself in the subject.

Freewriting

One way to immerse yourself in your subject is to do some "freewriting," quickly jotting down random thoughts that enter your head as you mull over a certain topic or idea. You may do freewriting anywhere, at any time, and for almost any reason— not just in a class notebook in your room or in the school library but even on napkins in the snack bar or cafeteria. Such writing is done usually in response to a stimulus; that is, some statement, overheard or read, or else some event, witnessed or learned about, causes you to pause momentarily and to check your mental bearings. You might have just learned something new or something that caused you to restructure the way you perceived the world, and the best way to fix that information in your mind for all time is to write down your response to it.

Sometimes the response is nothing more than a restatement of the stimulus in your own words: what Bill said yesterday at lunch; how the sun looked last evening; or what it means to think in the long term, like a mountain, which you learned from the Aldo Leopold essay (Chapter 1). But sometimes you will feel compelled to record your personal responses, feelings, or attitudes to these restatements: what you should have said in response to Bill; how the sunset made you feel or what it reminded you of; and perhaps how careless you have been recently about even the immediate, much less the remote, effects of your actions.

Of course, while in school you will often have to write in response to the stimulus of an assignment with a definite due date. Even then, however, you will find useful ideas coming to you at a variety of times, so that keeping writing paper—even a note card—handy at most times is a smart tactic. Too often a lost thought is never found again.

Journals

The best place for the kinds of responses we have just been discussing is in a journal—perhaps just a simple notebook, small enough for you to carry about with you in a pocket or purse. In this journal you can record your casual thoughts in response to the daily happenings of your life. More important, you can also use it to respond to your reading.

During this course, the stimulus for a great deal of your freewriting will likely come as responses to reading assignments made in this book by your instructor. You will also be assigned various writing tasks, and your journal is one good place to begin working on them.

If you're the kind of person described in Chapter 1 who prefers not to mark up your book, you'll probably be inclined to outline your reading in a notebook, responding to the study questions that follow each reading selection after you've completed an outline. The study questions are of two types, those dealing with the reading selection's content and those dealing with its form. In the last chapter, we suggested you would find it profitable, as a way of confirming your understanding of the material, to respond to the content questions after you'd read the assignment and marked the text or prepared an outline. After completing the content questions, you might quickly write down in your journal your personal response to the selection, your thoughts that arose as you read or as you tried to answer the questions, or perhaps questions that occurred to you as a result of the effect the reading had on you. Write them all down. Your journal is an excellent place to continue the dialogue that you began with the author in the margins of the book or on your outline page. Those random thoughts often prove to be useful starting points for your own papers.

Your journal is also a good place to jot down answers to the second group of questions that follow this book's reading selections—those on form. Just a quick glance through the remainder of this book or its table of contents will quickly reveal that it is organized around the various writing forms; indeed, all the remaining chapters are devoted to discussions of those individual forms, and the reading selections that appear in each chapter illustrate them. The questions of form that follow each selection help direct your attention to the ways in which that piece corresponds to the particular form.

You should also respond to the form questions, as well as those devoted to content, in your journal for two very good reasons. First, they will improve your understanding of each form of writing discussed in this book. Second, experimenting with a form (such as examples, comparison, or cause and effect) and letting it suggest ways to order your own experiences may prove to be just as useful in your freewriting exercises as are your responses to the reading selections' content. To see how that might work, have a look at the following sample form questions for the Aldo Leopold essay "Thinking Like a Mountain," which you encountered in Chapter 1. Before attempting to answer those questions, it would be wise to turn back and have another look at the marked-up version of the essay on pp. 4–7 and the branching diagram on p. 10.

DISCUSSION: FORM

1. What is the central thesis of this essay?
2. What is the purpose of the narrative in paragraphs 4–6 describing the killing of a wolf?
3. In how many places in the essay does Leopold repeat the idea of thinking like a mountain? Why does he do this?
4. What is Leopold's purpose in dividing his essay with asterisks into three sections of decreasing size?
5. In paragraphs 7–9, Leopold concentrates on immediate and remote effects. What other methods of development does he use to make his case in these three paragraphs?

The answer to question 1 can be determined very easily just by glancing at the marked essay or at the diagram. The thesis is something like this: Killing wolves has long-range effects that few people perceive. Leopold supplies those long-range effects in the essay, particularly in the section set off by asterisks.

Answering the remaining questions poses a bit more of a challenge. In question 2, the personal narrative creates reader interest by telling a brief story (we all like stories), and it also serves as a vantage point from which Leopold can view the reversal of his attitude toward wolves, and the beginning of his appreciation of the need to preserve a balance in nature.

Question 3 obliges you to scan the entire essay, searching out instances in which Leopold uses the phrase *thinking like a mountain.* That much is easily done; the instances occur in paragraphs 2, 3, 6, 8, and 10. You marked these in the text, either underscoring the references or marking the paragraphs with vertical lines. The second part of the question, dealing with Leopold's reason for the repetition, calls for some speculation. Clearly, things are repeated because they are important. Leopold uses this repetition to reinforce the notion that human ways of thinking are too short-sighted, that mountains can see longer and farther because they last longer. It's not an easy idea for us short-lived humans to grasp, and he needs to pound it home.

In response to question 4, you note that the asterisks serve to set off paragraphs 7 to 9 from the remainder of the essay. These paragraphs, treating the short-term and long-range effects of killing wolves, contain the core of Leopold's message, his explanation of what it means to think like a mountain. He uses the special marks to alert us to the importance of this portion of the essay. What precedes it has been a useful introduction, and what follows it serves as his conclusion.

The answer to the last question probably demands a greater understanding than you now have of the methods of development commonly used in writing. The question asks you to determine what methods, besides cause and effect, Leopold uses in the three crucial paragraphs of his essay. Nevertheless, it will serve you well to turn for a moment to the table of contents, where you will notice immediately that this book is arranged according to the various methods used in the development of writing: description, narration, exposition by examples, classification, process, comparison, and so on. As the weeks pass, you'll become familiar with each of these methods in turn, and you may expect that the form questions accompanying the reading assignments will often call your attention to the methods writers have used in developing the individual essays, just as the Leopold example does.

Thus, in paragraph 7, in addition to pointing out the immediate effects of exterminating wolves, Leopold also outlines the steps in the **process**, as the multiplying deer herd overgrazes the mountain. He uses **description** to show the effects, and he even uses an **analogy**, suggesting that the mountain looks as if God had taken pruning shears to it. In paragraph 8, Leopold makes a literal **comparison** between the mountain and the deer, suggesting that the mountain fears the deer in just the same way that the deer fear the wolves. He also compares the length of time it takes for a ravaged deer herd or a ravaged mountain to reestablish itself. Finally, in paragraph 9, Leopold again uses ***analogy,*** likening the service that the wolves provide in trimming the deer population to the cattlemen's obligation to keep their cattle herds trimmed to fit the range—an obligation they may neglect at their peril.

As you answer form questions such as these in your journal, you'll be preparing for any discussion of them that may arise in class, but you'll also be obliging your mind to range over the various cause and effect relationships that exist, not just in the events of the essay, but in all your daily activities. For example, in response to the content questions on Leopold's essay, you might have reflected on your own attitude toward wolves, deer, the ecological movement in America, or the general short-sightedness of most human beings. However, in response to this essay's form, you might very easily find yourself taking notes about a variety of other cause and effect relationships: your home town and why it has grown or failed to grow; your algebra class and why it is proving to be such a challenge; a party last weekend and why it turned out so well—or so badly. You might explore the immediate effects as well as the more remote effects of each of these situations.

You can make your journal a kind of personal diary of your random thoughts. At the same time, you can also make your journal the response log for your reading. Both of these approaches will prove useful in more ways than you can easily imagine.

For one thing, glancing back over the accumulated entries in your journal will quite often prove to be a good way of getting started on a piece of writing. Quite often you'll discover that you've already recorded some information or some attitude that will prove useful in the development of an assigned paper. That certainly was the case for one of our students, a white water canoeist, who had entries scattered throughout his journal that dealt with his avocation. When it came time, in response to a class assignment, to compare two activities, Gordon was more than ready. He merely had to reread his notes on canoeing and rafting and to make a simple outline in order to start the process of assembling ideas for his essay, used as a model in Chapter 8, "Comparison and Contrast" (see pp. 184–186).

Sometimes it will be your journal responses to class reading assignments that will touch off your thought processes and launch you into the prewriting step of your assignment. That happened to Gary (see pp. 316–319) when he looked over his responses to two of the essays in the Argumentation section. He could see the similarity in the approaches of two writers toward persuading their audiences, and therefore he was confident that he could use the same pattern.

Sometimes the daily events recorded in the journal will merge and blend with those triggered by the reading assignments in a very fortunate way. That was certainly the situation with Faye (see pp. 158–162), who had donated blood just the day before her process essay assignment was announced. A nursing major, she had made some journal notes about the event because it was a new experience for her, but the prospect of using that as the topic for her process paper was not confirmed until after she'd read and responded to the essay dealing with how a mosquito extracts blood from its victims. The two ideas reinforced one another, so Faye was ready to create a successful essay because she had both the idea and the pattern to develop that idea.

Often, you may not make any relevant journal entries until after an assignment has been made. Yet even then you can use the techniques that you've grown comfortable with in keeping your journal. Javon (see pp. 35–40) used the branching diagram we described in Chapter One to assemble his thoughts in describing his dormitory room. Neeife (see pp. 64–67) used a more traditional sort of outline to organize his narrative.

All of the students mentioned thus far have had one thing in common: they used their journals to stimulate their thoughts and to thereby begin the writing process. Once they'd begun to grapple with the issues, they already had a convenient starting place for transferring their thoughts onto paper.

There are, of course, a number of other thought-stimulating ways to perform the prewriting phase of composition. Your instructor may introduce you to such techniques as *webbing* or *clustering* (very similar to the outlining technique described and illustrated on pp. 9–10 and 36–38), *cubing, heuristics* (questions), or various other useful approaches for coming to terms with a topic and beginning to organize your thoughts on it.

Writing the First Draft

Sooner or later, you will have to select the most promising ideas, notes, or outlines generated by your prewriting attempts and actually begin to write. You may choose to make your first attempt at the assignment a part of your journal so you can refer more easily to your earlier jotting. Alternatively, you may feel it is time to start with a clean sheet of paper—or a blank diskette in your word processor. In either case, you will be starting the second phase, the actual writing of the piece, or at least of its first draft. You may be lucky and discover that an initial strategy or organizational plan works smoothly, with all the concrete details you jotted down earlier falling neatly into place. That seldom happens, however. More often you will have several false starts, plans whose promise evaporates almost as soon as you begin to put them into execution. Luckily, though, new and better ideas will frequently occur to you after you begin writing, further evidence that immersing yourself in your subject is crucial to writing success.

Whatever the case, you should strive to achieve three things in a first draft:

1. a suitable limiting of your topic (that is, a statement of thesis), along with a clear notion of your intended audience and your purpose in writing for it,
2. the inclusion of sufficient illustrations or evidence, and
3. an effective arrangement of your materials.

Of course, those were the things you were working toward when you were doing such things as freewriting, searching your journal, and creating outlines or organizational schemes in the prewriting phase. But you will never know for sure how effectively you have accomplished those three aims until you actually try to write the first draft. Quite often you are not the best judge of how satisfactory your efforts have been. That is why you may find it quite useful to have someone (or, better yet, a small group or circle of people) to turn to at crucial points in the writing process.

The Reading/Writing Group

In teaching our own classes, we often find it useful to divide students into groups of two, three, or four, to serve as mutual assistance groups for various stages of the writing process. Sometimes we schedule time in class for these groups to share their efforts and to respond to one another's progress, but we also encourage groups to meet outside of class, as well—at the library, at the snack bar, or in a dorm study room.

Usually the in-class meetings of these groups are dedicated to going over early stages of planning or of first drafts. One of us prefers to have his student groups gather in "helping circles" and merely "round-robin" each person's paper, passing it around for scrutiny until each paper reaches its creator again, with notes for improvement added by each person. But other teachers may prefer to have their students operate in a more structured way, perhaps following such simple guidelines as these:

1. Group members in turn pass out enough photocopies of their rough drafts so that each person has one.
2. Beginning with a selected paper, all members will read it silently. After the silent reading, the author will read the paper aloud while others follow along. Group members may mark their copies but may not interrupt the reading.
3. At the conclusion of each person's reading, each group member tries to make at least one positive or encouraging comment about the draft, usually focusing on how well it accomplished the three goals of the first draft: limiting the topic, adequacy of support, and arrangement. Only after everyone has commented positively is time allowed for suggestions or for the reader to ask for specific help with the piece of writing. Then the procedure is repeated for the next person in the circle until everyone's draft has been discussed by the group.

Suggestions usually deal with ways in which the writer might more effectively realize each of the three goals mentioned earlier. Often, some of the best, most convincing illustrations or evidence come from this sharing of ideas. Finally, in providing their responses, the readers are giving the writer valuable assistance about how effectively the draft has taken its audience into account—whether the illustrations were too sparse or simple or too general or difficult, or perhaps how they didn't seem relevant or were even an insult to some reader's intelligence. The comments will also reveal attitudes that members of the audience may have toward the topic, feelings that need to be taken into account for subsequent drafts of the paper.

Although we set aside the most class time for reading/writing groups to go over first drafts, we also allow time for groups to meet less formally during the prewriting stage of each assignment because we've learned that many profitable things can happen as a result of such meetings. For one thing, students are actually encouraged to begin working on the assignment soon after it's made, rather than putting it off. Sometimes, too, writers simply get stuck and need some help or some encouragement. Many of the case histories that precede the Student Work sections in each of the following chapters describe contributions made by members of the reading/writing groups at just such informal gatherings. Neeife (see p. 65) found the encouragement that he needed to get beyond the freewriting state. Margo (see p. 96) needed help in deciding which of two possible alternative paths she should follow in developing her illustration paper.

Once over the hurdle of composing the first draft, and after that draft has been reviewed and criticized, there comes the final phase (often several steps), which is revising the draft.

Revising the Draft

The foremost purpose of revision (literally "to see or view again") is to ensure that the objectives of the first draft have been adequately met. Once the reading/writing group (or any other objective reader) has had a chance to respond to your original draft, then you will need to review the suggestions for changes and adopt those that seem most likely to give your piece of writing sharper focus, adequate support, and effective organization. Seldom will you want to incorporate every suggestion, but quite often certain ones tend to trigger additional thought processes, making even better ideas emerge. Thus, revision at its best can become a very positive event in the writing process, a matter of selecting the best from a veritable cornucopia of information that has replaced the nearly blank page of the prewriting stage.

We find that it is helpful, if time allows, to schedule one or more additional meetings of the groups to go over subsequent drafts. Group members of course like to see just how many of their suggestions have been included—and how well. It is also good at this point, after all the larger parts have been put into place, to attend to matters of introductions, transitions, and conclusions, as well to the important matters of grammar and style.

Again, the same rules of conduct should prevail, with readings and positive comments preceding criticisms, but now group members should note any problems with grammar, spelling, or usage on their copies, as well as suggestions for stylistic changes.

During this revision phase, you should begin paying conscious attention to matters of grammar and style, thus minimizing the work that you and the reading group will need to do at second or subsequent readings of the revisions of this piece of writing. A standard reference grammar, such as your freshman handbook, will help you correct any usage errors that might have survived the prewriting and first draft steps, when your attention was more appropriately focused on transferring ideas from your brain onto paper. Now the time has come to begin making sure that subjects and verbs agree, to insert commas and semicolons, and to check for spelling faults. Just as important, though more difficult, is the matter of style, for now the choice is not between acceptable and unacceptable phrasing but between several alternatives, all of which are acceptable but some of which are more effective than others in conveying your ideas.

As you become more proficient, you will be able to juggle numerous grammatical and stylistic considerations as you write your first draft, pausing momentarily to determine the appropriate case of a pronoun, deciding between a semicolon or a period, or recasting a sentence for better effect. Nonetheless, in almost every case, you will find it best to avoid too much revision during the preparation of your initial draft. However, once that initial draft is completed, under no circumstances should the revision of that draft (or any later drafts) be slighted or, even worse, ignored altogether.

It should now be clear to you that this book's value lies chiefly in the assistance it offers you in the early phases of the writing process: in prewriting and in the preparation of your first draft. Studying it will provide two obvious benefits. First, you need to have something to write about, and the diverse array of reading selections furnishes a kind of launch pad for your prose flights by providing interesting, sometimes controversial, materials for you to think about and respond to. Second, these selections, chosen from the work of student and professional writers, illustrate a variety of writing strategies or organizational plans that you may adapt to your own writing projects.

It's now time to begin the careful exploration of those writing strategies and organizational plans. Let's start with an overview of the three essential types of writing.

Types of Writing

Prose writing may be divided into three types, based on the effect the writing is supposed to have on its audience. The first type, ***narrative-descriptive*** writing, strives to make readers see and feel as it presents a scene or series of actions witnessed or imagined by the writer. Travelogues, news accounts, short stories, and novels are familiar examples of narrative-descriptive writing.

The second kind of writing is called ***exposition.*** In expository writing, the writer presumes that readers do not know some piece of information and therefore seeks to explain it. Textbooks, essays, reports, instruction manuals, and legal documents furnish examples of expository writing. It is the most common type of writing both in school and in work situations, and you should therefore learn to master it to the best of your ability.

The third type of writing is ***argumentation,*** in which the writer presumes that readers either have no opinion concerning the subject matter or else they hold a contrary one. The purpose of argumentation then becomes the addition of new information (when this is all that is necessary), or more often the discussion of known information in a way that will persuade readers to change their minds about the subject, adopting instead the writer's opinion on the matter. Advertisements, scholarly and scientific treatises, debates, congressional speeches, and editorials provide examples of this kind of writing.

It is important that you understand these divisions, not only because they provide the framework for this book, but because they will help you answer the most important question that will confront you as a writer: What is my purpose in writing? If you want to make your audience see and feel, you will write in a narrative-descriptive mode and use narrative-descriptive techniques. If you want to inform, to educate, to expand your audience's fund of information, then you will write in an expository style, using expository techniques. If you want to change the minds of your readers—or at least open them to new ideas or viewpoints—you will write persuasively, using the techniques of argumentation.

You should now be ready to begin examining closely the writing models in this book, studying how both professional and student writers organize and present their materials by using these three major types or strategies. With the guidance of your instructor and this book, you will then learn to adapt these techniques to your own writing, in English class as well as in other classes, and at work as well as in school.

PART ONE

Narrative-Descriptive
Writing

Narrative-descriptive writing may be essentially either narration or description. Both have as their object an appeal to the senses. You want your reader to see and feel the scenes and actions that you are relating. When describing, you will concentrate primarily on things (nouns), rather than concerning yourself with the actions (verbs) in which things participate. Writing is purely descriptive when it catches a scene somewhat as a photograph does, frozen into a moment of time but full of things that recommend themselves for examination.

Narration, on the other hand, is more than mere description; it does as much yet goes beyond it. Where description focuses its attention on nouns, narration focuses on both nouns and verbs. It brings the still photograph to life so that the things described begin to move about and interact.

Here is a strictly descriptive sentence:

1. He was a skinny boy with protruding teeth and enormous freckles.

Notice how the key word *boy,* a noun, is enlarged upon by the other elements in the sentence. The writer is concentrating on description.

Similarly, the writer may concentrate on action:

2. He bounded into the room, throwing off his coat and muffler, tossing his books onto the sofa.

Observe how the phrases introduced by *throwing* and *tossing* enlarge on the action proposed by the main verb *bounded*, providing the reader with additional actions occurring simultaneously with the entry into the room.

But writers seldom concentrate on action alone. They usually combine the two techniques and concentrate on both things and actions—on nouns and verbs—as in this sentence:

  3. A skinny boy with protruding teeth and enormous freckles, he bounded into the room, throwing off his coat and muffler, tossing his books onto the sofa.

This combination, then, is what is generally understood to be narration (or narrative writing): the telling, however brief, of a story's events.

As you perhaps have ascertained, although description may exist apart from narration, narration cannot exist apart from description. To put it another way, you can describe a scene as a still life, as in a portrait or a photograph, without alluding to actions, but you cannot convey *action* without also *describing* the participants involved in those actions.

In accordance with the definitions provided here, description being the more fundamental of the two rhetorical methods, we'll begin with the chapter on description.

3

Description

Description is the place to begin when learning to write effectively because, as explained on page 30, it is fundamental, the foundation on which narration must build. As a consequence, *in writing a description you, like a painter or sculptor, must render in another medium—sentences—an accurate copy of what is experienced at one frozen moment in time.* In pure description, *you will not be concerned with actions.* There are three basic means by which you can achieve your goal of creating an accurate copy of an experience via description. You will rely exclusively on **qualities, details,** and **comparisons.**

Qualities

Descriptive terms usually involve **qualities,** words such as *dull, friendly, awkward,* or even such vague or general words as *good, bad, pretty,* or *nice.* But because these words are not specific, they only serve to point to a direction in which further development may go. In other words, they merely get things started. If, for example, you write

1. He was a peculiar fellow.

With no more information than this, your reader can get only a general sense of what you mean. You have attributed one quality to the noun *fellow.* Your reader knows that the fellow is not ordinary, that he's *peculiar*. But beyond that, your reader knows nothing. You have only managed to get a description started. And that is what qualities are chiefly good for: they get things started; they focus your reader's attention in some direction, frequently on one or the other of the five senses. For instance:

sight—colorful, gaudy, sparkly, picturesque
hearing—loud, quiet, noisy, grating
smell—rotten, acrid, noxious, pungent, savory
taste—sweet, sour, tangy, zesty, delicious
touch—hard, soft, rough, smooth, comfortable

But more often than not, the quality you start with will be one like *peculiar*, which is difficult to relate to any of the senses without some additional information. Clearly, you need something more than qualities if you expect any reader to see, feel, and experience the object or scene you wish to focus on. You need to add **details**.

Details

Providing details strengthens the description and makes it come alive. In sentence 1 the reader can see the subject, but dimly; you can improve the image, bring it into sharper focus, by adding details. These are words and phrases for specific colors, measurements, statistics, proper names (Nike, Blazer, Chicago Bulls), and the like. See what happens when you add such details as these:

2. He was a peculiar fellow, wearing a Ralph diLaurente dinner jacket with his stone-rubbed, kneeless jeans and sporting a head of spiked, chartreuse hair.

Here the added details verify and clarify the fellow's alleged peculiarity. To create a more complete description, you would continue to concentrate on other aspects of the fellow—eyes, teeth, earrings, footwear, and so on—until you had amassed sufficient details to convey to the reader your intended impression.

The details you choose will most often appeal to your reader's visual sense, as do the ones in sentence 2. But details may serve just as well, if less frequently, to focus the reader's attention on the other senses. Observe the following sentences:

3. He was a dirty and foul-smelling fellow, his wrinkled army fatigues reeking of stale sweat, a swarm of green flies hovering near his eyelids.
4. He uttered a shrill whistle, beginning high in the scale and descending slowly as it faded into silence.

Comparisons

The third element of description is not as immediately obvious as the preceding two, yet it will leap most readily to mind when we ask one of the most natural of questions about anything to be described: What does it look like? Suppose you asked this question about the peculiar fellow in sentence 2. You might come up with responses such as the following: "like a semi–tattered rock idol," "a tuxedoed chrysanthemum," "a seedy imitation of a television wrestler." Any of these would help to characterize or describe the image proposed by the noun *fellow* and the quality *peculiar.*

Comparisons are either *figurative* or *literal.* The ones we've looked at so far are figurative comparisons, for if we know he is none of these things, it is only figuratively that we can call the fellow described in sentence 2 a rock star, a chrysanthemum, or a TV wrestler. Two familiar figurative comparisons are the **simile** and the **metaphor.** The simile makes a comparison by asserting that something is *like* something else ("he looked *like* a semi–tattered rock idol"), while a metaphor implies the comparison ("he *was* a tuxedoed chrysanthemum"). A literal comparison differs from the figurative in that the comparison could prove to be literally or actually true ("he was dressed ridiculously, as though he were going to a masquerade party"). Literal comparisons usually begin with *as if* or *as though.*

Again, you'll be using comparisons most often to support the visual images on which you'll chiefly rely for description, but comparisons are useful in directing attention toward the other senses as well as in this sentence:

5. He uttered a shrill whistle, beginning high in the scale and descending slowly as it faded into silence, like the siren of an ambulance on the edge of the neighborhood.

Try as you might, you are not likely to discover other methods of description than these three just discussed. If you manage them properly, qualities, details, and comparisons will be sufficient for any descriptive task you undertake.

Organizing a Description

Each sentence in a description usually focuses on a particular aspect of the thing described. The overall effect is to produce a complete verbal picture. In order to accomplish this aim, you must proceed systematically to fill in the space occupied by the scene, so that the reader may see or visualize it clearly and completely. For example, if the object you intend to describe is a landscape, you may proceed from left to right, top to bottom, foreground to horizon, or vice versa. If the object is a room or other contained space, you may move more systematically around the area, examining each part in turn—walls, windows, floor, ceiling, furnishings. You can allow each sentence to linger over a certain feature or group of related features before giving way to the next sentence, which will bring into focus an adjoining portion of the scene. Think of yourself as an experienced video camera operator, someone who avoids rushing or jerking the camera and who is willing to pause and to use long shots, slow "pans" (panoramic or sweeping horizontal movements), pauses, and close ups.

Another technique that provides a description with direction and unity is the statement of a *dominant impression,* usually the *topic sentence* of a paragraph or, in extended descriptions, the *thesis statement.* (See **thesis** in the Glossary.) You, for example, might state that the New England farmhouse was bleak, that the dormitory room looked messy, or that the old judge appeared hateful. You would need to confirm each of these dominant impressions by providing just those qualities, details, and comparisons that will support the bleakness, the messiness, or the hatefulness, while other qualities, details, and comparisons not essential to the dominant impression may be omitted altogether.

Descriptive writing clearly has important practical applications, both in and out of school. Certainly, a biology student must describe the features of a laboratory specimen in precise, organized terms, a corporate recruiter's report must draw an accurate word picture of the prospective management trainee, a criminal investigator's report must systematically portray the scene of the murder, and so on.

Commentary on Student Work

This section contains examples of description written by students. You will find studying these examples is especially useful because the kinds of descriptive writing that you as a student will produce are more likely to resemble the student writing than the professional writing that appears later in this chapter.

We begin by presenting one essay (not necessarily the best, but something typical), along with a sort of "production history," showing how that piece reached its final form. We will repeat this procedure in each of the sections devoted to student work.

In this piece, Javon describes his room in Roberson Dormitory.

My Dormitory Room

When you walk into my room, you are immediately struck 1
by a profusion of colors. The black rug looks very appealing over the bright red mat, which forms a two-foot border all the way around. The brown paneled walls are dull by comparison and tend to subdue the colors on the floor.

The furniture has all the variety of a color wheel you see in 2
department stores. The easy chair, brought from home, is beige, white, and dirty brown, and it presses the rug snugly against the mat. The desk is the standard college-issue olive green, and it, together with my turquoise bedspread, keeps the black and red from taking charge.

Along one wall the makeshift bookcase (Pet Milk and orange 3
crate modern) contains an array of schoolbooks and paperbacks, some standing erect and gathering dust, others stacked on their sides and bristling with white and yellow notepaper.

A flick of the light switch brings the crazy ceiling into focus. 4
Some earlier occupant, perhaps a crazed student of interior design, painted every other white Celotex square a dark maroon. Or
maybe he was a chess fanatic who worked out his problems at
night with a flashlight. Whatever its origin, its effect is dazzling—and distracting.

One narrow window with its open venetian blind keeps real- 5
ity in place. Through it I can see the green lawn stretching down
toward the red brick library under a Carolina blue sky—a combination of colors a bit less shocking than those in my room.

When Javon received his assignment—to describe a local
interior space—he began by jotting down in his journal some
possible locations: his history classroom, his biology lecture hall,
a nearby sub shop, the computer lab in the library, Pressley's
Barber Shop. Among the items on his list was his dormitory
room, which he could observe in detail and at length without
making any extra effort. Javon began his brainstorming with a
diagram similar to the one recommended in Chapter 2, "The
Writing Process," in which he listed the chief features of his
room. It looked something like the outline that appears in "The
Reading Process," p. 10.

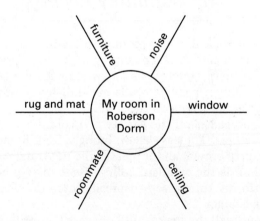

Javon then began to analyze each of the main features, thinking about each in turn, visualizing each in his mind's eye, and

searching for details. As they occurred to him, he added them to the spokes of his outline.

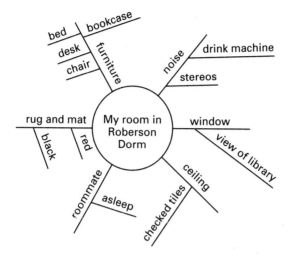

Next, he recalled the statements about the importance of qualities, comparisons, and details in producing accurate descriptions. He meditated on this for a moment and then added the following elements:

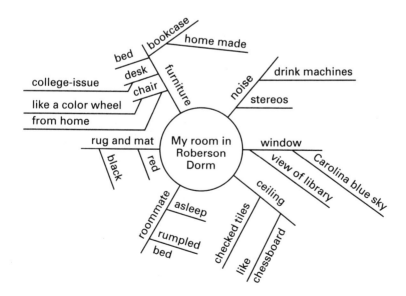

This was all the prewriting that Javon did before he began his initial draft. Here is that draft:

My room in Roberson Dorm is a pretty colorful place. The rug is black and the red mat underneath sticks out about two feet all around it. The brown paneled walls are dull by comparison.

My chair, which I brought from home, is colorful also, beige, white, and brown. It reminds me of one of those color wheels you get down at the hardware store.

The desk is college-issue. It's olive green. My bed has a turquoise bedspread on it and it clashes with the brown walls and the rug and mat.

My roommate's bed is a shambles. He's in it most of the time so it's usually messed up with just the white of the sheets showing and some of his body parts.

The noise is also something that can't be missed. It's usually deafening with the stereo from next door roaring. Then there's the drink machine outside the door always rumbling as the drinks drop down the chute. But it's a convenience to have it there.

My bookcases are made from things I've got free at a grocery store where I used to work: plastic milk crate, wooden box, plus some boards and bricks stacked up. Some of the books are standing erect in their places gathering dust. Others are stacked on their sides full of yellow and white papers used for book marks.

The ceiling is the most noticeable thing of all. The previous occupant painted every other Celotex tile maroon. It looks like a chess board. Maybe he was a chess player and worked out problems at night by staring at the ceiling. Anyway it's bizarre.

The one narrow window with its open venetian blind keeps reality in place. Through it I can see the green lawn stretching down to the red brick library under a Carolina blue sky. This combination is a bit less shocking than the colors in my room.

Javon ran the spell check on the word processor and brought this draft to class to share with the students in his writing group.

There was considerable discussion, and Javon was praised for the careful and orderly way that he had worked his way around the room, noting item after item. He was praised also for the almost consistent attention to the dominant impression established in the first paragraph—that of colorfulness. One student commented that the paragraph dealing with the noisiness tended to detract from that impression, and that paragraph was scrapped.

There was more discussion about the paragraph describing the roommate's bed. A couple of students felt that the less than lively roommate clashed with the rest of Javon's room and should be dumped as well. The other two felt that the paragraph belonged because it, after all, dealt with something that was there. Could the dominant impression dictate that things as big as beds and roommates be ignored? Javon went away pondering that one, and you can see what his decision turned out to be.

Finally, there were a number of stylistic revisions arising from the in-class discussion that week dealing with the use of free modifiers: noun phrases, participle phrases, and absolutes—structures that could be moved around to create special effects and to provide alternative ways of saying things. The first suggested free modifier was in the next to last paragraph, "a crazed student of interior design," inserted to describe the previous occupant of the dorm room. Other such changes were introduced: the relative clause in the second paragraph was reduced to "brought from home," and the final sentence was changed quite successfully into a noun phrase.

Discussion about vivid language brought praise for Javon's claim that the window "keeps reality in place." A fellow student suggested the way that the combination of colors in desk and bedspread might keep the red and black of the rug "from taking charge." Another's comment gave rise to the mention of the way the chair "presses the rug snugly against the mat."

Armed with these pieces of advice on several copies of his draft, Javon returned to the word-processing lab and produced a version that was very near the one that appears above. There were a few grammatical slips that the instructor noticed, a slightly confusing shift in point of view from second person (*you*) in the first two paragraphs to first person (*I*) by the last paragraph. There was also a suggestion that dashes might work better than commas in the last two paragraphs, and a hint that the essay might have been just a bit longer. Nonetheless, it received a good grade.

As we will also do in each chapter that follows, we now provide additional student work that uses and demonstrates the method of development just discussed.

STUDENT WORK

Evelyn's Drudgery

The smoky air, a grim reminder of Evelyn's drudgery, drifts slowly out of the window. The sewing machines surrounding her, racing and idling, sound like dragsters revving up their motors before a race. Ripping off old binding and sewing on new, Evelyn sits behind her machine toward the end of the second shift. Knuckles gnarled and crooked with arthritis brought on by her years of sewing blankets are another reminder as persistent as the smoke. Sweat rolls down her face like condensed water trickling down a glass. The plastic hairnet she wears to keep her hair out of her eyes only worsens the problem, collecting moisture in huge beads across her forehead and then releasing them to run down behind her frameless glasses. But the highlight of Evelyn's day is approaching, the sounding of the whistle that signals an end to another day at the mill.

DISCUSSION QUESTIONS

1. How many senses are appealed to in this description of Evelyn? Which do you find particularly effective? Ineffective? Why?
2. Circle the words that convey qualities. Underscore the portions that provide details, and enclose comparisons in brackets. Which of the descriptive techniques is used most?

Ruth

Ruth appears to be the typical no-nonsense college student. Her appearance is neat but not meticulous. Her clothing is smart-looking and color-coordinated, with her blue tennis shoes matching her Oxford cloth baby blue shirt, both set off by her white painter pants. No socks indicate she is prepared for a hot day, as does her short-sleeved shirt. Her hair is neatly braided in two sections along the sides and caught in the back by a yellow rubber band, allowing the rest to fall behind her. Although she does not wear much makeup, she is dramatic-looking with her dark brown eyes and hair and her creamy complexion, looking like she should be in an Ivory soap commercial. She doesn't wear fingernail polish, and for jewelry only has on one silver chain with a unique glass charm and, of course, a watch, which every no-nonsense student wears.

DISCUSSION QUESTIONS

1. "Ruth" begins with a topic sentence, a general statement that indicates the direction the rest of the paragraph will take. In this case the topic sentence conveys a dominant impression about a girl named Ruth. What is that dominant impression?
2. What details of the description serve to support or reinforce the dominant impression?
3. What, if anything, is gained by repeating the phrase "no-nonsense student" in the first and last sentences of the paragraph?

Dude

He walks slowly down the hall, with a flowing motion, rising slightly on the balls of his feet with each step. Beneath his white planter's hat, tilted to one side, his carefully groomed Afro flares out, framing a medium-brown face, with a high forehead, a slightly flattened nose, flaring nostrils, and a full, sensuous mouth. A moustache and goatee emphasize his prominent cheekbones, his unblemished skin, the polished glow of his face.

He wears a long-sleeved silky shirt with the throat open, its vivid colors shimmering as he moves. His high-waisted pants, which match the orange in his shirt, fit tightly, every muscle apparent as he walks. Off-white shoes with thick brown soles and heels complete his outfit, which is entirely color-coordinated and seems taken from an advertisement in *Ebony*.

Upon reaching his destination, a wall outside a classroom, he   3
leans back against it, his weight shifted off one foot, his pelvis
tilted forward. When an attractive girl walks by, he catches her
eye and gives her a slow, short nod, measuring her up and down,
taking in all her features. When she stops, he talks to her in a
deep, quiet voice, gesturing with his hands, the same flowing
motions. He smiles once, a small, secret smile, showing large,
even teeth. Every few moments he reaches out and lightly
touches the girl.

When the bell rings, the crowd comes noisily out of the   4
classroom; then he pushes himself lithely off the wall and strolls
in, a brown heel the last thing seen.

DISCUSSION QUESTIONS

1. "Dude" is a thorough description of a student—more complete,
   for instance, than Eudora Welty's of "Phoenix Jackson," in the
   following selection. Yet the writer has perhaps forgotten something that should have been in the description, something that
   would be carried by most students. Can you tell what is missing
   and explain why the omission is important or trivial? Suggest a
   sentence or two describing those missing items. Where could
   those sentences be inserted?
2. What kinds of grammatical constructions are "his weight shifted
   off one foot," "his pelvis tilted forward," "a brown heel the last
   thing seen"? What effect do they produce?
3. How is this description like the one Eudora Welty did of Phoenix
   Jackson? How are they different?

PARAGRAPHS

Phoenix Jackson

EUDORA WELTY

It was December—a bright frozen day in the early morning.
Far out in the country there was an old Negro woman with her
head tied in a red rag, coming along a path through the pine-

woods. Her name was Phoenix Jackson. She was very old and small and she walked slowly in the dark pine shadows, moving a little from side to side in her steps, with the balanced heaviness and lightness of a pendulum in a grandfather clock. She carried a thin, small cane made from an umbrella, and with this she kept tapping the frozen earth in front of her. This made a grave and persistent noise in the still air, that seemed meditative, like the chirping of a solitary little bird. She wore a dark striped dress reaching down to her shoetops, and an equally long apron of bleached sugar sacks, with a full pocket; all neat and tidy, but every time she took a step she might have fallen over her shoe-laces, which dragged from her unlaced shoes. She looked straight ahead. Her eyes were blue with age. Her skin had a pattern all its own of numberless branching wrinkles and as though a whole little tree stood in the middle of her forehead, but a golden color ran underneath, and the two knobs of her cheeks were illuminated by a yellow burning under the dark. Under the red rag her hair came down on her neck in the frailest of ringlets, still black, and with an odor like copper.

DISCUSSION QUESTIONS

1. Phoenix Jackson seems to come slowly into focus, as though the author were adjusting the lens of a camera. How does Welty use details to produce this effect? What qualities and comparisons figure in this description?
2. List the major comparisons that Welty uses in this paragraph. Other than sight, what senses are appealed to? Which are particularly effective, and why?

Detention House Cell, Shanghai

NIEN CHENG

I looked around the room, and my heart sank. Cobwebs dangled from the ceiling; the once whitewashed walls were yellow with age and streaked with dust. The single naked bulb was coated with grime and extremely dim. Patches of the cement floor were black with dampness. A strong musty smell pervaded the air. I hastened to open the only small window, with its rust-pitted iron bars. To reach it, I had to stand on tiptoe. When I succeeded in pulling the knob and the window swung open, flakes of peeling paint as well as a shower of dust fell to the floor. The only furniture in the room was three narrow beds of rough wooden planks, one against the wall, the other two stacked one on top of the other. Never in my life had I been in or even imagined a place so primitive and filthy.

DISCUSSION QUESTIONS

1. In this paragraph Cheng describes her first impression of the cell she would occupy alone for six and one-half years as a political prisoner in Shanghai during the so-called "Cultural Revolution." Which senses does she appeal to in her description? Which image seems strongest to you, and why?
2. Assume that with changing conditions in the People's Republic of China the time has come to convert this cell to a furnished room, and that you have the resources to change it into an inviting rather than a repulsive place. You can add furniture, hang curtains, paint the walls, and the like. Make notes to share in class for your version of the room, using qualities, details, and comparisons, trying also to appeal to the same senses as in the original description—but in a pleasant way.

The White Glove

WILLIAM PAULK

About that time I saw the glove lying there, cool and white and painfully neat. Somebody had left a glove, and a janitor or somebody else had picked it up and left it lying there on the table. It was a small glove, the kind a lady wears. I don't mean the kind of lady who drives a nice late model car; I don't mean the kind who has a chauffeur, either; still, a real lady. It was all flat and the thumb was folded over the palm, and it looked shy and retiring. I could almost imagine a little parlor with a high ceiling and a little marble-topped tea table in front of a Victorian sofa. But the glove wasn't by itself. It lay on a piece of paper, heavy white stationery of the kind elderly ladies prefer for important communications. The paper was sort of propped against the wall behind the table, and I could see that it had writing on it.

An entry at the top in an elegant, but spidery hand gave the name of a savings bank, and over to the side, heading a neat column, was written $235.58. Just below that line and indented a little were the words, "U.S. Govm't Bond, Series E, $100.00, cashed 1958," and on a third line, "U.S. Govm't Bond, Series E, $50.00, cashed 1958," with the interest listed just under the bank figure. Almost covered by the glove was a final entry, "Old Age Pension," written in a smaller, almost apologetic hand by the same person, and the amount was covered by the little white glove.

DISCUSSION QUESTIONS

1. It is evident that William Paulk is not so much describing a white glove as he is the imagined owner of the glove. What details hint at the character of the glove's owner?
2. What do you think he means by "a real lady"?
3. How does Paulk use comparison? How are the comparisons introduced?

Subway Station

GILBERT HIGHET

Standing in a subway station, I began to appreciate the place—almost to enjoy it. First of all, I looked at the lighting: a row of meager electric bulbs, unscreened, yellow, and coated with filth, stretched toward the black mouth of the tunnel, as though it were a bolt hole in an abandoned coal mine. Then I lingered, with zest, on the walls and ceiling: lavatory tiles which had been white about fifty years ago, and were now encrusted with soot, coated with the remains of a dirty liquid which might be either atmospheric humidity mingled with smog or the result of a perfunctory attempt to clean them with cold water; and, above them, gloomy vaulting from which dingy paint was peeling off like scabs from an old wound, sick black paint leaving a leprous white undersurface. Beneath my feet, the floor was a nauseating dark brown with black stains upon it which might be stale oil or dry chewing gum or some worse defilement; it looked like the hallway of a condemned slum building. Then my eye traveled to the tracks, where two lines

of glittering steel—the only positively clean objects in the whole
place—ran out of darkness into darkness above an unspeakable
mass of congealed oil, puddles of dubious liquid, and a mishmash
of old cigarette packets, mutilated and filthy newspapers, and
the débris that filtered down from the street above through a
barred grating in the roof. As I looked up toward the sunlight,
I could see more débris sifting slowly downward, and making
an abominable pattern in the slanting beam of dirt-laden sunlight. I was going on to relish more features of this unique
scene: such as the advertisement posters on the walls—here a
text from the Bible, there a half-naked girl, here a woman
wearing a hat consisting of a hen sitting on a nest full of eggs,
and there a pair of girl's legs walking up the keys of a cash
register—all scribbled over with unknown names and well-
known obscenities in black crayon and red lipstick; but then
my train came in at last, I boarded it, and began to read. The
experience was over for the time.

DISCUSSION QUESTIONS

1. How does Highet organize his description? What parts of the
   subway station does he focus upon and in what order?
2. How many comparisons do you count in Highet's third sentence,
   which begins, "Then I lingered . . ."? How are they related?
3. Which descriptive device does Highet use most frequently: qualities, details, or comparisons?

ESSAYS

The Woods and the Pacific

ROBERT LOUIS STEVENSON

*Robert Louis Stevenson (1850–1894) was Scotch-born and edu-
cated as a lawyer, but he became a world traveler, seeking
adventure and relief from tuberculosis, which he had from
childhood. Stevenson is best known for his first major work,*

the adventure novel Treasure Island *(1883). The descriptive essay below is from* Across the Plains *(1892), which records Stevenson's experiences in America in 1879 and 1880.*

The Bay of Monterey has been compared by no less a person than General Sherman to a bent fishing-hook; and the comparison, if less important than the march through Georgia, still shows the eye of a soldier for topography. Santa Cruz sits exposed at the shank; the mouth of the Salinas River is at the middle of the bend; and Monterey itself is cozily ensconced beside the barb. Thus the ancient capital of California faces across the bay, while the Pacific Ocean, though hidden by low hills and forest, bombards her left flank and rear with never-dying surf. In front of the town, the long line of sea-beach trends north and northwest, and then westward to enclose the bay. The waves which lap so quietly about the jetties of Monterey grow louder and larger in the distance; you can see the breakers leaping high and white by day; at night, the outline of the shore is traced in transparent silver by the moonlight and the flying foam; and from all around, even in quiet weather, the low, distant, thrilling roar of the Pacific hangs over the coast and the adjacent country like smoke above the battle.

These long beaches are enticing to the idle man. It would be hard to find a walk more solitary and at the same time more exciting to the mind. Crowds of ducks and sea-gulls hover over the sea. Sandpipers trot in and out by troops after the retiring waves, trilling together in a chorus of infinitesimal song. Strange sea-tangles, new to the European eye, the bones of whales, or sometimes a whole whale's carcase, white with carrion-gulls and poisoning the wind, lie scattered here and there along the sands. The waves come in slowly, vast and green, curve their translucent necks, and burst with a surprising uproar, that runs, waxing and waning, up and down the long keyboard of the beach. The foam of these great ruins mounts in an instant to the ridge of the sand glacis, swiftly fleets back again, and is met and buried by the next breaker. The interest is perpetually fresh. On no other coast that I know shall you enjoy, in calm, sunny weather, such a spectacle of Ocean's greatness, such beauty of changing colour, or such degrees of thunder in the sound. The very air is more than usually salt by this Homeric deep.

Inshore, a tract of sand-hills borders on the beach. Here and there a lagoon, more or less brackish, attracts the birds and hunters. A rough, spotty undergrowth partially conceals the sand.

The crouching, hardy live-oaks flourish singly or in thickets—
the kind of wood for murderers to crawl among—and here and
there the skirt of the forest extends downward from the hills
with a floor of turf and long aisles of pine-trees hung with Span-
iard's Beard. Through this quaint desert the railway cars drew
near to Monterey from the junction at Salinas City—though that
and so many other things are now forever altered—and it was
from here that you had the first view of the old township lying
in the sands, its white windmills bickering in the chill, perpetual
wind, and the first fogs of the evening drawing drearily around it
from the sea.

The one common note of all this country is the haunting   4
presence of the ocean. A great faint sound of breakers follows you
high up into the inland canyons; the roar of water dwells in the
clean, empty rooms of Monterey as in a shell upon the chimney;
go where you will, you have but to pause and listen to hear the
voice of the Pacific. You pass out of the town to the southwest,
and mount the hill among pine woods. Glade, thicket, and grove
surround you. You follow winding sandy tracks that lead now
thither. You see a deer; a multitude of quail arises. But the sound
of the sea still follows you, as you advance, like that of wind
among the trees, only harsher and stranger to the ear; and when
at length you gain the summit, out breaks on every hand and
with freshened vigour, that same unending, distant, whispering
rumble of the ocean; for now you are on the top of Monterey
peninsula, and the noise no longer only mounts to you from
behind along the beach towards Santa Cruz, but from your right
also, round by Chinatown and Pinos lighthouse, and from down
before you to the mouth of the Carmello River. The whole
woodland is begirt with thundering surges. The silence that immediately surrounds you where you stand is not so much broken
as it is haunted by this distinct, circling rumour. It sets your
senses upon edge; you strain your attention; you are clearly and
unusually conscious of small sounds near at hand; you walk
listening like an Indian hunter; and that voice of the Pacific is a
sort of disquieting company to you in your walk.

DISCUSSION: CONTENT

1. Find Monterey on a map of California. Locate as many other
   places named by Stevenson as you can.

2. Draw a rough map and label it to show the major landmarks around Monterey Bay. It might be a good idea just to draw a fish hook, and then locate the landmarks in and around it.
3. Who was General Sherman?
4. Stevenson's essay appeals particularly to which two senses?
5. What, according to Stevenson, dominates this entire area?

DISCUSSION: FORM

1. What logical order does Stevenson follow in describing the scenery around Monterey Bay? What does each paragraph contribute?
2. What transitional devices are used to link the paragraphs together?
3. Examine Stevenson's use of action verbs in one or two paragraphs; does he have at least one use that you would label unusual or creative?
4. Mark the topic sentence in each paragraph. Approximately how many distinct images does Stevenson supply to support the topic of each paragraph? Are these too few? Too many?

The Spinning Mills at Lowell

RICK BOYER

Rick Boyer (b. 1943) is the author of eight novels, seven of which chronicle the adventures of Doc Adams, an oral surgeon who manages to become embroiled in murder and mayhem. The first novel in this series, Billingsgate Shoal, *won the Edgar Award in 1982 for excellence in mystery writing. The most recent in the series,* Yellow Bird, *appeared in 1991. Rick Boyer teaches creative writing at Western Carolina University. This selection is taken from* Penny Ferry, *a Doc Adams mystery set in Lowell, Massachusetts.*

Lowell is not pretty; but it wasn't designed for aesthetics.   1
Like the other towns along the Merrimack River (Lawrence, Nashua, and Manchester), it was laid out in the early part of the last century to see how many big buildings could be squeezed along the sources of water power and barge traffic. Then a lot of effort was expended to see how much machinery each build-

ing could hold: looms, carding machines, spinning machines, and finishing machines, and how many immigrant workers—of all ages and sexes—could tend these machines for the maximum number of hours on scant wages without falling down and dying of exhaustion, hunger, disease, or grievous injury.

This cruel experiment in Social Darwinism lasted roughly   2 from the 1830s until the First World War. During its duration a few families and corporations made enormous fortunes, and many thousands of new Americans were chewed up and spit out by these gargantuan mill complexes. Then in the twentieth century, at an ever-increasing pace, the industries left for other places where they could find other people to tend the machines for less money and so do the whole ghastly thing all over again.

For all of its freedom and efficiency, capitalism can be a night   3 stalker. A benthic fish with gaping jaws and snaggle teeth. A Jabberwock. Looking into these old buildings can be enough to turn a hardened Republican into a trade unionist. If you ever get a glimpse of these mills in action (some of them are still working in these New England towns), it's a spectacle you won't soon forget. As you leave your car, even a block from the building, you can hear the giant locomotive thump of the looms. The walls of the mills are thick masonry, the windows shut or boarded, but the sound comes through: a monstrous syncopated two-stroke thumping of the swinging loom arms and frames. It is a pulsing mechanical heart that shakes the old wooden steps as you climb inside. Then go through two or three more doors and you see the huge interior halls with rows and rows of big metal machines, with racks of bobbins twirling off thread like fishing reels. And on the far side spills out cloth, inch by inch, made in thunder. The women who work here wear ear protectors, but they're deaf anyway.

You shout and cannot hear yourself. The women walk to and   4 fro on the old wooden floors, which are soaked with oozing oil and clotted with fibers. The machines are fuzzy-soft with grease-soaked lint. The floor shakes and trembles underfoot with the swinging metal and spinning flywheels. Sometimes even the old endless drive belts of wide leather remain overhead shrieking on the wooden drums. Perhaps the most depressing thing is that the women don't complain, don't plan to quit and move on to something else. They just serve out their time here on the gummy wooden floors, ears protected against the clank and thump, but already deaf.

And this scene makes you realize that there are two New 5
Englands. There's the one with kids dressed in blazers and madras blouses strolling on green lawns surrounded by ivy-colored walls, and there's this one trying to prop it all up. This one made of veiny-armed, pocked-faced kids in factories, of frowzy old ladies in cotton print dresses and torn stockings worn over purplish puckery legs, tending the machines in the din.

DISCUSSION: CONTENT

1. Boyer does not actually name in this passage the state where Lowell is to be found, although he does mention a river and three other cities. He later places the mills he is describing in New England. Consult an atlas to discover exactly where the cities mentioned are located. The textile mills, Boyer claims, were moved away from this area after World War I. What industries, if any, have replaced them? How might you find out this information?
2. In his description of the mill, Boyer has a purpose beyond the mere enumeration of details to deliver a clear mental image to the reader. What is that additional purpose?
3. Who are the employees of this mill? What characteristics do they share?

DISCUSSION: FORM

1. Which of the methods of description—qualities, comparisons, or details—does Boyer employ most frequently in his passage? Locate at least two examples of each method.
2. To what sense besides the visual does Boyer appeal in this passage? How does he incorporate that sort of imagery? Does he depend more heavily on nouns or verbs? Into what sorts of grammatical constructions does he work them?
3. The second and the concluding paragraphs contain some information that is not, strictly speaking, descriptive, but rather expository, or perhaps even argumentative. How does the description support the claims that are advanced in these paragraphs?

Boyhood Memories

MARK TWAIN

*Samuel Langhorne Clemens (1835–1910), better known as
Mark Twain, grew up in and around Hannibal, Missouri, along
the banks of the Mississippi River. One of America's greatest
writers, especially adept at humorous and descriptive writing,
Twain preserved memories of his boyhood for all time in his
two best-known novels,* The Adventures of Tom Sawyer *(1876)
and* The Adventures of Huckleberry Finn *(1885). In the passage
below, Twain displays his almost overwhelming descriptive
powers as he recalls youthful experiences on his Uncle John's
farm near Florida, Missouri.*

I spent some part of every year at the farm until I was twelve   1
or thirteen years old. The life which I led there with my cousins
was full of charm, and so is the memory of it yet. I can call back
the solemn twilight and mystery of the deep woods, the earthy
smells, the faint odors of the wild flowers, the sheen of rain-
washed foliage, the rattling clatter of drops when the wind shook
the trees, the far-off hammering of woodpeckers and the muffled
drumming of wood pheasants in the remoteness of the forest, the
snapshot glimpses of disturbed wild creatures scurrying through
the grass—I can call it all back and make it as real as it ever was,
and as blessed. I can call back the prairie, and its loneliness and
peace, and a vast hawk hanging motionless in the sky, with his
wings spread wide and the blue of the vault showing through the
fringe of their end feathers. I can see the woods in their autumn
dress, the oaks purple, the hickories washed with gold, the ma-
ples and the sumachs luminous with crimson fires, and I can hear
the rustle made by the fallen leaves as we plowed through them.
I can see the blue clusters of wild grapes hanging among the
foliage of the saplings, and I remember the taste of them and the
smell. I know how the wild blackberries looked, and how they
tasted; and the same with the pawpaws, the hazelnuts, and the
persimmons; and I can feel the thumping rain, upon my head, of
hickory nuts and walnuts when we were out in the frosty dawn
to scramble for them with the pigs, and the gusts of wind loosed
them and sent them down. I know the stain of blackberries, and
how pretty it is, and I know the stain of walnut hulls, and how

little it minds soap and water, also what grudged experience it had of either of them. I know the taste of maple sap, and when to gather it, and how to arrange the troughs and the delivery tubes, and how to boil down the juice, and how to hook the sugar after it is made; also how much better hooked sugar tastes than any that is honestly come by, let bigots say what they will. I know how a prize watermelon looks when it is sunning its fat rotundity among pumpkin vines and "simblins"; I know how to tell when it is ripe without "plugging" it; I know how inviting it looks when it is cooling itself in a tub of water under the bed, waiting; I know how it looks when it lies on the table in the sheltered great floor space between house and kitchen, and the children gathered for the sacrifice and their mouths watering; I know the crackling sound it makes when the carving knife enters its end, and I can see the split fly along in front of the blade as the knife cleaves its way to the other end; I can see its halves fall apart and display the rich red meat and the black seeds, and the heart standing up, a luxury fit for the elect; I know how a boy looks behind a yard-long slice of that melon, and I know how he feels; for I have been there. I know the taste of the watermelon which has been honestly come by, and I know the taste of the watermelon which has been acquired by art. Both taste good, but the experienced know which tastes best. I know the look of green apples and peaches and pears on the trees, and I know how entertaining they are when they are inside of a person. I know how ripe ones look when they are piled in pyramids under the trees, and how pretty they are and how vivid their colors. I know how a frozen apple looks, in a barrel down cellar in the wintertime, and how hard it is to bite, and how the frost makes the teeth ache, and yet how good it is, notwithstanding. I know the disposition of elderly people to select the specked apples for the children, and I once knew ways to beat the game. I know the look of an apple that is roasting and sizzling on a hearth on a winter's evening, and I know the comfort that comes of eating it hot, along with some sugar and a drench of cream. I know the delicate art and mystery of so cracking hickory nuts and walnuts on a flatiron with a hammer that the kernels will be delivered whole, and I know how the nuts, taken in conjunction with winter apples, cider, and doughnuts, make old people's old tales and old jokes sound fresh and crisp and enchanting, and juggle an evening away before you know what went with the time. I know the look of Uncle Dan'l's kitchen as it was on the privileged nights, when

I was a child, and I can see the white and black children grouped on the hearth, with firelight playing on their faces and the shadows flickering upon the walls, clear back toward the cavernous gloom of the rear, and I can hear Uncle Dan'l telling the immortal tales which Uncle Remus Harris was to gather into his book and charm the world with, by and by; and I can feel again the creepy joy which quivered through me when the time for the ghost story was reached—and the sense of regret, too, which came over me, for it was always the last story of the evening and there was nothing between it and the unwelcome bed.

I can remember the bare wooden stairway in my uncle's   2
house, and the turn to the left above the landing, and the rafters and the slanting roof over my bed, and the squares of moonlight on the floor, and the white cold world of snow outside, seen through the curtainless window. I can remember the howling of the wind and the quaking of the house on stormy nights, and how snug and cozy one felt, under the blankets, listening; and how the powdery snow used to sift in, around the sashes, and lie in little ridges on the floor and make the place look chilly in the morning and curb the wild desire to get up—in case there was any. I can remember how very dark that room was, in the dark of the moon, and how packed it was with ghostly stillness when one woke up by accident away in the night, and forgotten sins came flocking out of the secret chambers of the memory and wanted a hearing; and how ill chosen the time seemed for this kind of business; and how dismal was the hoohooing of the owl and the wailing of the wolf, sent mourning by on the night wind.

I remember the raging of the rain on that roof, summer   3
nights, and how pleasant it was to lie and listen to it, and enjoy the white splendor of the lightning and the majestic booming and crashing of the thunder. It was a very satisfactory room, and there was a lightning rod which was reachable from the window, an adorable and skittish thing to climb up and down, summer nights, when there were duties on hand of a sort to make privacy desirable.

I remember the 'coon and 'possum hunts, nights, . . . and the   4
long marches through the black gloom of the woods, and the excitement which fired everybody when the distant bay of an experienced dog announced that the game was treed; then the wild scrambling and stumblings through briers and bushes and over roots to get to the spot; then the lighting of a fire and the felling of the tree, the joyful frenzy of the dogs . . . and the weird

picture it all made in the red glare—I remember it all well, and
the delight that everyone got out of it, except the 'coon.

I remember the pigeon seasons, when the birds would come   5
in millions and cover the trees and by their weight break down
the branches. They were clubbed to death with sticks; guns were
not necessary and were not used. I remember the squirrel hunts,
and prairie-chicken hunts, and wild-turkey hunts, and all that;
and how we turned out, mornings, while it was still dark, to go
on these expeditions, and how chilly and dismal it was, and how
often I regretted that I was well enough to go. A toot on a tin horn
brought twice as many dogs as were needed, and in their happiness they raced and scampered about, and knocked small people
down, and made no end of unnecessary noise. At the word, they
vanished away toward the woods, and we drifted silently after
them in the melancholy gloom. But presently the gray dawn stole
over the world, the birds piped up, then the sun rose and poured
light and comfort all around, everything was fresh and dewy and
fragrant, and life was a boon again. After three hours of tramping
we arrived back wholesomely tired, overladen with game, very
hungry, and just in time for breakfast.

DISCUSSION: CONTENT

1. What details does Twain use to describe his room? What effect
   does that selection have or create?
2. How distinctly do you see other places? Uncle Dan'l's kitchen?
   The locales of hunts? Why?
3. Which of the many things mentioned in the long first paragraph
   receives the most space? What do you suppose this indicates?

DISCUSSION: FORM

1. Paragraph 1 seems intolerably long. Perhaps we are too used to
   the short paragraphs of newspaper articles. Nonetheless, if you
   were a modern editor, how would you suggest that Twain divide
   his paragraph? How would you justify these breaks?
2. Which of Twain's memories cause you to smile? How does Twain
   evoke this smile?
3. Comment on the overall organization of this description. What
   plan does Twain follow?

Shady Grove Cemetery

JAMES AGEE

James Agee (1909–1955) was an American journalist, screen-writer, and novelist. His posthumous novel, A Death in the Family, *won the Pulitzer Prize in 1958.* Agee on Film *(two volumes, 1958, 1960) is a collection of his film criticism and screenplays. The following essay is taken from* Let Us Now Praise Famous Men *(1941), a documentary, with photographs by Walker Evans, of the daily life of Alabama tenant farmers in 1936.*

The graveyard is about fifty by a hundred yards inside a wire   1
fence. There are almost no trees in it: a lemon verbena and a small magnolia; it is all red clay and very few weeds.

Out at the front of it across the road there is a cornfield and   2
then a field of cotton and then trees.

Most of the headboards are pine, and at the far end of the yard   3
from the church the graves are thinned out and there are many slender and low pine stumps about the height of the headboards. The shadows are all struck sharp lengthwise of the graves, to-ward the cornfield, by the afternoon sun. There is no one any-where in sight. It is heavily silent and fragrant and all the leaves are breathing slowly without touching each other.

Some of the graves have real headstones, a few of them so   4
large they must be the graves of landowners. One is a thick limestone log erected by the Woodmen of the World. One or two of the others, besides a headpiece, have a flat of stone as large as the whole grave.

On one of these there is a china dish on whose cover delicate   5
hands lie crossed, cuffs at their wrists, and the nails distinct.

On another a large fluted vase stands full of dead flowers,   6
with an inch of rusty water at the bottom.

On others of these stones, as many as a dozen of them, there   7
is something I have never seen before: by some kind of porcelain reproduction, a photograph of the person who is buried there; the last or the best likeness that had been made, in a small-town studio, or at home with a snapshot camera. I remember one well of a fifteen-year-old boy in Sunday pants and a plaid pullover sweater, his hair combed, his cap in his hand, sitting against a

piece of farm machinery and grinning. His eyes are squinted against the light and his nose makes a deep shadow down one side of his chin. Somebody's arm, with the sleeve rolled up, is against him; somebody who is almost certainly still alive: they could not cut him entirely out of the picture. Another is a studio portrait, close up, in artificial lighting, of a young woman. She is leaned a little forward, smiling vivaciously, one hand at her cheek. She is not very pretty, but she believed she was; her face is free from strain or fear. She is wearing an evidently new dress, with a mail-order look about it; patterns of beads are sewn over it and have caught the light. Her face is soft with powder and at the wings of her nose lines have been deleted. Her dark blonde hair is newly washed and professionally done up in puffs at the ears which in that time, shortly after the first great war of her century, were called cootie garages. This image of her face is split across and the split has begun to turn brown at its edges.

I think these would be graves of small farmers.   8

There are others about which there can be no mistake: they   9
are the graves of the poorest of the farmers and of the tenants. Mainly they are the graves with the pine headboards; or without them.

When the grave is still young, it is very sharply distinct, and   10
of a peculiar form. The clay is raised in a long and narrow oval with a sharp ridge, the shape exactly of an inverted boat. A fairly broad board is driven at the head; a narrower one, sometimes only a stob, at the feet. A good many of the headboards have been sawed into the flat simulacrum of an hourglass; in some of these, the top has been roughly rounded off, so that the resemblance is more nearly that of a head and shoulders sunken or risen to the waist in the dirt. On some of these boards names and dates have been written or printed in hesitant letterings, in pencil or in crayon, but most of them appear never to have been touched in this way. The boards at some of the graves have fallen slantwise or down; many graves seem never to have been marked except in their own carefully made shape. These graves are of all sizes between those of giants and of newborn children; and there are a great many, so many they seem shoals of minnows, two feet long or less, lying near one another; and of these smallest graves, very few are marked with any wood at all, and many are already so drawn into the earth that they are scarcely distinguishable. Some of the largest, on the other hand, are of heroic size, seven and eight feet long, and of these more are marked, a few, even, with

the smallest and plainest blocks of limestone, and initials, once or twice a full name; but many more of them have never been marked, and many, too, are sunken half down and more and almost entirely into the earth. A great many of these graves, perhaps half to two-thirds of those which are still distinct, have been decorated, not only with shrunken flowers in their cracked vases and with bent targets of blasted flowers, but otherwise as well.

Some have a line of white clamshells planted along their 11 ridge; of others, the rim as well is garlanded with these shells. On one large grave, which is otherwise completely plain, a blown-out electric bulb is screwed into the clay at the exact center. On another, on the slope of clay just in front of the headboard, its feet next the board, is a horseshoe; and at its center a blown bulb is stood upright. On two or three others there are insulators of blue-green glass. On several graves, which I presume to be those of women, there is at the center the prettiest or the oldest and most valued piece of china: on one, a blue glass butter dish whose cover is a setting hen; on another, an intricate milk-colored glass basket; on others, ten-cent-store candy dishes and iridescent vases; on one, a pattern of white and colored buttons. On other graves there are small and thick white butter dishes of the sort which are used in lunch-rooms, and by the action of rain these stand free of the grave on slender turrets of clay. On still another grave, laid carefully next the headboard, is a corncob pipe.

On the graves of children there are still these pretty pieces of 12 glass and china, but they begin to diminish in size and they verge into the forms of animals and into homuncular symbols of growth; and there are toys: small autos, locomotives and fire engines of red and blue metal; tea sets for dolls, and tin kettles the size of thimbles; little effigies in rubber and glass and china, of cows, lions, bulldogs, squeaking mice, and the characters of comic strips; and of these I knew, when Louise told me how precious her china dogs were to her and her glass lace dish, where they would go if she were soon drawn down, and of many other things in that home, to whom they would likely be consigned; and of the tea set we gave Clair Bell, I knew in the buying in what daintiness it will a little while adorn her remembrance when the heaviness has sufficiently grown upon her and she has done the last of her dancing: for it will only be by a fortune which cannot be even hoped that she will live much longer; and only by great chance that they can do for her what two parents have done here for their little daughter: not only a tea set, and a Coca-Cola bottle, and a milk bottle, ranged on her short grave, but a stone at the head and a stone at the foot, and in the headstone her six month image as she lies sleeping dead in her white dress, the head sunken delicately forward, deeply and delicately gone, the eyes seamed, as that of a dead bird, and on the rear face of this stone the words:

> We can't have all things to please us,
> Our little Daughter, Joe An, has gone to Jesus.

DISCUSSION: CONTENT

1. Based on their size and number, it appears that the greatest number of graves contain the bodies of members of what age group: adults, teenagers, or babies?
2. Name three unusual items or objects decorating the Shady Grove, Alabama, graves. Have you ever seen graves similarly decorated?
3. The three photographs mentioned include which persons?
4. How do the grave markers of tenant farmers differ from those of landowners?

DISCUSSION: FORM

1. In the earlier paragraph, "The White Glove," William Paulk is able to describe the glove's owner by concentrating on specific details of the glove and its surroundings. In this description Agee seems to be doing the same thing. What are you able to infer about the area's residents, their lives, their hopes, and their pleasures, based on the cemetery description? Be specific. What details support your impressions?
2. Examine the last sentence in paragraph 3. Here Agee attributes to inanimate objects, leaves, an ability they lack—breathing. What is the effect of such a tactic? Does he employ similar methods elsewhere?
3. Notice in paragraph 7 of Agee's essay on the graveyard that he doesn't stop after he describes the basic subjects of the porcelainized photographs, but goes further; why do you suppose he does, and is that good or bad?
4. Returning to the imaginary role of motion picture photographer a moment, analyze what Agee has done in his last paragraph, moving from the general to the particular or specific. What is gained by this move?

4

Narration

In the introduction to Chapter 3, we mentioned that not only does narration focus on action or verbs, but it must also include description. A moment's thought will convince you of this need. You cannot portray the actions of an event or story very effectively unless you relate to the reader a description of the people or things participating in those actions. You also learned earlier that there are three basic ways to describe these participants: by assigning qualities, by providing details, and by making comparisons. How do you portray the actions in which these participants engage? The answer is simple, because it is exactly the same: qualities, details, and comparisons.

Qualities

When you read our discussion of how qualities expanded the basic images proposed by nouns, you noticed that we came up with words like *good, dull, friendly*—in other words, adjectives. Similarly, if you want to enlarge on the idea involved in an action or a verb, you must turn to adverbs. A great many of these adverbs, particularly those that grammarians call adverbs of manner, refer to qualities—characteristics that attach less general, more concrete meaning to the stated action. Such adverbs describe how something is done. Take, for example, the following sentence:

1. Roscoe sneezed.

61

As it is, the sentence delivers a fact to your reader, but not very clearly. But if you were to attach to that sentence any of the possible adverbs of manner that appear in Sentence 2, you would create a much clearer picture of the event in your reader's imagination:

> 2. Roscoe sneezed violently.
>   repeatedly.
>   surreptitiously.
>   noisily.
>   wetly.

Again, recalling the earlier chapter on descriptive writing, you will remember that qualities merely get things started, pointing the direction for further descriptive development. The same is true for qualities assigned to verbs. In order to help your reader see vividly the actions involved in a sentence, you will need to amplify with details.

Details

Often, details associated with actions involve accompanying circumstances or movements that occur at the same time as the action being described. Look at the concrete impression that would emerge if you added details to sentence 2:

> 3. *Closing his eyes, placing his index finger under his nose,* Roscoe sneezed violently, *his shoulders hunched up and forward, his knees bent.*

The italicized portions of the sentence supply details that enable your reader to visualize more clearly "what happened." Each detail concentrates on circumstances surrounding the sneeze, with the result that your reader may see the event with much greater clarity than before.

Comparisons

Although less valuable than details, comparisons are also helpful in creating an impression, particularly a visual one. For example, in the preceding sentence you might further characterize Roscoe's act of sneezing by including the italicized comparison in sentence 4:

4. Closing his eyes and placing his index finger under his nose, Roscoe sneezed violently, his shoulders hunched up and forward, his knees bent, *his lips emitting a fine geyser of spray.*

Here the metaphor of a geyser describes one effect of the sneeze. In a similar fashion you might have employed other comparisons involving nouns. You could have used a simile to say the sneeze was *like the report of a rifle,* or you could have compared it with a *thunderclap* or a *diesel horn,* either of which would have been helpfully descriptive. On the other hand, you might use verbs or verbals to create useful descriptive comparisons. You might say, for instance, that Roscoe's sneeze *thundered,* or you might have added such participle phrases as *exploding abruptly, honking noisily,* or *barking ferociously,* thus calling to mind the sounds of dynamite, geese, or dogs.

Organizing a Narrative

Each sentence, each main verb of a narrative passage, advances the narrative step by step through time. For this reason, a narrative episode is usually one of the simplest forms of writing to arrange or organize. As the writer, you merely take the familiar routine of telling a story, arranging the events in chronological order.

Occasionally, of course, you may find it useful to break away from a straightforward chronological order to heighten the effect of an episode or story. Two ways to do so are by using a *flashback* (a jump back in time) or a *flashforward* (a jump forward in time), before beginning or resuming the normal sequence of events.

You will also find that compressing or expanding the elapsed time for certain portions of your story can sometimes be a useful tactic since that can be most faithful to your perception of certain events. For instance, if you have been in an automobile accident, you might recall so vividly the separate phases of it that it seems as if time almost stood still. You would, of course, want your readers to share that experience if possible, and thus you would dwell on these vivid moments at length, thus slowing time down for the best narrative effect.

In any event, the chief difficulty in narration is the need to include enough descriptive material—qualities, details, and comparisons—so that your reader will experience the actions that you are relating. To achieve this goal, you must learn to make each sentence count. Short stories and novels often provide examples of narrative writing at its best. However, narration has practical uses too. For instance, a sportswriter must concisely but correctly relate the key plays of a game or match, just as a social worker must accurately recount a child's tale of parental abuse, or a law enforcement officer must report all that happened during the surveillance of a drug deal. Clearly, narration plays a vital part in life beyond school, and you should learn to use it effectively.

Commentary on Student Work

This section on student work begins with a piece written by Neeife, an exchange student from Nigeria. The event he describes took place some time ago, but it was still very clear in his memory. It did, however, take some time to tease out the final product.

The assignment to which Neeife responded was to narrate an event in which he was a participant. He began by writing in his journal several responses to the assignment: coming to America, my first job, winning the big race. For each of these he did some freewriting, trying to discover which topic best suited his mood at the time. The first two attempts turned out halting and stiff, but when Neeife turned to the race, this is what his freewriting produced:

At the sound of the starting gun, the crowd on the infield began surging toward my position at the far end of the track, where I would receive the baton for the final leg. Jogging in place, I tried to focus on the finish line 100 meters away, but before I could make it out, here came five boys running neck-and-neck. In the next second my signal came: GO! I had the baton in my hand and headed for the tape. I could hear the rhythm of the other runners' steps beside me; then they were behind me. Then I hit the tape.

Neeife brought this entry to share with his writing group. The instructor sat in with the group for a while that day, and together they made these observations:

1. There are three scenes in this narrative: the opening one that finds Neeife in his place when the gun sounds, the commencement of the last leg of the race, and the moment of victory.
2. The group agreed that each of these moments needed further elaboration, using additional details and perhaps some qualities and comparisons.
3. The group also agreed that the piece would need an introduction that set the stage, providing background information about the race—its location, its importance, and Neeife's part in it. Neeife agreed with these, but held strongly to his conviction that his role in the race should not be revealed until the starting gun goes off, which is what he had done in his freewriting.

Next, Neeife set up four headings in his journal to assist him in focusing on each of the parts of his narrative. Then beneath each of these he wrote down the thoughts that came to mind. Here are the results:

The Setting	*The Start*	*The Last Leg*	*Victory*
date	alert	taking baton	crowd
location	calm	hearing footsteps	reaction
people in	like a snake	like talking	Mother's
attendance	jogging in place	drums	comment
	glance toward	running like	
	finish line	Carl Lewis in	
	approaching	Helsinki	
	runners	footsteps falling	
	like thorough-	behind me	
	bred race horses		

Armed with this outline, Neeife was ready to begin his next draft, which he again shared with his reading group. The reaction was again favorable. Several suggestions were made concerning the use of free modifiers, such as the two that appear in the second sentence of the first paragraph, and then Neeife wrote his final draft. Here it is, with the title he gave to it:

Going for the Gold

The 14th of April, 1979, was for me a day of joy, victory, and self-realization. The chanting, cheering, and joyous noise that filled the Nigerian evening that day were the result of an event—a track and field meet—that had been properly scheduled and widely advertised, allowing people from many villages and from many walks of life to converge on Arondizuogu Community Stadium after their day's work. Moreover, their hometown hero was going to bring home the gold medal—the most prized trophy in the competition.   1

I was nervous and tense inside, but my body was physically and mentally wide awake, calm on the outside, like a snake enjoying the sun. At the blast of the starting gun, the crowd on the infield started surging toward my position at the far end of the track where the staggered lines marked the starting points for the final leg of the 400 meters. Jogging in place, I tried one last time to focus on the tape marking the finish line, but before I could make it out, there came out of the near corner of my eye five able-bodied boys, running neck and neck like thoroughbreds. In a split second my signal came—"Go!"   2

As soon as I got a feel of the baton in my hand, I was heading for the tape. In my mind's eye was the newsreel of my idol, Carl Lewis, dashing to victory in Helsinki. That borrowed feeling of triumph invigorated my nerves. I was running for joy. Like the sound of an African talking drum, I could hear very clearly the rhythm of my opponents' steps abusing the track alongside me—then behind me.   3

When I hit the tape, my home crowd went wild. Mama said that I performed like her dad the day he won the village wrestling championship. "It is in the family," she said.   4

DISCUSSION QUESTIONS

1. The second sentence in the first paragraph is long and complicated. Does it work well or might it be revised to make it work better?
2. The first paragraph sets the stage for the actions that are to be narrated. But the narrator's actual participation in the race does not begin until paragraph 3. What purpose, then, does the second paragraph serve?
3. What clever tactic does the narrator employ to describe the way he pulls ahead of his opponents?

STUDENT WORK

On-the-Job Training

Seeing the obvious mistake from across the warehouse, the gray-haired supervisor walked up to the newest of the crew in hopes of enlightening him in the correct way of doing his job. As his pace slowed, the air of hopelessness enveloping him made him resemble the Saturday matinee sheriff ready for the showdown. Scanning the young man's output with a critic's eye, the old man slowly began to nod his head as he silently scrutinized the new boy's work. Finally, like a father having decided on a course of discipline, he reached out his hand to pat the boy's back. Breaking the silence with his patient voice, the knowledgeable elder commended his junior on his work, while making advice about how to remedy an obvious flaw seem like a mere digression. Having diplomatically resolved this problem, old Sharp Eyes took only a moment to glance at his watch before heading toward me.

DISCUSSION QUESTIONS

1. Writers of narrative sentences almost always add additional information to their sentences' main clauses. This additional infor-

mation will appear in any of three positions: (1) before the main clause (*Rustling the pages noisily,* Martha thumbed through the book); (2) after the main clause (Martha thumbed through the book, *rustling the pages noisily*); (3) between the subject and the predicate of the main clause (Martha, *rustling the pages noisily,* thumbed through the book). Which of these three positions does the writer of "On-the-Job Training" seem to prefer?

2. The additional information set off from the main clause, as described in question 1 above, is usually called a *free modifier* (see Glossary). Compare the use of free modifiers in "On-the-Job Training" and in the professionally written paragraph "Mating Flight" on p. 74. Determine how many free modifiers are used by each writer and in which position(s) each writer tends to place them.

On the Intermediate Slope

I glanced excitedly over to the rolling mountainsides surrounding me, peering through the large flakes of snow that danced downward toward my face. The trees nearby looked cold and lonesome, their bare, brown branches reaching tautly upward and outward, as if seeking warmth and companionship. Farther up, conical evergreens were bunched together, their outer limbs dipping heavily with the weight of the ever-increasing snow, pure in appearance due to its newness and feathered whiteness. The falling snow forced me to lower my face, and I looked down the slope. Like a giant white blanket it stretched in front of me, wide and soft, patterned with brightly colored figures growing constantly smaller, until they disappeared in the haze. Some of the figures moved quickly away, zigzagging efficiently, bent forward slightly, arms akimbo and poles slanting outward in a "V." Others moved more slowly, as if unsure, falling on occasion, only to rise, reclamp their bindings, and proceed on. Haltingly I sidled over to the starting point, my skis sifting the dry powder so that the wind sent it into twisting snake curls. Gathering my mounting courage, and pulling my thick scarf more tightly around my neck, its woolly fibers warming me, I pushed off down the inviting slope, leaving my doubts behind as a fledgling leaves its nest forever.

DISCUSSION QUESTIONS

1. "On the Intermediate Slope" lets us play video camera operator again, this time through the eyes of the narrator. When does the focus of attention shift? Is the shift necessary? Is it a good idea?
2. Is the ending of the one-paragraph narrative satisfactory? Why, or why not?

The Kiss

I couldn't believe it. It was like a dream come true. Finally, after drooling over Tom for all my high school years, he had asked me for a date. All my girlfriends looked starry-eyed at Tom whenever he strutted down the halls between classes, though other guys claimed that Tom was not that great. However, they always kept their girlfriends at a distance from him, and they took dance lessons, hoping to become as impressive as Tom was on the dance floor. With his olive skin, jet black hair, and sparkling blue bedroom eyes, Tom was the idol and heart throb of every girl I knew.

The few lucky girls that had the grand opportunity to go out with Tom said that he was the perfect date. Now I had the chance of a lifetime. To go out with Tom would be heaven, and I was sure it would be a night to remember always.

On Monday I had been failing an advanced math test because of goggling at Tom in the next row when he handed me a note that said, "Are you free Saturday night? I would like to take you out." My eyes still fixed on the paper in shock, I automatically nodded a yes, unconscious that he was there and had seen my mouth drop to the floor.

Later that afternoon when I came back down to the ground and the numbness had gone away, I realized I had a lot of preparing to do for my perfect date. A new fifty-dollar dress, a crash diet, a new haircut, exercises, and a new pair of three-inch heels were all part of my plan to win Tom's heart on Saturday night. Insomnia set in as I paced the floor and counted down the hours until the big event. Saturday morning I woke up with an awful surprise. I had large spots all over my face from not eating right. Dark circles under my swollen eyes proved that I had been the victim of sleepless nights. All day I worked on my horrid face, trying to make it look halfway presentable, and succeeding in the end. I had to wash my hair three times to get the new cut to look right. Stiff and sore from the exercises I had begun that week, I soaked in hot bath water for an hour in hopes that I wouldn't groan every time I had to move. My best jewelry and most expensive perfume were used lavishly. By 4:30 I was ready, sitting in the living room looking out the window, though Tom wasn't to arrive until 6:00. Finally he came driving up in his silver Porsche.

With weak knees I ran to the door and flung it open, ready for   5
my night in paradise. There Tom stood, a Greek god, in straight-legged Levis, a flannel shirt, and Adidas tennis shoes. He looked fantastic, but it was totally embarrassing when I remembered that I was very dressed up. As we started out the door, I realized that my new shoes made me about an inch taller than Tom, an obvious fact I was sure he would notice. I couldn't remember any of the conversations I had practiced in front of the mirror, and it seemed like eternity before we reached the restaurant, even though it was only about five or six miles. He took me to a German-type tavern where he ordered sauerkraut, hot potato salad, and a large German sausage. Since I was near the point of starvation from my diet, the heavy, hot German food made me not only lose my appetite, but become nauseated as well. However, poking bites into my dry mouth and forcing them down my throat gave me a chance to avoid conversation. When the meal was over, the movie theater was our next stop. Inside, the darkness was pleasant, hiding my blemished face and my over-dressy attire. So far the evening just wasn't going the way I had planned. Then Tom casually put his arm around me and took my hand in his, looking over to give me one of his flirtatious grins. I was floating again, and I still don't remember what movie we saw. On the way home I felt more at ease and relaxed with Tom than ever before. Maybe too relaxed, for as I remember back, I chattered the whole time, not letting him get in a word.

When we pulled into my driveway, however, I nervously   6
clammed up. It was almost time for the good-night kiss—the grand finale that I had longed to experience since the day I had first seen Tom. He stopped the car and came around the side to open my door. From my seat I looked up at him as he was romantically gazing down into the car at me. It seemed that he

was moving downward as if to kiss me through the window. I was eager to meet his kiss and started to lift my face upward to his. I closed my eyes to receive his kiss, and then my lips pressed against the cold, hard glass—the window had not been rolled down.

Totally humiliated when I realized what I had done and that Tom was only intending to open my door, I rushed to the house as quickly as my new three-inch heels could carry me, without looking back to see if the Greek god was following me to the door.   7

DISCUSSION QUESTIONS

1. This first-person narrative does not actually begin to unfold until paragraph 3. What function do the first two paragraphs serve?
2. Paragraph 4 is devoted to the preparations for the big date. They are listed in great detail. What effect does this listing have on the reader?
3. Paragraph 5, which narrates the events of the evening, is also slanted so that the writer's anxiety is always in the foreground. How many other instances of anxiety are added to the narrative?
4. Comment on the effective use of dashes in the crucial sixth paragraph.
5. Could the narrative have ended effectively with paragraph 6? What is the purpose of the last paragraph?

PARAGRAPHS

Granny's Fall

RICHARD WRIGHT

On one lazy, hot summer night Granny, my mother, and Aunt Addie were sitting on the front porch, arguing some obscure point of religious doctrine. I sat huddled on the steps, my cheeks resting sullenly in my palms, half listening to what the grownups were saying and half lost in a daydream. Suddenly the dispute evoked an idea in me and, forgetting that I had no right to speak without permission, I piped up and had my say. I must have sounded reekingly blasphemous, for Granny said, "Shut up, you!" and leaned forward promptly to chastise me with one of her casual, back-handed slaps on my mouth. But I had by now become adept at dodging blows and I nimbly ducked my head. She missed me; the force of her blow was so strong that she fell down the steps, headlong, her aged body wedged in a narrow space between the fence and the bottom step. I leaped up. Aunt Addie and my mother screamed and rushed down the steps and tried to pull Granny's body out. But they could not move her. Grandpa was called and he had to tear the fence down to rescue Granny. She was barely conscious. They put her to bed and summoned a doctor.

DISCUSSION QUESTIONS

1. This paragraph, taken from Wright's autobiography *Black Boy*, is a first-person narrative; that is, the speaker is telling a story in which he himself is a character. What other pieces of writing that you have examined earlier in this text have employed this first-person technique? How is this example different?
2. What is the effect of the short sentence, "I leaped up," which occurs a little past the midpoint of the paragraph?
3. Wright uses a peculiar figurative comparison when he says that his remark must have "sounded reekingly blasphemous." How exactly is this a comparison? Why is it peculiar, and how effective is it?

Morning Ballet

JANE JACOBS

The stretch of Hudson Street where I live is each day the scene of an intricate sidewalk ballet. I make my own first entrance into it a little after eight when I put out the garbage can, surely a prosaic occupation, but I enjoy my part, my little clang, as the droves of junior high school students walk by the center of the stage dropping candy wrappers. (How do they eat so much candy so early in the morning?) While I sweep up the wrappers I watch the other rituals of morning: Mr. Halpert unlocking the laundry's handcart from its mooring to a cellar door, Joe Comacchia's son-in-law stacking out the empty crates from the delicatessen, the barber bringing out his sidewalk folding chair, Mr. Goldstein arranging the coils of wire which proclaim the hardware store is open, the wife of the tenement's superintendent depositing her chunky three-year-old with a toy mandolin on the stoop, the vantage point from which he is learning the English his mother cannot speak. Now the primary children, heading for St. Luke's, dribble through to the south; the children for St. Veronica's cross, heading to the west, and the children for P.S. 41, heading toward the east. Two new entrances are being made from the wings: well-dressed and even elegant women and men with brief cases emerge from doorways and side streets. Most of these are heading for the bus and subways, but some hover on the curbs, stopping taxis which have miraculously appeared at the right moment, for the taxis are part of a wider morning ritual: having dropped passengers from midtown in the downtown financial district, they are now bringing downtowners up to midtown. Simultaneously, numbers of women in housedresses have emerged and as they crisscross with one another they pause for quick conversations that sound with either laughter or joint indignation, never, it seems, anything between. It is time for me to hurry to work too, and I exchange my ritual farewell with Mr. Lofaro, the short, thick-bodied, white-aproned fruit man who stands outside his doorway a little up the street, his arms folded, his feet planted, looking solid as earth itself. We nod; we each glance quickly up and down the street, then look back to each other and smile. We have done this many a morning for more than ten years, and we both know what it means: All is well.

DISCUSSION QUESTIONS

1. In this paragraph it is never clearly stated where Hudson Street is located. Yet there are some clues that suggest its location. What are they?
2. What details suggest the ethnic makeup of the neighborhood?
3. What technique does Jacobs use to sustain the notion that the street scene she is describing is like a ballet?

Mating Flight

N. SCOTT MOMADAY

They were golden eagles, a male and a female, in their mating flight. They were cavorting, spinning and spiraling on the cold, clear columns of air, and they were beautiful. They swooped and hovered, leaning on the air, and swung close together, feinting and screaming with delight. The female was full-grown, and the span of her broad wings was greater than any man's height. There was a fine flourish to her motion; she was deceptively, incredibly fast, and her pivots and wheels were wide and full-blown. But her great weight was streamlined and perfectly controlled. She carried a rattlesnake; it hung shining from her feet, limp and curving out in the trail of her flight. Suddenly her wings and tail fanned, catching full on the wind, and for an instant she was still, widespread and spectral in the blue, while her mate flared past and away, turning around in the distance to look for her. Then she began to beat upward at an angle from the rim until she was small in the sky, and she let go of the snake. It fell slowly, writhing and rolling, floating out like a bit of silver thread against the wide backdrop of the land. She held still above, buoyed up on the cold current, her crop and hackles gleaming like copper in the sun. The male swerved and sailed. He was younger than she and a little more than half as large. He was quicker, tighter in his moves. He let the carrion drift by; then suddenly he gathered himself and stooped, sliding down in a blur of motion to the strike. He hit the snake in the head, with not the slightest deflection of his course or speed, cracking its long body like a whip. Then he rolled and swung upward in a great pendulum arc, riding out his momentum. At the top of his glide he let go of the snake in turn, but the female did not go for it. Instead she soared out over the plain, nearly out of sight, like a mote receding into the haze of the far mountain. The male followed and Abel watched them go, straining to see, saw them veer once, dip and disappear.

DISCUSSION QUESTIONS

1. Many of the actions involved in "Mating Flight" occur simultaneously. How does Momaday manage to portray these actions so clearly and without confusion?

2. Contrast these simultaneous actions with the consecutive actions in "Granny's Fall." How are they different?
3. Read this passage aloud when you are alone. Do not hurry your reading and pause very briefly at the commas, a little longer at the semicolons and periods. You should notice that Momaday's prose has qualities we associate more with poetry. What are some of these?

ESSAYS

The Soul of a Dog

DANIEL M. PINKWATER

Daniel M. Pinkwater (b. 1941) is an artist and illustrator of children's books who lives in upstate New York. Also a prolific writer, he is the author of over twenty books for children (some under the name Manus Pinkwater). With his wife, Jill, he is the coauthor of Superpuppy: How to Choose, Raise, and Train the Best Possible Dog for You. *Pinkwater is also a regular contributor to National Public Radio's "All Things Considered." The following essay first aired on that program and was later included in Pinkwater's anthology* Fishwhistle *(1989).*

Once, Jill had fun with our Alaskan malamute, Arnold, by 1
pretending that she was teaching him a nursery song. It was pure nonsense—Jill was tending our old-fashioned, nonautomatic clothes washer, and Arnold was keeping her company.

Jill sang him the song about the eensy beensy spider, and 2
indicated where he was supposed to join in. He did so, with something between a scream of anguish and the call of a moose in rut.

The next time she had laundry to do, Arnold appeared, and 3
sat squirming excitedly until she sang him the song. He came in on cue. Arnold learned a number of songs. His vocal range was limited, but his ear was good.

It was also Arnold who taught Juno, our other dog, to set up 4
a howl whenever we passed a McDonald's. On a vacation trip, we'd breakfasted on Egg McMuffins for a week, and the dogs always got an English muffin. They never forgot.

I once observed Arnold taking care of an eight-week-old kit- 5
ten. The kitten was in a cage. Arnold wanted to go and sleep in
his private corner, but every time the kitten cried, he'd drag
himself to his feet, slouch over the cage and lie down with his
nose between the wires, so the kitten could sink its tiny claws
into it. When the kitten became quiet, Arnold would head for his
corner and flop, exhausted. Immediately the kitten would cry,
and Arnold would haul himself back to the cage. I counted this
performance repeated over forty times.

Arnold acquired friends. People would visit him.   6

My friend Don Yee would borrow Arnold sometimes, and   7
they'd drive to the White Castle and eat hamburgers.

He was the sort of dog you could talk things over with.   8

But he was not just a good listener, affable eccentric and bon   9
vivant. He was a magnificent athlete. While Juno was tireless and
efficient on the trail, Arnold made locomotion an art—a ballet.

Watching Arnold run flat-out in a large open space was un-   10
forgettable, and opened a window to something exceedingly ancient and precious—a link to the first time men followed dogs,
and hunted to live.

He was a splendid companion—and he would pull you up a   11
steep hill, if you were tired.

In a way, the hardest thing about living with dogs in modern   12
times is related to the excellent care we give them.

Vast sums are spent by pet food companies devising beauti-   13
fully balanced, cheap, palatable diets. Vet care these days is
superb—and most pet owners take advantage of it.

As a result, dogs live longer than they may have done, and   14
survive illnesses that they would not have survived in earlier
times. And it very often falls to us to decide when a dog's life has
to end—when suffering has come to outweigh satisfaction.

When it came Arnold's time to die, it was I who decided it. I   15
called the vet and told him I was bringing Arnold in.

He knew about malamute vigor. He prepared a syringe with   16
twice the dose it would take to put a dog Arnold's size to sleep.
"Put to sleep" is an apt euphemism. It's simply an overdose of a
sleeping drug. The dog feels nothing.

"There's enough in here for a gorilla," the vet wisecracked   17
weakly. He was very uncomfortable with what he had to do.

Arnold, of course, was completely comfortable—doing his   18
best to put everyone else at ease.

I held Arnold while the vet tied off a vein.   19

"This will take six, maybe eight seconds at most," the vet   20
said. He injected the fluid.

Nothing happened. Arnold, who had been completely re-   21
laxed, was now somewhat intent—but not unconscious, not
dead.

"Sometimes it takes a little longer," the vet said. It had been   22
a full half minute. Arnold was looking around.

The vet was perspiring—getting panicky. I knew what he was   23
thinking. Some ghastly error. The wrong stuff in the syringe.
More than a minute had passed.

A crazy thought occurred to me. Was it possible? Was Arnold   24
waiting for me to give him leave to go? I rubbed his shoulders
and spoke to him. "It's OK, Arnold, I release you." Instantly he
died.

I swear I felt his spirit leave his body.   25

The vet and I went outside and cried for a quarter of an hour.   26

He was an awfully good dog.   27

DISCUSSION: CONTENT

1. In the first five paragraphs, Pinkwater narrates three brief anecdotes about his dog Arnold, an Alaskan malamute. What is his
   purpose in relating these anecdotes?
2. Why, according to Pinkwater, do pets live longer and healthier
   lives today? What adverse effect does this produce for their owners?
3. The last twelve paragraphs describe a scene at the veterinary
   clinic. What is being narrated there besides Arnold's euthanasia?

DISCUSSION: FORM

1. Pinkwater uses very short paragraphs throughout. What effect is
   produced by this strategy? If you were to combine the last four
   paragraphs into one, how would the effect be altered?
2. This brief essay may be neatly divided into three segments. What
   is the purpose of each? What transitions mark the movements
   from one segment to the next?
3. If you were emotionally affected by this essay, you might try to
   discover how Pinkwater managed to create the effect and ma-
   nipulate your feelings. In what places in the narrative does Pinkwater tell you directly how you are supposed to feel about

Arnold? Why do you accept those directions? Having accepted
them, how do you respond to the last sentence? Would the essay
be as effective without it?

Nonnie's Day

MARY E. MEBANE

*Mary E. Mebane (b. 1933) was born in Durham, North Caro-
lina. She attended North Carolina College (now North Carolina Central University), and received her M.A. and Ph.D. from
the University of North Carolina at Chapel Hill. She has
taught high school and college English in North Carolina,
South Carolina and Wisconsin. Her writing includes a play,*
Take a Sad Song *(1975), and her autobiography,* Mary: An
Autobiography *(1981) (from which this selection describing her
mother was taken), as well as* Mary, Wayfarer *(1983), a second
installment of her autobiography.*

Nonnie led a structured, orderly existence. Before six o'clock   1
in the morning, she was up, starting her day. First she turned on
WPTF and listened to the news and the weather and the music.
Later, when WDNC in Durham hired Norfleet Whitted, the first
black announcer in the area, she listened first to one station, then
to the other. Some mornings it would be "They Traced Her Little
Footprints in the Snow," and other mornings it would be black
gospel-singing and rhythm-and-blues. Then she would make a
fire in the wood stove and start her breakfast. She prepared some
meat—fried liver pudding or fatback, or a streak-of-fat streak-of-
lean—and made a hoecake of bread on top of the stove, which she
ate with either Karo syrup or homemade blackberry preserves,
occasionally with store-bought strawberry preserves, or sometimes with homemade watermelon-rind preserves that she had
canned in the summer. Then she would drink her coffee, call me
to get up, and leave the house in her blue uniform, blue apron,
and blue cap—it would still be dark when she left on winter
mornings—and go to catch her ride to the tobacco factory (with
Mr. Ralph Baldwin at first, and then, when he retired, with Mr.
James Yergan). When Miss Delilah still lived in Wildwood, before
she and Mr. Leroy separated, she would come by and call from

the road and the two of them would walk together to the end of the road near the highway and wait for Mr. Ralph there.

My job after she left was to see that the fire didn't go out in the wood stove, to see that the pots sitting on the back didn't burn—for in them was our supper, often pinto beans or black-eyed peas or collard greens or turnip salad. Occasionally there was kale or mustard greens or cressy salad. The other pot would have the meat, which most often was neck bones or pig feet or pig ears, and sometimes spareribs. These would cook until it was time for me to go to school; then I would let the fire die down, only to relight it when I came home to let the pots finish cooking.

After Nonnie left, I also had the task of getting Ruf Junior up so that he could get to school on time. This presented no problem to me until Ruf Junior was in high school and started playing basketball. Often he would travel with the team to schools in distant towns, sometimes getting home after midnight, and the next morning he would be tired and sleepy and wouldn't want to get up. I sympathized, but I had my job to do. If I let him oversleep, I knew that Nonnie would fuss when she got home. But on the other hand, no matter how often I called to him, he would murmur sleepily, "All right, all right," then go back to sleep. I solved this problem one bitter-cold winter morning. I jerked all the covers off his bed and ran. I knew that the only place he could get warm again would be in the kitchen. (The only fire was in the wood stove.) The fire was already out, so he'd have to make one. After that, I didn't have such a hard time getting him up.

My mother worked as a cutter, clipping the hard ends off each bundle of tobacco before it was shredded to make cigarettes. At noon she ate the lunch she had brought from home in a brown paper bag: a biscuit with meat in it and a sweet potato or a piece of pie or cake. Some of the women ate in the cafeteria, but in her thirty years at the Liggett and Myers factory, she never once did. She always took her lunch. Then she worked on until closing time, caught her ride back to Wildwood, and started on the evening's activities. First she had supper, which I had finished preparing from the morning. After I got older we sometimes had meat other than what had to be prepared in a "pot." It would be my duty to fry chicken or prepare ham bits and gravy.

After supper, she'd read the Durham *Sun* and see to it that we did the chores if we hadn't done them already: slop the hogs,

feed the chickens, get in the wood for the next day. Then we were
free. She'd get her blue uniform ready for the next day, then listen
to the radio. No later than nine o'clock, she would be in bed. In
the morning she would get up, turn on the radio, and start frying
some fatback. Another day would have started.

DISCUSSION: CONTENT

1. What do you learn about Nonnie from the description of her radio
   listening habits?
2. What may we infer about Nonnie from her breakfast routine?
3. What do you make of the references to the four people mentioned
   at the end of paragraph 1? Is there any significance to be attached
   to the fact that the first two have their complete names mentioned along with their titles while the last two are called by title
   and first name?
4. What further facts about Nonnie's impoverished state are implied
   by the facts mentioned in paragraphs 2 and 3?
5. What evidence do you find in the final two paragraphs that Nonnie is doing more than surviving, that she is working and planning for a better life for her children?

DISCUSSION: FORM

1. Mebane uses free modifiers less often than Momaday, but when
   she does use them, in what position does she most frequently
   place them—before or after the main clause?
2. Examine paragraphs 2–5 and point out the transitional devices
   that Mebane uses in each paragraph to show the steady passage
   of time during Nonnie's day.
3. Other than the thesis statement, which begins the selection,
   what sentences underscore the cyclical, repetitive nature of Nonnie's existence?

Christmas

FLOYD DELL

*Floyd James Dell (1887–1969), a high school dropout at 17,
became a reporter for a Davenport, Iowa, newspaper in 1905.
By 1911 he was editor of Chicago's* Friday Literary Review,

during a burst of interest in the arts known as the Chicago Renaissance, and he helped to foster the careers of such notable writers as Sherwood Anderson and Carl Sandburg. In 1913 Dell published his first book, Women as World-Builders, *signalling his lifelong interest in women's rights. That year he also moved to New York City, settling in Greenwich Village as managing editor of the radical magazine* The Masses. *Throughout the 1920s and early 1930s he published a succession of books, including eleven novels, collections of short stories and essays, and four nonfiction books. Always a rebel (he joined the Socialist Party at 16) and champion of a variety of social and human rights causes, he nevertheless spent his last active working years inside the Federal bureaucracy in Washington as a writer for the Works Progress Administration, 1935–1947. Dell recounted his early experiences in autobiographical novels as well as in* Homecoming: An Autobiography *(1933), from which the following essay is taken.*

(Memories of childhood are strange things. The obscurity of the past opens upon a little lighted space—a scene, unconnected with anything else. One must figure out when it happened. There may be anomalies in the scene, which need explanation. Sometimes the scenes are tiny fragments only. Again they are long dramas. Having once been remembered, they can be lived through again in every moment, with a detailed experiencing of movement and sensation and thought. One can start the scene in one's mind and see it all through again. Exactly so it was—clearer in memory than something that happened yesterday, though it was forty years ago. And, oddly enough, if there is some detail skipped over, lost out of the memory picture, no repetition of the remembering process will supply it—the gap is always there.)

That fall, before it was discovered that the soles of both my shoes were worn clear through, I still went to Sunday school. And one time the Sunday-school superintendent made a speech to all the classes. He said that these were hard times, and that many poor children weren't getting enough to eat. It was the first that I had heard about it. He asked everybody to bring some food for the poor children next Sunday. I felt very sorry for the poor children.

Also, little envelopes were distributed to all the classes. Each little boy and girl was to bring money for the poor, next Sunday.

The pretty Sunday-school teacher explained that we were to write our names, or have our parents write them, up in the left-hand corner of the little envelopes. . . . I told my mother all about it when I came home. And my mother gave me, the next Sunday, a small bag of potatoes to carry to Sunday school. I supposed the poor children's mothers would make potato soup out of them. . . . Potato soup was good. My father, who was quite a joker, would always say, as if he were surprised, "Ah! I see we have some nourishing potato soup today!" It was so good that we had it every day. My father was at home all day long and every day, now; and I liked that, even if he was grumpy as he sat reading Grant's "Memoirs." I had my parents all to myself, too; the others were away. My oldest brother was in Quincy, and memory does not reveal where the others were: perhaps with relatives in the country.

Taking my small bag of potatoes to Sunday school, I looked   4
around for the poor children; I was disappointed not to see them. I had heard about poor children in stories. But I was told just to put my contribution with the others on the big table in the side room.

I had brought with me the little yellow envelope, with some   5
money in it for the poor children. My mother had put the money in it and sealed it up. She wouldn't tell me how much money she had put in it, but it felt like several dimes. Only she wouldn't let me write my name on the envelope. I had learned to write my name, and I was proud of being able to do it. But my mother said firmly, *no*, I must *not* write my name on the envelope; she didn't tell me why. On the way to Sunday school I had pressed the envelope against the coins until I could tell what they were; they weren't dimes but pennies.

When I handed in my envelope, my Sunday-school teacher   6
noticed that my name wasn't on it, and she gave me a pencil; I could write my own name, she said. So I did. But I was confused because my mother had said not to; and when I came home, I confessed what I had done. She looked distressed. "I told you not to!" she said. But she didn't explain why. . . .

I didn't go back to school that fall. My mother said it was   7
because I was sick. I did have a cold the week that school opened; I had been playing in the gutters and had got my feet wet, because there were holes in my shoes. My father cut insoles out of cardboard, and I wore those in my shoes. As long as I had to stay in the house anyway, they were all right.

I stayed cooped up in the house, without any companionship. 8
We didn't take a Sunday paper any more, but the Barry *Adage*
came every week in the mails; and though I did not read small
print, I could see the Santa Clauses and holly wreaths in the
advertisements.

There was a calendar in the kitchen. The red days were 9
Sundays and holidays; and that red 25 was Christmas. (It was on
a Monday, and the two red figures would come right together in
1893; but this represents research in the World Almanac, not
memory.) I knew when Sunday was, because I could look out
of the window and see the neighbor's children, all dressed up,
going to Sunday school. I knew just when Christmas was going
to be.

But there was something queer! My father and mother didn't 10
say a word about Christmas. And once, when I spoke of it, there
was a strange, embarrassed silence; so I didn't say anything more
about it. But I wondered, and was troubled. Why didn't they say
anything about it? Was what I had said I wanted (memory refuses
to supply that detail) too expensive?

I wasn't arrogant and talkative now. I was silent and fright- 11
ened. What was the matter? Why didn't my father and mother
say anything about Christmas? As the day approached, my chest
grew tighter with anxiety.

Now it was the day before Christmas. I couldn't be mistaken. 12
But not a word about it from my father and mother. I waited in
painful bewilderment all day. I had supper with them, and was
allowed to sit up for an hour. I was waiting for them to say
something. "It's time for you to go to bed," my mother said
gently. I *had* to say something.

"This is Christmas Eve, isn't it?" I asked, as if I didn't know. 13

My father and mother looked at one another. Then my 14
mother looked away. Her face was pale and stony. My father
cleared his throat, and his face took on a joking look. He pretended
he hadn't known it was Christmas Eve, because he hadn't been
reading the papers. He said he would go downtown and find out.

My mother got up and walked out of the room. I didn't want 15
my father to have to keep on being funny about it, so I got up and
went to bed. I went by myself without having a light. I undressed
in the dark and crawled into bed.

I was numb. As if I had been hit by something. It was hard to 16
breathe. I ached all through. I was stunned—with finding out the
truth.

My body knew before my mind quite did. In a minute, when   17
I could think, my mind would know. And as the pain in my body
ebbed, the pain in my mind began. I *knew*. I couldn't put it into
words yet. But I knew why I had taken only a little bag of
potatoes to Sunday school that fall. I knew why there had been
only pennies in my little yellow envelope. I knew why I hadn't
gone to school that fall—why I hadn't any new shoes—why we
had been living on potato soup all winter. All these things, and
others, many others, fitted themselves together in my mind, and
meant something.

Then the words came into my mind and I whispered them   18
into the darkness:

"We're poor!"

That was it. I was one of those poor children I had been sorry   19
for, when I heard about them in Sunday school. My mother
hadn't told me. My father was out of work, and we hadn't any
money. That was why there wasn't going to be any Christmas at
our house.

Then I remembered something that made me squirm with   20
shame—a boast. (Memory will not yield this up. Had I said to
some Nice little boy, "I'm going to be President of the United
States"? Or to a Nice little girl: "I'll marry you when I grow up"?
It was some boast as horribly shameful to remember.)

"We're poor." There in bed in the dark, I whispered it over   21
and over to myself. I was making myself get used to it. (Or—just
torturing myself, as one presses the tongue against a sore tooth?
No, memory says, not like that—but to keep myself from ever
being such a fool again: suffering now, to keep this awful thing
from ever happening again. Memory is clear on that; it was more
like pulling the tooth, to get it over with—never mind the pain,
this will be the end!)

It wasn't so bad, now that I knew. I just *hadn't known!* I had   22
thought all sorts of foolish things: that I was going to Ann
Arbor—going to be a lawyer—going to make speeches in the
Square, going to be President. Now I knew better.

I had wanted (something) for Christmas. I didn't want it, now.   23
I didn't want anything.

I lay there in the dark, feeling the cold emotion of renuncia-   24
tion. (The tendrils of desire unfold their clasp on the outer world
of objects, withdraw, shrivel up. Wishes shrivel up, turn black,
die. It is like that.)

It hurt. But nothing would ever hurt again. I would never let   25
myself want anything again.

I lay there stretched out straight and stiff in the dark, my fists   26
clenched hard upon Nothing. . . .

In the morning it had been like a nightmare that is not clearly   27
remembered—that one wishes to forget. Though I hadn't hung up
any stocking, there was one hanging at the foot of my bed. A bag
of popcorn, and a lead pencil, for me. They had done the best they
could, now they realized that I knew about Christmas. But they
needn't have thought they had to. I didn't want anything.

DISCUSSION: CONTENT

1. What hints are given during the first half of the narrative that the
   Dell family has economic problems?
2. Dell seems to have stopped going to Sunday school after the
   episode involving the pennies in the envelope for the poor. What
   are at least two reasons his parents probably kept him at home?
3. Examine Dell's reactions, physical and psychological, after he
   goes to bed on Christmas Eve (paragraphs 15–26). Make a list of
   words that come to mind to describe his emotional state in
   particular, and be prepared to discuss those and how they are or
   are not typical of a young child.
4. Examine your own reaction to Dell's story. Write down a word or
   phrase that describes your emotional reaction(s) to each of these
   sections of the essay: paragraphs 2–6; 9–15; 16–19; 20–26; 27.
5. This narrative describes a real incident when Dell was six, early
   in the depression of 1893 to 1896, one of the most difficult
   economic periods in American history besides the Great Depression of the 1930s. What public and private social services now
   commonly available could have eased the plight of the Dell
   family?

DISCUSSION: FORM

1. What purpose seems to be served in the essay by paragraphs 1 and
   27, which Dell emphasizes by using extra space to set them off
   from the rest of the essay?
2. Clearly Dell, even forty years afterward, finds the memory of this
   childhood Christmas to be painful. How does he use word choice,

point of view, and irony to touch our emotions without presenting his experience as overly sentimental?
3. The tension of the story builds until paragraph 17, when Dell
suddenly puts together all of the pieces of the intellectual puzzle
that he could not figure out in the previous months, thereby
solving it. How is paragraph 18 used to emphasize Dell's discovery of that solution?
4. What does the narrative gain by Dell's use of very short paragraphs (paragraphs 22–26) at the end of the Christmas eve episode?

Look at Your Fish

SAMUEL H. SCUDDER

*Samuel H. Scudder (1837–1911) was an American naturalist, a
graduate of Williams College who then attended Lawrence
Scientific School at Harvard, where he came under the influence of Professor Jean Louis R. Agassiz, as reported in the essay
below. Professor Agassiz (1807–1873) was Swiss-born, an outstanding European scientist, especially in the field of compara-
tive anatomy, who came to America and, from 1848 until his
death, was a great and famous teacher at Harvard. Beyond his
influence on future generations of scientists, such as Scudder,
Professor Agassiz was also one of the founders of the National
Academy of Sciences.*

It was more than fifteen years ago that I entered the labora- 1
tory of Professor Agassiz, and told him I had enrolled my name
in the Scientific School as a student of natural history. He asked
me a few questions about my object in coming, my antecedents
generally, the mode in which I afterwards proposed to use the
knowledge I might acquire, and, finally, whether I wished to
study any special branch. To the latter I replied that, while I
wished to be well grounded in all departments of zoology, I
purposed to devote myself specially to insects.

"When do you wish to begin?" he asked.   2
"Now," I replied.   3
This seemed to please him, and with an energetic "Very   4
well!" he reached from a shelf a huge jar of specimens in yellow
alcohol." Take this fish," he said, "and look at it; we call it a
haemulon; by and by I will ask what you have seen."

With that he left me, but in a moment returned with explicit   5
instructions as to the care of the object entrusted to me.

"No man is fit to be a naturalist," said he, "who does not   6
know how to take care of specimens."

I was to keep the fish before me in a tin tray, and occasionally   7
moisten the surface with alcohol from the jar, always taking care
to replace the stopper tightly. Those were not the days of ground
glass stoppers and elegantly shaped exhibition jars; all the old
students will recall the huge neckless glass bottles with their
leaky, wax-besmeared corks, half eaten by insects, and begrimed
with cellar dust. Entomology was a cleaner science than ichthy-
ology, but the example of the Professor, who had unhesitatingly
plunged to the bottom of the jar to produce the fish, was infectious, and though this alcohol had a "very ancient and fishlike
smell," I really dared not show any aversion within these sacred
precincts, and treated the alcohol as though it were pure water.
Still I was conscious of a passing feeling of disappointment, for
gazing at a fish did not commend itself to an ardent entomolo-
gist. My friends at home, too, were annoyed when they discovered that no amount of eau-de-Cologne would drown the perfume
which haunted me like a shadow.

In ten minutes I had seen all that could be seen in that fish,   8
and started in search of the Professor—who had, however, left the
Museum; and when I returned, after lingering over some of the
odd animals stored in the upper apartment, my specimen was dry
all over. I dashed the fluid over the fish as if to resuscitate the
beast from a fainting fit, and looked with anxiety for a return of
the normal sloppy appearance. This little excitement over, nothing was to be done but to return to a steadfast gaze at my mute
companion. Half an hour passed—an hour—another hour; the
fish began to look loathsome. I turned it over and around; looked
it in the face—ghastly; from behind, beneath, above, sideways, at
a three-quarters' view—just as ghastly. I was in despair; at an
early hour I concluded that lunch was necessary; so, with infinite
relief, the fish was carefully replaced in the jar, and for an hour I
was free.

On my return, I learned that Professor Agassiz had been at   9
the Museum, but had gone, and would not return for several
hours. My fellow-students were too busy to be disturbed by
continued conversation. Slowly I drew forth that hideous fish,
and with a feeling of desperation again looked at it. I might not
use a magnifying-glass; instruments of all kinds were interdicted.

My two hands, my two eyes, and the fish: it seemed a most limited field. I pushed my finger down its throat to feel how sharp the teeth were. I began to count the scales in the different rows, until I was convinced that that was nonsense. At last a happy thought struck me—I would draw the fish; and now with surprise I began to discover new features in the creature. Just then the Professor returned.

"That is right," said he; "a pencil is one of the best of eyes. I   10
am glad to notice, too, that you keep your specimen wet, and your bottle corked."

With these encouraging words, he added: 11

"Well, what is it like?

He listened attentively to my brief rehearsal of the struc-   12
ture of parts whose names were still unknown to me; the fringed gill-arches and movable operculum; the pores of the head, fleshy lips and lidless eyes; the lateral line, the spinous fins and forked tail; the compressed and arched body. When I finished, he waited as if expecting more, and then, with an air of disappointment:

"You have not looked very carefully; why," he continued   13
more earnestly, "you haven't even seen one of the most con-spicuous features of the animal, which is as plainly before your eyes as the fish itself; look again, look again!" and he left me to my misery.

I was piqued; I was mortified. Still more of that wretched   14
fish! But now I set myself to my task with a will, and discovered one new thing after another, until I saw how just the Professor's criticism had been. The afternoon passed quickly; and when, towards its close, the Professor inquired:

"Do you see it yet?"

"No, I replied, "I am certain I do not, but I see how little I   15
saw before."

"That is next best," said he, earnestly, "but I won't hear you   16
now; put away your fish and go home; perhaps you will be ready with a better answer in the morning. I will examine you before you look at the fish."

This was disconcerting. Not only must I think of my fish all   17
night, studying, without the object before me, what this un-known but most visible feature might be; but also, without reviewing my discoveries, I must give an exact account of them the next day. I had a bad memory; so I walked home by Charles River in a distracted state, with my two perplexities.

The cordial greeting from the Professor the next morning was   18
reassuring; here was a man who seemed to be quite as anxious as
I that I should see for myself what he saw.

"Do you perhaps mean," I asked, "that the fish has symmet-   19
rical sides with paired organs?"

His thoroughly pleased "Of course! of course!" repaid the   20
wakeful hours of the previous night. After he had discoursed
most happily and enthusiastically—as he always did—upon
the importance of this point, I ventured to ask what I should
do next.

"Oh, look at your fish!" he said, and left me again to my own   21
devices. In a little more than an hour he returned, and heard my
new catalogue.

"That is good, that is good," he repeated; "but that is not all;   22
go on"; and so for three long days he placed that fish before my
eyes, forbidding me to look at anything else, or to use any artificial aid. "Look, look, look," was his repeated injunction.

This was the best entomological lesson I ever had—a lesson   23
whose influence has extended to the details of every subsequent
study; a legacy the Professor had left to me, as he has left it to
many others, of inestimable value, which we could not buy, with
which we cannot part.

A year afterward, some of us were amusing ourselves with   24
chalking outlandish beasts on the Museum blackboard. We drew
prancing starfishes; frogs in mortal combat; hydra-headed
worms; stately crawfishes, standing on their tails, bearing aloft
umbrellas; and grotesque fishes with gaping mouths and staring
eyes. The Professor came in shortly after, and was as amused as
any at our experiments. He looked at the fishes.

"Haemulons, every one of them," he said; "Mr. ——— drew   25
them."

True; and to this day, if I attempt a fish, I can draw nothing   26
but haemulons.

The fourth day, a second fish of the same group was placed   27
beside the first, and I was bidden to point out the resemblances
and differences between the two; another and another followed,
until the entire family lay before me, and a whole legion of jars
covered the table and surrounding shelves; the odor had become
a pleasant perfume; and even now, the sight of an old, six-inch,
worm-eaten cork brings fragrant memories.

The whole group of haemulons was thus brought in review;   28
and, whether engaged upon the dissection of the internal organs,

the preparation and examination of the bony framework, or the description of the various parts, Agassiz's training in the method of observing facts and their orderly arrangement was ever accompanied by the urgent exhortation not to be content with them.

"Facts are stupid things," he would say, "until brought into   29 connection with some general law."

At the end of eight months, it was almost with reluctance   30 that I left these friends and turned to insects; but what I had gained by this outside experience has been of greater value than years of later investigation in my favorite groups.

DISCUSSION: CONTENT

1. Describe Professor Agassiz's teaching method. Which of your instructors has used a similar method? How well did it work for you?
2. What did Professor Agassiz say about a pencil?
3. Why was Scudder's lengthy study of a single fish the best *entomological* lesson he ever had?

DISCUSSION: FORM

1. This essay, like those that precede it in this chapter, is a narration, relating to a series of events. But in actuality it is more than a narrative, and you as the reader soon realize this fact. In what paragraph do you begin to suspect that Scudder is telling the story to illustrate some point rather than just to be entertaining? What is his point? Write a single sentence that states Scudder's thesis in general terms.
2. Eventually, Scudder's fish takes on a symbolic value. What does it symbolize?
3. What lesson does Professor Agassiz's method of instruction hold for student writers? Could you profit in a similar way if you were told by an instructor to "look at your paragraph"? What sort or sorts of paragraphs might be the most profitable for close study?

PART TWO

Expository Writing

Exposition is the second major type of prose writing. Its purpose is to inform or instruct and to make readers understand. To achieve its purpose, exposition frequently relies on the techniques of narration and description. Likewise, exposition often has a persuasive or even an argumentative "edge," intending not only to make readers understand, but to change opinions they hold. This is particularly true when such opinions are based on limited information.

In learning how to write good expository prose, you should become familiar with methods of development that date back to Aristotle, who first gave them names. (He called all these methods *topoi,* or "topics.") They may be thought of as convenient ways of thinking—grooves or channels in which the human mind naturally runs. We are going to give you a brief explanation of each of the methods, so you can begin at once to understand their basic features and their relationships to one another.

The first method of development in expository writing is *illustration by example.* It is very closely related to narration. If you want to explain a principle or confirm an observation, a convenient way is to use **exemplification.** You may offer numerous short examples or may choose to develop several, or a single one, more thoroughly.

The second method of expository development is **classification.** Here you clarify a subject by separating or grouping it into its constituent elements or classes. That is precisely what we are doing right now—dividing expository writing into seven classes or categories.

Process development, the third method, is related to classification and to narration in that it arranges events in logical order, putting them in a step-by-step sequence.

The fourth method is **comparison.** Comparison was mentioned earlier in Part One in connection with narrative-descriptive writing, but it is also useful in exposition. In applying this method of development, you will examine the features of two or more objects, places, persons, or ideas in an organized fashion, determining what characteristics they have, or do not have, in common.

Analogy, the fifth method, is similar to comparison in that it looks at two subjects (in fact, it's an extended comparison), but it differs in its effort to explain an unfamiliar subject by comparing it with a familiar one.

The sixth method involves **cause and effect.** Confronted with a given situation such as rising prices for food and fuel, you may ask, "Why does this situation exist? What will happen if it persists?" In asking these questions and answering them, you expect to ascertain a causal chain, a series of causes and effects, which will suggest an appropriate arrangement of ideas for writing.

A seventh method of exposition, **definition,** is most useful when you want to introduce to the reader a new and unfamiliar term or concept, such as *quarks* or *legal entailments.* This method of development, most often associated with dictionaries, is frequently used along with one or more of the other methods to furnish brief explanations of terms. But on occasion it may be employed as the chief organizing device for an entire essay.

We have discussed these seven methods of development separately, in their "pure" forms. You must understand, however, that writers frequently will combine several of these methods— along with description and narration, plus the persuasive techniques discussed later in this book—both to present their ideas and to help their readers understand those ideas more fully. After all, writers are more interested in communicating their ideas successfully than in furnishing illustrations for effective writing techniques.

Sometimes, however, a single method of development is clearly dominant in a piece of writing, whether it takes the form of a paragraph, an essay, or even a book. This has allowed us to furnish sample paragraphs and essays, by professional and student writers whose work is clearly dominated by one of the seven methods, so that you can study that method in a model that approaches the "pure" form.

5

Examples

Examples and Your Thesis

Development by examples is probably the method of exposition you will use most, especially when your objective is to present new or unfamiliar information.

Once you have decided on the new or unfamiliar information you wish to relate, you must state your case as briefly as possible. A single sentence is best:

1. Studying differential equations can be a terrifying experience.
2. Ellen Brown is clever as well as attractive.
3. Basketball is now a popular sport in many countries around the world.
4. Neanderthal man practiced a rudimentary form of democracy.

Each of these statements might well serve as the *topic sentence* for an expository paragraph or as the *thesis sentence* for an expository essay. The purpose of such sentences is to state a fact or an opinion about which some readers may know little or nothing and hence may want or need to know more. Notice that each statement is somewhat abstract; a reader, having read it, probably understands your intentions only vaguely. The reader needs something more, and you must supply it. That is where examples come in. If you are trying to amaze a hometown friend with the rigors of college life, you might very easily claim that

93

differential equations are difficult to the point of impossibility. If the friend is unimpressed, you might supply evidence by offering several pages of typical homework, bristling with radicals, integrals, summations, and other mysterious mathematical symbols. Then there would surely follow a tale of some length and detail, describing the unreadable textbook, cataloging the hours of frustration spent in preparing that assignment, and ending with a terrifying confrontation with the math professor in class. At this point the hometown friend may not be convinced of the intrinsic difficulty of differential equations, but at least the hardship they pose for you can hardly be questioned. Information has changed hands, and that, after all, is the principal aim of exposition: to inform.

Notice that the examples used in the situation just described were of two sorts: short examples delivered in quantity—the homework problems—and the single, more fully developed example—the story surrounding the assignment. By using both types of examples, you're on familiar ground, because both types depend on the techniques you already observed in your analysis of description and narration. In supplying brief examples, you were concentrating chiefly on details; in writing a longer example, you were telling a story, or narrating.

The other three thesis statements presented in the sentence examples may be handled in a similar fashion. If you were to write that Ellen is clever and attractive, you would then want to list at least some of her charms and graces for verification, or to retell a particularly exemplary chapter in her life. Similarly, if you claim that basketball enjoys international popularity, you might enumerate countries on every continent around the globe to support your point, or perhaps describe the competition at the most recent Summer Olympic Games. Finally, a series of cultural traits attributed to Neanderthals may prove to be a good way of confirming their practice of democracy; then again, narrating the reconstruction of a day in the life of a Neanderthal community might well be more useful and more interesting.

Obviously, generating interest is important. Examples, because they are concrete, remove the reader from the dull generality of the thesis statement. Examples bring readers face to face with real events, ideas, and people. They make the experience more real and more interesting. Furthermore, in practical terms, learning to use examples effectively is crucial to your own future success, since development by examples is the most common feature of all serious expository and argumentative writing, both in school and at work. Your instructors and your employers will want you to support your ideas with relevant examples—facts, quotations, statistics, and the like. A claim of increased sales by your division will need to be bolstered by the actual dollar figures, just as a report asserting the effectiveness of a new antibiotic that you helped develop must include clinical data. Failure to provide such support will likely mean your own failure, in one way or another, while providing it should result in success, for your ideas and for you. Of course, examples will seldom provide the only method of development in an essay. Almost always they will be mingled with comparisons, definitions, causes and effects, and so on, as we shall see in the following sections.

Commentary on Student Work

This was the assignment that prompted the first paper in this section: Think about life on this campus, and then make some general statement about classes or customs or teachers or students or the like that you feel deserves an explanation, especially for those who do not live here (such as parents or friends back home). Then use examples, either a number of brief ones or an extended one, to explain your statement.

Margo, the author of this paper, began by drawing on her assignment sheet four columns, one for each of the suggested subjects in the assignment: *classes, customs, teachers, students.* In later discussion, Margo admitted that she could have added other elements to this list, but she had to start somewhere. These, after all, were the ones that had come first to the teacher's mind and were stated in the assignment itself.

Under *classes* Margo noted that Advanced Drawing classes had nude models, and under *teachers* she observed that the sociologists and criminal justice professors who had offices in the building that housed the Art Department were generally better dressed and more conservative in appearance than her art professors. *Customs* did not receive an entry, but *students* evoked this brief sentence: "Art majors are freaks."

When she shared her thoughts with her writing group, it was this last observation that stirred the greatest interest. The nude models, they felt, did not need much explanation, and the claim about the contrasting fashion trends among sociologists and artists was more likely to result in a comparison than a simple illustration. The statement about freaky art majors seemed worthy of further attention, and the group began to brainstorm. The members challenged Margo to provide some examples of freaky art students she had met so far, and she immediately responded with a description of a guy named Jock, who wore eye shadow. And then there was Glenda, the doll-maker, who made deformed and mangled dolls that were very much in her own image.

These were the two freaks that Margo obviously had in mind, but further prompting caused her to admit that perhaps she was one herself. After all, she was an art major who had dyed her hair purple last semester as part of her work with colors.

Three examples were probably enough to make the paper work, but one of the members supplied a fourth—Charlene, the girl with the weird hair-do. It was fairly certain that she was an art major too. Exactly what the hair-dos had to do with her art was not very clear, but creative license could surely supply something. So Margo was sent back to work it out.

Several rewrites were required to get the paper into the shape in which it appears here. First, Margo had to give the paper a tighter focus than the original "Art majors are freaks." She began with an introductory paragraph in which she established the thesis that art majors are easy to pick out because of their peculiar modes of dress. But this proved to be not quite the right fit for the examples that she and her group had amassed. The weirdness or freakiness of the art majors' dress or appearance seemed to have some definite connection to their art work. That insight eventually led to a tightening of the thesis and the creation of the second paragraph.

Because she could not type and was more than a little frightened by the word-processing lab, Margo's revisions were more laborious than most. She tried several orderings of her examples before arriving at the final version. She also had some trouble attempting to use the exotic modifiers that the instructor was anxious for everyone to experiment with. Furthermore, punctuation, always a problem for her, needed considerable fine-tuning. Eventually, though, Margo produced the following paper, which the writing group agreed was ready to be submitted.

Art Majors Are Different

It seems that most of the art majors at this college enjoy being   1
as different as possible from everyone else on campus. The Art
Department has a long-standing reputation for attracting a certain
type of person: tie-dyed shirts, peasant blouses, black China shoes,
and frizzy uncombed hair are typical traits of many art majors. This
is not to say that no other department on campus has students that
fit this description, but a tour through the Art Building is sure to
turn up more such students than can be found elsewhere.

Being an art major myself, it is easy for me to see why people   2
tend to think we are weirded out. We are encouraged to be different,
to take things to extremes, to push things to the limit. Our teachers
give us assignments that force us to think creatively and differently,
assuring us that the more wrapped up in our projects we become,
the better and more creative they will be.

Last year Glenda, a girl from Salem, did a series of drawings   3
of mangled and deformed dolls. She worked on the project all
semester, and it is no wonder that before the year was over she
had begun to look like a zombie herself. Charlene, a printmaker
from Florida, was experimenting with methods of portraying hair
texture. Each of her efforts featured subjects with increasingly
bushy and extravagant hairdos. And sure enough, Charlene's own
hair got wilder and wilder. Stranger still was Jock, who became
so engrossed in his attempts to capture facial highlights that he
started to wear brown eye shadow and a pale blush.

Even I, who consider myself something of a conservative, have   4
been drawn into the madness. I have been doing a lot of work with
color this semester, and I just couldn't resist tinting my hair purple—to express what I have learned by working on my project.

It becomes so easy to live what we are trying so hard to learn   5
that we often get laughed at and talked about, but I have yet to
meet a business or accounting major with half the guts and
character that art majors have.

DISCUSSION QUESTIONS

1. What is the thesis of this essay as it is stated in the opening
   paragraph? How does the second paragraph serve to reinforce the
   thesis?

2. Why does the writer use a separate paragraph to present the fourth example in the series that started in paragraph 3?
3. The second paragraph contains a couple of improprieties that you might wish to correct—a dangling modifier and a slang expression. Or is it possible to make a case for the effectiveness of either of these constructions?

STUDENT WORK

Accelerated Incubation

Scientists often experiment with life—its beginning in particular. Some organisms begin development in an egg, and scientists will try to speed up this process by simulated conditions in order to deduce whether or not any abnormalities or impairments will result.   1

But occurrences such as these need not be made in sparkling laboratories to be effective, nor by professionals in white lab coats to be observed. In fact, they may happen quite by accident!   2

A good friend of mine brought to school a small, pungent evergreen bough off her family's Christmas tree. Firmly attached to one side was a white, slightly papery mass of eggs which she recognized as those of a praying mantis. Realizing their valuable quality of devouring crop-eating insects, she resolved to keep them for a professor she knew who would appreciate them in spring. She placed the bough gingerly on her small, high bookshelf, only a few feet above a none-too-cool heater, thinking they would keep until spring.   3

Now, one factor in the early development of organisms is warmth—coolness induces dormancy, warmth induces growth. Insect eggs wait over winter until the warm spring weather mysteriously triggers a mechanism to incubate the offspring to the hatching stage. The papery clump of eggs resting over the heater underwent accelerated incubation. Perfectly formed, slender, green praying mantises with bulging brown eyes, spindly legs, and folded arms emerged in January instead of May. Jumping upon the shelves, walls, down into the window, crawling swiftly over the desk, stereo, and record albums, these tiny crea-   4 tures had come under bizarre conditions to give us an "experiment." It was quite by nature's accident, and quite to our surprise.

DISCUSSION QUESTIONS

1. "Accelerated Incubation" furnishes a clear model of the use of extended example. Notice that the example is really created by the combination of description and narration. What story from your experience could you substitute in order to support the same thesis statement?
2. How well is this student writer applying the lessons of the section on description? Can you spot qualities, details, and comparisons in the essay?

Fear

Fear can be used as a powerful tool. I use fear myself when I need to complete assignments for school. By reminding myself of the dreaded F or the embarrassment of being behind, I can frighten myself into completing my work on time. A foreman can use fear as a tool at work to keep production booming. A worker who needs his job to survive will usually work harder when there is fear of losing it. But the most natural kind of fear is that which nature provides. Adrenaline flows quickly when something unexpected happens, allowing fear to be used as a tool by a sudden burst of energy. I once read of a man who lifted the end of a car, freeing a victim wedged beneath. Through fear the man had become a tool—more effective than the jack, which had failed.

DISCUSSION QUESTIONS

1. Does the writer use an extended example or a series of brief examples to develop the topic?
2. In the topic sentence the writer states that fear is like a tool. How is this comparison maintained throughout the remainder of the paragraph; that is, how does the writer remind the reader about this crucial similarity?

Beyond Words

Perhaps the most striking example of a nonverbal message was not communicated by a professional actor, but by five-year-old Caroline Kennedy. As the world kept vigil at the graveside for John F. Kennedy, Caroline, brave and quiet, stood beside her mother. The child squinted in the blinding flash as cameras tried to record her mute grief, but she stubbornly defended the dignity of her emotions by pulling her black veil over her face. After a long, tense silence, the Kennedy widow knelt solemnly beside the coffin, crossed herself, and bowed her head sadly against the cold, gray box. Now slipping up beside her mother, Caroline also knelt and bowed her head. People were staring and cameras were flashing, when suddenly the child glanced up, straight at the coffin. Slowly, one tiny, white-gloved hand came forward, hesitated, then slipped beneath the flag draping the coffin. And in that gesture, Caroline Kennedy gave us the eloquent image of a child grappling with the enormous, bewildering finality of death. She shed no tears, uttered not a word; she reached out, somberly, poignantly, a child saying good-bye forever in the only way she knew.

DISCUSSION QUESTIONS

1. What is meant here by "nonverbal message"? What are some everyday or familiar examples?
2. What familiar nonverbal messages were conveyed by Mrs. Kennedy? How do Caroline's actions differ?
3. Besides being an extended example in support of the topic sentence (the first sentence), this paragraph also uses which two familiar writing modes, introduced in earlier sections of this book?

PARAGRAPHS

The Disadvantages of Human Anatomy

BERGEN EVANS

There are disadvantages [in the human anatomy] that would generally be perceived were it not for the concept of the "divinity" of the human form. The backbone, in its vertical position, is subject to strains and jars and pressures which it—particularly in the intervertebral discs—is not fully adapted to sustain, and from this fact proceed a hundred ills that not all of the liniment in the world can wash away. The arched foot absorbs some of the shocks, but the foot itself cannot always bear its burden and millions of flat-footed wretches shuffle along in undignified woe. The pelvis, called on "to serve simultaneously the incompatible functions of pillar and portal," made a halfhearted compromise, spreading enough to make women knock-kneed but not enough to prevent squeezing the heads of their children as they emerge. And when we get old and fall, where four-footed animals rarely fall, the pelvis breaks.

DISCUSSION QUESTIONS:

1. Evans names three shortcoming of the human anatomy in this paragraph. What others can you think of? What personal anecdotes can you recount involving a "disadvantage of human anatomy"?
2. What does Evans mean by the "divinity" of the human form? How about his comment that the human pelvis is called on "to serve simultaneously the incompatible functions of pillar and portal"?

American Women in Wartime

MARGARET TRUMAN

Although American women have never been officially involved in combat, a surprising number of them have distinguished themselves in wartime. Deborah Sampson Gannett disguised herself as a man, enlisted in the Continental Army, and fought in several engagements before her true sex was discovered. Bridget Divers, wife of a Civil War private in the First Michigan Cavalry, often rode with the men on scouting and raiding expeditions. Once, traveling with a wagon train that was attacked by Confederate cavalry, she took command of the poorly armed teamsters and fought off the rebel assault. Jacqueline Cochran ferried planes to the U.S. Eighth Air Force in England during World War II.

DISCUSSION QUESTIONS

1. The stark simplicity of this paragraph is striking. It contains the barest, yet most essential, elements of expository writing: (a) a statement in general terms about which the reader is not expected to be knowledgeable—a topic sentence, and (b) specific examples which reduce the general statement to a succession of concrete instances. What is the topic sentence, and how many examples does the paragraph contain?
2. Why do you suppose Truman did not mention such better known American historical figures as Molly Pitcher or Clara Barton among her examples of women who distinguished themselves in wartime?

Argument Is War

GEORGE LAKOFF AND MARK JOHNSON

To give some idea of what it could mean for a concept to be metaphorical and for such a concept to structure an everyday activity, let us start with the concept *argument* and the conceptual metaphor *Argument Is War*. This metaphor is reflected in our everyday language by a wide variety of expressions:

ARGUMENT IS WAR
Your claims are *indefensible.*
He *attacked every weak point* in my argument.
His criticisms were *right on target.*
I *demolished* his argument.
I've never *won* an argument with him.
You disagree? Okay, *shoot!*
If you use that *strategy*, he'll *wipe you out.*
He *shot down* all of my arguments.

DISCUSSION QUESTIONS

1. This paragraph furnishes a number of examples of war-related terms used to describe arguments. What examples can you add to this list? How about metaphors drawn from poker, like "ante up," "the chips are down," and "blue chips"? With what activity, besides poker, are these expressions associated? Can you name at least one more example of such an association?

2. What sorts of metaphors are commonly used to describe such topics as politics, sex, education, or sports?

The Actor's Voice

STANLEY KAHAN

It is obvious that the voice can be an important asset to any actor. One of the famous legends of the theater tells of the wonderful vocal expressiveness of the great Polish actress Helena Modjeska. Once at a dinner party, when asked to perform one of her famous scenes for the assembled guests, the actress complied by giving a very brief monologue. Many onlookers were moved to tears by the gripping effect of Modjeska's eloquence, despite the fact that she performed the "scene" in Polish! After she had finished she was asked which great and touching selection she had chosen to move her audience so deeply. It must have been with a sly wink that she confided that in fact she had recited the Polish alphabet. Such effectiveness was made possible not only by her sense of the dramatic but by a supple and expressive voice, delicately tuned to a great versatility and the needs of every occasion.

DISCUSSION QUESTIONS

1. How does the way Kahan uses the example technique differ from the way Margaret Truman employed it in "American Women in Wartime"?
2. The last sentence in this paragraph is not a part of the example used to support the topic sentence. What is its purpose?

ESSAYS

We "Talk That Talk" on Any Subject

CAROLE CURRIE

A native of Western North Carolina, Carole Currie (b. 1941) is a Duke University graduate who began her journalism career at the Durham Morning Herald, *where she was a staff writer for five years. Since 1968 Currie has been at the Asheville* Citizen-Times, *where she now serves as editor of that newspaper's Lifestyles section.*

It's hard to know a lot about a little but it's not hard to know   1
a little about a lot. In fact, it's almost required in these complicated times to pretend to know more than we do when we get
cornered conversationally.

Take wines. To me, I like them or I don't. They are dry or   2
sweet, white or red. But oenologists (that's the word for wine
scientists) have a vocabulary all their own to describe the fra-
grances and flavors of wine. "Heady, assertive, fruity with an
aftertaste of bananas and pineapple" are typical words used by
wine writers to describe wine, but I'm sure I've never tasted any
wine like that. Does wine really taste buttery, oaky, flinty? Does
its flavor fade on the back of the palate? Maybe, but for me, it's
hard to say for sure. If you can catch onto a favorite all-purpose
wine phrase like "crisp and light" and use it with discretion to
describe the wine you sample, you may be able to fool some of
the people some of the time.

And take sports. Men (and women) who don't know how to   3
talk the line are at an extreme disadvantage because there's
almost no way to escape talking about sports—at the barber shop,
at the gym, at lunch. It's un-American not to know who's leading
the league. That's why the question "How 'bout them Dawgs?"
has always struck me as perfect for the non-sports buff. It really
doesn't say anything, but it implies a lot of knowledge. Substitute any team for Dogs, as in, "How 'bout them Braves?" or
"How 'bout them Cubs?" and you're off and running and you can
let someone else take the conversational lead from there. This is
all assuming you know some basics like what sports season it is
and that you don't get a hockey team name mixed up with a
baseball team.

Computers are another area of expertise where a little can   4
mean, well, a little. Everything is computerized now and many
of us have worked with computers enough to do what we have
to do on them without really understanding too much about the
inner workings. When it comes to talk of the main frame, cold
starts and warm starts and "booting up," knowing what it means
isn't as important as *seeming* to know what it means. When I

heard myself asking someone the other day if she had a modem hookup and I got a serious answer, I knew I'd finessed the art of computerspeak.

Farming is also an area for potential *faux pas* for the uninitiated. There aren't as many farmers around as there used to be, sad to say, but when in the company of farmers, it pays to know a little about blue mold, haying, and cutting silage. If someone asks, "How many head do you have?" the answer is not "one." It means how many head of cattle, and you should know the difference between a Holstein and a Guernsey. It's always safe to talk about low milk prices and the travails of dairy farmers everywhere.

In education, the Basic Education Plan and Senate Bill Two get a pretty good going-over when school people get together. It is always safe to talk about the sorry state of teachers' salaries and personnel cuts and hiring freezes. It's extremely safe to say what you think the solution to the country's education crisis is. If you don't have an opinion on how to educate our country's children more effectively and more cheaply, you're the only one who doesn't.

The final rule of deceptive gab is to flutter around the outskirts of the conversation. Don't get left holding the conversational bag on a subject about which you know little. If you do, change the subject.

How 'bout them Dawgs?

DISCUSSION: CONTENT

1. What five basic topics of conversation does Currie present as examples?
2. Which of Currie's topics would you feel most comfortable discussing, and why? Which topic would you be least likely to bring up, and why?
3. What topics not mentioned by Currie would you and your friends be most likely to use as substitutes for one or more of hers?
4. Currie often uses the specialized vocabulary associated with a particular subject or profession to make her examples more convincing. Be prepared to discuss at least one such use for any three of her five examples.

DISCUSSION: FORM

1. Currie's essay follows preferred newspaper practice in maintaining an overall balance between being concise and providing specific, concrete details. Which of her five supporting example paragraphs (paragraphs 2–6) seems to have best reached that goal, and why?
2. Although she does not, for instance, number her five examples, Currie still achieves significant coherence in her essay. Where do you notice transitions or other coherence-creating techniques, such as repetition of key words or phrases?
3. Starting with the *paradox* (see Glossary) of her opening sentence, Currie manages to create a light **tone** for a subject that might otherwise be dull. See if you can find a playful place in each of her five example paragraphs.
4. Besides unity, what else is gained by ending her essay with the single question "How 'bout them Dawgs?" already used earlier in paragraph 3?

The Ultimate Key to Success

SUZANNE CHAZIN

Suzanne Chazin is a senior editor for Reader's Digest. *Her articles and essays have also appeared in* American Health, Money, *the New York* Times, People, *and* The Utne Reader.

Every day, a fatherless boy gazed at the fence separating his 1 family's ramshackle cabin from the Glen Lakes Country Club golf course on the outskirts of Dallas. What chance did a poor Chicano with a seventh-grade education have of being welcomed into that world?

Yet the boy was determined. First, he gained entrance to the 2 grounds as a gardener. Then he began caddying and playing a few holes at dusk. He honed his putting skills by hitting balls with a soda bottle wrapped in adhesive tape.

Today no fence keeps Lee Trevino, two-time U.S. Open winner, 3 from being welcomed into any country club in the nation.

Sure, Trevino had talent. But talent isn't what kept him from 4 quitting after he placed an embarrassing 54th in his first U.S. Open. His secret was perseverance.

Persistent people know they can succeed where smarter and   5
more talented people fail. You can succeed, too, if you follow
their strategies. As author Christopher Morley once said, "Big
shots are only little shots that keep shooting."

Achievers may lose their jobs, get rejected, watch their com-   6
panies fail or see their ideas founder. But they take advantage of
adversity, carving opportunities from change.

In her 30-year career, one broadcaster has been fired 18 times.   7
But every time, she set her sights on something bigger and better.
When no mainland radio station would hire her because they
thought women couldn't attract an audience, she moved to
Puerto Rico and polished her Spanish. When a wire service refused to send her to an uprising in the Dominican Republic, she
scraped together money to fly there and sell her own stories.

In 1981 she was fired by a New York radio station for not   8
having kept up with the times and was out of work for more than
a year. One day she pitched her idea for a new talk show to a man
who worked for NBC radio.

"I'm sure the network would be interested," he said—and   9
then left NBC. She met another man at NBC radio and presented
her idea for the show. He also praised her ideas, and then disappeared. So she persuaded a third man to hire her—but he wanted
her to host a show on a political radio station.

"I don't know enough about national politics to make this   10
work," she told her husband. Yet in the summer of 1982, she
went on the air. Drawing on her familiarity with a microphone
and her easy, confessional style, she talked about what the
Fourth of July meant to her and invited callers to do the same.

Listeners connected immediately, and she became known as   11
the "Dear Abby" of the airwaves. Today, Sally Jessy Raphaël is
the two-time Emmy award-winning host of her own television
show, reaching eight million viewers daily throughout the
United States, Canada and the United Kingdom.

"I could have let those 18 firings prevent me from doing what   12
I wanted," she says. "Instead, I let them spur me on."

Successful people radiate a positive attitude that inspires   13
others to help them realize their dreams.

He was the son of a seamstress and an impoverished trunk   14
maker. He worked his way through high school in a New York
neighborhood of tenements and sweatshops. He loved theater

and longed to see a Broadway show. But he couldn't afford a ticket.

Through sheer energy and will, he rose to become a televi-   15
sion stage manager. But he wanted to produce plays for people
like himself, who could never afford to see one on Broadway.

He started a drama group in a church basement and later   16
rented an outdoor amphitheater on New York's Lower East Side.
One of his company's early plays, a boisterous production of
Shakespeare's *The Taming of the Shrew*, attracted enthusiastic
crowds—but not one drama critic. Without publicity, how could
he attract donations?

So one day, he showed up at the New York *Times*, demanding   17
to see drama critic Brooks Atkinson. Atkinson was in London,
his assistant, Arthur Gelb, told the young man.

"Then I'll wait here until Mr. Atkinson returns," he said   18
firmly.

Gelb decided to hear him out. The trunk maker's son pas-   19
sionately spoke of his fine cast of actors, and the applause of his
audience, mostly immigrants who had never seen live theater.
Yet if the *Times* didn't review his production, he'd have to pack
up by week's end.

Moved by the man's determination and spirit, Gelb agreed to   20
review the production that night.

The evening sky darkened with clouds as Gelb showed up at   21
the outdoor theater. At intermission, rain drenched the stage.
The young man grabbed Gelb as he ran for cover: "I know critics
don't normally review half a show, but I beg you to make an
exception."

That night, Gelb wrote a small, favorable review of the first   22
half of the play and explained the production company's need for
financing. A day later, Herman Levin, producer of *My Fair Lady*,
sent a messenger to the production company with a check for
$750—enough in 1956 to keep the show afloat until summer's
end. When Brooks Atkinson returned, he saw the play and raved
about it in his Sunday column.

Soon Joe Papp was giving free Shakespeare productions to all   23
of New York. He became, until his death [in 1991], perhaps the
greatest modern influence in American theater, producing such
shows as *A Chorus Line, Hair* and *The Threepenny Opera*. He
once said the cornerstone of his persistence was a conviction that
the theater is important to other people's lives. "If you don't
believe this, you might as well give up."

Successful people know that being persistent involves mak- 24
ing choices. And choice involves risk, as this 58-year-old Indiana
farm-products salesman discovered.

For years, he had experimented with different strains of pop- 25
corn to produce a lighter, fluffier variety with few unpopped
kernels. When he finally grew his ideal strain, no seed buyers
wanted it because it cost more to produce.

"If I could just get the public to *try* the popcorn, I know 26
they'd buy it," he told his partner.

"If you feel that strongly about it, why don't you sell it 27
yourself?" his partner replied.

If "Red Bow" failed, he might lose lots of money. At his age, 28
did he really want to take such a risk?

He hired a marketing firm to develop a name and image for 29
his popcorn. Soon Orville Redenbacher was selling his Gourmet
Popping Corn across the nation. Today, it's the best-selling popcorn in the world—all because Redenbacher was willing to risk
what he already had to get what he wanted.

"I think most of my drive comes from people telling me I 30
can't do something," says Redenbacher, now 84. "That just
makes me want to prove them wrong."

At times, even the most persistent person feels over- 31
whelmed, and needs the support of others who really believe.
Consider this presser in an industrial laundry.

He lived in a trailer and earned $60 a week. His wife worked 32
nights, but even with both jobs they barely made ends meet.
When their baby developed an ear infection, they had to give up
their telephone to pay for antibiotics.

The laundry worker wanted to be a writer. Nights and week- 33
ends the clack-clack of his typewriter filled the trailer. He spent
all his spare money on sending his manuscripts to publishers and
agents.

Everyone rejected them. The form letters were short and 34
impersonal. He couldn't even be certain his work was being read.

One day, the laundry worker read a novel that reminded him 35
of his own work. He sent his manuscript to Doubleday, the
book's publisher. The manuscript was given to Bill Thompson.

A few weeks later, a warm, personal reply came in the mail. 36
The manuscript had too many flaws. But Thompson did believe
the laundry worker had promise as a writer and encouraged him
to try again.

Over the next 18 months, the laundry worker sent the editor   37
two more manuscripts. The editor rejected both. The laundry
worker began work on a fourth novel. But with bills mounting,
he began to lose hope.

One night, he threw his manuscript into the garbage. The   38
next day, his wife fished it out. "You shouldn't be quitting," she
told him. "Not when you're so close."

The laundry worker stared at the pages. Perhaps he no longer   39
believed in himself, but his wife did. And so did a New York
editor he'd never met. So, every day, he wrote another 1500
words.

When he finished, he sent the novel to Bill Thompson—but   40
he was sure it wouldn't sell.

He was wrong. Thompson's publishing house handed over a   41
$2500 advance, and Stephen King's horror classic, *Carrie*, was
born. It went on to sell five million copies and was made into one
of the top-grossing films of 1976.

Successful people understand that no one makes it to the top   42
in a single bound. What truly sets them apart is their willingness
to keep putting one step in front of the other—no matter how
rough the terrain.

Just ask the kid from the South Bronx who batted over .500   43
in his senior year in high school, and yet was passed over by all
26 Major League teams. Undaunted, he tried out for a position on
a high-school all-star baseball team and did so well that a tryout
with the Pittsburgh Pirates was arranged.

Today, that kid is still batting baseballs in New York. Only   44
now Bobby Bonilla has a five-year contract with the Mets worth
$29 million, making him the highest-paid player on the field.

DISCUSSION: CONTENT

1. From what five different areas of human activity does Chazin
   draw her examples?
2. Why do you suppose she provides examples from so many different areas?
3. Besides persistence, what four other factors are shown by Chazin
   to be related to success?
4. Which of Chazin's narrative extended examples do you think best
   supports her thesis, and why?

DISCUSSION: FORM

1. Why do you suppose Chazin delayed announcing her thesis until paragraph 4?
2. Three of Chazin's examples are significantly longer than her other three. Why do you suppose she has spent more time on these?
3. Chazin clearly depends on *narrative* examples (those built around a story). What does she gain by using these?
4. Besides extensive use of examples to explain her point, Chazin also depends on another expository mode. Look again at the part introduction to expository writing (pp. 91–92) and see if you can identify that other mode.

Solve That Problem—With Humor

WILLIAM D. ELLIS

*William D. Ellis (b. 1918) is an Ohioan who since combat service in World War II has been a writer of best-selling fiction—*The Bounty Lands, *(1952),* Jonathan Blair, Bounty Lands Lawyer, *(1954)—and various nonfiction books, such as* The Cuyahoga *("Rivers of America" series, 1967);* Clarke of St. Vith: The Sergeant's General *(1974);* More: The Rediscovery of American Common Sense *(1986); and* The Ordinance of 1787: The Nation Begins *(1987). Ellis is also a frequent contributor of fiction and nonfiction to major American magazines, the following essay being one such example.*

A lot of us lose life's tougher confrontations by mounting a frontal attack—when a touch of humor might well enable us to chalk up a win. Consider the case of a young friend of mine, who hit a traffic jam en route to work shortly after receiving an ultimatum about being late on the job. Although there was a good reason for Sam's chronic tardiness—serious illness at home—he decided that this by-now-familiar excuse wouldn't work any longer. His supervisor was probably already pacing up and down with a dismissal speech rehearsed. 1

He was. Sam entered the office at 9:35. The place was as quiet as a loser's locker room; everyone was hard at work. Sam's supervisor approached him. Suddenly, Sam forced a grin and shoved 2 out his hand. "How do you do!" he said. "I'm Sam Maynard. I'm applying for a job I understand became available just 35 minutes ago. Does the early bird get the worm?"

The room exploded in laughter. The supervisor clamped off a smile and walked back to his office. Sam Maynard had saved his job—with the only tool that could win, a laugh.   3

Humor is a most effective, yet frequently neglected, means of handling the difficult situations in our lives. It can be used for patching up differences, apologizing, saying "no," criticizing, getting the other fellow to do what you want without his losing face. For some jobs, it's the *only* tool that can succeed. It is a way to discuss subjects so sensitive that serious dialogue may start a riot. For example, many believe that comedians on television are doing more today for racial and religious tolerance than are people in any other forum.   4

Humor is often the best way to keep a small misunderstanding from escalating into a big deal. Recently a neighbor of mine had a squabble with his wife as she drove him to the airport. Airborne, he felt miserable, and he knew she did, too. Two hours after she returned home, she received a long-distance phone call. "Person-to-person for Mrs. I. A. Pologize," intoned the operator. "That's spelled 'P' as in . . ." In a twinkling, the whole day changed from grim to lovely at both ends of the wire.   5

An English hostess with a quick wit was giving a formal dinner for eight distinguished guests whom she hoped to enlist in a major charity drive. Austerity was *de rigueur* in England at the time, and she had drafted her children to serve the meal. She knew that anything could happen—and it did, just as her son, with the studied concentration of a tightrope walker, brought in a large roast turkey. He successfully elbowed the swinging dining-room door, but the backswing deplattered the bird onto the dining-room floor.   6

The boy stood rooted: guests stared at their plates. Moving only her head the hostess smiled at her son, "No harm, Daniel," she said. "Just pick him up and take him back to the kitchen"— she enunciated clearly so he would think about what she was saying—"and bring in the *other* one."   7

A wink and a one-liner instantly changed the dinner from a red-faced embarrassment to a conspiracy of fun.   8

The power of humor to dissolve a hostile confrontation often lies in its unspoken promise: "You let me off the hook, my friend, and I'll let you off." The trick is to assign friendly motives to   9 your opponent, to smile just a little—but not too much. Canada's Governor-General Roland Michener, master of the technique, was about to inspect a public school when he was faced with a truculent picket line of striking maintenance personnel. If he backed away from the line, he would seriously diminish his office's image; if he crossed it, he might put the government smack into a hot labor issue.

While he pondered the matter, more strikers gathered across his path. Suddenly, the graying pencil-line mustache on Michener's weathered face stretched a little in Cheshirean complicity. "How very nice of you all to turn out to see me!" he boomed. "Thank you. Shall we go in?" The line parted and, by the time the pickets began to chuckle, the governor-general was striding briskly up the school steps.   10

Next time you find yourself in an ethnically awkward situation, take a lesson from the diplomatic delegates to Europe's Common Market. In the course of history, nearly every member nation has been invaded or betrayed by at least one of the others, and the Market's harmony must be constantly buttressed. One method is the laugh based on national caricatures. Recently, a new arrival at Market headquarters in Brussels introduced himself as a minister for the Swiss navy. Everybody laughed. The Swiss delegate retorted, "Well, why not? Italy has a minister of finance."   11

Of course, humor is often more than a laughing matter. In its more potent guises, it has a Trojan-horse nature: no one goes on guard against a gag; we let it in because it looks like a little wooden toy. Once inside, however, it can turn a city to reform, to rebellion, to resistance. Some believe, for instance, that, next to the heroic British RAF, British humor did the most to fend off German takeover in World War II. One sample will suffice: that famous story of the woman who was finally extracted from the rubble of her house during the London blitz. Asked, "Where is your husband?" she brushed brick dust off her head and arms and answered, "Fighting in Libya, the bloody coward!"   12

Similarly, whenever we Americans start taking ourselves a bit too seriously, a grassroots humor seems to rise and strew banana peels in our path. The movement is usually led by professionals: Mark Twain penlancing the boils of pomposity ("Man was made at the end of the week's work, when God was tired"); Will Rogers deflating our lawmakers ("The oldest boy became a Congressman, and the second son turned out no good, too"); Bill   13

Mauldin needling fatuous officers (one second lieutenant to another, on observing a beautiful sunset: "Is there one for enlisted
men, too?"). Such masters of comic deflation restore the balance.
They bring us back to ourselves.

When life has us in a tight corner, one of the first questions   14
we might ask is, "Can I solve this with a laugh?" Men with giant
responsibilities have frequently used this approach to solve giant
problems—often with sweeping effect. As Gen. George C. Marshall, U.S. Army Chief of Staff, labored to prepare this then-un-
ready nation to enter World War II, he met stiff opposition from
his commander-in-chief regarding the elements that called for
the most bolstering. Marshall felt that what we needed most
were highly developed ground forces. President Roosevelt was a
Navy man who believed that our principal need was for a powerful navy, plus a large air force. In increasingly tense debates with
the President, Marshall pushed his argument so hard that he
began to foster ever stronger resistance. Finally, during a particularly hot session, the usually stonefaced Marshall forced a grin.
"At least, Mr. President," he said, "you might stop referring to
the Navy as 'us' and the Army as 'them.' "

Roosevelt studied Marshall over his glasses, then unlipped a   15
great show of teeth and laughter. Shortly thereafter, he made a
more objective study of Marshall's recommendations and eventually bought the ground-force concept.

Occasionally, humor goes beyond saving arguments, saving   16
face or saving jobs; it can save life itself. Viktor E. Frankl was a
psychiatrist imprisoned in a German concentration camp during
World War II. As the shrinking number of surviving prisoners
descended to new depths of hell, Frankl and his closest prisoner
friend sought desperately for ways to keep from dying. Piled on
top of malnutrition, exhaustion and disease, suicidal despair was
the big killer in these citadels of degradation.

As a psychiatrist, Frankl knew that humor was one of the   17
soul's best survival weapons, since it can create, if only for
moments, aloofness from horror. Therefore, Frankl made a rule
that once each day he and his friend must invent and tell an
amusing anecdote, specifically about something which could
happen after their liberation.

Others were caught up in the contagion of defiant laughter.   18
One starving prisoner forecast that in the future he might be at
a prestigious formal dinner, and when the soup was being served,

he would shatter protocol by imploring the hostess, "Ladle it from the *bottom!*"

Frankl tells of another prisoner, who nodded toward one of   19
the most despised *capos*—favored prisoners who acted as guards and became as arrogant as the SS men. "Imagine!" he quipped. "I knew him when he was only the president of a bank!"

If humor can be used successfully against such odds, what   20
can't you and I do with it in daily life?

DISCUSSION: CONTENT

1. How does the clever young man whose story is told in paragraphs 1–3 use humor to save being fired for tardiness?
2. Where does Ellis explain in nonhumorous terms exactly why humor is such an effective problem-solving device?
3. What is funny about the Swiss delegate's comment in paragraph 11 that the Swiss should have a naval minister if the Italians have a minister of finance?
4. What rule did the Jewish concentration camp prisoners make about the type of anecdotes that they would invent daily?

DISCUSSION: FORM

1. What is Ellis's thesis in this essay, and where exactly does he state it?
2. Which illustration receives the most space? Why do you suppose it does?
3. In an earlier version of this book Ellis's essay was placed in the argumentative section. What justification is there for the decision to move it to this section in expository writing?

Los Chinos *Discover* El Barrio

LUIS R. TORRES

Luis R. Torres (b. 1950) is a journalist who works in Southern California. Formerly a journalism professor at California State University, Los Angeles, he is now a producer at the National Latino Communications Center, Los Angeles. His essay first appeared in the Los Angeles Times.

There's a colorful mural on the asphalt playground of Hillside   1
Elementary School, in the neighborhood called Lincoln Heights.
Painted on the beige handball wall, the mural is of life-sized
youngsters holding hands. Depicted are Asian and Latino kids
with bright faces and ear-to-ear smiles.

The mural is a mirror of the makeup of the neighborhood   2
today: Latinos living side-by-side with Asians. But it's not all
smiles and happy faces in this Northeast Los Angeles community, located just a couple of miles up Broadway from City Hall.
On the surfaces there's harmony between Latinos and Asians.
But there are indications of simmering ethnic-based tensions.

That became clear to me recently when I took a walk through   3
the old neighborhood—the one where I grew up. As I walked
along North Broadway, I thought of a joke that comic Paul Ro-
driguez often tells on the state. He paints the picture of a young
Chicano walking down a street on L.A.'s Eastside. He comes
upon two Asians having an animated conversation in what
sounds like babble. "Hey, you guys," he says, "knock off that
foreign talk. This is America—speak Spanish!"

When I was growing up in Lincoln Heights 30 years ago most   4
of us spoke Spanish—and English. There was a sometimes uneasy coexistence in the neighborhood between brown and white.
Back then we Latinos were moving in and essentially displacing
the working-class Italians (to us, they were just *los gringos*) who
had moved there and thrived after World War II.

Because I was an extremely fair-skinned Latino kid I would   5
often overhear remarks by gringos in Lincoln Heights that were
not intended for Latino ears, disparaging comments about
"smelly wetbacks," and worse. The transition was, for the most
part, a gradual process. And as I recall—except for the slurs that
sometimes stung me directly—a process marked only occasionally by outright hostility.

A trend that began about 10 years ago in Lincoln Heights   6
seems to have hit a critical point now. It's similar to the ethnic
tug-of-war of yesteryear, but different colors, different words are
involved. Today Chinese and Vietnamese are displacing the Latinos who, by choice or circumstance, had Lincoln Heights virtually to themselves for two solid generations.

Evidence of the transition is clear.   7

The bank where I opened my first meager savings account in   8
the late 1950s has changed hands. It's now the East-West Federal
Bank, an Asian-owned enterprise.

The public library on Workman Street, where I checked out 9 *Charlotte's Web* with my first library card, abounds with signs of the new times: It's called "La Biblioteca del Pueblo de Lincoln Heights," and on the door there's a notice advising that the building is closed because of the Oct. 1 earthquake; it's written in Chinese.

The white, wood-frame house on Griffin Avenue that I once 10 lived in is now owned by a Chinese family.

What used to be a Latino-run mortuary at the corner of Sichel 11 Street and North Broadway is now the Chung Wah Funeral Home.

A block down the street from the funeral home is a *panad-* 12 *eria*, a bakery. As I would listen to radio reports of the U.S. war in faraway Indochina while walking from class at Lincoln High School, I often used to drop in the *panaderia* for a snack.

The word *panaderia*, now faded and chipped, is still painted 13 on the shop window that fronts North Broadway. But another sign, a gleaming plastic one, hangs above the window. The sign proclaims that it is a Vietnamese-Chinese bakery. The proprietor, Sam Lee, bought the business less than a year ago. With a wave of his arm, he indicates that *La Opinion,* the Spanish-language daily newspaper, is still for sale on the counter. Two signs hang side-by-side behind the counter announcing in Spanish and in Chinese that cakes are made to order for all occasions.

Out on North Broadway, Fidel Farrillas sells *raspadas* (snow- 14 cones) from his pushcart. He has lived and worked in Lincoln Heights "for 30 years, and a pinch more," he says, his voice nearly whistling through two gold-framed teeth. He has seen the neighborhood change. Twice.

Like many older Latinos he remembers the tension felt be- 15 tween *los gringos y la raza* years ago—even though most people went about their business ostensibly coexisting politely. And others who have been around as long will tell an inquiring reporter scratching away in his notebook, "We're going out of our way to treat the *chinos* nice—better than the *gringos* sometimes treated us back then." But when the notebook is closed, they're likely to whisper, "But you know, the thing is, they smell funny, and they talk behind your back, and they are so arrogant—the way they're buying up everything in our neighborhood."

Neighborhood transitions can be tough to reconcile. 16

It isn't easy for the blue-collar Latinos of Lincoln Heights. 17 They haven't possessed much. But they had the barrio, "a little

chunk of the world where we belonged," as one described it.
There may be some hard times and hard feelings ahead as *los
chinos* continue to make inroads into what had been an exclusively Latino enclave. But there are hopeful signs as well.

On one recent Saturday afternoon a Latino fifth-grader, wear- 18
ing the same type of hightop tennis shoes I wore as a 10-year-old
on that same street corner, strode up to Senor Farrillas's snow-
cone pushcart. The kid pulled out a pocketful of dimes and
bought two *raspadas*. One for himself, and one for his school
chum—a Vietnamese kid. He was wearing hightops, too. They
both ordered strawberry, as I recall.

DISCUSSION: CONTENT

1. The events of this essay take place in Lincoln Heights. In what
   city is that neighborhood? What does Torres mean by the term
   barrio?
2. Who is moving into Lincoln Heights to displace the Latinos?
   Whom did the Latinos displace earlier? How much earlier did
   that displacement occur?
3. Torres lists a number of changes that have taken place in his old
   neighborhood. How many does he list? What is his attitude toward those changes?
4. What hopeful sign does Torres mention that would lead us to
   believe that the changes underway in Lincoln Heights will not
   lead to violence?

DISCUSSION: FORM

1. How many paragraphs are devoted to introduction in this essay?
   What is the thesis statement? How effectively is it located?
2. What is the purpose of paragraph 7? Why do you suppose Torres
   chose to cast that paragraph as just a single sentence? After that
   paragraph, how many short examples does Torres provide before
   he pauses to provide an extended one?
3. What is the relationship in this essay between the last paragraph
   and the opening paragraph?

6

Classification and Division

Where there is no order, human beings attempt to impose it. We look at the welter of stars in the night sky and see bears, dippers, crabs, and scorpions. When we look at a roomful of students, we automatically begin to arrange them into groups. We classify or group them variously by sex, into male and female; by race, into whites, blacks, and Asians; or by size, into big and little or fat and thin. The campus playboy, looking right past his male classmates, will arrange the coeds into an elaborate hierarchy of desirability. And, no doubt, his female counterpart will devise a similar classification for the males in the room. The instructor, in the meantime, is more than likely making still other classifications according to dress, attentiveness, or mannerisms. One instructor went so far as to classify students into three groups: those who were above distractions, those who were looking for distractions, and those who *were* distractions. Eventually, the instructor will make another sort of classification based on performance, arranging students into groups by grades: those who earned A's, those who earned B's, and so forth.

Classification and Division

Some rhetoricians make a distinction between what they call *classification* and *division*. Classification, they say, is an attempt to bring order out of disorder. Division, on the other hand, creates diversity out of unity. Sometimes the distinction is important; sometimes it is trivial. Suppose you were to view a roomful of students as a unit; then you might *divide* that class into those who are bright, average, or dull. If, however, you examined the roomful of students one by one, you might then *classify* each one according to his or her membership in the three groups just named.

To use a less trivial example, the Bible may be *classified* as a religious work; but it is *divided* into the Old and New Testaments. Actually, the hierarchy (or ordered grouping) that includes the Bible can be very instructive; it is worth a closer examination. See Figure 6.1.

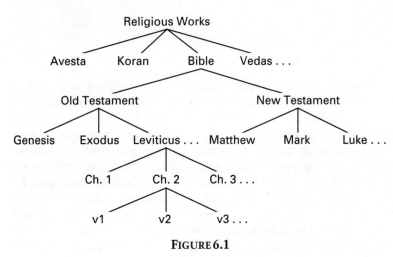

FIGURE 6.1

Here the Bible can be clearly seen as part of a hierarchy whose highest element is religious works; thus, looking *up* the hierarchy, you see that the Bible is classified as a religious work. You could also say the same thing about the Koran, the Avesta, and the Vedas—sacred scriptures of other world religions. But if you look *down* the hierarchy, you see that the Bible is divided into the Old and New Testaments. And although the hierarchy does not show it, the other sacred scriptures may also be divided into component parts. If next you were to choose another point in the hierarchy, perhaps Leviticus this time, you could look upward and say that Leviticus is *classified* as a part of the Old Testament and downward to note that it is *divided* into chapters.

Put simply, an element *within* a hierarchy—at neither extreme, top or bottom—may be either classified or divided. We classify an element by looking *up* the hierarchy to determine the next highest class to which it belongs. We divide an element by looking *down* the hierarchy to determine its component elements.

There must be a consistent rationale or basis for setting up the divisions within a hierarchy. It would make little sense to divide a group of students into underachievers, overachievers, and athletes. The basic rationale here might seem to be academic achievement, but setting up a category for athletes clearly conflicts with that presumed rationale for division. An athlete might belong to either of these other two groups—or might belong to neither. And this last possibility points out another shortcoming present in this particular division: the division should be complete, accounting for all the elements in the group. A group of students may contain underachievers and overachievers, but it will also surely contain members belonging to neither of these extremes, and these average achievers must also figure in the division. Generally speaking then, every classification must have a *consistent rationale,* and it must be *complete.*

The rationale may be thought of as a plan for cutting up or dividing an object. The experienced butcher cuts up a steer according to a preconceived plan and furnishes us with steaks, roasts, and other cuts. The apprentice butcher or backward farmer who does his own butchering sometimes ends up with many pieces of stew meat or a hunk of beef too large for the pot. A carefully determined rationale for making a division will produce the desired results; a haphazard one will produce, at worst, confused or conflicting results and, at best, only ordinary results.

Ordinary or uninteresting results often arise when you choose a too common rationale. Finding an unusual method of classification is the key. We generally cut up apples in the same way, slicing them longitudinally into quarters or eighths, and we come up with very ordinary slices of apple. However, if you cut the apple latitudinally into round slices, you will have, first of all, unusual slices, and you will discover something you may never have noticed: The seeds in the core are arranged in a star-shaped pattern, a fact concealed by the usual method of slicing. Similarly, a well-chosen rationale will often reveal many aspects of the subject that would otherwise have remained hidden.

In each of the following classification paragraphs and essays you should be able to determine fairly early what is being classified or divided and what rationale is being used. Having done that, you should next ascertain whether the rationale is followed consistently and whether the classification is complete. Then later, when using classification in your own writing—for instance, to organize a paper on personality types for a psychology course or to organize a report on advertising strategies for a marketing course—you will want to be sure you follow a rationale consistently and make your classification complete.

When you enter the world of work, you will find classification and division in use at every turn: in computer spreadsheet programs, in the separate sections of newspapers and professional journals, in the stock market exchanges (New York, American, Over-the-Counter), in organizations (executive vice-president, vice-president, assistant vice-president), and so on. Therefore, your own writing must take into account the diversity and complexity that surrounds you and, via thoughtful use of classification and division, impose order on it.

Commentary on Student Work

After reading the introductory material about classification and division, Paula jotted down some items on which she might try to use this method of development. Her journal contained the following list: basketball players, coworkers, English professors, sorority sisters, gossips, and—lastly—noseblowers. She had tinkered with some hierarchical arrangements involving basketball players, then professors, and finally sorority sisters. Eventually, she drew the following structure tree as Figure 6.2.

FIGURE 6.2

In this case Paula was looking *up* the hierarchy; that is, she was trying to determine what was *above* basketball players in the hierarchy, or—to say it another way—what larger class of things basketball players belonged to. Athletes was obvious and occurred to her immediately; then she went on to supply the remaining kinds of athletes she was familiar with as in Figure 6.3.

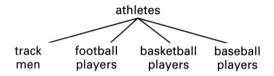

FIGURE 6.3

In doing so she was looking *down* the hierarchy. She pondered for a moment to determine whether the classification was complete and decided that her paper, if she ever wrote it, would need some qualifying statements. Certainly, what she was dealing with here was *male* athletes, and more important, she realized that there were more kinds of athletes than the four she had in the tree, but these had occurred to her because they represented the four major sports at the college she was attending. This explanation would need to be stated also.

Next, Paula tried to locate a rationale for this arrangement. It was obvious that she had already divided athletes according to the sports they played, but that was hopelessly ordinary and uninteresting. At last she hit on this rationale: male college athletes could be divided according to the way they dressed for class. Anyway, to her it seemed that you could always spot the football players by their cut-off jerseys, their shower shoes, and their beltless bermudas.

This looked promising, but Paula veered abruptly away from this approach and next applied the same rationale to college professors. After first listing a few distressing facts about the outmoded clothing of English professors she had seen, she went on to demonstrate that biologists are, as a rule, much more casually dressed, and that education professors have a preference for cheap-looking neckties.

But soon Paula tired of this promising approach (one we wish she had pursued further) and hit on the last item on her list, noseblowing, even though she never could satisfactorily explain how or why she had arrived at this topic. She constructed this hierarchy (see Figure 6.4) and soon was off and writing.

Her initial draft elicited some mixed responses from Paula's classmates. Two people in her reading group felt that the subject matter was too repulsive for presentation, unless she planned a career as a writer for a television show like *Saturday Night Live.*

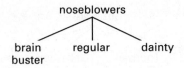

FIGURE 6.4

Others, however, felt that because it was so unusual it deserved attention, especially since the first cold days of winter had arrived and there was already some noseblowing going on in class. In fact, they felt that Paula might well find other types to discuss. The group worked out a concluding paragraph together that did two things: (1) it dealt with the possibility of other types and apologized for their possible oversight, and (2) it provided a mild apology for treating a "gross" subject. Here is Paula's final draft.

Noseblowing

Blowing one's nose is a job, especially when a person has a cold. From my observations I have decided there are three major types of noseblowing.

First, there is what I call the "brain buster." This type is usually demonstrated by a large man or a young child. This person, leaning way back, pointing his chin toward the ceiling, taking a deep breath, bringing an especially strong tissue to his face, blows his nose with the force of a hurricane, sometimes putting a hole in the tissue. Because of his forceful effort, this person sometimes injures his sinuses.

The second type, probably the most popular, is regular noseblowing, and it is done by almost everyone. In this case, a person takes a Kleenex, tilts his head slightly, takes a medium-sized breath, and blows his nose just hard enough to clear his sinuses. This type doesn't endanger himself when he blows his nose.

The third type is what I call the "easy-does-it" blower. This person is most often a very young child or a delicate, mannerly lady. This type, acting as if she doesn't want to be seen, slowly picks up a Scottie, looks slowly around, carefully slips the tissue up to her nose, gives it a quick, soft sniff outward, and then lowers her hand quickly so no one will notice her blowing her nose.

I have just described what I think are the three major types ⁵ of noseblowing. Of course, these types can be broken down further, but, like most people, I don't enjoy talking about blowing noses.

DISCUSSION QUESTIONS

1. What is the writer's rationale in classifying types of noseblowing? Could you suggest a different one?
2. Why might the descriptions of the types of noseblowing be labeled as narrative in form?
3. In the last paragraph, the writer suggests that the topic might be further divided. Do you agree or disagree?

STUDENT WORK

Cat Fanciers

All who enter my home can be divided into four types based on their reaction to my cats. Obviously terror-struck, some hold an apparent loathing for felines. Others whose reaction is less severe are still extremely reluctant and cautious, somehow feeling very threatened by the common domestic cat. Some people, reacting with complete indifference, carry on as if there weren't a fat calico rubbing against their ankles or a gray shadow darting behind the chairs. My favorite visitors are the enthusiastic, who immediately begin to relate stories of their cats' antics, jabbering away contentedly while one of my cats picks away at their double-knits.

DISCUSSION QUESTIONS

1. The student writer of this paragraph states the rationale for division in the topic sentence. What is it?
2. Is the rationale followed consistently?
3. How many classes of cat fanciers does the writer enumerate, and is there any order or method in their arrangement?

Popular Diets

I'm not sure which of the five most popular diets to try in order to lose ten pounds. My first choice is to take stimulants—speed, diet pills, or caffeine—to decrease my appetite, causing rapid pulse, insomnia, and restlessness in many dieters. Another choice is a liquid diet—water, fruit juices, or high-protein drinks—which results in excessive coldness, sleepiness, and urination. A third choice is a diet high in nutrients, featuring foods rich in protein and carbohydrates. The lack of variety—eating only eggs, nuts, fish, or potatoes—makes this diet hard to maintain. The vegetarian diet, a meatless regimen, has gained favor in the last few years. This diet is designed for a lifetime of health and not for a quick weight loss. The last and most popular diet, the one that everybody tries to stick to, is the avoidance diet, abstaining from various high-calorie foods and beverages. This diet requires a lot of willpower, especially if you have small children, eat out, or attend many social functions. After reviewing the five most popular courses of action, I think I'll save myself the trouble of failure and take up running.

DISCUSSION QUESTIONS

1. The writer mentions five types of diets, but is there a clear-cut basis for the division?
2. In addition to naming each type of diet, what extra information does the writer provide?
3. There is a sixth alternative for weight control that the writer introduces obliquely. What is it?

T-Shirt Inscriptionalia

The sight of people wearing T-shirts with slogans, mottoes, phrases, and pictures on their chests and backs has fascinated me for years. The immense variety of T-shirt inscriptionalia and the obvious lack of research about it has led me to begin a taxonomy of this facet of our society.

I have labeled the first category *Scholarly Prestige by Identification,* and it includes all references to schools or colleges or institutions of higher learning. This is perhaps the earliest form of the T-shirt message, but it began not with the lowly T-shirt (it was considered underwear in those early days), but with a sweat shirt. In order to gain scholarly prestige by identification, every incoming freshman bought a sweat shirt with the school's crest and colors just as soon as the bookstore was located, and then wore it and washed it and wore it and washed it until it became properly faded and limp. When the elbows gave way, the sleeves were cut off, but it was proudly worn until its emblem of eminence was no longer discernible.

These sweat shirts lost their uniqueness when they began to be produced in all sizes—even infant's—and the whole idea of scholarly prestige suddenly was covered with Pablum. Then somebody started printing T-shirts, and nowadays a student can own an entire wardrobe of T-shirts bearing the name of the institution with which identification is desired. This can be expressed any number of ways, such as "Western Carolina University," "Western," "The Cats," "WCU," even "Western Carolina Is for Lovers."

The next category is *Advertising*, containing the most presuming types of T-shirts, those bearing the names of various products. Although these are nothing more than free commercials, the wearer seems to gain an element of status by association with these products. This category includes not only the most blatant form of advertising, which is simply stating the name of the product, such as "Coors," "Levis," or "Adidas"; but it also comprises the sneaky, snooty practice of using a high-class designer's trademark embroidered prominently yet discreetly. It all started with the Izod alligator and now includes Givenchy's, Pierre Cardin's, and Geoffrey Beene's initials, as well as Sears' Winnie-the-Pooh.

A related category also involves advertising, but the product seems to be the person wearing the T-shirt. It embraces such mottoes as "Try me, " "WOW, " "Dangerous Curves, " "Bad Company, " and (I'm still blushing at this one) "Red Breast."

Another category is based on *Identification with Personalities*, where we find pictures of Shaun Cassidy, Wonder Woman, Holly Hobble, Charlie's Angels, the Marshall Tucker Band, Darth Vader, etc. Anybody, really, who is somebody can be depicted. This is a relatively new category, for certainly the likenesses of Babe Ruth or Bing Crosby were never displayed upon someone's chest. Now, however, press agents measure success by how well T-shirts with their clients' pictures sell.

The next classification is one I've labeled *Esoterica*. Some examples are the portrait of Beethoven, "Think Snow," "Frodo

Lives," "Ecologize," "Jojoba Saves Whales" (by providing a substitute for whale oil), "Chemists Have Solutions," and my favorite, "Love a Nurse PRN."

However carefully and comprehensively I have tried to categorize this wealth of trivia, I still find that I have some examples of T-shirt designs which I will necessarily have to lump into a *Miscellaneous* class. Included here are a realistic picture of a splattered tomato, a frog with his feet propped on his desk and a sour look on his face saying, "I'm so happy I could just s____!", "Love is lending a helping hand," "Pigs Is Beautiful," and "Baby ↓." 8

The printing of T-shirts goes on relentlessly, and as I continue my avocation of researching and categorizing, my knowledge and understanding of the subject broaden. However, a few weeks ago I saw an inscription that still defies classification, because I cannot, for the life of me, figure out what it means. The T-shirt said, simply, "Moss Stuffers." 9

DISCUSSION QUESTIONS

1. Is there such a word as *inscriptionalia?* What does it mean? How do you know?
2. Can you state a consistent rationale for this classification of T-shirt messages?
3. At one point the writer shows obvious concern for the completeness of the classification. How does the writer preclude the possible charge that the classification is incomplete?
4. The writer of this essay is older than the average freshman, a faculty wife who had returned to college to complete a degree. Are there any clues to the writer's age?
5. Discuss the writer's use of parentheses in this essay.

PARAGRAPHS

Three Kinds of Book Owners

MORTIMER J. ADLER

There are three kinds of book owners. The first has all the standard sets and best-sellers—unread, untouched. (This deluded individual owns woodpulp and ink, not books.) The second has a great many books—a few of them read through, most of them dipped into, but all of them as clean and shiny as the day they were bought. (This person would probably like to make books his own, but is restrained by a false respect for their physical appearance.) The third has a few books or many—every one of them dog-eared and dilapidated, shaken and loosened by continual use, marked and scribbled in from front to back. (This man owns books.)

DISCUSSION QUESTIONS

1. What is the basis or rationale that Adler uses in classifying book owners?
2. Is the classification complete?
3. What effect does Adler achieve by enclosing three of his sentences in parentheses?

Intellectuals

SEYMOUR MARTIN LIPSET

[Intellectuals] are all those who create, distribute and apply culture—the symbolic world of man, including art, science and religion. Within this group, three different levels can be set out. There is the hard core who are the creators of culture—authors, artists, philosophers, scholars, editors, some journalists. Second, there are those who distribute what others create—performers of various arts, most teachers, most reporters. Third, and the most peripheral group, are those who apply culture as part of their jobs—professionals such as physicians and lawyers.

DISCUSSION QUESTIONS

1. Where does Lipset reveal the basis or rationale for his classification of intellectuals?
2. How does Lipset define culture?
3. Whom does Lipset include among the distributors of culture? Among those who apply it?

The Three New Yorks

E. B. WHITE

There are roughly three New Yorks. There is, first, the New York of the man or woman who was born here, who takes the city for granted and accepts its size and its turbulence as natural and inevitable. Second, there is the New York of the commuter— the city that is devoured by locusts each day and spat out each night. Third, there is a New York of the person who was born somewhere else and came to New York in quest of something. Of these three trembling cities the greatest is the last—the city of final destination, the city that is a goal. It is this third city that accounts for New York's high-strung disposition, its poetical deportment, its dedication to the arts, and its incomparable achievements. Commuters give the city its tidal restlessness, natives give it solidity and continuity, but the settlers give it passion. And whether it is a farmer arriving from Italy to set up a small grocery store in a slum, or a young girl arriving from a small town in Mississippi to escape the indignity of being observed by her neighbors, or a boy arriving from the Corn Belt with a manuscript in his suitcase and a pain in his heart, it makes no difference: each embraces New York with the intense excitement of first love, each absorbs New York with the fresh eyes of an adventurer, each generates heat and light to dwarf the Consolidated Edison Company.

DISCUSSION QUESTIONS

1. What single nouns used by White in "The Three New Yorks" best describe the three types of persons who perceive New York's "three trembling cities"?
2. Which of the three groups has the most significant vision of and effect on New York, according to White? How does he use the paragraph's form and organization to emphasize that dominance?
3. What is the Consolidated Edison Company, and why does White refer to it?
4. White uses a figurative comparison in the third sentence when he refers to the New York of the commuter as a city "devoured by

locusts each day and spat out each night." Why is this comparison, perhaps based on Exodus 10: 12–15 in the Bible, particularly
appropriate?

Types of Whales

RACHEL CARSON

Eventually the whales, as though to divide the sea's food
resources among them, became separated into three groups: the
plankton-eaters, the fish-eaters, and the squid-eaters. The plank-
ton-eating whales can exist only where there are dense masses of
small shrimp or copepods to supply their enormous food requirements. This limits them, except for scattered areas, to arctic and
antarctic waters and the high temperate latitudes. Fish-eating
whales may find food over a somewhat wider range of ocean, but
they are restricted to places where there are enormous populations of schooling fish. The blue water of the tropics and of the
open ocean basins offers little to either of these groups. But that
immense, square-headed, formidably toothed whale known as
the cachalot or sperm whale discovered long ago what men have
known for only a short time—that hundreds of fathoms below
the almost untenanted surface waters of these regions there is an
abundant animal life. The sperm whale has taken these deep
waters for his hunting grounds; his quarry is the deep-water
population of squids, including the giant squid Architeuthis,
which lives pelagically at depths of 1500 feet or more. The head
of the sperm whale is often marked with long stripes, which
consist of a great number of circular scars made by the suckers
of the squid. From this evidence we can imagine the battles that
go on, in the darkness of the deep water, between these two huge
creatures—the sperm whale with its 70-ton bulk, the squid with
a body as long as 30 feet, and writhing, grasping arms extending
the total length of the animal to perhaps 50 feet.

DISCUSSION QUESTIONS

1. What is Carson's rationale for dividing up the whale population?

2. Is her classification complete? Why do you suppose her discussion of squid-eating whales is more extensive than those of the other two classes?
3. Could Carson possibly have used a different rationale—for example, geographical habitat—for her classification? Would the paragraph have been as effective? Why, or why not?

ESSAYS

The Duration of Human Relationships

ALVIN TOFFLER

Alvin Toffler (b. 1928) is an American writer who has popularized futurology or speculative sociology in such books as The Futurists *(1972),* Learning for Tomorrow *(1973),* The Third Wave *(1980),* Previews and Premises *(1983),* The Adaptive Corporation *(1984), and* Power Shift *(1990). The following essay, which examines one aspect of the changing pace of modern life, is from* Future Shock *(1970). The book has sold over seven million copies in over fifty countries.*

Sociologists like Wirth have referred in passing to the transitory nature of human ties in urban society. But they have made no systematic effort to relate the shorter duration of human ties to shorter durations in other kinds of relationships. Nor have they attempted to document the progressive decline in these durations. Until we analyze the temporal character of human bonds, we will completely misunderstand the move toward super-industrialism. 1

For one thing, the decline in the *average* duration of human relationships is a likely corollary of the increase in the number of such relationships. The average urban individual today probably comes into contact with more people in a week than the feudal villager did in a year, perhaps even a lifetime. The villager's ties with other people no doubt included some transient relationships, but most of the people he knew were the same 2 throughout his life. The urban man may have a core group of people with whom his interactions are sustained over long periods of time, but he also interacts with hundreds, perhaps thousands of people whom he may see only once or twice and who then vanish into anonymity.

All of us approach human relationships, as we approach other 3 kinds of relationships, with a set of built-in durational expectancies. We expect that certain kinds of relationships will endure longer than others. It is, in fact, possible to classify relationships with other people in terms of their expected duration. These vary, of course, from culture to culture and from person to person. Nevertheless, throughout wide sectors of the population of the advanced technological societies something like the following order is typical:

Long-duration relationships. We expect ties with our imme- 4 diate family, and to a lesser extent with other kin, to extend throughout the lifetimes of the people involved. This expectation is by no means always fulfilled, as rising divorce rates and family break-ups indicate. Nevertheless, we still theoretically marry "until death do us part" and the social ideal is a lifetime relationship. Whether this is a proper or realistic expectation in a society of high transience is debatable. The fact remains, however, that family links are expected to be long term, if not lifelong, and considerable guilt attaches to the person who breaks off such a relationship.

Medium-duration relationships. Four classes of relationships 5 fall within this category. Roughly in order for descending durational expectancies, these are relationships with friends, neighbors, job associates, and co-members of churches, clubs and other voluntary organizations.

Friendships are traditionally supposed to survive almost, if 6 not quite, as long as family ties. The culture places high value on "old friends" and a certain amount of blame attaches to dropping a friendship. One type of friendship relationship, however, acquaintanceship, is recognized as less durable.

Neighbor relationships are no longer regarded as long-term 7 commitments—the rate of geographical turnover is too high. They are expected to last as long as the individual remains in a single location, an interval that is growing shorter and shorter on average. Breaking off with a neighbor may involve other difficulties, but it carries no great burden of guilt.

On-the-job relationships frequently overlap friendships, and,   8
less often, neighbor relationships. Traditionally, particularly
among white-collar, professional and technical people, job relationships were supposed to last a relatively long time. This expectation, however, is also changing rapidly, as we shall see.

Co-membership relationships—links with people in church   9
or civic organizations, political parties and the like—sometimes
flower into friendship, but until that happens such individual
associations are regarded as more perishable than either friendships, ties with neighbors or fellow workers.

Short-duration relationships. Most, though not all, service   10
relationships fall into this category. These involve sales clerks,
delivery people, gas station attendants, milkmen, barbers, hair-
dressers, etc. The turnover among these is relatively rapid, and
little or no shame attaches to the person who terminates such a
relationship. Exceptions to the service pattern are professionals
such as physicians, lawyers and accountants, with whom relationships are expected to be somewhat more enduring.

This categorization is hardly airtight. Most of us can cite   11
some "service" relationship that has lasted longer than some
friendship, job or neighbor relationship. Moreover, most of us can
cite a number of quite long-lasting relationships in our own
lives—perhaps we have been going to the same doctor for years
or have maintained extremely close ties with a college friend.
Such cases are hardly unusual, but they are relatively few in
number in our lives. They are like long-stemmed flowers tower-
ing above a field of grass in which each blade represents a short-
term relationship, a transient contact. It is the very durability of
these ties that makes them noticeable. Such exceptions do not
invalidate the rule. They do not change the key that, across the
board, the *average* interpersonal relationship in our life is shorter
and shorter in duration.

DISCUSSION: CONTENT

1. What comment does Toffler make about the average length of
   human relationships?
2. Did the residents of feudal villages have more or fewer human
   relationships than modern man?

3. What examples does Toffler cite for each of his divisions?
4. Toffler admits that there may be exceptions to his classification, but he likens them to what?

DISCUSSION: FORM

1. Alvin Toffler divides human relationships according to their du-ration, an interesting and fairly unusual rationale, particularly when we consider the ways in which we most frequently think of our relationships with others: professional, romantic, aca-demic, casual, and so on. How many ways of classifying human relationships can you think of? How interesting or unusual are they? Do any of them reveal anything about the nature of human relationships that you did not already know?
2. Toffler further subdivides medium-duration relationships. What is his rationale for the subdivision? Could the job of dividing and subdividing have been done differently? What would be the effect of a six-part division based on duration that uses Toffler's divi-sions and subdivisions?
3. In making his divisions and subdivisions Toffler clearly uses duration of the relationship as his basis for division, but there is yet another factor that figures in his rationale. He mentions it in each major division. What is it?
4. What is the purpose of paragraphs 2 and 3? What is Toffler doing in the last two sentences of paragraph 3?
5. What is the effect of the concluding paragraph? How does it show Toffler's awareness of the demands imposed by the use of classi-fication as a rhetorical device?
6. What additional rhetorical device does Toffler use in the last paragraph to explain some of the exceptions he mentions?

The Origins of College Slang

CONNIE EBLE

Connie Eble (b. 1941) teaches English at the University of North Carolina at Chapel Hill. Her scholarly interests include general linguistics, dialectology, and especially college slang. This selection is taken from her book College Slang 101 *(1989).*

Recycling Old Words

Slang items usually arise by the same means in which new words   1
enter the general vocabulary—by recycling words and parts of
words which are already in the language. In the recycling process
either the shape or the sense of a word, or both, can be altered to
yield a new and different union between sound and meaning.
This is the way that standard English has recently added words
like *AIDS* (acquired immune deficiency syndrome), *fax* (to trans-
mit a facsimile electronically over telephone lines), and *micro-
wave* (to cook by heat produced by short electromagnetic waves).

By the same kinds of processes, slang has created *TAN* (tough   2
as nails), *preesh* (appreciate) and *megabread* (large amount of
money). This essay shows the various productive processes that
give rise to college slang.

Slangdom: Adding Prefixes and Suffixes

Ordinary English uses prefixes and suffixes to make new words.   3
Prearrange, predate, and *pretrial* are made by adding the prefix
pre- to different words. The suffix *-er*, which means "one who or
that which," turns a verb into a noun in words like *dancer, joker,
player,* and *singer*. Slang uses many of the same prefixes and
suffixes as ordinary English but sometimes with greater freedom
and slightly different meanings or grammatical functions.

MEGA-	A large quantity of: *megabitch, megabooks, megabucks, megagood, megawork.* "That teacher is such a *megabitch.*"
PERMA-	Permanent: *permagrin, permagross, permanerve, permaproblem.* "After just two beers, she had *permagrin.*"
-AGE	Noun suffix which does not change the meaning of the word to which it is attached: *bookage, buckage, fundage, snowage, tunage.* "I'm desperate for *foodage.*"
-AHOLIC	A person who indulges excessively in the noun to which the suffix is attached: *bookaholic, cokeaholic, foodaholic, hoopaholic.* "Sue is such a *hoopaholic* she carries a basketball in her car at all times."

-DOM	The domain of: *fratdom, geekdom, jockdom.* "Walking through the computer building is a trip through *geekdom.*"
-ER	One who or that which.
BUMMER	Depressing experience. "Studying on Thursday nights is a *bummer.*"
DOPER	Associated with smoking marijuana. "The *doper* music is loud tonight."
HOOKER	Tow truck. "The *hooker* got me for parking in the state vehicles' spot."
LOOKER	Attractive male or female. "There are a couple of *lookers* in my English class."
WANKER	Undesirable person, thing, or situation. "Don't read that book—it's a real *wanker.*"
-FEST	An abundance of: *beerfest, pizzafest, sleepfest.* "I just got paid. *Pizzafest,* everyone!"
-EY, -IE	One who or that which.
DESKIE	Desk attendant in a dormitory. "He's a *deskie* at James."
GROUPIE	Follower, idolizer. "Granville Towers is filled with basketball *groupies.*"
GRUNGIE	Someone who wears old, shabby, dirty-looking clothes. "Those motorcycle freaks are *grungies.*"
HOMEY	Someone from the same town or a longtime friend. "I want you to meet one of my *homies.*"
VEGGIE	Someone who *vegs out,,* i.e., acts like a vegetable. "When I finish this paper, I'm just going to be a *veggie.*"
-OMATIC	Emphatic suffix: *cramomatic, dunkomatic, jamomatic, jogomatic.* "I have to *cramomatic* for Dr. Joyner's English test."
-ORAMA	Emphatic suffix: *barforama, funorama, geekorama, sexorama.* "She gave us a fourteen-page take-home test—*barforama!*"

Word Action: Putting Words Together

Putting words together into a new compound word or into a   4
unified phrase is an ancient and ongoing process in English. The
three categories of words and phrases in this section show that
compounding is a productive process in slang as well. In the first
group, the nouns that form the second member of the compound
have general, stereotypic meanings like suffixes and combine
freely with a wide range of words.

For example, the element -*city* indicates merely "a presence   5
or abundance of," not "a metropolis," and can be added to almost
any kind of word. The second group illustrates less predictable
combinations of two words into one, sometimes with figurative
meanings, e.g., *lunchbox* (one who is not aware of what is going
on). The third type of compound is the most frequent, combining
a word of any part of speech with a little invariant word like *out*,
up, down, on, off.

[Type 1 Compounds]

-ACTION	Activity. "I'm ready for some Chinese *food action*." "Check out the *volleyball action*."
-ANIMAL	One who does something excessively. "That *party animal* cruises Franklin Street every night." "The *study animals* are complaining about the noise."
-CITY	A presence or abundance of. "The day after spring break it was *tan city*." "Even when she plays tennis, she's *jewelry city*."
-DUDE	A person. "Somebody pay the *pizza dude*." (The one who delivers pizza.)
-DWELLER	Someone who frequents a particular place. "She's one of the *stand dwellers*." (She hangs around the life guard stand.) "I could hardly get into Lenoir Hall because of the *step dwellers*."
-HEAD	Person. "Check out the shoes on that *tackhead*." (Male who dresses in pimp-like clothes and thinks he's cool.) "The *potheads* were in the corner mellowing out." (One who smokes marijuana, i.e., pot.)

-MACHINE	An enthusiast, a devotee. "After Thanksgiving I'll be a *study-machine.*" "That *sex-machine* keeps phoning Karen even though I told him she went home this weekend."
-QUEEN	Female enthusiast. "Miss *Partyqueen* woke me up when she came in at 5 AM." "The *datequeen* slept through class this morning and wanted to copy my notes."
-WAD	Dense, dull, foolish person. "Joe is such a *dip-wad*—who invited him to the party?" "*Mike-wad* here locked himself out of the room."

[Type 2 Compounds]

ALL-NIGHTER	Entire night spent without sleep to study or write a paper. "After I pulled an *all-nighter* to finish the paper, the teacher gave the whole class an extension."
BAT CAVE	To sleep. "Tim's been *bat caving* all afternoon because he partied all night."
BONG-BREATH	Someone who takes advantage of another. "Leave my cigarettes alone, you *bong-breath.*" (A *bong* is a pipe used to smoke marijuana and other herbs.)
BUTTLOAD	Large quantity. "It just cost me a *buttload* of money to get my motorcycle fixed."
CHEESEMAN	An out of style, socially inept person. Also CHEESEBAG, CHEESEFACE, CHEESEHEAD, CAPTAIN CHEDDAR, CHEESE WHIZ. "That stereo salesman was a real *cheeseman.*"
COOL WHIP	Something new and appealing. "That new flick is *cool whip.*"
DINGLE-BERRY	A socially inept person. "Tell that *dingleberry* I'm not here."
DOY-BURGER	Someone who is dim-witted or physically uncoordinated. "That usher-dude is such a *doyburger.*"
EARTH DADDY	Older-than-college-age male who displays a 60's style mellowness, wears a beard, and attends college parties.

HOMEBOY   Someone from the same hometown, a longtime
               friend, or someone who shares the same
               values. Also HOME, HOMESLICE, HOMES,
               SHERLOCK (from Sherlock Holmes). "One of
               my *homeboys* is coming for the weekend."

HOME   Good friend. "Yo, *home biscuit*, let's go shoot
BISCUIT   some hoop."

HOT DOG   One who tries to impress others by dominating
               a situation. To show off, particularly in sports.
               "Coach Smith doesn't allow *hot dogging* on
               his team."

JACKSHIT   Nothing. "I didn't do *jackshit* on my paper this
               weekend."

MOUNTAIN   High induced by drugs. "Don't mess with this
CLIMBER   *mountain climber.*"

RAGMAN/   Person in a bad mood. "Jim is such a *ragman*
RAG-   that I hate to be around him."
WOMAN

REDNECK   Conservative, white, rural Southerner. "I'm a
               wreck. Some *redneck* in a pickup kept riding
               my bumper all the way from Pittsboro."

RICEBURNER   Japanese motorcycle.

ROAD TRIP   A spur-of-the-moment trip anywhere, usually
               after a party. "We took a *road trip* to the
               beach this morning to get some donuts."

SAND-   Thrown out of one's room so that one's roomate
BAGGED   can have an amorous encounter. "Bill's
               girlfriend came up for the weekend and Bob
               got *sandbagged* again."

ZIPPERHEAD   A male with an out-of-style haircut, e.g., parted
               down the middle. "That *zipperhead* needs to
               catch the CLUE BUS."

[Type 3 Compounds]

BEAM OUT   To daydream. "Oh, I'm sorry. I was *beaming
               out* and didn't hear what you said."

BLOW OUT   To shock, embarrass. "When she got drunk at
               the party, she really *blew* her date *out.*"

BOMB OUT   To fail, perform poorly. "He really *bombed out* by forgetting their date."

BUM OUT   To cause or experience unpleasant feelings or bad reaction. "This English 2 research paper really *bums* me *out*."

BURN OUT   To become mentally or physically exhausted. "Rush was fun, but I'm *burned out* from it."

CHECK OUT   To look at, observe. "Let's go *check out* the fox factor at the mixer."

CHILL OUT   To relax, calm down. "Hey, *chill out,* man, I was only kidding." Also CHILL, TAKE A CHILL PILL.

CRANK OUT   To produce large amounts of work, energy, volume. "The band at the all-campus could really *crank out* the jams."

GEEK OUT   To study hard.

GOOB OUT   To cause repulsion or disgust. "Joe got sick in the car—he really *goobed* me *out*."

JELL OUT   To relax by doing nothing, i.e., by acting like jello. "Bob just *jelled out* all weekend." Also VEG OUT.

LAY OUT   To sunbathe. "Check the babes *laying out* behind the dorm."

LUDE OUT   To become unable to function or physically incapacitated. (Probably derived from the drug name *Quaalude*.) "He was so *luded out* he couldn't get the key in his door."

PHASE OUT   To become unware, as if asleep. "I *phased out* during that lecture about footnotes this morning."

PLASTIC   To assume temporarily an artificial behavior or
OUT   personality. "Beth began to *plastic out* when she realized it was Dave's mother on the phone."

RAG OUT   To become tired. "I *ragged out* when I ran those four miles on just two hours of sleep."

RAUNCH OUT	To offend by making sexual remarks or using offensive language. "Peter thinks he's cool, but he just *raunches* me *out.*"
ROCK OUT	To play music loudly. "My roomate loves to *rock out* when she does her homework."
SMELL OUT	To interview. "We're going to *smell out* the rush chairman today."
SNORT OUT	To overeat. "The four of us ordered pizza and really *snorted out.*"
SPAZ OUT	To lose mental control. "I *spazzed out* during the Chem final."
SCHIZ OUT	To lose emotional control, to act crazed. "Lisa started *schizzing out* about three hours before the exam."
SUE OUT	To dress and look like a stereotypic sorority member. "I think I'll *sue out* today and wear my add-a-beads."
TANG OUT	To abandon, put an end to. "I'm going to *tang out* on the books and catch some Z's."
TRIP OUT	To strike as funny, crazy, or extraordinary. "That film last night *tripped me out.*"
WEIRD OUT	To feel confused and at a loss because of someone's or something's strangeness. "I was *weirded out* when she said she was looking forward to a painful death."
WIG OUT	To become astonished. "When I saw the price of my textbooks I *wigged out.*"
WIMP OUT	To let someone down; to fail to live up to a commitment. "You promised not to tell anyone. Now don't *wimp out* on us."
BAMAED UP	Very ugly. "Her boyfriend is one *bamaed up* dude."
BEAM UP	To die. "The doctors tried to save him, but he just *beamed up.*"
BURN UP	To put in a complete effort or do fast. "I was so hungry I *burned up* Wendy's taco bar."
CAFF UP	To become hyperactive because of too much caffeine. "During my English exam I was so *caffed up* I could hardly sit still."

CASH UP	To solve, think through, analyze. "Louie aked me to *cash up* the Chem problems for him."
EAT UP	Temporarily physically unattractive. "Laura pulled an ALL-NIGHTER and looked *eat up* in her 9 o'clock class."
JACK UP	To use force. "You do that again, and I'll *jack* you *up*."
LIGHTEN UP	To stop annoying or bothering. "Would you *lighten up* about my smoking?"
MOMMY UP	To love, hug, comfort. "His girlfriend *mommied* him *up* when he stepped off the plane."
PUMP UP	Inspire, energize, stimulate. "Phil Ford could always *pump up* the team."
SCREW UP	To bungle, to make a mistake. "They really *screwed up* student seating in the Dean Dome."
BITE ON	To copy someone else, particularly in clothing. "Susan is *biting on* my earrings."
BUST ON	To criticize, poke fun at. "Would you quit *busting on* my date?"
CRACK ON	To embarrass or humiliate. "Bill kept *cracking on* Joan about locking the keys in the car." To make romantic overtures. "That geek kept *cracking on* Jane, so we had to leave."
DISS ON	To criticize, belittle. "I'm tired of John *dissing on* her all the time."
HARSH ON	To criticize, belittle, act ungraciously. "Don't *harsh on* me for making noise—It's almost noon."
LATCH ON	To understand. "If I can't *latch on* to physics soon, I'm in big trouble."
LIVE ON	To take pleasure from the embarrassment of another. "When I fell off my bike in the middle of campus, my roomate *lived on* it all day."
RAG ON	To reprimand, insult. "Our professor *ragged on* us for reading the DTH in class." Also RAIL ON.

RIFF ON	To take advantage of another. "Hey don't *riff on* me, man, just because I'm sick."
TURN ON	To use some sort of drugs. "My roommate *turns on* every day before grammar class." To cause interest or excitement. "The Red Clay Ramblers can *turn* this local audience *on*."
BLOW OFF	To forget, ignore, absent oneself. "I haven't read the novel we're talking about, so I'm going to *blow off* English class."
DINK OFF	To make angry. "It *dinks* me *off* when you yell at me."
GET OFF	To become excited, have fun. "Coye was *getting off* at Purdy's last night."
GO OFF ON	To show anger at. "Pat *went off on* John for breaking the exercise bike."

Slanguage: Putting Pieces of Words Together

Sometimes new words are made by putting pieces of words to- 6 gether and combining the meanings of the original words. Examples from everyday language are *brunch,* from *breakfast* and *lunch,* and names created for products like *apple-cran* juice and the *croissandwich.*

BUEL	Food; to eat voraciously. From *body + fuel.* "Let's go *buel* on some Hector's."
DRONED	Unaware because of alcohol or drugs. From *drink + stoned.* "He was so *droned* he thought his date was his mother."
HOMECHOP	An endearing term for a close friend, usually of the opposite sex. From *homeboy/homegirl + lambchop.* "Yo, Michelle. What's up, *homechop*?"
SPADET	A student preoccupied with studies. From *space + cadet.* "My roomate's off booking with the other *spadets* in the class."
SPORK	Eating implement. From *spoon + fork.* "I wonder why someone invented these stupid plastic *sporks.*"

SWEAVE	To have difficulty walking straight. From *swerve* + *weave*. "Scot was *sweaving* after pounding a six-pack."
VOMATOSE	Disgusting. From *vomit* + *comatose*. "Sean downed so many mixed drinks he was *vomatose* the whole weekend."

To the min: Shortening Words and Phrases

By the process of shortening, sounds are eliminated from words without a loss of meaning. Many ordinary English words have been formed in this way: *fan* from fanatic, flu from *influenza*, and *phone* from *telephone*. Most of the time, the meaning of the shortened form is the same as that of the longer word from which it was derived.

BOD	From *body*.
BRARY	From *library*.
BRO, BROTH	From *brother*.
CATCH A VID	To watch music videos on MTV. "Let's go to the lounge and *catch a vid*." From *catch a music video*.
CAZH	Relaxing, conducive to good times. "I heard this was a *cazh* birthday party." From *casual*.
COKE	From *cocaine*.
FEEB	Dull-witted or absent-minded person. From *feeble*.
FILE	To show off; to dress up. "Did you see what Nicholas has on? Man, he's *filing*." From *profile*.
FRIZ	From *frisbee*.
GIG	From *gigolo*.
HYPER	From *hyperactive*.
IG	From *ignore*.
MESC	From *mescaline*.
NARK	From *narcotics agent*.
OBNO	From *obnoxious*.

PREESH	Thanks. "*Preesh* for telling my mom I was at the library." From *appreciate*.
PRESH	Favorable, enjoyable. "That late night was *presh*." From *precious*. Also rhymes with *fresh*.
RAD	Excellent. From *radical*.
RENT, RENTAL UNIT	From *parental unit*, mock sociological jargon popularized by *Saturday Night Live*.
RENTS	From *parents*.
SPAZ	A clumsy person, usually said jokingly. From *spastic*.
TIVES	From *relatives*.
TO THE MAX	From *to the maximum*.
VIBES	Inaudible signals that people and places emit. From *vibrations*.
WELK	From *you're welcome*.

N.B.D.: Words from Letters

In an extreme form of shortening called acronymy, words are made from the initial letters of the words in a phrase. For example, the United States of America is named by the letters U.S.A.; however, in the acronym SCUBA, from *self-contained underwater breathing apparatus,* the letters are pronounced together as a word. Both ways of forming words from letters also occur in slang.

B.K. LOUNGE	From *Burger King*.
B.L.	From *Big Library*.
D.H.C.	From *deep heavy conversation*.
G.H.	From the soap opera *General Hospital*.
G.Q.	Fashionably and tastefully dressed. "Dean Floyd always looks so *G.Q.*" From *Gentlemen's Quarterly*.
H.D.	Male who mooches off a female. From the military designation *husband dependent*.

J.	Marijuana cigarette. From *joint*.
K.O.	Die. From *kick off*.
M.D.G.	Strong physical attraction, not dependent on feelings of love or friendship. "Libby and Billy have an *M.D.G.*" From *mutual desire to grope*.
M.L.A.	Passionate kissing. From *massive lip action*.
M.R.A.	Unsociable behavior. From *major reeb action*.
N.B.D.	From *no big deal*.
N.C.	A boorish person. From *no class*.
N.C.A.A.	From *no class at all*. Pronounced "n.c. double a."
N.F.	From *no fun*.
N.T.S.	Good-looking male. From *name tag shaker*. "That Jack is one power *N.T.S.*"
O.D.	From *overdose*.
O.O.C.	Drunk, high on drugs, or acting crazy. From *out of control*.
O.T.L.	Inattentive, unaware. From *out to lunch*.
O.T.R.	Snappish, in a bad mood. Originally applied to females but now can apply to either sex. "I think Bill's *O.T.R.* today because of problems at home." From *on the rag*.
P.D.K.	Someone who is out of date or out of touch. From *polyester double knit*.
P.F. MATERIAL	Good looking male. From *pledge formal material*.
P.Q.	Someone who is out of date. From *polyester queen*.
R. & I.	Extremely exciting and enjoyable. From *radical and intense*.
S.A.B.	From *social airhead bitch*.
TAN	Aggressively masculine. From *tough as nails*.
T.S.H.	From *that shit happens*.
V.P.L.	From *visible panty lines*, from a Woody Allen film.

DISCUSSION: CONTENT

1. What does Eble mean when she says that slang usually arises from the recycling of words or parts of words already in the language?
2. What are some examples that Eble presents of slang words based on the use of prefixes or suffixes? Are any of these terms in use on your campus? Are you familiar with any slang terms that Eble doesn't mention that feature these prefixes or suffixes?
3. What examples can you provide of your own campus slang words based on compounds? How about shortenings or initials?
4. Which types of college slang described here are totally new to your experience? Try to discover whether examples of them exist on your campus.

DISCUSSION: FORM

1. Eble's purpose in this essay is to describe the various *types* of college slang. In doing so, is she both classifying and dividing—creating a hierarchy—like the one on p. 120? Could you represent Eble's hierarchy in the form of just such a branching diagram?
2. How many different types of slang does she describe? Are they all separate, distinct types, or do some tend to cluster together, sharing certain characteristics? In other words, are some of the types that she mentions actually sub-types of a larger grouping?
3. After briefly identifying and discussing each type of slang, what does Eble do next? What method of exposition is she using?
4. Is Eble's essay consistent? That is, does it have a governing rationale? If so, what is it? Is it complete? Can you suggest any other types that she has failed to examine?

Can People Be Judged by Their Appearance?

ERIC BERNE

Eric Berne (1910–1970) was a psychiatrist who practiced in New York and then California. He was also the author of numerous articles and books, including the best-seller Games People Play *(1964). The essay below is from* A Layman's Guide to Psychiatry and Psychoanalysis *(1968).*

Everyone knows that a human being, like a chicken, comes   1
from an egg. At a very early stage, the human embryo forms a
three-layered tube, the inside layer of which grows into the
stomach and lungs, the middle layer into bones, muscle, joints,
and blood vessels, and the outside layer into the skin and nervous
system.

Usually these three grow about equally, so that the average   2
human being is a fair mixture of brains, muscles, and inward
organs. In some eggs, however, one layer grows more than the
others, and when the angels have finished putting the child
together, he may have more gut than brain, or more brain than
muscle. When this happens, the individual's activities will often
be mostly with the overgrown layer.

We can thus say that while the average human being is a   3
mixture, some people are mainly "digestion-minded," some
"muscle-minded," and some "brain-minded," correspondingly
digestion-bodied, muscle-bodied, or brain-bodied. The digestion-
bodied people look thick, the muscle-bodied people look wide,
and the brain-bodied people look long. This does not mean the
taller a man is the brainier he will be. It means that if a man,
even a short man, looks long rather than wide or thick, he will
often be more concerned about what goes on in his mind than
about what he does or what he eats; but the key factor is slender-
ness and not height. On the other hand, a man who gives the
impression of being thick rather than long or wide will usually
be more interested in a good steak than in a good idea or a good
long walk.

Medical men use Greek words to describe these types of   4
body-build. For the man whose body shape mostly depends on
the inside layer of the egg, they use the word *endomorph*. If it
depends mostly upon the middle layer, they call him a *mesomorph*. If it depends upon the outside layer they call him an
ectomorph. We can see the same roots in our English words
"enter," "medium," and "exit," which might just as easily have
been spelled "ender," "mesium," and "ectit."

Since the inside skin of the human egg, or endoderm, forms   5
the inner organs of the belly, the viscera, the endomorph is
usually belly-minded; since the middle skin forms the body tis-
sues, or soma, the mesomorph is usually muscle-minded; and
since the outside skin forms the brain, or cerebrum, the ectomorph is usually brain-minded. Translating this into Greek, we

have the viscerotonic endomorph, the somatotonic mesomorph, and the cerebrotonic ectomorph.

Words are beautiful things to a cerebrotonic, but a viscero-   6
tonic knows you cannot eat a menu no matter what language it is printed in, and a somatotonic knows you cannot increase your chest expansion by reading a dictionary. So it is advisable to leave these words and see what kinds of people they actually apply to, remembering again that most individuals are fairly equal mixtures and that what we have to say concerns only the extremes. Up to the present, these types have been thoroughly studied only in the male sex.

Viscerotonic Endomorph

If a man is definitely a thick type rather than a broad or long type,   7
he is likely to be round and soft, with a big chest but a bigger belly. He would rather eat than breathe comfortably. He is likely to have a wide face, short, thick neck, big thighs and upper arms, and small hands and feet. He has overdeveloped breasts and looks as though he were blown up a little like a balloon. His skin is soft and smooth, and when he gets bald, as he does usually quite early, he loses the hair in the middle of his head first.

The short, jolly, thickset, red-faced politician with a cigar in   8
his mouth, who always looks as though he were about to have a stroke, is the best example of this type. The reason he often makes a good politician is that he likes people, banquets, baths, and sleep; he is easygoing, soothing, and his feelings are easy to understand.

His abdomen is big because he has lots of intestines. He likes   9
to take in things. He likes to take in food, and affection and approval as well. Going to a banquet with people who like him is his idea of a fine time. It is important for a psychiatrist to understand the natures of such men when they come to him for advice.

Somatotonic Mesomorph

If a man is definitely a broad type rather than a thick or long type,   10
he is likely to be rugged and have lots of muscle. He is apt to have big forearms and legs, and his chest and belly are well formed and firm, with the chest bigger than the belly. He would rather breathe than eat. He has a bony head, big shoulders, and a square

jaw. His skin is thick, coarse, and elastic, and tans easily. If he gets bald, it usually starts on the front of the head.

Dick Tracy, Li'l Abner, and other men of action belong to this type. Such people make good lifeguards and construction workers. They like to put out energy. They have lots of muscles and they like to use them. They go in for adventure, exercise, fighting, and getting the upper hand. They are bold and unrestrained, and love to master the people and things around them. If the psychiatrist knows the things which give such people satisfaction, he is able to understand why they may be unhappy in certain situations.

Cerebrotonic Ectomorph

The man who is definitely a long type is likely to have thin bones and muscles. His shoulders are apt to sag and he has a flat belly with a dropped stomach, and long, weak legs. His neck and fingers are long, and his face is shaped like a long egg. His skin is thin, dry, and pale, and he rarely gets bald. He looks like an absent-minded professor and often is one.

Though such people are jumpy, they like to keep their energy and don't fancy moving around much. They would rather sit quietly by themselves and keep out of difficulties. Trouble upsets them, and they run away from it. Their friends don't understand them very well. They move jerkily and feel jerkily. The psychiatrist who understands how easily they become anxious is often able to help them get along better in the sociable and aggressive world of endomorphs and mesomorphs.

In the special cases where people definitely belong to one type or another, then, one can tell a good deal about their personalities from their appearance. When the human mind is engaged in one of its struggles with itself or with the world outside, the individual's way of handling the struggle will be partly determined by his type. If he is a viscerotonic he will often want to go to a party where he can eat and drink and be in good company at a time when he might be better off attending to business; the somatotonic will want to go out and do something about it, master the situation, even if what he does is foolish and not properly figured out, while the cerebrotonic will go off by himself and think it over, when perhaps he would be better off doing something about it or seeking good company to try to forget it.

Since these personality characteristics depend on the growth of   15
the layers of the little egg from which the person developed, they
are very difficult to change. Nevertheless, it is important for the
individual to know about these types, so that he can have at least
an inkling of what to expect from those around him, and can make
allowances for the different kinds of human nature, and so that he
can become aware of and learn to control his own natural tendencies, which may sometimes guide him into making the same mistakes over and over again in handling his difficulties.

DISCUSSION: CONTENT

1. What are the three main types into which Berne divides human
   appearances?
2. Explain the derivation of each of the terms for the types.
3. Berne furnishes examples of each type. Name one for each type.
   Supply at least two additional examples of your own for each
   type.
4. According to Berne, how is this classification of human appearances useful to the psychiatrist? To other persons? What danger
   is there in classifying people by their appearances? Does Berne
   warn us about that danger, at least in part?

DISCUSSION: FORM

1. What is Berne's basis for classification in this essay?
2. In which paragraph does he define his terms?
3. On what basis are the three major divisions divided further? Is he
   consistent in his application of these criteria to each class?
4. Which of Berne's examples for each type is most effective? Why?

Three Kinds of Discipline

JOHN HOLT

*John Caldwell Holt (1923–1985), a graduate of Yale, served as
a submarine officer during World War II. His most notable
books,* How Children Fail *(1964) and* How Children Learn
*(1967), were based on his diaries and letters from experiences
as an elementary school teacher and called for radical reform*

of American schools. He also taught education theory at Harvard University and the University of California at Berkeley. Among his other books are The Underachieving Child *(1969),* Escape from Childhood *(1974),* Instead of Education *(1976), his fictionalized autobiography* Never Too Late: My Musical Life Story *(1978), and* Freedom and Beyond *(1972), from which this essay is taken.*

A child, in growing up, may meet and learn from three different kinds of disciplines. The first and most important is what we might call the Discipline of Nature or of Reality. When he is trying to do something real, if he does the wrong thing or doesn't do the right one, he doesn't get the result he wants. If he doesn't pile one block right on top of another, or tries to build on a slanting surface, his tower falls down. If he hits the wrong key, he hears the wrong note. If he doesn't hit the nail squarely on the head, it bends, and he has to pull it out and start with another. If he doesn't measure properly what he is trying to build, it won't open, close, fit, stand up, fly, float, whistle, or do whatever he wants it to do. If he closes his eyes when he swings, he doesn't hit the ball. A child meets this kind of discipline every time he tries to *do* something, which is why it is so important in school to give children more chances to do things, instead of just reading or listening to someone talk (or pretending to). This discipline is a great teacher. The learner never has to wait long for his answer; it usually comes quickly, often instantly. Also it is clear, and very often points toward the needed correction; from what happened he can not only see that what he did was wrong, but also why, and what he needs to do instead. Finally, and most important, the giver of the answer, call it Nature, is impersonal, impartial, and indifferent. She does not give opinions, or make judgments; she cannot be wheedled, bullied, or fooled; she does not get angry or disappointed; she does not praise or blame; she does not remember past failures or hold grudges; with her one always gets a fresh start; this time is the one that counts.

The next discipline we might call the Discipline of Culture, of Society, of What People Really Do. Man is a social, a cultural animal. Children sense around them this culture, this network of agreements, customs, habits, and rules binding the adults together. They want to understand it and be a part of it. They watch very carefully what people around them are doing and want to do the same. They want to do right, unless they become convinced they can't do right. Thus children rarely misbehave seriously in church, but sit as quietly as they can. The example of all those grownups is contagious. Some mysterious ritual is going on, and children, who like rituals, want to be part of it. In the same way, the little children that I see at concerts or operas, though they may fidget a little, or perhaps take a nap now and then, rarely make any disturbance. With all those grownups sitting there, neither moving nor talking, it is the most natural thing in the world to imitate them. Children who live among adults who are habitually courteous to each other, and to them, will soon learn to be courteous. Children who live surrounded by people who speak a certain way will speak that way, however much we may try to tell them that speaking that way is bad or wrong.

The third discipline is the one most people mean when they speak of discipline—the Discipline of Superior Force, of sergeant to private, of "you do what I tell you or I'll make you wish you had." There is bound to be some of this in a child's life. Living as we do surrounded by things that can hurt children, or that children can hurt, we cannot avoid it. We can't afford to let a small child find out from experience the danger of playing in a busy street, or of fooling with the pots on the top of a stove, or of eating up the pills in the medicine cabinet. So, along with other precautions, we say to him, "Don't play in the street, or touch things on the stove, or go into the medicine cabinet, or I'll punish you." Between him and the danger too great for him to imagine we put a lesser danger, but one he can imagine and maybe therefore want to avoid. He can have no idea of what it would be like to be hit by a car, but he can imagine being shouted at, or spanked, or sent to his room. He avoids these substitutes for the greater danger until he can understand it and avoid it for its own sake. But we ought to use this discipline only when it is necessary to protect the life, health, safety, or well-being of people or other living creatures, or to prevent destruction of things that people care about. We ought not to assume too long, as we usually do, that a child cannot understand the real nature of the danger from which we want to protect him. The sooner he avoids the danger, not to escape our punishment, but as a matter of good sense, the better. He can learn that faster than we think. In Mexico, for example, where people drive their cars with a good deal of spirit, I saw many children no older than five or four walking unattended on the streets. They understood about cars;

3

they knew what to do. A child whose life is full of the threat and fear of punishment is locked into babyhood. There is no way for him to grow up, to learn to take responsibility for his life and acts. Most important of all, we should not assume that having to yield to the threat of our superior force is good for the child's character. It is never good for *anyone's* character. To bow to superior force makes us feel impotent and cowardly for not having had the strength or courage to resist. Worse, it makes us resentful and vengeful. We can hardly wait to make someone pay for our humiliation, yield to us as we were once made to yield. No, if we cannot always avoid using the Discipline of Superior Force, we should at least use it as seldom as we can.

There are places where all three disciplines overlap. Any very   4 demanding human activity combines in it the disciplines of Superior Force, of Culture, and of Nature. The novice will be told, "Do it this way, never mind asking why, just do it that way, that is the way we always do it." But it probably *is* just the way they always do it, and usually for the very good reason that it is a way that has been found to work. Think, for example, of ballet training. The student in a class is told to do this exercise, or that; to stand so; to do this or that with his head, arms, shoulders, abdomen, hips, legs, feet. He is constantly corrected. There is no argument. But behind these seemingly autocratic demands by the teacher lie many decades of custom and tradition, and behind that, the necessities of dancing itself. You cannot make the moves of classical ballet unless over many years you have acquired, and renewed every day, the needed strength and suppleness in scores of muscles and joints. Nor can you do the difficult motions, making them look easy, unless you have learned hundreds of easier ones first. Dance teachers may not always agree on all the details of teaching these strengths and skills. But no novice could learn them all by himself. You could not go for a night or two to watch the ballet and then, without any other knowledge at all, teach yourself how to do it. In the same way, you would be unlikely to learn any complicated and difficult human activity without drawing heavily on the experience of those who know it better. But the point is that the authority of these experts or teachers stems from, grows out of their greater competence and experience, the fact that what they do *works*, not the fact that they happen to be the teacher and as such have the power to kick a student out of class. And the further point is that children are always and everywhere attracted to that competence, and ready and eager to submit themselves to a discipline that grows out of it. We hear constantly that children will never do anything unless compelled to by bribes or threats. But in their private lives, or in extracurricular activities in school, in sports, music, drama, art, running a newspaper, and so on, they often submit themselves willingly and wholeheartedly to very intense disciplines, simply because they want to learn to do a given thing well. Our Little-Napoleon football coaches, of whom we have too many and hear far too much, blind us to the fact that millions of children work hard every year getting better at sports and games without coaches barking and yelling at them.

DISCUSSION: CONTENT

1. Name the three kinds of discipline that Holt describes, and give an example of each.
2. Why, according to Holt, do most children behave well in church?
3. Which of the three disciplines that Holt discusses most closely resembles the discipline most people think of when they hear the word?
4. Holt asserts that in most situations all three types of discipline are blended together. He offers an example to illustrate that point. What is the example? Show how it provides a blend of the three disciplines.
5. Holt suggests that modern education often fails because teachers do not make sufficient use of which of the disciplines?

DISCUSSION: FORM

1. What consistent rationale guides Holt in his division of discipline into three types?
2. Is the classification complete? What about discipline that comes from God or religion? What about self-discipline?
3. After making his classification, how does Holt substantiate it?
4. Holt's essay ends quite abruptly with criticism of Little-Napoleon football coaches. Compose a more effective concluding paragraph for the essay.

7

Process

Process analysis is similar to classification in that it divides a subject into parts. It is similar to narration in that it orders those parts into a step-by step sequence. However, your purpose in process analysis is to do one or the other of two things: (1) explain to your reader how to do something, or (2) inform your reader about how something works, happens, is organized, or was accomplished.

How To Do It

Cookbooks furnish familiar and precise examples of the first type of process analysis. Typically, recipes are processes described in barest detail—a list of ingredients, followed by step-by-step instructions detailing when and how to mix and cook them. This same "how-to-do-it" formula will confront you at almost every turn in daily life: simple instructions telling how to assemble the thing that you got for Christmas; more complicated directions spelling out how to declare an academic major or how to apply for graduation; bewildering booklets on how to file state and federal income taxes or how to qualify for food stamps; even books promising to tell you how to enjoy Europe on $25 a day.

In addition, you'll frequently need to use a version of this formula in your own writing, for instance when you describe the steps in double-entry bookkeeping for an accounting class or explain the various ways to amend the U.S. Constitution for a political science class.

How It Works, How It Happened

Histories are an example of the second type of process analysis, that is, how events happened. The process described may be as simple as how one team defeated another in a sports event, or as complicated as how America pursued its so-called "manifest destiny" from sea to shining sea. Quite often, though, this type of process involves more than just a simple listing of steps. In retrospect it's easy to see that events often occur simultaneously rather than in sequence. And it's frequently necessary to discuss *why* events occurred as well as *how* they occurred. Thus, as you prepare your process analysis, you'll often find it necessary to employ the techniques of cause and effect analysis (to be discussed in Chapter 10). You'll need to make allowances for such possibilities as you organize process analyses, when writing for history or other classes. If you are planning a scientific or technical career, perhaps as a biochemist or systems analyst or chemical engineer, you especially must be able not only to read and understand complicated process analyses fully, but also to write them effectively. The selections and exercises that follow will help you to begin developing those skills.

Commentary on Student Work

As we pointed out in Chapter 2, "The Writing Process," one of this book's chief advantages is in the assistance that its readings can provide during the prewriting stage. Quite often the readings will trigger thought processes or associations that will lead quite quickly and easily into the development of your own ideas.

Such was the case with the first of our student selections. The class had just discussed Alice Gray's essay "Mosquito Bite" (p. 169), and the assignment was to write a process paper using the step-by-step procedures illustrated in Gray's piece. In this instance, for the paper by Faye that follows, the essay provided more than just the framework; it provided something of the subject matter.

As the students in Faye's reading/writing group brainstormed the assignment, which was to complete a process analysis involving some activity in which the student had been involved, the subject of blood—and how the mosquito collected it—was still fresh in each mind. Faye spontaneously recalled aloud the experience of donating blood, which she and two of her friends had shared the day before. As freshman nursing majors, they were required to volunteer during the three-day blood drive. While she recalled the experience, a couple of the group members wrote down the steps of the procedure:

1. check-in with volunteer
2. medical history
3. the blood-letting
4. afterward

These four major divisions of the blood-donating procedure served as the beginning of an outline that Faye later expanded in this way:

1. Check-in with volunteer
   a. identification check and filling out forms
   b. first sight of blood donors
   c. recording of temperature, pulse, and blood pressure
2. Medical history and finish preliminaries
   a. medical history—diseases—recorded
   b. blood sample taken from finger
   c. plastic bag issued
3. The actual blood-letting by a nurse
   a. inspection of arm
   b. lying down on special lounge chair
   c. strap put around arm
   d. placing antiseptic on arm
   e. rubber ball to squeeze
   f. insertion of needle in arm
4. After donating
   a. removal of needle
   b. instructions about care of arm
   c. snacks and soft drinks
   d. feeling of satisfaction

After completing this outline, Faye glanced back over "Mosquito Bite" and was pleased to notice how similar its structure was to the one that she had just completed: each of that essay's paragraphs was devoted to a major step in the process, and each of the paragraphs was expanded into a series of subparts, listing the steps involved.

Faye felt confident now as she completed the initial draft of her paper, which she then shared with her reading group. In this first effort, Faye's paper consisted of four paragraphs corresponding to the outline. With the assistance of her classmates, Faye added transitional paragraphs 3 and 5 and divided the final portion of the process into two parts so that the last paragraph provided a fitting conclusion. Similarly, she divided her initial paragraph into two parts, so that the first of these served as her introduction. Here is that final paper:

Donating Blood

1 Yesterday my roommate, another friend, and I gave blood to the American Red Cross, each of us donating a pint of blood in an almost painless process.

2 Just inside the Grand Room, on the top floor of the University Center, volunteers seated at the first of a series of tables asked if we were first-time donors and for our identification. While we answered some other questions, beyond them we could see people in various sections of the large ballroom. The area that caught my eye was where people were actually giving blood; a moment of fear struck me, and butterflies fluttered to life in my stomach.

3 From those first tables we were sent with a form bearing our names, addresses, and other personal information to the next long table. There other volunteers, with medical training, took and recorded our temperatures, pulse rates, and blood pressures, and then directed us on to the next station.

4 In this section of the room a uniformed medical professional then proceeded to inquire about our medical histories and enter our answers on our individual forms. Such questions as "Have you had heart trouble, respiratory diseases, epilepsy?" were asked. Then blood samples were taken from a finger, checked for white cell count, and recorded. Now accepted as donors, we were directed to another table nearby.

5 There each of us handed our forms to one of several volunteers, who put stickers with identifying numbers on our forms. We then each received a plastic pint donor bag with a personal identifying number and a form that told us what to do if we decided later to notify the Red Cross that our donated blood

should not be used, perhaps because we might have had prior exposure to a sexually-transmitted disease, such as AIDS. We read that form and then took seats in a row of chairs to wait for a vacancy in one of the special lounge chairs where the actual donations were taking place, just twenty-five or thirty feet away. As I chatted with my two friends and watched the donors in the chairs, my butterflies began to stir again.

As vacancies occurred, each of us went to a different section 6 of chairs. Every section contained three adjustable chairs arranged to make a U, plus a small supply table across the top of the U's open space. A registered nurse sitting on a stool on rollers managed each section. My section's nurse looked up from attending to another donor and greeted me with a smile and a few friendly words, while I settled down on the vacant chair.

The chairs were similar to common outdoor lounging chairs 7 but were made from heavier painted metal tubing and had beds of plastic ribbons. These allowed us to lean back comfortably at a 45-degree angle with our legs raised parallel to the floor. (If necessary, as when a donor begins feeling faint, the chair back can also be lowered to parallel with the floor, and the leg section raised, so that the donor's feet will be higher than his or her head. I saw this done for a husky male student, who turned white as typing paper and was very sheepish about his weakness after he recovered.) As I sat on one of these soft chairs and considered all that was soon to happen, it seemed as if a bushel of butterflies fluttered wildly in my stomach.

The nurse had me roll up both sleeves, and while examining 8 the undersides of my arms, tried to start a conversation, for she must have sensed how scared I was. After I settled back into the chair with my feet up, she stretched out my left arm with the elbow down on an arm rest and adjusted it until I felt comfortable. At this point, she tightened a strap with a Velcro fastener around my left upper arm. Then she rubbed first red and then clear antiseptic solutions on the middle inner crook of my left arm with sterile pads, at the same time talking quietly with me about my plans to become a pediatric nurse. Then she handed me a hard red rubber ball and showed me how to put its loop over my left middle finger while I squeezed the ball in my palm.

Telling me to relax and suggesting that I look away, the nurse 9 inserted a large needle, connected to my donor bag by tubing, in the largest vein in the crook of my left arm. The butterflies really went wild for a time then, because the needle felt like the jab of a knife, and it continued to sting a little as the bag began to fill with blood. I was directed to squeeze the rubber ball at five-second intervals, to help the blood flow more readily from my vein into the tubing and bag.

About ten or so minutes later, when the nurse prepared to 10 remove the needle, my butterflies stirred again. But to my surprise, I felt no pain; my left arm was simply a little numb. When she had the needle out, she covered the prick wound with a gauze pad and asked me to press the pad with my right hand while holding my left arm up in the air for a few minutes. Soon the nurse had me lower my arm so she could check to be sure all bleeding from the needle wound had stopped. Then she covered the spot with a Band-Aid and warned me not to do heavy lifting or to wash that part of my arm until the next day. By then the process was clearly over, and my butterflies lay down to rest.

After being escorted to the refreshment tables and seated by 11 a volunteer, I joined my two friends in sipping soft drinks and nibbling cookies and snack crackers. Later, as we walked back to the dorm, a great feeling of warmth and satisfaction beamed inside me.

DISCUSSION QUESTIONS

1. "Donating Blood" is more than a simple process essay. What other writing modes are used?
2. How many major steps in the process does the student describe?
3. How is figurative language used to connect the steps of the process/experience?
4. What effect may the student writer's intended profession have had on the amount of specific detail included in her description of this particular process?

STUDENT WORK

Registration

Registration on this campus is a classic headache. The lines are long, and you must wait for hours while people take the last seats in most of the courses that you intended to sign up for. When you finally get to the computer terminal, the actual registration is almost over before it has begun because only half the classes you asked for are available. Nevertheless, you are asked to move on to make room for the next in line. As you leave the registration area, you encounter first a bitchy lady requesting that you fill out an address card. After you have filled out this card, there will be more forms to complete, such as forms to get a parking sticker, forms to get an I.D. made, and forms to get back into the registration hall for Drop-Add so that you can complete your schedule. When you have completed this hectic filling out of forms, advisor-hunting begins. (The season on advisor-hunting begins in late August and continues until Drop-Add is over.) Yet it isn't really over until you receive your error-filled printed schedule back from the computer center, with courses meeting at the same hour, with the lab section but not the lecture section listed, or with courses that you signed up for missing completely.

DISCUSSION QUESTIONS

1. "Registration" demonstrates that using process as a writing strategy may also require the use of another expository strategy. What is it?
2. How many problems does this student encounter, as described here? What other problems can you think of, perhaps unique to your own campus?
3. The sentence beginning "After you have filled . . ." uses the word *forms* four different times. The word might have been used just once, with the sentence consequently much shortened. What justification can you provide for keeping the repetition?

Successful Sketching

When beginning a drawing, often putting the first mark down on the empty piece of paper is the hardest part of all. The way I have overcome this problem is to take my pencil and very loosely and lightly make several marks going across the page. This more or less frames my subject, directing my concentration on the view that I wish to capture. Next I start to sketch in the large areas. Working very fast and freely, I concentrate on getting these large areas in the right place with respect to one another. When this is done, I begin putting in the different values that I see. Using the side of my pencil, I quickly color in the largest, darkest areas, being very careful with placement and trying to get the exact shape of the shadows. Next, I take my eraser and begin picking up the highlighted areas. Switching back and forth between putting down the shadows and picking up the highlights, I watch the picture as it emerges. What most people do not realize is that the details of a drawing are the very last thing to be put in; what must come first is the large areas reduced to flat planes of light and dark.

DISCUSSION QUESTIONS

1. According to this student, what is often the hardest part of sketching?
2. What is the first step the writer suggests?
3. What comes next?
4. What are the last things to be added to a drawing?
5. Sometimes a description of a process must be converted into instructions. To manage that in this case will require shifting the point of view from first to second person and changing some verbs from passive to active voice and imperative mood (commands). How, for example, would you restate the second sentence in this paragraph? How many separate commands would you need to restate the whole paragraph?

I Remember, Granner

My mother's mother probably made the best apple pies I ever tasted. As a tiny girl, I used to watch my Granner make them, and I marveled at her sure, swift movements. Granner needed no recipes, yet her pies always came out delicious, fragrant with love and goodness. I was never too interested in making the crust, but by the time Granner brought out eight plump red apples, she had my full attention. 1

Peeling the apples was my job, and each round, firm apple yielded up its crisp skin in a long spiral. Meanwhile, Granner quartered and cored the apples I had peeled and began slicing 2 them into the crust-lined pans. Often, I pilfered a thick, tangy slice and popped it into my mouth, but she pretended not to notice.

When the two pans were heaped full of apples, Granner   3
dusted them generously with cinnamon, then sprinkled a scoopful of sugar over the cinnamon. Next, she dotted each piece with small squares of butter, sprinkled on a pinch or two of ground nutmeg and cloves, then drizzled on the juice of half a lemon.

Finally, Granner was ready to place the top crust. She did this   4
by folding the rolled-out dough in half, slipping it over the pie, then flipping the folded half into place. I always felt quite capable and efficient as I then carefully trimmed the excess crust from around each rim and slit six steam holes in each pie-top. When I proudly handed the perfect pies over to Granner, she smiled and slid them into a 375° oven.

After twenty minutes, the spicy warmth crept into the living   5
room and enticed us toward the kitchen. My eager taste buds were convinced that the pies were ready, but Granner said it would be twenty minutes more. Finally, it was time to take the steamy prizes from the oven, and I could scarcely wait for them to cool. But with that first bite, I was in a child's heaven, eating in the nippy-sweet warmth of that kitchen, surrounded by an aura of well-being and love.

Ten years ago, my Granner died. I grieved over her death for   6
more than a year, until the day my mother called me into the kitchen. On the counter sat two crust-lined pans and eight plump red apples. For a long moment, we just gazed at each other, our eyes glistening. Then we sat down together and made two perfect apple pies, just the way Granner always did. That day, working out those loving memories, my broken, lonely heart began to heal. But often, especially when I make an apple pie, I remember. Oh, yes, I remember, Granner.

DISCUSSION QUESTIONS

1. The writer uses verbs and verbals very effectively in this essay. The tensed verbs, coming in a series, show consecutive actions (Granner *dusted* them . . . then *sprinkled* them . . .). On the other hand, tenseless verbs, or verbals, are used to capture simultaneous actions (I was in a child's heaven, *eating* the nippy-sweet . . . ,

surrounded by an aura . . .). Locate at least two additional examples for each of these strategies.
2. To keep the statement of process from becoming too laborious,
    the writer dismisses part of it in a rather clever way. Can you spot
    this maneuver?
3. The first five paragraphs of this essay enumerate the steps of a
    process, but in the sixth paragraph a new objective is introduced.
    How would you characterize it?
4. The last paragraph is very moving; it appeals to readers' emo-
    tions. How exactly is this accomplished?

PARAGRAPHS

French Bread

VERONICA NICHOLAS

1 tablespoon butter
1 tablespoon sugar
2 teaspoons salt

Dissolve the above in one cup boiling water (be sure the
water is at a boiling boil when you pour it over the butter, sugar,
and salt). Cool with 3/4 cup cold water; add 1 package yeast
which has been dissolved in 1/4 cup quite warm water. Immediately add about six cups flour. Stir until stiff, then put on floured
surface and knead until shiny and elastic. Place in a buttered
bowl and let rise until about doubled in size. Then make into two
round or traditional long loaves and place on a cookie sheet or
pizza tin that has been lightly sprinkled with corn meal. Score
the loaves with a sharp knife (about 3 cuts per loaf), then brush
the tops with egg white. You can either put the loaves immediately into the oven, or let them rise until about double in size
before baking them. Put them in at 425 degrees for about 30 to
40 minutes more. Cool on a rack, or serve immediately. This
bread is wonderful because it seems to get better if you're a little
absent-minded—you can let it rise and beat it down indefinitely!

DISCUSSION QUESTIONS

1. Most recipes exhibit a so-called "telegraphic style" in which short or predictable words have been left out. Do you note any instances of telegraphic style in this recipe? Cite at least two or three instances. How would you revise those sentences to make them conform to standard usage?
2. Most recipes will usually begin with a complete listing of ingredients. Do you think this one suffers from its failure to do so? What would a complete listing include? Why do you suppose that this recipe begins with only a partial listing?

How They Put Stripes on Toothpaste

CAROLINE SUTTON

Although it's intriguing to imagine the peppermint stripes neatly wound inside the tube, actually the stripes don't go into the paste until it's on its way out. A small hollow tube, with slots running lengthwise, extends from the neck of the toothpaste tube back into the interior for a short distance. When the toothpaste tube is filled, red paste—the striping material—is inserted first, thus filling the conical area around the hollow tube at the front. (It must not, however, reach beyond the point to which the hollow tube extends into the toothpaste tube.) The remainder of the dispenser is filled with the familiar white stuff. When you squeeze the toothpaste tube, pressure is applied to the white paste, which in turn presses on the red paste at the head of the tube. The red then passes through the slots and into the white, which is moving through the inserted tube—and which emerges with five red stripes.

DISCUSSION QUESTIONS

1. What two or three additional household items can you name whose familiarity, like that of striped toothpaste, actually conceals a poorly understood process? You might wish to explore one of these in a paragraph of your own.

2. What purpose is served in this process statement by such words as *when, then,* and *in turn?*
3. Why do you suppose Sutton chooses to enclose one of the sentences in parentheses?

Brewing Coors

GRACE LICHTENSTEIN

Like other beers, Coors is produced from barley. Most of the big Midwestern brewers use barley grown in North Dakota and Minnesota. Coors is the single American brewer to use a Moravian strain, grown under company supervision on farms in Colorado, Idaho, Wyoming and Montana. At the brewery, the barley is turned into malt by being soaked in water—which must be biologically pure and of a known mineral content—for several days, causing it to sprout and producing a chemical change—breaking down starch into sugar. The malt is toasted, a process that halts the sprouting and determines the color and sweetness (the more the roasting, the darker, more bitter the beer). It is ground into flour and brewed, with more pure water, in huge copper-domed kettles until it is the consistency of oatmeal. Rice and refined starch are added to make mash; solids are strained out, leaving an amber liquid malt extract, which is boiled with hops—the dried cones from the hop vine which add to the bitterness, or tang. The hops are strained, yeast is added, turning the sugar to alcohol, and the beer is aged in huge red vats at nearfreezing temperatures for almost two months, during which the second fermentation takes place and the liquid becomes carbonated, or bubbly. (Many breweries chemically age their beer to speed up production; Coors people say only naturally aged brew can be called a true "lager.") Next, the beer is filtered through cellulose filters to remove bacteria, and finally is pumped into cans, bottles or kegs for shipping.

DISCUSSION QUESTIONS

1. In the process of brewing Coors (or any beer), just as in many other processes, the materials and equipment involved are just as

important as the steps in the process. What are the key ingredients, equipment, and steps in "Brewing Coors"?
2. What extra efforts are taken to make Coors beer special?
3. As is the case with almost any process description, Lichtenstein finds it necessary to explain briefly some elements in further detail for readers unfamiliar with the process. What are a couple of elements receiving such explanations?

ESSAYS

Mosquito Bite

ALICE GRAY

Alice Gray (b. 1914) majored in entomology and English at Cornell, did a master's in the teaching of natural science at Columbia, and completed the course work for a Ph.D. in entomology at the University of California, Berkeley. From 1937 to 1984 she was associated with the Department of Entomology at the American Museum of Natural History in New York City. Over the years Gray became the department's "Answer Woman," acting as liaison between the staff entomologists and the general public; she talked about insects in the museum and on radio and television shows, and answered a wide range of questions about insects in person and by letter. Gray has contributed numerous articles to natural science publications and also wrote The Adventure Book of Insects *(1956). Another area of expertise is origami, the Japanese art of paperfolding; that interest led to coauthorship of a second book,* The Magic of Origami *(1977). In this entomological essay, Gray effectively describes a familiar natural process whose results most of us have felt.*

You are now taking a last turn around your yard before going in to dinner. Insect eyes are more sensitive to contrast and motion than to form or color. In your shirt of faded blue denim, you are a moving target no insect could miss. A mosquito zeroes in for a landing. The warmth, moisture and odor of your skin assure her that she has arrived, and the convection currents set up in the cool air by the heat of your body prompt her to cut the motor and let down the landing gear.

On six long legs, she puts down so lightly that you feel 2 nothing. Sensors on her feet detect the carbon dioxide that your skin exhales. Down comes the long proboscis; up go the long back legs, as though to balance it. The little soft lobes at the tip of the proboscis are spread to test the surface. It will do. A sudden contraction of the legs with the weight of the body behind it bends the proboscis backward in an arc while the six sharp blades it has unsheathed are thrust into your skin. Two of the blades are tipped with barbs. These work alternately, shove and hold, shove and hold, pulling the insect's face down and carrying their fellows deeper into your skin.

Once the skin is penetrated, all the blades bend forward and 3 probe as far as they can reach in all directions. (A scientist learned all this by watching through a microscope while a mosquito bit the transparent membrane between the toes of a frog.) With luck, the blades strike a capillary. If they don't, saliva pumped into the wound through a channel in one of the blades stimulates the flow of blood into a pool. And still you feel nothing. Your continued ignorance of attack is probably due, not to any anesthetic effect (although a few mosquitoes do have an anesthetic saliva) but rather to the minute size of the mouthparts, which have simply passed between nerve endings without touching any.

The taste of blood turns on two pumps in the insect's throat. 4 The broadest blade of the mouthparts is rolled lengthwise to form a tube. Through it, blood passes upward into the mouth. In a blood meal, volume is what counts—the more blood, the more eggs—and even while the pumping is going on, excess water is passing out at the insect's other end.

In three to five minutes, her body is so swollen that your 5 blood shows pinkly through the taut skin. The stretching of the stomach wall stimulates nerves that turn on a pair of glands in the thorax; the glands, in turn, release a hormone that sets the ovaries to work. Finally, when she has filled herself so full that she can't force in a single additional corpuscle, Madam Mosquito withdraws her mouthparts with a tug and drifts away.

All this time you may have felt nothing, but soon you will 6 begin to itch and later a welt will appear.

DISCUSSION: CONTENT

1. What attracts the mosquito to humans?
2. Why do we seldom feel the bite of the mosquito until after the insect has flown away?
3. How long does it take a mosquito to gorge itself?
4. How did scientists learn of the blade structure of a mosquito's proboscis?

DISCUSSION: FORM

1. Which type of process is this—a how-to type or a how-it-was-done type?
2. This essay lacks a thesis statement. Does it suffer for not having one? Write an appropriate thesis statement. Where would you place it?
3. State the purpose of each paragraph in this process; i.e., explain why the author divided up the process in the way she did.

Making Tappa

HERMAN MELVILLE

Herman Melville (1819–1891) was an American writer who based his early works on his youthful adventures as a sailor. His most famous and greatest work, Moby Dick *(1851), draws on those experiences. During his lifetime Melville's most popular book was a novel about life among the cannibals of the Marquesan Islands,* Typee *(1846), from which this selection was taken.*

Although the whole existence of the inhabitants of the valley   1
seemed to pass away exempt from toil, yet there were some light employments which, although amusing rather than laborious as occupations, contributed to their comfort and luxury. Among these, the most important was the manufacture of the native cloth,—"tappa,"—so well known, under various modifications, throughout the whole Polynesian Archipelago. As is generally understood, this useful and sometimes elegant article is fabri-

cated from the bark of different trees. But, as I believe that no
description of its manufacture has ever been given, I shall state
what I know regarding it.

In the manufacture of the beautiful white tappa generally   2
worn on the Marquesan Islands, the preliminary operation consists in gathering a certain quantity of the young branches of the
cloth-tree. The exterior green bark being pulled off as worthless,
there remains a slender fibrous substance, which is carefully
stripped from the stick, to which it closely adheres. When a
sufficient quantity of it has been collected, the various strips are
enveloped in a covering of large leaves, which the natives use
precisely as we do wrapping paper, and which are secured by a
few turns of a line passed round them. The package is then laid
in the bed of some running stream, with a heavy stone placed
over it, to prevent its being swept away. After it has remained for
two or three days in this state, it is drawn out, and exposed, for
a short time, to the action of the air, every distinct piece being
attentively inspected, with a view of ascertaining whether it has
yet been sufficiently affected by the operation. This is repeated
again and again, until the desired result is obtained.

When the substance is in a proper state for the next process,   3
it betrays evidences of incipient decomposition; the fibers are
relaxed and softened, and rendered perfectly malleable. The different strips are now extended, one by one, in successive layers,
upon some smooth surface—generally the prostrate trunk of a
cocoa-nut tree—and the heap thus formed is subjected, at every
new increase, to a moderate beating, with a sort of wooden
mallet, leisurely applied. The mallet, made of a hard heavy wood
resembling ebony, is about twelve inches in length, and perhaps
two in breadth, with a rounded handle at one end, and in shape
is the exact counterpart of one of our four-sided razor-strops. The
flat surfaces of the implement are marked with shallow parallel
indentations, varying in depth on the different sides, so as to be
adapted to the several stages of the operation. These marks produce the corduroy sort of stripes discernible in the tappa in its
finished state. After being beaten in the manner I have described,
the material soon becomes blended in one mass, which, mois-
tened occasionally with water, is at intervals hammered out, by
a kind of gold-beating process, to any degree of thinness required.
In this way the cloth is easily made to vary in strength and
thickness, so as to suit the numerous purposes to which it is
applied.

When the operation last described has been concluded, the 4
new-made tappa is spread out on the grass to bleach and dry, and
soon becomes of a dazzling whiteness. Sometimes, in the first
stages of the manufacture, the substance is impregnated with a
vegetable juice, which gives it a permanent color. A rich brown
and a bright yellow are occasionally seen, but the simple taste of
the Typee people inclines them to prefer the natural tint.

DISCUSSION: CONTENT

1. According to Melville, what are the distinct steps in making
   tappa? How many steps are there?
2. What tool is used in making tappa? Has Melville described it fully
   enough so that you could make a copy? What is the weakness in
   the description's comparison of the tool to "our four-sided razor-
   strops"?
3. What is the most common color for finished tappa cloth?

DISCUSSION: FORM

1. What is the basis for each of the paragraphs in the selection? Does
   the paragraph arrangement suggest to you that Melville saw tappa
   making as consisting of a certain number of processes that contained subprocesses? How would the distinct steps that you enumerated above (in response to the first content question) fit into
   such an arrangement?
2. Other than by describing the process steps chronologically, how
   does Melville achieve unity in his essay, especially within individual paragraphs? Mark the words serving transitional functions
   in paragraphs 2 and 3.

How Dictionaries are Made

S. I. HAYAKAWA

*Samuel I. Hayakawa (1906–1992) was born in Canada, but he
moved to the United States in 1929 and completed a Ph.D. at
the University of Wisconsin in 1935. A semanticist and an
educator, he was associated the longest with San Francisco
State University, where he served as Professor of English and*

*then as President. In the latter post Hayakawa drew national
attention with his combative attitude toward campus demon-
strations. From 1977 to 1982 he represented California in the
U.S. Senate. The following essay is from his most popular book
on verbal communication,* Language in Thought and Action
(1949), originally published as Language in Action *(1939),
which made the best-seller lists on both appearances and continues to be widely read.*

It is widely believed that every word has a correct meaning,   1
that we learn these meanings principally from teachers and
grammarians (except that most of the time we don't bother to, so
that we ordinarily speak "sloppy English"), and that dictionaries
and grammars are the supreme authority in matters of meaning
and usage. Few people ask by what authority the writers of
dictionaries and grammars say what they say. I once got into a
dispute with an Englishwoman over the pronunciation of a word
and offered to look it up in the dictionary. The Englishwoman
said firmly, "What for? I am English. I was born and brought up
in England. The way I speak *is* English." Such self-assurance
about one's own language is not uncommon among the English.
In the United States, however, anyone who is willing to quarrel
with the dictionary is regarded as either eccentric or mad.

Let us see how dictionaries are made and how the editors   2
arrive at definitions. What follows applies, incidentally, only to
those dictionary offices where first-hand, original research goes
on—not those in which editors simply copy existing dictionaries.
The task of writing a dictionary begins with reading vast
amounts of the literature of the period or subject that the dictionary is to cover. As the editors read, they copy on cards every
interesting or rare word, every unusual or peculiar occurrence of
a common word, a large number of common words in their
ordinary uses, and also the sentences in which each of these
words appear, thus:

pail
The dairy *pails* bring home increase of milk

Keats, Endymion
I, 44–45

That is to say, the context of each word is collected, along   3
with the word itself. For a really big job of dictionary-writing,

such as the *Oxford English Dictionary* (usually bound in about twenty-five volumes), millions of such cards are collected, and the task of editing occupies decades. As the cards are collected, they are alphabetized and sorted. When the sorting is completed, there will be for each word anywhere from two or three to several hundred illustrative quotations, each on its card.

To define a word, then, the dictionary-editor places before him the stack of cards illustrating that word; each of the cards represents an actual use of the word by a writer of some literary or historical importance. He reads the cards carefully, discards some, rereads the rest, and divides up the stack according to what he thinks are the several senses of the word. Finally, he writes his definitions, following the hard-and-fast rule that each definition *must* be based on what the quotations in front of him reveal about the meaning of the word. The editor cannot be influenced by what *he* thinks a given word *ought* to mean. He must work according to the cards or not at all.

The writing of a dictionary, therefore, is not a task of setting up authoritative statements about the "true meanings" of words, but a task of *recording*, to the best of one's ability, what various words have meant to authors in the distant or immediate past. *The writer of a dictionary is a historian, not a lawgiver.* If, for example, we had been writing a dictionary in 1890, or even as late as 1919, we could have said that the word "broadcast" means "to scatter" (seed, for example), but we could not have decreed that from 1921 on, the most common meaning of the word should become "to disseminate audible messages, etc., by radio transmission." To regard the dictionary as an "authority," therefore, is to credit the dictionary-writer with gifts of prophecy which neither he nor anyone else possesses. In choosing our words when we speak or write, we can be *guided* by the historical record afforded us by the dictionary, but we cannot be *bound* by it, because new situations, new experiences, new inventions, new feelings are always compelling us to give new uses to old words. Looking under a "hood," we should ordinarily have found, five hundred years ago, a monk; today, we find a motorcar engine.

DISCUSSION: CONTENT

1. What are the steps in the process of making a dictionary?

2. What effect does the changing nature of language have on the dictionary maker and on the dictionaries that already exist?

DISCUSSION: FORM

1. Hayakawa waits till paragraph 2 before announcing his thesis; what does he accomplish by including paragraph 1?
2. Hayakawa clarifies the importance of the dictionary writer as historian by using two examples. Can you think of additional examples he might use, assuming he were to revise the essay today?

Building a Hopi House

HELEN SEKAQUAPTEWA

Helen Sekaquaptewa (b. 1898) is a Native American who grew up on the Hopi Reservation in northeastern Arizona. She has described her personal, family, and social life there in Me and Mine: The Life Story of Helen Sekaquaptewa *(1969), where the following selection first appeared.*

The newly married Hopi couple usually went to live at the home of the bride's mother until such time as they could build a house of their own, the speed of which depended upon the pressure from within and the ambition of the young husband. The youngest daughter would likely stay and gradually take over the mother's household, and in a few years it would be the mother who would be living with her daughter in the latter's home.

Hopis build their houses close to each other to remind them that they are supposed to love each other. If one should build his house away from the others, they would say, "He is selfish. He does not love his neighbors." When a man decided to build a house he did not draw money from his bank account to pay for materials and labor. He gathered the materials provided by nature and drew from his reserve of good will (and that of his relatives) among his clan and friends, acquired from his own participation in such cooperative projects. The nearby sandstone cliffs invited the hammer and wedge to furnish rock for the walls. Logs for the beams that would support the roof could be obtained from nearby cedar trees if the room was not too large, but if the room was a big one, from the pines in the mountains sixty miles away. The materials for the roof were to be had from the trees and brush and earth at hand.

The house was built one room at a time, the existing wall of 　3 another house was used for one side, and thus only three walls had to be built. When a second room was added it often was built at the rear of the first; the third room would be built on top of the second, leaving the roof of the first room as a terrace porch.

The first step was to get out the sandstone. This the builder 　4 did by himself, working at cutting the blocks at odd times for as long as a year, depending upon how much time he had to devote to this task and how diligently he applied himself. When he had enough stone cut, he might kill a sheep from his own flock or buy one, and his wife and her family started cooking. The husband then invited his friends and neighbors to help transport the stone to the site of the proposed house. They formed a brigade and passed the building stone from hand to hand to the point where it was to be laid into the walls. This part of the project was usually completed in one day, with dinner served at noon to all the workers. It was sometimes several weeks later before the walls were erected.

Whenever the community came to help they had to be fed. 　5 After each operation, the builder sometimes needed time in which to acquire the necessary food. It was easier to feed the women when they worked; they would settle for corn and beans, while the men would want meat and something better.

The women made the mortar and sometimes helped lay the 　6 walls; even sometimes it was all women working. As many as could find room to work helped lay up the stone. To make the mortar, first they dug a hole about a foot deep and three feet in diameter near the new house. Sand and clay were carried and piled near this hole. If there was a puddle of rain-water nearby everyone carried water in her jug. If there was no rainwater, they carried the water from the well; everyone had her jug full, so there was a lot of water on hand before they started mixing. Water and clay were put into the hole and let soak a while. Then sand was added, and the women sat around the hole and mixed the mortar with their hands, until it was satiny and smooth, when they lifted it out and piled it nearby. This process was repeated until there was a big pile of mortar. (The men make mortar now with hoes, but it is not as good.) Next the women formed a line and passed the mortar in double hands full to the men working at the walls. This clay and sand set hard like cement.

After the walls were laid, the beams for the flat roof were put   7 in place about three feet apart. Next, little cedar logs about two inches in diameter, gathered and ready, were laid at right angles to the beams, three to four inches apart.

Now, there must be more mortar for the roof. While the   8 women made the mortar, the men gathered fresh, green rabbit brush and arms full of bee plant, which they carried in bundles on their backs to the house being born. A six-inch layer of green brush was carefully packed at right angles to the little logs, and over the brush was spread a six-inch layer of mortar, again passed from hand to hand and up the ladder to the roof, in double hands full. Men were ready on the roof to take the mortar and carefully place it over the brush and tamp it down; lastly, three inches of dry clay well tamped by the feet finished the fine waterproof roof. Days later, the women made more mortar and with it smoothly plastered the inside walls; they then put a thick layer on the floor and smoothed it down, which when hardened made a good hard floor. So, after many weeks and the labor of many hands and many meals served, the house was ready for occupancy.

DISCUSSION: CONTENT

1. The process of building a Hopi house is clearly a communal process, with ten distinct stages. Identify those in order, from (1) getting the sandstone blocks for the walls to (10) plastering the walls and floor.
2. Identify the stages or steps traditionally performed by groups of men and by groups of women. What seem to be some reasons for this division of labor?
3. How do the Hopi methods of getting materials and labor contrast with those of most other Americans?
4. What Hopi architectural design and construction custom reduces the number of walls to be built for a room to three?

DISCUSSION: FORM

1. The actual process of building a Hopi house is described in paragraphs 4 and 6–8. What purposes are served by paragraphs 1–3 and 5?

2. Why was it probably necessary to describe the mortar mixing and roof building stages in more detail and as separate processes?
3. Why, as a Hopi woman, might Sekaquaptewa have been unable to describe the building stone and log beam procurement stages in any detail? Is any harm done to the house building description by those omissions?
4. How does the final sentence of paragraph 8 serve as a satisfactory conclusion for this process essay?

8

Comparison and Contrast

You are already familiar with comparison, having studied it as a useful strategy for description and narration. In narrative-descriptive writing you used metaphors or similes, calling attention to resemblances or similarities, letting your reader know what something looked like, or perhaps what it sounded or smelled like. In expository writing, you will also find it useful to deal with similarities, but differences will also prove to be of equal importance. That is why this chapter treats both **comparison and contrast,** emphasizing the usefulness of both similarities and differences as devices for informing the reader.

At this point a gentle warning is in order. In expository writing it has become customary to speak of *comparing* two subjects or of the *comparison* of two or more ideas without making any reference to *contrasts*—although the enumeration of both similarities and differences is ordinarily what is expected. Thus, when you encounter the term *comparison,* you must first determine whether you are expected to describe (write descriptively, emphasizing only resemblances) or to inform (write expositorily, emphasizing both resemblances and differences). Here is how expository comparison is done.

Topics versus Points

Suppose you want to inform your readers about the relative merits of two or more people, places, or concepts. There is a procedure that must be followed if the comparison is to be understandable. First, determine the subjects or *topics* to be compared (let us say two baseball teams); then decide what *points* shared by the teams need to be examined. A rough sketch of possible ideas might look like this:

Topic to be compared	Points of comparison	Topic to be compared
Braves	hitting fielding base-running pitching coaching depth	Giants

To *compare and contrast by topics,* begin with the Braves and discuss that team's performance with respect to each of the points of comparison. Then repeat the procedure for the Giants. The similarities and the differences will be readily apparent. On the other hand, you may choose to *compare and contrast by points,* in which case you start with the first point of comparison (hitting) and discuss the Braves' performance at the plate and then the Giants'. Then you do the same for fielding, base-running, and so on. Again, it will be easy to see how well each team measures up—how similar or different they are with respect to each point.

As a general rule, if the points of comparison are few, it's a good idea to work by topics. If the points of comparison are many, say four or more, or if any part is complex enough to require detailed discussion that may extend to a paragraph or more, it's wise to compare by points; then your reader will be better able to keep the points of comparison clear and distinct.

Familiar to Unfamiliar

Comparison and contrast techniques are helpful when you are attempting to inform your reader about familiar things, such as baseball teams, but also when you are trying to explain less familiar things. This technique enables you to lead your reader into the unfamiliar by way of the familiar. Suppose, for example, you want to explain how the South Sea Islanders you have been studying in Anthropology 201 reckon their standing in their community. You may suppose that your readers know very little about South Sea Islanders, but you can also assume that they have some ideas about how their own prestige as Americans is determined. Your first step is to enumerate important status markers for Americans—education, wealth, landholdings, lodgings, and means of transportation. These familiar items will make up a partial list of points of comparison. Next, you should add those status markers that apply to that South Seas culture, noting overlaps when they occur. A sketch of the comparison might look like Figure 8.1.

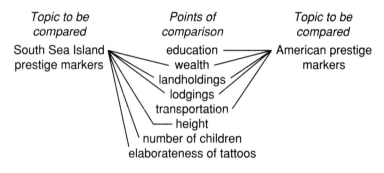

FIGURE 8.1

As the arrows show, wealth, landholdings, and lodgings are of equal importance to Islanders and Americans. This much your readers might have suspected. They may be surprised to learn, however, that Islanders do not share the American's reverence for education and transportation. And your readers may be amazed to learn that such unusual considerations as height, number of children, and elaborateness of tattoos become measures of prestige for these distant people.

Examine the following selections, paying attention to the ways that the authors have organized their materials by their use of topics and points. The technique of comparison and contrast is often useful, so practice applying both means of comparison organization in your own writing. Your English teacher may ask you to compare two characters in a short story, your chemistry teacher may ask you to compare the characteristics of two compounds, and your psychology professor may ask you to compare two personality types. When you have left school and are perhaps a management trainee, your supervisor may ask for a report comparing two products or two pieces of equipment. You'll need to be ready.

Commentary on Student Work

The first student essay in this section was done by Gordon, who worked as a guide on one of the white-water rivers in the Appalachian Mountains near the campus. When comparison was introduced as a method of development, Gordon made several scratch outlines in his journal. One compared two such rivers, the Nantahala and the Ocoee, and a second compared two classes of rapids, Class III and Class IV. Although he completed fairly elaborate outlines for these two comparisons, neither progressed any further than that. Gordon's third outline, however, furnished a more promising prospect—one that eventually grew into the theme that appears on p. 185. But first, let's look at that third outline, in which Gordon listed the topics to be compared along with the points of the intended comparison. It looked like this:

white water rafting	construction stability maneuverability danger skill required	white water canoeing

Based on this outline, Gordon wrote a quick paragraph. Setting aside for later such matters as introductions and conclusions, he plunged right in. He produced this effort, which he carried with him to discuss with his reading group during the next class meeting:

A raft is made of tear-resistant rubber, so you can hit a lot of rocks and simply bounce off. A canoe is made of fiber glass or aluminum, so it is necessary to miss as many rocks as possible. A raft is very stable, but a canoe is not very stable at all, tipping over quite easily. Rafts can negotiate Class I and II rapids without much need for maneuvering, but these rapids require canoeists to be practiced to stay on course. Even Class III and IV rapids can be handled by rafters without precise maneuvering; however, these rapids will damage or destroy a canoe, along with its occupants, unless they are skilled and careful. Rafts are very safe; canoes are dangerous.

Gordon's reading group approved of his initial effort and asked a number of enthusiastic questions about his white water guide's job and about some of the terms he had used. Everyone agreed that he would need to define the different classes of rapids he had mentioned, since the average reader could not be expected to attach much significance to these terms.

One member of the group even raised the prospect of drinking beer while rafting, which led to the rather successful conclusion that Gordon eventually wrote for his essay. Here is his final product:

Traveling the White Water

There are at least two ways to travel down a river containing white water. One way is in a raft; the other is in a canoe.   1

A raft is made of tear-resistant rubber; therefore, you can   2 hit a lot of rocks and simply bounce off. A river canoe is made of fiber glass or aluminum, so it is necessary to miss as many rocks as possible. A raft is half as wide as it is long, a design that makes it very stable. On the other hand, a canoe is not stable, its length exceeding its width by a factor of five or seven to one. Not surprisingly, careless and unbalanced lateral motion, which is no big deal in a raft, causes a canoe to tip over quite easily.

Class I and II rapids—small regular waves with small drops   3 and clear passages that require no maneuvering—can be successfully negotiated in a raft by any beginner. A canoe is altogether different. Class I and II rapids do require the canoeist to be practiced in order to keep the canoe straight on course.

Class Ill and IV rapids—large, numerous, and irregular waves   4 with narrow passages, significant drops, and crosscurrents of fast and powerful water—can be successfully negotiated by the novice rafter without super-precise maneuvering. However, these rapids will quickly damage, if not destroy, a canoe along with its occupants, unless they are skilled and careful.

A white-water raft trip is relatively safe. You can even get   5
slightly intoxicated along the way. A white-water canoe trip is a challenge. You can even get slightly killed.

DISCUSSION QUESTIONS

1. Here is a comparison of raft and canoe travel that is arranged by points. What are these points?
2. The writer has to describe or define items as the comparison is made. What are these items?
3. The conclusion of this essay might strike you as being quite clever. What makes it so?

STUDENT WORK

Private and Public Bathrooms

A bathroom is one place where most American girls spend a tremendous amount of time. At home, I have my own bathroom, and it is usually overflowing with various types of makeup, hair dryers, electric curlers, and other items which females use to improve their appearance. Because no one else uses my bathroom, I never have to wait for the shower, and I am able to hop in whenever I feel the need. I am also responsible for the cleanliness of my bathroom, so if I feel like having my personal items scattered in it, I can do so. On the other hand, sharing a community bath in a dorm is strikingly different. For example, there is seldom a moment when I am in the bathroom alone. I have even brushed my teeth as late as 2:30 a.m. and discovered that someone else was taking an early morning shower. In addition, I frequently wait in line for the use of a shower in the mornings. Of course, the only reason waiting in line upsets me is that I begin to run behind in my schedule and miss breakfast. Furthermore, in using a community bath, one has to carry her personal items with her on each trip. I can recall several occasions when

I stepped into the shower only to realize that my soap was in my room. Another difference in a community bath is the fact that some people on the hall do not keep it clean. In this case all those involved suffer.

DISCUSSION QUESTIONS

1. Is this paragraph organized by topics or by points? How many points are covered? What is gained by this method of organization? What, if anything, is lost by this choice?
2. To help you better understand organization of comparison writing, try creating the appropriate two-level outline, by topics or by points, for this paragraph. Fill in the blanks below, then rearrange the topics and points to create an outline for the other form of organization.

Topics	*Points*
I.	I.
A.	A.
B.	B.
C.	II.
D.	A.
II.	B.
A.	III.
B.	A.
C.	B.
D.	IV.
	A.
	B.

3. After completing the outline above based on the student's original organization of her material, what flaws, if any, do you notice in her plan?

Comparing Mechanics

When comparing professional mechanics to the more common variety of backyard shade-tree mechanics, one will certainly notice a number of differences. First, one might look at how each group gains its knowledge. The professional mechanic's knowledge comes from vocational schools and instruction manuals, each emphasizing the latest techniques in sophisticated analysis. The shade-tree mechanic, hanging around service stations and garages, accepts anything he hears as fact until trial and error prove it wrong. Style of dress and general appearance present another contrast. The professional, well groomed and tidy even in his grease spots, wears a uniform of coveralls, the name of his garage stenciled across the back and his own first name above the pencil-filled pocket. His counterpart is more likely to be dressed in nondescript blue jeans, covered with grease from head to toe, his hair slicked back Elvis style, and a cigarette stuck behind his ear. The manner in which the two groups work is also different: the professional going about his work in a quiet and orderly manner, responding politely to the customers' questions, while our friend the shade-tree mechanic will beat and bang, shouting over the noise, "&#%$ this" and "bleep that," as he pounds away. A final point of comparison is the fees charged by each group: the professional working a half hour, taking a break, then working another fifteen minutes and charging $200 for two hours' labor, and the shade-tree mechanic working all day for an honest fee.

DISCUSSION QUESTIONS

1. The writer never defines "backyard shade-tree mechanic." What does the term mean and why is it not defined?
2. How is "Comparing Mechanics" organized, by points or by topics?
3. How many points are covered in the discussion? Why do you suppose the writer used fees charged as the final point?

The Changing World of Women

The life-styles of women have changed drastically in the last   1
thirty years and are still changing today. Basically, there have
been four major changes. These have been in sexual attitudes,
marriage ideas, marriage roles, and career opportunities.

The first major change has been in sexual attitudes. Thirty   2
years ago it was considered taboo for a woman even to say the

word "sex" in public. Today women as well as men are able to discuss sex and its problems and joys freely and openly. Additionally, women are now emphasizing their roles as sexual partners and leaders rather than inferiors and followers, and men are accepting that change, too.

Another change has been in the idea of marriage. Formerly it was believed that a woman must either marry young or risk becoming a spinster. And a woman who did not marry was thought to be inferior and abnormal. However, today's woman has numerous options open to her besides early marriage. Most important, a single woman is no longer looked down upon by society.

A third change has been in the woman's role in marriage. In the past it was generally agreed that a mother's place was in the home and a father's was at work. Today, though, it is perfectly acceptable for a mother to work outside the home. In fact, in some cases the traditional roles have been reversed, so that the homemaker wears a beard with his apron.

The last major change has been in career opportunities. Thirty years ago the only jobs available to women were domestic work and, if properly educated, teaching jobs. But today's woman is no longer stereotyped into certain jobs. She has many opportunities open to her, as a business executive, engineer, government leader, and on and on. One notable recent change is that the United States military academies have opened their doors to women, and many are accepting this new challenge.

Although the life-styles of women have changed drastically, there are still other changes to come. Yet most women are now accepting the changes and challenges of today's world.

DISCUSSION QUESTIONS

1. Is "The Changing World of Women" organized clearly? Comment on the use of transitional devices. How many points are covered?
2. Which points are developed most adequately? What examples could be used to clarify or develop the points in each instance? What would be gained by the addition of such examples?
3. A weakness of this student's paper, beyond its lack of specific examples, is the tendency to overgeneralize. Cite one example of this tendency.

PARAGRAPHS

Listening and Reading

CHARLES OSGOOD

There is a big difference between listening to something on broadcast and reading it in print. If something doesn't make sense to you on the air, you just shrug and figure you must have missed something. But if something doesn't make sense in print, you can go back a few lines and try to pick up the thread. If it still doesn't make any sense the reader has every reason to conclude that it never made any sense in the first place. What I'm saying is that you can get away with more in hot air than you can in cold print.

DISCUSSION QUESTIONS

1. Look up the terms **abstract** and **concrete** in this book's Glossary. How are those two contrasting concepts related to listening and reading?
2. What does Osgood mean by "pick up the thread" in his third sentence?
3. What does Osgood gain by repeatedly using the word *something* in his first three sentences and the word *if* in sentence two, three, and four?
4. Why are the opposing adjectives *hot* and *cold* appropriate choices in Osgood's final sentence?

The Natural Superiority of Women

ASHLEY MONTAGU

Physically and psychically women are by far the superior of men. The old chestnut about women being more emotional than men has been forever destroyed by the facts of the two great wars. Women under blockade, heavy bombardment, concentration camp confinement, and similar rigors withstand them vastly more successfully than men. The psychiatric casualties of civilian populations under such conditions are mostly masculine, and there are far more men in our mental hospitals than there are women. The steady hand at the helm is the hand that has had the practice of rocking the cradle. Because of their greater size and weight, men are physically more powerful than women—which is not the same thing as saying that they are stronger. A man of the same size and weight as a woman of comparable background and occupational status would probably not be any more powerful than a woman. As far as constitutional strength is concerned, women are stronger than men. Many diseases from which men suffer can be shown to be largely influenced by their relation to the male Y-chromosome. More males die than females. Deaths from almost all causes are more frequent in males of all ages. Though women are more frequently ill than men, they recover from illness more easily and more frequently than men.

DISCUSSION QUESTIONS

1. What is the topic sentence of this paragraph?
2. What does Montagu mean by the phrase "the old chestnut" in his second sentence?
3. How many points of comparison does Montagu examine? What are they? Could you supply additional ones?

Women and Blacks

ELLEN WILLIS

Like the early feminist movement, which grew out of the campaign to end slavery, the present-day women's movement has been inspired and influenced by the black liberation struggle. The situation of women and blacks is similar in many ways. Just as blacks live in a world defined by whites, women live in a world defined by males. (The generic term of human being is "man"; "woman" means "wife of man.") To be female or black is to be peculiar; whiteness and maleness are the norm. Newspapers do not have "men's pages," nor would anyone think of discussing the "man problem." Racial and sexual stereotypes also resemble each other: women, like blacks, are said to be childish, incapable of abstract reasoning, innately submissive, biologically suited for menial tasks, emotional, close to nature.

DISCUSSION QUESTIONS

1. Clearly the topics to be compared are revealed in the title. What are the points assigned to each?
2. Willis says, "To be female or black is to be peculiar; whiteness and maleness are the norm." How does she support this idea?
3. Willis claims that both women and blacks are the targets of stereotyped thinking. What are some of the examples of such stereotypes that she mentions?

The Old Practitioner and the Young

OLIVER WENDELL HOLMES

May I venture to contrast youth and experience in medical practice? The young man knows the rules, but the old man knows the exceptions. The young man knows his patient, but the old man knows also his patient's family, dead and alive, up and down for generations. He can tell beforehand what diseases their unborn children will be subject to, what they will die of if they live long enough, and whether they had better live at all, or remain unrealized possibilities, as belonging to a stock not worth being perpetuated. The young man feels uneasy if he is not continually doing something to stir up his patient's internal arrangements. The old man takes things more quietly, and is much more willing to let well enough alone. All these superiorities, if such they are, you must wait for time to bring you. In the meanwhile, the young man's senses are quicker than those of his older rival. His education in all the accessory branches is more recent, and therefore nearer the existing condition of knowledge. He finds it easier than his seniors to accept the improvements which every year is bringing forward. New ideas build their nests in young men's brains. "Revolutions are not made by men in spectacles," as I once heard it remarked, and the first whispers of a new truth are not caught by those who begin to feel the need of an ear-trumpet. Granting all these advantages to the young man, he ought, nevertheless, to go on improving, on the whole, as a medical practitioner, with every year, until he has ripened into a well-mellowed maturity. But, to improve, he must be good for something at the start. If you ship a poor cask of wine to India and back, if you keep it half a century, it only grows thinner and sharper.

DISCUSSION QUESTIONS

1. Has Holmes organized his comparison by topics or by points?
2. How many points are enumerated?
3. Near the end of the paragraph Holmes uses the related technique of analogy. How effective is that use? Do you understand the point he is making?

ESSAYS

Different Worlds of Words

DEBORAH TANNEN

Deborah F. Tannen (b. 1945), a native of Brooklyn, got her education at SUNY-Binghamton, Wayne State University, and the University of California-Berkeley, where she earned a Ph. D. in linguistics. She has taught in Greece and at U.S. colleges and universities. Since 1979, she has been at Georgetown University, where she serves as professor of linguistics. A published poet and short story writer, Tannen has edited six books and written five others, the most notable being the best-selling You Just Don't Understand: Women and Men in Conversation *(1990), which is the source for the following selection.*

Even if they grow up in the same neighborhood, on the same   1
block, or in the same house, girls and boys grow up in different worlds of words. Others talk to them differently and expect and accept different ways of talking from them. Most important, children learn how to talk, how to have conversations, not only from their parents but from their peers. After all, if their parents

have a foreign or regional accent, children do not emulate it; they learn to speak with the pronunciation of the region where they grow up. Anthropologists Daniel Maltz and Ruth Borker summarize research showing that boys and girls have very different ways of talking to their friends. Although they often play together, boys and girls spend most of their time playing in same-sex groups. And, although some of the activities they play at are similar, their favorite games are different, and their ways of using language in their games are separated by a world of difference.

Boys tend to play outside, in large groups that are hierarchically structured. Their groups have a leader who tells others what to do and how to do it, and resists doing what other boys propose. It is by giving orders and making them stick that high status is negotiated. Another way boys achieve status is to take center stage by telling stories and jokes, and by sidetracking or challenging the stories and jokes of others. Boys' games have winners and losers and elaborate systems of rules that are frequently the subjects of arguments. Finally, boys are frequently heard to boast of their skill and argue about who is best at what.

Girls, on the other hand, play in small groups or in pairs; the center of a girl's social life is a best friend. Within the group, intimacy is key: Differentiation is measured by relative closeness. In their most frequent games, such as jump rope and hopscotch, everyone gets a turn. Many of their activities (such as playing house) do not have winners or losers. Though some girls are certainly more skilled than others, girls are expected not to boast about it, or show that they think they are better than the others. Girls don't give orders; they express their preferences as suggestions, and suggestions are likely to be accepted. Whereas boys say, "Gimme that!" and "Get outta here!" girls say, "Let's do this," and "How about doing that?" Anything else is put down as "bossy." They don't grab center stage—they don't want it— so they don't challenge each other directly. And much of the time, they simply sit together and talk. Girls are not accustomed to jockeying for status in an obvious way; they are more concerned that they be liked.

DISCUSSION: CONTENT

1. Tannen makes clear in her first paragraph that differences in how females and males talk begin in childhood. What two groups of

persons does she say are typically the most important influences on how one talks? How well is this confirmed by your own experience?

2. According to Tannen, how different are the sizes and structures of groups most often played in by boys and by girls? How well do those stated differences conform to your memories of your own pre-teen play groups?

3. Which of the two gender play groups values status more? How do you see this reflected in teenage and in adult behavior?

4. How is gender also reflected in the different sorts of games that groups of boys and of girls typically play? What effect do their contrasting game experiences apparently have on boasting and on arguing in groups?

DISCUSSION: FORM

1. How does the organization of this short essay emphasize that "girls and boys grow up in different worlds of words" (paragraph 1)?

2. Notice Tannen's frequent use of transitional words and phrases, both within and between paragraphs. Pick out the use of a transitional device in each paragraph and comment on its value in helping to guide the attention of readers to the subject matter.

3. This simple three-paragraph essay clearly lacks a conclusion; what might you add to create a closing paragraph of one or two sentences, remembering to provide a transition from the essay's body into your conclusion?

Fable for Tomorrow

RACHEL CARSON

Rachel Carson (1907–1964) was a scientist and author whose book Silent Spring *(1962) is generally recognized as having begun the "save our environment" movement in the United States. That book, which made Americans aware of the dangers of pesticides, is the source for the following essay. Carson's writing earned her many honors, including the National Book Award for nonfiction, won by her earlier best-selling book,* The Sea Around Us *(1951).*

There was once a town in the heart of America where all life   1
seemed to live in harmony with its surroundings. The town lay
in the midst of a checkerboard of prosperous farms, with fields of
grain and hillsides of orchards where, in spring, white clouds of
bloom drifted above the green fields. In autumn, oak and maple
and birch set up a blaze of color that flamed and flickered across
a backdrop of pines. Then foxes barked in the hills and deer
silently crossed the fields, half hidden in the mists of the fall
mornings.

Along the roads, laurel, viburnum and alder, great ferns and   2
wildflowers delighted the traveler's eye through much of the
year. Even in winter the roadsides were places of beauty, where
countless birds came to feed on the berries and on the seed heads
of the dried weeds rising above the snow. The countryside was,
in fact, famous for the abundance and variety of its bird life, and
when the flood of migrants was pouring through in spring and fall
people traveled from great distances to observe them. Others
came to fish the streams, which flowed clear and cold out of the
hills and contained shady pools where trout lay. So it had been
from the days many years ago when the first settlers raised their
houses, sank their wells, and built their barns.

Then a strange blight crept over the area and everything   3
began to change. Some evil spell had settled on the community:
mysterious maladies swept the flocks of chickens; the cattle and
sheep sickened and died. Everywhere was a shadow of death. The
farmers spoke of much illness among their families. In the town
the doctors had become more and more puzzled by new kinds of
sickness appearing among their patients. There had been several
sudden and unexplained deaths, not only among adults but even
among children, who would be stricken suddenly while at play
and die within a few hours.

There was a strange stillness. The birds, for example—where   4
had they gone? Many people spoke of them, puzzled and disturbed. The feeding stations in the backyards were deserted. The
few birds seen anywhere were moribund; they trembled violently
and could not fly. It was a spring without voices. On the mornings that had once throbbed with the dawn chorus of robins,
catbirds, doves, jays, wrens, and scores of other bird voices there
was now no sound; only silence lay over the fields and woods and
marsh.

On the farms the hens brooded, but no chicks hatched. The   5
farmers complained that they were unable to raise any pigs—the

litters were small and the young survived only a few days. The apple trees were coming into bloom but no bees droned among the blossoms, so there was no pollination and there would be no fruit.

The roadsides, once so attractive, were now lined with   6
browned and withered vegetation as though swept by fire. These, too, were silent, deserted by all living things. Even the streams were now lifeless. Anglers no longer visited them, for all the fish had died.

In the gutters under the eaves and between the shingles of the   7
roofs, a white granular powder still showed a few patches; some weeks before it had fallen like snow upon the roofs and the lawns, the fields and streams.

No witchcraft, no enemy action had silenced the rebirth of   8
new life in this stricken world. The people had done it themselves.

This town does not actually exist, but it might easily have a   9
thousand counterparts in America or elsewhere in the world. I know of no community that has experienced all the misfortunes I describe. Yet every one of these disasters has actually happened somewhere, and many real communities have already suffered a substantial number of them. A grim specter has crept upon us almost unnoticed, and this imagined tragedy may easily become a stark reality we all shall know.

DISCUSSION: CONTENT

1. What animals are affected by the blight described in "Fable for Tomorrow"?
2. Why do the apple trees fail to produce?
3. Is there any clue to the source of blight?
4. What or who is responsible for the blight?
5. What do you suppose has caused the transformation of this town and countryside?

DISCUSSION: FORM

1. Is this comparison accomplished by points or by topics?
2. Why is this method particularly suitable?
3. What transitional word serves as a turning point? Where is it?

4. When does the comparison end?
5. Why do you suppose Carson's paragraphs become consistently shorter from 2 through 8? What purpose is served by the longer paragraph 9?

Columbus and the Moon

TOM WOLFE

Tom Wolfe (b. 1931), a native of Virginia and graduate of Washington and Lee University, began his professional career as a newspaperman, working for the Washington Post *and the* New York Herald. *Some of his books include* The Kandy-Kolored Tangerine-Flake Streamline Baby *(1965),* The Electric Kool-Aid Acid Test *(1968),* Radical Chic and Mau-Mauing the Flak Catchers *(1970),* The Right Stuff *(1977),* From Bauhaus to Our House *(1981), and* The Bonfire of the Vanities *(1987). The following essay first appeared in the New York* Times *in 1979.*

The National Aeronautics and Space Administration's moon landing ten years ago today was a Government project, but then so was Columbus's voyage to America in 1492. The Government, in Columbus's case, was the Spanish Court of Ferdinand and Isabella. Spain was engaged in a sea race with Portugal in much the same way that the United States would be caught up in a space race with the Soviet Union four and a half centuries later.

The race in 1492 was to create the first shipping lane to Asia. The Portuguese expeditions had always sailed east, around the southern tip of Africa. Columbus decided to head due west, across open ocean, a scheme that was feasible only thanks to a recent invention—the magnetic ship's compass. Until then ships had stayed close to the great land masses even for the longest voyages. Likewise, it was only thanks to an invention of the 1940's and early 1950's, the high-speed electronic computer, that NASA would even consider propelling astronauts out of the Earth's orbit and toward the moon.

Both NASA and Columbus made not one but a series of voyages. NASA landed men on six different parts of the moon. Columbus made four voyages to different parts of what he remained convinced was the east coast of Asia. As a result both NASA and Columbus had to keep coming back to the Government with their hands out, pleading for refinancing. In each case the reply of the Government became, after a few years: "This is all very impressive, but what earthly good is it to anyone back home?"

Columbus was reduced to making the most desperate claims. When he first reached land in 1492 at San Salvador, off Cuba, he expected to find gold, or at least spices. The Arawak Indians were awed by the strangers and their ships, which they believed had descended from the sky, and they presented them with their most prized possessions, live parrots and balls of cotton. Columbus soon set them digging for gold, which didn't exist. So he brought back reports of fabulous riches in the form of manpower; which is to say, slaves. He was not speaking of the Arawaks, however. With the exception of criminals and prisoners of war, he was supposed to civilize all natives and convert them to Christianity. He was talking about the Carib Indians, who were cannibals and therefore qualified as criminals. The Caribs would fight down to the last unbroken bone rather than endure captivity, and few ever survived the voyages back to Spain. By the end of Columbus's second voyage, in 1496, the Government was becoming testy. A great deal of wealth was going into voyages to Asia, and very little was coming back. Columbus made his men swear to return to Spain saying that they had not only reached the Asian mainland, they had heard Japanese spoken.

Likewise by the early 1970's, it was clear that the moon was in economic terms pretty much what it looked like from Earth, a gray rock. NASA, in the quest for appropriations, was reduced to publicizing the "spinoffs" of the space program. These included Teflon-coated frying pans, a ball-point pen that would write in a weightless environment, and a computerized biosensor system that would enable doctors to treat heart patients without making house calls. On the whole, not a giant step for mankind.

In 1493, after his first voyage, Columbus had ridden through Barcelona at the side of King Ferdinand in the position once occupied by Ferdinand's late son, Juan. By 1500, the bad-mouthing of Columbus had reached the point where he was put in chains at the conclusion of his third voyage and returned to Spain in disgrace. NASA suffered no such ignominy, of course, but by July 20, 1974, the fifth anniversary of the landing of Apollo 11, things were grim enough. The public had become gloriously bored by space exploration. The fifth anniversary celebration consisted mainly of about two hundred souls, mostly NASA

people, sitting on folding chairs underneath a camp meeting
canopy on the marble prairie outside the old Smithsonian Air
Museum in Washington listening to speeches by Neil Armstrong, Michael Collins, and Buzz Aldrin and watching the ca-
loric waves ripple.

Extraordinary rumors had begun to circulate about the astro-   7
nauts. The most lurid said that trips to the moon, and even into
Earth orbit, had so traumatized the men, they had fallen victim
to religious and spiritualist manias or plain madness. (Of the
total seventy-three astronauts chosen, one, Aldrin, is known to
have suffered from depression, rooted, as his own memoir makes
clear, in matters that had nothing to do with space flight. Two
teamed up in an evangelical organization, and one set up a foundation for the scientific study of psychic phenomena—interests
the three of them had developed long before they flew in space.)
The NASA budget, meanwhile, had been reduced to the light-bill
level.

Columbus died in 1509, nearly broke and stripped of most of   8
his honors as Spain's Admiral of the Ocean, a title he preferred.
It was only later that history began to look upon him not as an
adventurer who had tried and failed to bring home gold—but as
a man with a supernatural sense of destiny, whose true glory was
his willingness to plunge into the unknown, including the remot-
est parts of the universe he could hope to reach.

NASA still lives, albeit in reduced circumstances, and   9
whether or not history will treat NASA like the admiral is hard
to say.

The idea that the exploration of the rest of the universe is its   10
own reward is not very popular, and NASA is forced to keep
talking about things such as bigger communications satellites
that will enable live television transmission of European soccer
games at a fraction of the current cost. Such notions as "building
a bridge to the stars for mankind" do not light up the sky today—
but may yet.

DISCUSSION: CONTENT

1. From what historical perspective on the moon landing is Wolfe
   writing? How, if at all, have attitudes toward NASA and space
   exploration changed since Wolfe wrote this essay?

2. What country was Spain's competitor in the race to win riches in the New World?
3. What invention, perfected in the late 1940s and early 1950s, allowed astronauts to venture out of Earth's orbit?
4. Why has NASA focused increasingly on the importance of the spinoffs from the space exploration rather than on the explorations themselves?
5. Why did Columbus suffer such ill fame in his lifetime?

DISCUSSION: FORM

1. In this essay we have a strikingly clear example of comparison by points. What are the topics that Wolfe is comparing, and what points do they have in common?
2. The comparison is not quite complete. What point raised in paragraph 8 with respect to Columbus is not countered with a corresponding point for the space program?
3. List some examples Wolfe cites of the "desperate claims" that both Columbus and the space program were forced to make in order to keep their expeditions funded.

How Asian Teachers Polish
Each Lesson to Perfection

JAMES W. STIGLER AND
HAROLD W. STEVENSON

James W. Stigler is professor of psychology at UCLA. A recipient of the Boyd R. McCandless Young Scientist Award from the American Psychological Association in 1990, he was awarded a Guggenheim Fellowship for research in mathematics education. Harold N. Stevenson (b. 1924) is a professor of psychology at the University of Michigan, where he directs the program in Child Development and Social Policy. He is president of the International Society for the Study of Behavioral Development. This essay is drawn from their 1992 book, The Learning Gap: Why Our Schools Are Failing and What We Can Learn from Japanese and Chinese Education.

Although there is no overall difference in intelligence, the   1
differences in mathematical achievement of American children
and their Asian counterparts are staggering.

Let us look at the results of a study we conducted in 120   2
classrooms in three cities: Taipei (Taiwan); Sendai (Japan); and
the Minneapolis metropolitan area. First and fifth graders from
representative schools in these cities were given a test of mathematics that required computation and problem solving. Among
the one hundred first-graders in the three locations who received
the lowest scores, fifty-eight were American children; among the
one hundred lowest-scoring fifth graders, sixty-seven were
American children. Among the top one hundred first graders in
mathematics, there were only fifteen American children. And
only one American child appeared among the top one hundred
fifth graders. The highest-scoring American classroom obtained
an average score lower than that of the lowest-scoring Japanese
classroom and of all but one of the twenty classrooms in Taipei.
In whatever way we looked at the data, the poor performance of
American children was evident.

These data are startling, but no more so than the results of a   3
study that involved 40 first- and 40 fifth-grade classrooms in the
metropolitan area of Chicago—a very representative sample of
the city and the suburbs of Cook County—and twenty-two
classes in each of these grades in metropolitan Beijing (China). In
this study, children were given a battery of mathematics tasks
that included diverse problems, such as estimating the distance
between a tree and a hidden treasure on a map, deciding who won
a race on the basis of data in a graph, trying to explain subtraction
to visiting Martians, or calculating the sum of nineteen and
forty-five. There was no area in which the American children
were competitive with those from China. The Chinese children's
superiority appeared in complex tasks involving the application
of knowledge as well as in the routines of computation. When
fifth graders were asked, for example, how many members of a
stamp club with twenty-four members collected only foreign
stamps if five-sixths of the members did so, 59 percent of Beijing
children, but only 9 percent of the Chicago children, produced
the correct answer. On a computation test, only 2.2 percent of
the Chinese fifth graders scored at or below the mean for their
American counterparts. All of the twenty Chicago area schools
had average scores on the fifth-grade geometry test that were
below those of the Beijing schools. The results from all these

tasks paint a bleak picture of American children's competencies in mathematics.

The poor performance of American students compels us to try to understand the reasons why. We have written extensively elsewhere about the cultural differences in attitudes toward learning and toward the importance of effort vs. innate ability and about the substantially greater amounts of time Japanese and Chinese students devote to academic activities in general and to the study of math in particular. Important as these factors are, they do not tell the whole story. For that we have to take a close look inside the classrooms of Japan, China, and the United States to see how mathematics is actually taught in the three cultures. 4

Lessons Not Lectures

If we were asked briefly to characterize classes in Japan and China, we would say that they consist of coherent lessons that are presented in a thoughtful, relaxed, and nonauthoritarian manner. Teachers frequently rely on students as sources of information. Lessons are oriented toward problem solving rather than rote mastery of facts and procedures and utilize many different types of representational materials. The role assumed by the teacher is that of knowledgeable guide, rather than that of prime dispenser of information and arbiter of what is correct. There is frequent verbal interaction in the classroom as the teacher attempts to stimulate students to produce, explain, and evaluate solutions to problems. These characteristics contradict stereotypes held by most Westerners about Asian teaching practices. Lessons are not rote; they are not filled with drill. Teachers do not spend large amounts of time lecturing but attempt to lead the children in productive interactions and discussions. And the children are not the passive automata depicted in Western descriptions but active participants in the learning process. 5

We begin by discussing what we mean by the coherence of a lesson. One way to think of a lesson is by using the analogy of a story. A good story is highly organized; it has a beginning, a middle, and an end; and it follows a protagonist who meets challenges and resolves problems that arise along the way. Above all, a good story engages the reader's interest in a series of interconnected events, which are best understood in the context of the events that precede and follow it. 6

Such a concept of a lesson guides the organization of instruc-   7
tion in Asia. The curricula are defined in terms of coherent
lessons, each carefully designed to fill a forty- to fifty-minute
class period with sustained attention to the development of some
concept or skill. Like a good story, the lesson has an introduction,
a conclusion, and a consistent theme.

We can illustrate what we are talking about with this account of a fifth-grade Japanese mathematics class:

> The teacher walks in carrying a large paper bag full of clinking
> glass. Entering the classroom with a large paper bag is highly
> unusual, and by the time she has placed the bag on her desk the
> students are regarding her with rapt attention. What's in the
> bag? She begins to pull items out of the bag, placing them,
> one-by-one, on her desk. She removes a pitcher and a vase. A
> beer bottle evokes laughter and surprise. She soon has six con-
> tainers lined up on her desk. The children continue to watch
> intently, glancing back and forth at each other as they seek to
> understand the purpose of this display.
>
> The teacher, looking thoughtfully at the containers, poses a
> question: "I wonder which one would hold the most water?"
> Hands go up, and the teacher calls on different students to give
> their guesses: "the pitcher," "the beer bottle," "the teapot."
> The teacher stands aside and ponders: "Some of you said one
> thing, others said something different. You don't agree with
> each other. There must be some way we can find out who is
> correct. How can we know who is correct?" Interest is high, and
> the discussion continues.
>
> The students soon agree that to find out how much each
> container holds they will need to fill the containers with some-
> thing. How about water? The teacher finds some buckets and
> sends several children out to fill them with water. When they
> return, the teacher says: "Now what do we do?" Again there is
> a discussion, and after several minutes the children decide that
> they will need to use a smaller container to measure how much
> water fits into each of the larger containers. They decide on a
> drinking cup, and one of the students warns that, they all have
> to fill each cup to the same level—otherwise the measure won't
> be the same for all of the groups.
>
> At this point the teacher divides the class into their groups
> *(ban)* and gives each group one of the containers and a drinking
> cup. Each group fills its container, counts how many cups of
> water it holds, and writes the result in a notebook. When all of
> the groups have completed the task, the teacher calls on the
> leader of each group to report on the group's findings and notes

the results on the blackboard. She has written the names of the containers in a column on the left and a scale from 1 to 6 along the bottom. Pitcher, 4.5 cups; vase, 3 cups; beer bottle, 1.5 cups; and so on. As each group makes its report, the teacher draws a bar representing the amount, in cups, the container holds.

Finally, the teacher returns to the question she posed at the beginning of the lesson: Which container holds the most water? She reviews how they were able to solve the problem and points out that the answer is now contained in the bar graph on the board. She then arranges the containers on the table in order according to how much they hold and writes a rank order on each container, from 1 to 6. She ends the class with a brief review of what they have done. No definitions of ordinate and abscissa, no discussion of how to make a graph preceded the example—these all became obvious in the course of the lesson, and only at the end did the teacher mention the terms that describe the horizontal and vertical axes of the graph they had made.

With one carefully crafted problem, this Japanese teacher has guided her students to discover—and most likely to remember— several important concepts. As this article unfolds, we hope to demonstrate that this example of how well-designed Asian class lessons are is not an isolated one; to the contrary, it is the norm. And as we hope to further demonstrate, excellent class lessons do not come effortlessly or magically. Asian teachers are not born great teachers; they and the lessons they develop require careful nurturing and constant refinement. The practice of teaching in Japan and China is more uniformly perfected than it is in the United States because their systems of education are structured to encourage teaching excellence to develop and flourish. Ours is not. We will take up the question of why and what can be done about this later in the piece. But first, we present a more detailed look at what Asian lessons are like. 8

Coherence Broken

Asian lessons almost always begin with a practical problem, such as the example we have just given, or with a word problem written on the blackboard. Asian teachers, to a much greater degree than American teachers, give coherence to their lessons by introducing the lesson with a word problem. 9

It is not uncommon for the Asian teacher to organize the   10
entire lesson around the solution to this single problem. The
teacher leads the children to recognize what is known and what
is unknown and directs the students' attention to the critical
parts of the problem. Teachers are careful to see that the problem
is understood by all of the children, and even mechanics, such as
mathematical computation, are presented in the context of solving a problem.

Before ending the lesson, the teacher reviews what has been   11
learned and relates it to the problem she posed at the beginning
of the lesson. American teachers are much less likely than Asian
teachers to begin and end lessons in this way. For example, we
found that fifth-grade teachers in Beijing spent eight times as
long at the end of the class period summarizing the lessons as did
those in the Chicago metropolitan area.

Now contrast the Japanese math lesson described above with   12
a fifth-grade American mathematics classroom that we recently
visited. Immediately after getting the students' attention, the
teacher pointed out that today was Tuesday, "band day," and that
all students in the band should go to the band room. "Those of
you doing the news report today should meet over there in the
corner," he continued. He then began the mathematics class
with the remaining students by reviewing the solution to a computation problem that had been included in the previous day's
homework. After this brief review, the teacher directed the students' attention to the blackboard, where the day's assignment
had been written. From this point on, the teacher spent most of
the rest of the period walking about the room monitoring the
children's work, talking to individual children about questions or
errors, and uttering "shushes" whenever the students began talking among themselves.

This example is typical of the American classrooms we have   13
visited, classrooms where students spend more time in transition
and less in academic activities, more time working on their own
and less being instructed by the teacher; where teachers spend
much of their time working with individual students and attending to matters of discipline; and where the shape of a coherent
lesson is often hard to discern.

American lessons are often disrupted by irrelevant interrup-   14
tions. These serve to break the continuity of the lesson and add
to children's difficulty in perceiving the lesson as a coherent

whole. In our American observations, the teacher interrupted the flow of the lesson with an interlude of irrelevant comments or the class was interrupted by someone else in 20 percent of all first-grade lessons and 47 percent of all fifth-grade lessons. This occurred less than 10 percent of the time at both grade levels in Sendai, Taipei, and Beijing. In fact, no interruptions of either type were recorded during the eighty hours of observation in Beijing fifth-grade classrooms. The mathematics lesson in one of the American schools we visited was interrupted every morning by a woman from the cafeteria who polled the children about their lunch plans and collected money from those who planned to eat the hot lunch. Interruptions, as well as inefficient transitions from one activity to another, make it difficult to sustain a coherent lesson throughout the class period.

Coherence is also disrupted when teachers shift frequently   15 from one topic to another. This occurred often in the American classrooms we observed. The teacher might begin with a segment on measurement, then proceed to a segment on simple addition, then to a segment on telling time, and then to a second segment on addition. These segments constitute a math class, but they are hardly a coherent lesson. Such changes in topic were responsible for 21 percent of the changes in segments that we observed in American classrooms but accounted for only 4 percent of the changes in segments in Japanese classrooms.

Teachers frequently capitalize on variety as a means of cap-   16 turing children's interest. This may explain why American teachers shift topics so frequently within the lesson. Asian teachers also seek variety; but they tend to introduce new activities instead of new topics. Shifts in materials do not necessarily pose a threat to coherence. For example, the coherence of a lesson does not diminish when the teacher shifts from working with numerals to working with concrete objects, if both are used to represent the same subtraction problem. Shifting the topic, on the other hand, introduces variety, but at the risk of destroying the coherence of the lesson.

DISCUSSION: CONTENT

1. What proof do Stigler and Stevenson offer to support their claim that Asian children outperform American ones in math?

2. How would you characterize the basic differences between teaching practices in the United States and those in Asia?
3. What, according to Stigler and Stevenson, is the difference between a lesson and a lecture? How do they illustrate that distinction?
4. In what ways do American instructors fail to achieve coherence in their teaching? What adjustments might they make? What factors militate against them?

DISCUSSION: FORM

1. How do the authors formulate their comparison in this essay: by topics or by points?
2. In addition to comparison, what other methods of development did you encounter in this essay?
3. Do you find the subheadings useful? What reasons do the authors have for grouping their material this way?

9

Analogy

In the last chapter we examined comparison as an expository or informative tool. Another expository technique, closely related to comparison, is **analogy.** To understand analogy it would be helpful to review briefly some of the things that you know about comparison. Remember that a useful distinction can be made between descriptive and expository comparisons. Descriptive comparisons focus chiefly on resemblances; in using similes or metaphors, you attempt to show your readers what something looks, sounds, smells, or behaves like. On the other hand, expository comparisons focus not just on similarities but on contrasts; in using comparison to inform, you tell your readers how two or more subjects (called *topics*) resembled or differed from one another with respect to selected points.

Another fact that you should recall about descriptive comparisons is that they can be either *literal,* or possible ("He looked as though he had tasted something sour"), or *figurative,* or fantastic ("His face resembled a prune").

Literal Comparison

Literal descriptive comparisons bear a certain resemblance to the informative comparisons discussed in the last chapter. Baseball teams are literally alike. They have certain points in common—personnel, hitting, pitching, fielding, and so on. The teams may differ with respect to these points, but baseball teams are essentially alike. Similarly, human societies can be literally compared with respect to their status symbols—wealth, real estate, education, transportation, and the like—even though those societies are as widely separated as those of United States and Polynesia. Again, the differences are important, and they can be readily observed because the common points of comparison help the readers to focus on those differences. In other words, we think of baseball teams or human societies as things that can be logically or literally compared because they are essentially alike and can be distinguished chiefly by their few differences.

Figurative Comparisons or Analogies

On the other hand, we often are inclined to make comparisons between things that cannot be logically compared. In descriptive writing this is what figurative comparisons—metaphors and similes—are all about. A human face, however withered and wrinkled, will never, literally, look like a prune. The suggestion is that the face you are describing shares with a prune at least one striking characteristic—deep wrinkles. And that comparison is highly descriptive. Likewise, if a person is described as having a face shaped like a pumpkin, then the round, full look of that person's cheeks and jawline gets emphasized in a concrete, useful manner.

Such figurative comparisons can also be highly informative, and when they are, they are called *analogies.* They are like the descriptive comparisons because they focus chiefly on resemblances, but the resemblances are figurative or fantastic. On the other hand, analogies, especially when they are expanded at some length, are organized like informative comparisons, featuring points of comparison enumerating all the fantastic resemblances that have been observed.

To summarize this discussion, you might say this: *Informative comparisons focus on the differences that exist among essentially similar things, while analogies focus on the similarities shared by essentially dissimilar things.*

A very common analogy is the comparison of an echo to a rubber ball bouncing off a wall. Sound waves and bouncing rubber balls have very little in common and cannot logically be compared in the same way that baseball teams or human societies can. Nevertheless, such a figurative comparison is informative simply because the average reader can be expected to envision the movement of a rubber ball more clearly than the movement of sound waves, and separate points might be singled out for special attention—the approach to the wall, the moment of impact, the return to the place of origin.

A great many difficult or complicated explanations employ the strategy of analogy because it is so helpful in assisting readers to understand an unfamiliar subject in relation to a more familiar one. For example, your chemistry teacher may compare the structures of atoms with electrons and protons to solar systems with orbiting planets, although planets have nothing else in common with the electrons revolving around the atomic nuclei. Similarly, human brains are often compared with computers, even though the resemblance is imperfect, to say the least. Nevertheless, you might very well be able, with a little thought, to determine several useful points of comparison that a brain and a computer share: memory storage, indexing strategies, and retrieval systems, to suggest a few. Electrical current moving through a wire is almost always explained in terms of water flowing through a pipe, its volume, pressure, and the resistance it encounters being likened to electrical voltage, amperage, and the ohms of electrical resistance. Such analogies are successful informative tools because readers, however little they may know about solar systems, computers, or plumbing, will normally know more about them than they will about atomic structures, human brains, or electricity.

As a writer, you always must take into account what your readers know, or what they are likely to know. This is especially true when using analogy as an expository writing device, for you must base or ground your analogy's comparison on one subject that is—at least to some extent—quite familiar to your readers. If you do not choose wisely, then your analogy is bound to fail, as you try to explain one unfamiliar subject in terms of another. Remember that Jesus was a successful teacher because he recognized that his listeners knew more about sheep herding, farming, or money lending than they did about the kingdom of heaven. So he used analogies based on such common and familiar activities to explain his vision—and changed the world.

The paragraphs and essays that follow all employ the strategy of analogy, for they compare entities or subjects that are essentially dissimilar. But the purpose of each is to lead readers to a better understanding of something unfamiliar by comparing it to something most people already know about. As implied above, you probably have already encountered analogies in your textbooks for chemistry, physics, or other technical and scientific courses. More practice will make you an even better reader of such material. You will also find occasion to use analogy in your own writing, especially as you are called on to explain concepts learned in your studies: how psychologists view a child's mind as a blank tablet, how biologists view each ecological system as a separate small world, and so forth. Clearly, then, analogy is an explanatory technique whose proper use you need to understand if your writing is to be successful.

Commentary on Student Work

The student work on p. 214 never developed further than a single paragraph. It had its beginnings in a classroom discussion the day that analogy was introduced as a possible model for development. The class had discussed the Carroll essay, "Feeding the Mind," which likened reading to eating, and the Lukas essay, which compared life to a game of pinball. In each case the students had determined the points of comparison that were shared by each of these seemingly unrelated topics.

Once the class was comfortable with the notion of comparing seemingly unlike things, they were divided into their reading groups where they were given these instructions: (1) choose some familiar things or activities around the campus that everyone would be well acquainted with, and (2) try to compare those chosen topics with something essentially dissimilar, thereby creating an effective metaphor (an apt analogy that would provide some unusual insights into a topic that had grown stale from familiarity). Some suggestions were offered: cafeteria meals, math teachers, the football team, cheerleaders, Greek letter organizations, and even freshman English classes.

The students brainstormed in groups for the remainder of the period, trying to think of unusual comparisons on which to base their analogies. Some fairly uninteresting matches were tried before anything managed to click. You can imagine the typical sorts of false starts, such as these generated by one group:

Cafeteria food is like pig swill.
The football team is like the Keystone Kops.
Fraternities are like big businesses.
Female cheerleaders are like Greek priestesses.
Math professors are like medieval torturers.

None of these analogies was exceptionally interesting, although the last two did have a bit of promise. That, at least, was the observation made by the instructor, who stopped by the group. Those comparisons, he said, were more likely to develop into a successful analogy because they were more apt to stretch the imagination in searching for shared points. Nevertheless, he continued, the differences were not really great enough yet to produce anything terribly imaginative. "Why don't you try something really off-the-wall," he said, "like comparing the football team to a computer . . . or the cafeteria to a jet plane?"

And that was when it happened. "Yeah," Donald, a student in the group, responded, "or a fraternity to a set of long underwear!"

"That just might work. What did you have in mind?"

"Well, they both make you feel warm and cozy," Donald answered.

"But they both get mighty uncomfortable, too," someone else chimed in.

"How exactly?" another asked.

"Wool underwear can itch like hell."

"And some of the brothers can make pledges awfully uncomfortable, too," Donald admitted.

They were warming up now, and the instructor moved away to another group. The next class meeting, Donald brought with him something very like the paragraph that follows; it needed only a small amount of polishing to bring it to its present form. The group decided that this analogy probably would not stand much expansion; it was a successful paragraph because it had made its point quickly and efficiently. Stretching it into an essay, they felt, would detract from its overall effect.

Here is Donald's paragraph. On page 214 you'll also encounter another student paragraph, "Freshmen English," that arose from a similar discussion during another semester.

Fraternal Itch

Being in a fraternity or sorority is like putting on wool underwear. The benefits do not always compensate for the discomfort. There is the warm, snug feeling of having ready-made friends, but there is always the nagging itch of those two or three that a person simply does not like and cannot get away from. A good brother or sister has to tolerate these itches—to grin and bear them—because to do otherwise would violate established customs. It is not polite to scratch. But after a while, getting rid of the itch becomes a very urgent matter—to get away for the weekend, away for the summer, or out of the organization altogether—a body just has to get out of that underwear.

DISCUSSION QUESTIONS

1. List the points that wearing wool underwear and being in a fraternity or sorority have in common.
2. Where does the writer state the thesis of the paragraph?
3. If you are a contented member of a fraternity, sorority, or similar social organization, you may want to challenge this analogy in writing. You may do so by constructing your own analogy whose points of comparison are positive and attractive rather than negative.

STUDENT WORK

Freshman English

Freshman English is very much like going to the dentist. The due dates for paragraphs and essays are as ugly on your calendar as dental appointments, and as each one approaches, anxiety increases. You begin each paper with the same feeling of resignation that brings you to the dentist's office, and trying to think of a topic is usually as shallow an activity as the reading of last year's magazines in the waiting room. Anyway, you're too worried about the outcome to think straight. But the most painful part is just getting started, and it's the same at the dentist's: after the painful stab of Novocain, everything settles into dullness. And just as that numbed feeling hangs on while the dentist probes around in your mouth, doing things you can't see, you also have that drugged feeling while you wait to get your paper back, knowing that the teacher is probing around among your sentences. Finally, getting the paper back is like having the Novocain wear off, so that you're now painfully aware of each little probing that has gone on—and even more anxious about the next scheduled appointment.

DISCUSSION QUESTIONS

1. In most analogies the points of comparison are few because the subjects to be compared are essentially dissimilar. Here, freshman English and a visit to the dentist are certainly dissimilar topics, and yet the student writer has come up with a surprising number of points. How many do you count?
2. One technique that the writer uses effectively is the repetition of key words common to both freshman English and dental visits. *Anxiety* is one such word. Can you discover three more such words or expressions?

Sunbathing on Scott Beach

Sunbathing on Scott Beach is in many respects just like   1
roasting a pig. It is not at all easy for the sunbather or the pig to become well done, but in the event of success, the result in either case is an appetizing delight. To insure success a number of steps must be taken.

First, the sunbather must be properly dressed and spitted—   2
with as much surface area exposed as possible and situated to receive as much direct radiation as possible. Next, the sunbather begins by marinating her body with browning oils and basting it with aromatic spices, both to arouse the appetite of onlookers and to prevent the tender meat from drying out. To achieve an even cooking, continual rotation is necessary.

During the final stages careful observation of the skin must   3
be maintained to determine whether it is ready or not. This is a most difficult step, and only the most trained eye can tell when

it is time to remove the carcass from the fire. The sunbather who is reckless in her first roasting will turn out with a skin that is blistered or charred and generally discolored—extremely tender to the touch. And if someone should slap her burnt back, her expression will not be unlike that of a roasted pig with an apple in its mouth.

DISCUSSION QUESTIONS

1. Notice how the language used to describe the preparation of the sunbather overlaps the terminology for pig roasting. What effect is thus created?
2. In addition to analogy the writer is making use of another rhetorical method of development already discussed. What is it? What transitional devices clearly point out the writer's concern for this technique?

Fishing for the Buyer

A good salesman in many respects is just like a good fisherman. It is not easy to attract that wary buyer to a lure of merchandise when he does not hunger for the goods offered, yet the good salesman can hook the consumer almost every time.

First, like any good fisherman, the salesman entices the buyer with good bait. Some salesmen prefer natural bait, but the majority these days use the much cheaper artificials, with a lot of doubletalk for smell. When he has turned the unlucky customer's head and has his interest, it is then time for the second stage in this delicate process of catching the buyer.

The salesman must then make his prey believe the bait is about to escape. There are several ways of doing this. One effective method is to tell the customer that he is not sure he wants to sell this fine object, since it once belonged to his grandmother and perhaps the salesman should keep it in the family and pass it on to his heirs. This shake of the bait seldom fails to make the customer twice as eager to get his jaws around that delightful tidbit that is trying to evade his waiting stomach. Another way to jiggle the bait is to say that the expected new shipment of this item will have to sell for a higher price or will be of inferior quality. In any case, the way is prepared for the final stage.

This last stage, perhaps the most difficult, is one that results 4
in a trophy-sized sale if successful. It is easy to get the customer
to bite, but hard to get him landed, where he will pay. Many
salesmen swear by the "let-'em-run-with-it" method. This enables the customer to take the bait "on time." He is allowed to
make monthly payments or to use a charge card. In either case
he does not realize what a trap he is getting into until it is too
late. One advantage of this method is that in many cases it
enables the salesman to use the law as a kind of landing net, not
only for gaining the trophy but in some cases for recovering the
bait as well!

Yes, a salesman, especially a novice, can learn much from an 5
experienced fisherman, for a buyer is just as eager to take some
attractive merchandise bait as a mountain trout is for the right
kind of fly. The proof can be found in the thousands of green
trophies that fill the wallet-creels of thousands of successful
salesmen.

DISCUSSION QUESTIONS

1. Where does the writer of this essay pause to give concrete *examples?* How does he make clear the steps of the process?
2. Overlapping terminology is also used in "Fishing for the Buyer."
Mark the passages that display this "overlapping" language in
this model, and then try to incorporate this technique in your
own analogy papers.

PARAGRAPHS

The Flight of a Sparrow

BEDE

Another of the king's chief men . . . soon added: "The present
life of man, O king, seems to me, in comparison to that time
which is unknown to us, like the swift flight of a sparrow

through the room wherein you sit at supper in winter, with your commanders and ministers, and a good fire in the midst, whilst the storms of rain and snow prevail abroad; the sparrow, flying in at one door, and immediately out at another, whilst he is within, is safe from the wintry storm; but after a short space of fair weather, he immediately vanishes out of your sight, into the dark winter from which he had emerged. So this life of man appears for a short space, but of what went before, or what is to follow, we are utterly ignorant."

DISCUSSION QUESTIONS

1. Analogy is frequently a successful expository tool, for the complex or the unfamiliar may be made understandable by comparison with something simple or familiar. In this regard, the life of man is nothing like the flight of a sparrow, except at the crucial point of resemblance that concerns the king's counselor. This analogy must have been extremely successful, though, because Bede (?673–735), who included this episode in the first history of England, credits it with the conversion of the Northumbrians (in northeast England) to Christianity. How do you suppose this analogy helped convince people to adopt Christianity?
2. What other analogies can you think of that have been used to explain religious principles? What is suggested by the frequent use of analogies to explain religious principles?

The Ego and the Id

SIGMUND FREUD

One might compare the relation of the ego to the id with that between a rider and his horse. The horse provides the locomotor energy, and the rider has the prerogative of determining the goal and of guiding the movements of his powerful mount towards it. But all too often in the relations between the ego and the id we find a picture of the less than ideal situation in which the rider is obliged to guide his horse in the direction in which it itself wants to go.

DISCUSSION QUESTIONS

1. Are you familiar with the terms *ego* and *id*? If you are not, look them up in a dictionary or, better yet, in an introductory psychology textbook. What other names might nonpsychologists use to refer to these facets of one's personality?
2. Examine the sentences of this paragraph carefully. In each sentence Freud is guilty of "sexist diction," or of using "sexual reference," when one is not really called for. Look up these terms in a grammar handbook. How might you revise the sentences to escape the criticism?
3. When Freud created this analogy to explain ego and id, horses were a common means of transportation. Since that is no longer true, you might expect his analogy to be ineffective now, since modern readers are not nearly so familiar with the experience of riding a horse. How well does the analogy carry its point to you now? If the analogy were switched to *driver* and *car*, what would be gained—or lost?

A Good Relationship

ANNE MORROW LINDBERGH

A good relationship has a pattern like a dance and is built on some of the same rules. The partners do not need to hold on tightly, because they move confidently in the same pattern, intricate but gay and swift and free, like a country dance of Mozart's. To touch heavily would be to arrest the pattern and to freeze the movement, to check the endlessly changing beauty of its unfolding. There is no place here for the possessive clutch, the clinging arm, the heavy hand; there is only the barest touch in passing. Now arm in arm, now face to face, now back to back—it does not matter which. They know they are partners moving to the same rhythm, creating a pattern together, and being invisibly nourished by it.

DISCUSSION QUESTIONS

1. Lindbergh compares a desirable relationship between two persons to a couple in a certain kind of dance, describing it with some care by using contrasts; what contrasts do you notice?

2. To reinforce the idea of unity, Lindbergh often uses phrasal repetition, repeating parallel grammatical structures. Try to find at least two of these and notice how they give her descriptive analogy a graceful counterpoint movement not unlike the sort of dance she wants her readers to imagine.
3. To appreciate more Lindbergh's accomplishment and her point, consider how you might create your own negative comparison, describing a *bad* relationship (perhaps even a psychologically or physically abusive one) in terms of a different sort of dance or other activity.

Daedalus and Icarus

ARTHUR EDDINGTON

In ancient days two aviators procured for themselves wings. Daedalus flew safely through the middle air and was duly honoured on his landing. Icarus soared upwards to the sun till the wax melted which bound his wings, and his flight ended in fiasco. In weighing their achievements, there is something to be said for Icarus. The classical authorities tell us that he was only "doing a stunt," but I prefer to think of him as the man who brought to light a serious constructional defect in the flying-machines of his day. So, too, in Science. Cautious Daedalus will apply his theories where he feels confident they will safely go; but by his excesses of caution their hidden weaknesses remain undiscovered. Icarus will strain his theories to the breaking point till the weak joints gape.

DISCUSSION QUESTIONS

1. Eddington takes the mythological story of the inventor Daedalus and his son, Icarus, and uses it to explain a more difficult and poorly understood point about science. What exactly is that point? Who or what do Daedalus and Icarus represent?
2. The pivotal sentence in the paragraph turns out not to be a sentence at all. What is it? Does it upset the paragraph?

ESSAYS

Pinball

J. ANTHONY LUKAS

J. Anthony Lukas (b. 1933) is an American journalist who has written for the Baltimore Sun *and the New York* Times; *he won the Pulitzer Prize for local reporting in 1968. He has written two best-selling books,* Don't Shoot: We Are Your Children! *(1971) and* Nightmare: The Underside of the Nixon Years *(1976), and in 1985 he was awarded a second Pulitzer Prize for the year's best nonfiction book,* Common Ground: A Turbulent Decade in the Lives of Three American Families. *Since 1972 he has been a free-lance writer, his work appearing in such national magazines as* Esquire, Harper's, New Republic, Psychology Today, *and* Atlantic Monthly, *from which the following essay has been excerpted.*

Pinball is a metaphor for life, pitting man's skill, nerve, persistence, and luck against the perverse machinery of human existence. The playfield is rich with rewards: targets that bring huge scores, bright lights, chiming bells, free balls, and extra games. But it is replete with perils, too: culs-de-sac, traps, gutters, and gobble holes down which the ball may disappear forever.   1

Each pull of the plunger launches the ball into a miniature universe of incalculable possibilities. As the steel sphere hurtles into the ellipse at the top of the playfield, it hangs for a moment in exquisite tension between triumph and disaster. Down one lane lies a hole worth thousands, down another a sickening lurch to oblivion. The ball trembles on the lip, seeming to lean first one way, then the other.   2

A player is not powerless to control the ball's wild flight, any more than man is powerless to control his own life. He may nudge the machine with hands, arms, or hips, jogging it just enough to change the angle of the ball's descent. And he is armed with "flippers" which can propel the ball back up the playfield,   3 aiming at the targets with the richest payoffs. But, just as man's boldest strokes and bravest ventures often boomerang, so an ill-timed flip can ricochet the ball straight down "death alley," and a too vigorous nudge will send the machine into "tilt." Winning pinball, like rewarding life, requires delicate touch, fine calibrations, careful discrimination between boldness and folly.

DISCUSSION: CONTENT

1. Lukas begins by calling pinball a metaphor for life. What does he mean by that? Is a metaphor the same as an analogy?
2. To what extent does Lukas suggest that man can govern his own destiny in life?

DISCUSSION: FORM

1. Aside from the opening sentence, Lukas offers us few overt reminders that there is an analogy at work. How many times and where does Lukas again call the reader's attention to the analogy?
2. If overt reminders are few or absent altogether, as they are in paragraph 2, how is the analogy sustained so that the reader does not forget the ongoing comparison?

The Salmon Instinct

WILLIAM HUMPHREY

William Humphrey (b. 1924) is a Texas native who attended Southern Methodist University and the University of Texas. His first novel, Home from the Hill *(1958), brought widespread critical attention. It was followed by* The Ordways *(1965) and* Proud Flesh *(1973). His favorite subject is the American Southwest, and he has chronicled its literature in* Ah Wilderness: The Frontier in American Literature *(1977). His more recent books include* Hostages of Fortune *(1984),* Open Season: Sporting Adventures *(1986), and* No Resting Place *(1989).*

When James I, King of England, was asked why he was going back, after a long absence, to visit his native Scotland, he replied, "The salmon instinct."

The salmon is in his early adolescence when he leaves his   2
native stream, impelled by an irresistible urge for something
he has never known, the salt, salt sea. There he stays for the
rest of his life, until he feels another prompting equally irresistible, the urge to reproduce himself. This the salmon can do
only in that same stream in which he was born. And so, from
distances as great as fifteen hundred miles, the old salmon
heads for home.

Many things can, and do, kill the salmon on his long voyage   3
home, but nothing can deter or detour him. Not the diseases and
parasites he is prone to, not fishermen, commercial or sporting,
not the highest falls. He endures them, he eludes them, he leaps
them, impelled by his ardent homesickness. Though long an
expatriate, he knows his nationality as a naturalized American
knows his, and back to the country of his birth he goes, as though
throughout all the years away he has kept his first passport.
Through the pathless sea he finds his way unerringly to the river
down which he came on his voyage out long ago, and past each
of its tributaries, each more temptingly like the one he is seeking
the nearer he gets to that special one, as towns in the same
county are similar but not the same. When he gets to his, he
knows it—as I, for instance, know Clarksville, and would know
it even if, like the salmon, I had but one sense to lead me to it.
The name given the salmon in Latin is *Salmo salar:* the fish that
will leap waterfalls to get back home. Some later Linnaeus of the
human orders must have classed me at birth among the Hum-
phreys: in Welsh the name means "One who loves his hearth and
home."

But I began to doubt my homing instincts, to think I had   4
wandered too far away, stayed gone too long, when, after crossing
the ocean, I went back those thirty-two years later.

I had spent a few days in Dallas first, as the homecoming   5
salmon spends a few days in the estuary to reaccustom himself
to sweet water after all his years at sea before ascending to his
native stream; for although this is what he now longs for, those
uterine waters of his, too sudden a change from the salt is a shock
to him. Dallas had always been brackish to me.

The nearer I got to Clarksville the farther from it I seemed to   6
be. This was not where I was spawned. Strange places had
usurped the names of towns I used to know. It was like what the
British during World War II, fearing an invasion, had done, setting
real but wrong place-names and roadsigns around the country-

side so that the enemy in, say, Kent would find himself in villages belonging to Lancashire.

Gone were the spreading cottonfields I remembered, though   7
this was the season when they should have been beginning to
whiten. The few patches that remained were small and sparse,
like the patches of snow lingering on in sunless spots in New
England in March and April. The prairie grass that had been there
before the fields were broken for cotton had reclaimed them. The
woods were gone . . . grazing land now, nearly all of it. For in a
move that reverses Texas history, a move totally opposite to
what I knew in my childhood, one which all but turns the world
upside down, which makes the sun set in the East, Red River
Country has ceased to be Old South and become Far West. I who
for years had had to set my Northern friends straight by pointing
out that I was a Southerner, not a Westerner, and that I had never
seen a cowboy or for that matter a beefcow any more than they
had, found myself now in that Texas of legend and the popular
image which when I was a child had seemed more romantic to
me than to a boy of New England precisely because it was closer
to me than to him and yet still worlds away. Gone from the
square were the bib overalls of my childhood when the farmers
came to town on Saturday. Ranchers now, they came in high-
heeled boots and rolled-brim hats, a costume that would have
provoked as much surprise, and even more derision, there, in my
time, as it would on Manhattan's Madison Avenue.

You can never ascend the same river twice, an early philoso-   8
pher tells us. Its course, its composition are ever changing. Even
so, one of its natives knows it, even one, like the salmon, who
has spent most of his life away. I had been away from Clarksville
since my father's death, and although ever since then I had been
surprised each day to find myself alive, I was now an older man
than he had lived to be. In that time much had changed in
Clarksville; still, it was where I belonged.

Just as the salmon must leave home when the time comes,   9
so he must return to round out his life. There where he was born,
he dies.

DISCUSSION: CONTENT

1. What activity involving Humphrey personally prompted him to
   contemplate the instinctive behavior of salmon?

2. Following Humphrey, briefly describe the amazing life cycle of the salmon.
3. How do salmon find their way back to their spawning grounds?
4. What surprising changes does Humphrey observe about the land surrounding Clarksville?
5. Why does Humphrey say that the Texas of legend—its cowboys and beef cattle—was more romantic to him as a boy than it was to others?

DISCUSSION: FORM

1. What points do the author's behavior and that of a salmon have in common?
2. What additional similarity does Humphrey contemplate in the last two paragraphs?
3. What expository purpose does the analogy involving the salmon serve in this essay?
4. To make his analogy more successful, Humphrey on occasion personifies salmon, giving them human attributes, and likewise refers to himself using terminology more suitable to salmon. Cite some instances of both uses.

Feeding the Mind

LEWIS CARROLL

Lewis Carroll was the pseudonym for Charles L. Dodgson (1832–1898), a British mathematician, logician, and teacher at Oxford University. He is best known for nonsense verse, mathematical riddles, fantasies, and children's stories, especially Alice's Adventures in Wonderland *(1865) and* Through the Looking-Glass *(1872). Carroll's wit and unconventional viewpoint may also be seen in the following essay.*

Breakfast, dinner, tea; in extreme cases, breakfast, luncheon, dinner, tea, supper, and a glass of something hot at bedtime. What care we take about feeding the lucky body! Which of us does as much for his mind? And what causes the difference? Is the body so much the more important of the two?

By no means; but life depends on the body being fed, whereas   2
we can continue to exist as animals (scarcely as men) though the
mind be utterly starved and neglected. Therefore Nature provides
that, in case of serious neglect of the body, such terrible consequences of discomfort and pain shall ensue as will soon bring us
back to a sense of our duty; and some of the functions necessary
to life she does for us altogether, leaving us no choice in the
matter. It would fare but ill with many of us if we were left to
superintend our own digestion and circulation. "Bless me!" one
would cry, "I forgot to wind up my heart this morning! To think
that it has been standing still for the last three hours!" "I can't
walk with you this afternoon," a friend would say, "as I have no
less than eleven dinners to digest. I had to let them stand over
from last week, being so busy—and my doctor says he will not
answer for the consequences if I wait any longer!"

Well it is, I say, for us, that the consequences of neglecting   3
the body can be clearly seen and felt; and it might be well for
some if the mind were equally visible and tangible—if we could
take it, say, to the doctor and have its pulse felt!

"Why, what have you been doing with this mind lately? How   4
have you fed it? It looks pale, and the pulse is very slow."

"Well, doctor, it has not had much regular food lately. I gave   5
it a lot of sugar-plums yesterday."

"Sugar-plums! What kind?"   6

"Well, they were a parcel of conundrums, sir."   7

"Ah! I thought so. Now just mind this: if you go on playing   8
tricks like that, you'll spoil all its teeth, and get laid up with
mental indigestion. You must have nothing but the plainest
reading for the next few days. Take care now! No novels on any
account!"

Considering the amount of painful experience many of us   9
have had in feeding and dosing the body, it would, I think, be
quite worth our while to try to translate some of the rules into
corresponding ones for the mind.

First, then, we should set ourselves to provide for our mind   10
its *proper kind* of food; we very soon learn what will, and what
will not, agree with the body, and find little difficulty in refusing
a piece of the tempting pudding or pie which is associated in our
memory with that terrible attack of indigestion, and whose very
name irresistibly recalls rhubarb and magnesia; but it takes a
great many lessons to convince us how indigestible some of our

favorite lines of reading are, and again and again we make a meal
of the unwholesome novel, sure to be followed by its usual train
of low spirits, unwillingness to work, weariness of existence—in
fact by mental nightmare.

Then we should be careful to provide this wholesome food in   11
proper amount. Mental gluttony, or overreading, is a dangerous
propensity, tending to weakness of digestive power, and in some
cases to loss of appetite; we know that bread is a good and
wholesome food, but who would like to try the experiment of
eating two or three loaves at a sitting?

I have heard of a physician telling his patient—whose com-   12
plaint was merely gluttony and want of exercise—that "the earliest symptom of hypernutrition is a deposition of adipose
tissue," and no doubt the fine long words greatly consoled the
poor man under his increasing load of fat.

I wonder if there is such a thing in nature as a *fat mind!* I   13
really think I have met with one or two minds which could not
keep up with the slowest trot in conversation, could not jump
over a logical fence to save their lives, always got stuck fast in a
narrow argument, and, in short, were fit for nothing but to wad-
dle helplessly through the world.

Then, again, though the food be wholesome and in proper   14
amount, we know that we must not consume *too many kinds at
once.* Take the thirsty haymaker a quart of beer, or a quart of
cider, or even a quart of cold tea, and he will probably thank you
(though not so heartily in the last case!). But what think you his
feelings would be if you offered him a tray containing a little mug
of beer, a little mug of cider, another of cold tea, one of hot tea,
one of coffee, one of cocoa, and corresponding vessels of milk,
water, brandy-and-water, and buttermilk? The sum total might
be a quart, but would it be the same thing to the haymaker?

Having settled the proper kind, amount, and variety of our   15
mental food, it remains that we should be careful to allow *proper
intervals* between meal and meal, and not swallow the food
hastily without mastication, so that it may be thoroughly di-
gested; both of which rules for the body are also applicable at
once to the mind.

First as to the intervals: these are as really necessary as they   16
are for the body, with this difference only, that while the body
requires three or four hours' rest before it is ready for another
meal, the mind will in many cases do with three or four minutes.

I believe that the interval required is much shorter than is generally supposed, and from personal experience I would recommend anyone who has to devote several hours together to one subject of thought to try the effect of such a break, say once an hour—leaving off for five minutes only, each time, but taking care to throw the mind absolutely "out of gear" for those five minutes, and to turn it entirely to other subjects. It is astonishing what an amount of impetus and elasticity the mind recovers during those short periods of rest.

And then as to the mastication of the food: the mental process answering to this is simply *thinking over* what we read. This is a very much greater exertion of mind than the mere passive taking in the contents of our author—so much greater an exertion is it, that, as Coleridge says, the mind often "angrily refuses" to put itself to such trouble—so much greater, that we are far too apt to neglect it altogether, and go on pouring in fresh food on the top of the undigested masses already lying there, till the unfortunate mind is fairly swamped under the flood. But the greater the exertion, the more valuable, we may be sure, is the effect; one hour of steady thinking over a subject (a solitary walk is as good an opportunity for the process as any other) is worth two or three of reading only.   17

And just consider another effect of this thorough digestion of the books we read; I mean the arranging and "ticketing," so to speak, of the subjects in our minds, so that we can readily refer to them when we want them. Sam Slick tells us that he has learned several languages in his life, but somehow "couldn't keep the parcels sorted" in his mind; and many a mind that hurries through book after book, without waiting to digest or arrange anything, gets into that sort of condition, and the unfortunate owner finds himself far from fit really to support the character all his friends give him.   18

"A thoroughly well-read man. Just you try him in any subject, now. You can't puzzle him!"   19

You turn to the thoroughly well-read man, you ask him a question, say, in English history (he is understood to have just finished reading Macaulay); he smiles good-naturedly, tries to look as if he knew all about it, and proceeds to dive into his mind for the answer. Up comes a handful of very promising facts, but on examination they turn out to belong to the wrong century, and are pitched in again; a second haul brings up a fact much more like the real thing, but unfortunately along with it   20 comes a tangle of other things—a fact in political economy, a rule in arithmetic, the ages of his brother's children, and a stanza of Gray's "Elegy"; and among all these the fact he wants has got hopelessly twisted up and entangled. Meanwhile everyone is waiting for his reply, and as the silence is getting more and more awkward, our well-read friend has to stammer out some half-answer at last, not nearly so clear or so satisfactory as an ordinary schoolboy would have given. And all this for want of making up his knowledge into proper bundles and ticketing them!

Do you know the unfortunate victim of ill-judged mental 21 feeding when you see him? Can you doubt him? Look at him drearily wandering around a reading-room, tasting dish after dish—we beg his pardon, book after book—keeping to none. First a mouthful of novel—but, no, faugh! he has had nothing but that to eat for the last week, and is quite tired of the taste; then a slice of science, but you know at once what the result of that will be—ah, of course, much too tough for *his* teeth. And so on through the old weary round, which he tried (and failed in) yesterday, and will probably try, and fail in, tomorrow.

Mr. Oliver Wendell Holmes, in his very amusing book *The* 22 *Professor at the Breakfast-table,* gives the following rule for knowing whether a human being is young or old. "The crucial experiment is this. Offer a bulky bun to the suspected individual just ten minutes before dinner. If this is easily accepted and devoured, the fact of youth is established." He tells us that a human being, "if young, will eat anything at any hour of the day or night."

To ascertain the healthiness of the *mental* appetite of a hu- 23 man animal, place in its hands a short, well-written, but not exciting treatise on some popular subject—a mental *bun,* in fact. If it is read with eager interest and perfect attention, *and if the reader can answer questions on the subject afterwards,* the mind is in first-rate working order; if it be politely laid down again, or perhaps lounged over for a few minutes, and then, "I can't read this stupid book! Would you hand me the second volume of *The Mysterious Murder?*" you may be equally sure that there is something wrong in the mental digestion.

If this paper has given you any useful hints on the important 24 subject of reading, and made you see that it is one's duty no less than one's interest to "read, mark, learn, and inwardly digest" the good books that fall in your way, its purpose will be fulfilled.

DISCUSSION: CONTENT

1. List Carroll's five rules for the proper feeding of the mind.
2. To what process involved in feeding the body does Carroll liken thinking over what we have read?
3. The supposedly well-read person who cannot summon up a piece of needed information is suffering from what failure?
4. How does Oliver Wendell Holmes distinguish a young person from an old one? How does Carroll apply Holmes's rule to the readers he is discussing?

DISCUSSION: FORM

1. Although the central analogy here is Carroll's likening reading to eating, he uses at least one other analogical comparison. Locate it.
2. Into how many parts does Carroll *divide* his analogy?
3. Where does he use overlapping language, as the students did in "Sunbathing on Scott Beach" and "Fishing for the Buyer"?
4. What comment would you make about the **tone** of this essay (Carroll's attitude toward his subject and audience)? How does he achieve this stance? What words and phrases reveal this tone?

The Iks

LEWIS THOMAS

Lewis Thomas (b. 1913) is an American physician and medical researcher who has held various important administrative posts at medical schools and medical research centers. A frequent contributor to medical journals and science periodicals, Dr. Thomas has published six books of essays. The Lives of a Cell (1974), in which the following essay first appeared, won the National Book award that year. His other books include The Medusa and the Snail (1979), The Youngest Science (1983), Late Night Thoughts on Listening to Mahler's Ninth Symphony (1983), Et Cetera, Et Cetera (1990), and The Fragile Species (1992).

The small tribe of Iks, formerly hunters and gatherers in the   1
mountain valleys of northern Uganda, have become celebrities,

literary symbols for the ultimate fate of disheartened, heartless mankind at large. Two disastrously conclusive things happened to them: the government decided to have a national park, so they were compelled by law to give up hunting in the valleys and become farmers on poor hillside soil, and then they were visited for two years by an anthropologist who detested them and wrote a book about them.

The message of the book is that the Iks have transformed themselves into an irreversibly disagreeable collection of unattached, brutish creatures, totally selfish and loveless, in response to the dismantling of their traditional culture. Moreover, this is what the rest of us are like in our inner selves, and we will all turn into Iks when the structure of our society becomes unhinged. 2

The argument rests, of course, on certain assumptions about the core of human beings, and is necessarily speculative. You have to agree in advance that man is fundamentally a bad lot, out for himself alone, displaying such graces as affection and compassion only as learned habits. If you take this view, the story of the Iks can be used to confirm it. These people seem to be living together, clustered in small, dense villages, but they are really solitary, unrelated individuals with no evident use for each other. They talk, but only to make ill-tempered demands and cold refusals. They share nothing. They never sing. They turn the children out to forage as soon as they can walk, and desert the elders to starve whenever they can, and the foraging children snatch food from the mouths of the helpless elders. It is a mean society. 3

They breed without love or even casual regard. They defecate on each other's doorsteps. They watch their neighbors for signs of misfortune, and only then do they laugh. In the book they do a lot of laughing, having so much bad luck. Several times they even laughed at the anthropologist, who found this especially repellent (one senses, between the lines, that the scholar is not himself the world's luckiest man). Worse, they took him into the family, snatched his food, defecated on his doorstep, and hooted dislike at him. They gave him two bad years. 4

It is a depressing book. If, as he suggests, there is only Ikness at the center of each of us, our sole hope for hanging on to the name of humanity will be in endlessly mending the structure of our society, and it is changing so quickly and completely that we may never find the threads in time. Meanwhile, left to ourselves 5

alone, solitary, we will become the same joyless, zestless, un-
touching lone animals.

But this may be too narrow a view. For one thing, the Iks are 6
extraordinary. They are absolutely astonishing, in fact. The anthropologist has never seen people like them anywhere, nor have
I. You'd think, if they were simply examples of the common
essence of mankind, they'd seem more recognizable. Instead,
they are bizarre, anomalous. I have known my share of peculiar,
difficult, nervous, grabby people, but I've never encountered any
genuinely, consistently detestable human beings in all my life.
The Iks sound more like abnormalities, maladies.

I cannot accept it. I do not believe that the Iks are repre- 7
sentative of isolated, revealed man, unobscured by social habits.
I believe their behavior is something extra, something laid on.
This unremitting, compulsive repellence is a kind of complicated
ritual. They must have learned to act this way; they copied it,
somehow.

I have a theory then. The Iks have gone crazy. 8

The solitary Ik, isolated in the ruins of an exploded culture, 9
has built a new defense for himself. If you live in an unworkable
society you can make up one of your own, and this is what the
Iks have done. Each Ik has become a group, a one-man tribe on
its own, a constituency.

Now everything falls into place. This is why they do seem, 10
after all, vaguely familiar to all of us. We've seen them before.
This is precisely the way groups of one size or another, ranging
from committees to nations, behave. It is, of course, this aspect
of humanity that has lagged behind the rest of evolution, and this
is why the Ik seems so primitive. In his absolute selfishness, his
incapacity to give anything away, no matter what, he is a successful committee. When he stands at the door of his hut, shouting insults at his neighbors in a loud harangue, he is a city
addressing another city.

Cities have all the Ik characteristics. They defecate on door- 11
steps, in rivers and lakes, their own or anybody else's. They leave
rubbish. They detest all neighboring cities, give nothing away.
They even build institutions for deserting elders out of sight.

Nations are the most Iklike of all. No wonder the Iks seem 12
familiar. For total greed, rapacity, heartlessness, and irresponsi-
bility there is nothing to match a nation. There is no such thing
as affection between nations, and certainly no nation ever loved
another. They bawl insults from their doorsteps, defecate into

whole oceans, snatch all the food, survive by detestation, take joy in the bad luck of others, celebrate the death of others, live for the death of others.

That's it, and I shall stop worrying about the book. It does not signify that man is a sparse, inhuman thing at his center. He's all right. It only says what we've always known and never had enough time to worry about, that we haven't yet learned how to stay human when assembled in masses. The Ik, in his despair, is acting out this failure, and perhaps we should pay closer attention. Nations have themselves become too frightening to think about, but we might learn some things by watching these people.

DISCUSSION: CONTENT

1. Who are the Iks? Where do they live? What two things happened to the Iks that changed their lives forever?
2. How did the Iks respond to the changes in their lives?
3. Thomas suggests that the Iks have all gone crazy. He is not serious, of course, but he does use this comment to introduce his central observation about human beings. What is that observation?
4. Thomas has learned about the Iks by reading the report of the anthropologist who lived with them and wrote about them. How do his conclusions about the behavior of the Iks differ from those expressed by the anthropologist?

DISCUSSION: FORM

1. Thomas constructs an analogy that compares the behavior of each individual Ik to the behavior of modern cities and nations. What kinds of behavior do these entities have in common?
2. At what point does Thomas begin to draw his analogy? What had he been doing before that point?
3. Analogies are very much like comparisons. How would you describe Thomas's analogy in terms of the comparison it makes; that is, does Thomas proceed by points or by topics?

10

Cause and Effect

Hardly a day goes by that we are not confronted with some perplexing situation, one that moves us to ask the question *Why?* In asking *why*, we are following a natural line of reasoning, another of those convenient channels in which human thoughts flow; we are performing *causal analysis.* Since our tendency to ask *why* is so natural, it follows that causal analysis—explaining causes and effects—is one of the most useful and valuable tasks you can perform as a writer.

When you set out to answer any question involving *why*, you will be seeking to make a statement of cause. Why did the Japanese attack Pearl Harbor? Why did the cake fail to rise? Why did the team lose the game? Any useful answers to these questions will clearly be reasons or causes. Some of these questions need only a single answer. For instance, the reason for the cake's not rising was the failure of the cook to follow the recipe, which called for baking powder. The reasons for the assault on Pearl Harbor or the team's loss may be much more complicated. Yet whatever the causes may be and however complex they may appear, you should be prepared to make some fairly clear observations about them.

Immediate and Remote Causes

Causes may be divided into *immediate* causes and *remote* causes. For example, we might assert that the attack on Pearl

Harbor was precipitated by the Japanese nation's abiding commitment to sea power—especially control of the Pacific seaways. If this was true, then the U.S. Pacific fleet based at Pearl Harbor posed a threat to their control of the Pacific. So it follows that the desire to eliminate a presumed obstacle was an immediate cause, while the commitment to sea power was a more remote cause. We might go on to claim that the commitment to sea power arose from the geographical isolation Japan as a nation had always enjoyed, an even more remote cause.

You should understand that for any given effect there can be a number of immediate and remote causes. The threat posed by the U.S. Pacific fleet was not the only immediate cause for the attack on Pearl Harbor; vast petroleum reserves stored at Pearl Harbor might also have been used by land and air forces to threaten Japan. Likewise, Japan's commitment to nautical supremacy would have been more tolerant of the U.S. Pacific Fleet had the Japanese government not entered into an alliance with the Axis bloc of Nazi Germany and Fascist Italy, whose implicit aim was world domination.

Immediate and Remote Effects

The situations just analyzed—the simple case of the fallen cake and the attack on Pearl Harbor—are effects of the causes we have at least partially enumerated. But just as causes may be both immediate and remote, so may be the effects. More remote effects of the lack of baking powder, beyond the immediate effect of the fallen cake, might be the ruination of supper and a loss of esteem for the cook. Less trivially, the attack on Pearl Harbor, while it was the result of Japan's fear of American sea power, was also the cause of a more colossal effect, America's entry into World War II, together with a galvanizing of American sentiments against the Axis powers. So, as you see, effects in turn become causes and lead to other effects, and so on.

As you can easily imagine, causal analysis is not only useful in determining what happened and why after an actual event, but it is also very useful in a number of theoretical situations. The emphasis then is on finding solutions to problems. Again, this is a natural human tendency. Just as the conscientious cook will try to determine why the cake fell, with the intent of ensuring that the next attempt will be successful, so do you often find yourself proposing ways to correct or to avoid unsatisfactory effects or results. For instance, when you fasten your seatbelt before driving off, you are practicing this sort of causal analysis. You theorize that *if* you are in an accident, you are less likely to be injured if you have buckled up.

Naturally, this same tendency finds expression in writing at all levels, from letters pointing out flaws in public policy through technical instructions that warn of dangers if certain procedures are not followed. Clearly, then, causal analysis is an expository writing technique that you'll want to master.

Therefore, while you read and analyze the following selections, try to determine in each instance whether the writer is informing you of the cause or causes of a particular event or situation, or whether it is the writer's purpose to discuss the effects arising from an event or situation. Or is the writer dealing with *both* causes and effects? Furthermore, is the writer's emphasis on an event that has already occurred, or on one that may or should occur?

Bear in mind too just how useful the techniques of cause and effect can be in your own writing. As a student, you may be called on to list the causes for a particular chemical reaction or the reasons why at some point in history a certain political institution failed. You may also be obliged to explain the effects of behavioral psychology on American education or the effects of increased protein consumption in a family's diet. Furthermore, because of its obvious usefulness in problem-solving, your mastery of this technique is especially crucial if you have plans for a career in a scientific, engineering, or other technical field. Clearly, then, the section that follows is an important one. Study it carefully.

Commentary on Student Work

The following student paper was written after a classroom discussion had focused on the treatment of effects arising from a particular causal event in Aldo Leopold's "Thinking Like a Mountain" (Chapter 1), and on the treatment of several causes that produce a particular effect in Donna Kaminski's "Where Are the Female Einsteins?" (p. 254).

Delisa began her prewriting exercises by copying onto a page of her journal several personal problems, one of which was titled "procrastination about studies." Next, she began to assemble some notions associated with this problem, arranging them to the right or left of it, depending on whether she viewed them as causes of that situation or effects arising from it. After awhile, her work took on the shape of an outline that looked like Figure 10.1.

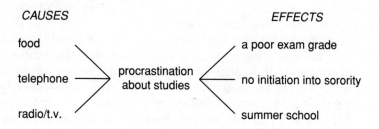

CAUSES   *EFFECTS*

food   a poor exam grade

telephone → procrastination ← no initiation into sorority
              about studies

radio/t.v.   summer school

FIGURE 10.1

Delisa studied the outline for a while and settled on treating only half of the topic posed by the brainstorming exercise (the first half), the part dealing with the several causes for her tendency to procrastinate at study time. it seemed, at least, to be the lighter of the two possibilities; the other was too filled with unpleasant outcomes. She began free-writing and produced this paragraph, which she took to class for discussion:

Whenever I get serious about sitting down to study, I get distracted. I get hungry just looking at the refrigerator, and I have to take time out to satisfy my taste buds. Another distraction is the telephone. I will be in the middle of some important piece of study, and the telephone rings. Of course, I have to answer it and talk for a while. I can't be rude. Finally, I get distracted by the television or by the radio. I can't study until the latest episode of my favorite soap opera has ended or until the top forty songs have been played.

Delisa's paragraph enjoyed an enthusiastic reception from her student group. They suggested that she could easily expand it into a full essay with at least one paragraph devoted to each of the three distractions. An introduction and a conclusion would round the essay off. Each of the paragraphs dealing with distractions needed concrete examples of the kinds of foods, the kinds of calls, and the kinds of television and radio shows that proved to be the worst distractions. There was some talk about favorite foods and television shows, and soon Delisa had a page full of notes.

With the addition of the suggested examples, Delisa's single paragraph grew to three, but there she was stymied for the weekend. Finally, on Monday morning she took the paper to the writing lab, where the graduate student who helped her suggested more attention to the transitional devices that linked the three example paragraphs together. The subject turned next to the introduction and conclusion, and the tutor asked Delisa which cause/effect essays in the collection she had read. Together they looked again at the Leopold essay, and it was Delisa who noticed the clever way that Leopold had begun his essay with a discussion of the predator wolf and had concluded by returning to it. Turning this notion over in her mind, she went back to her room. In time for class, she completed this essay.

Study Habit Blues

"Just one more cookie and then I *will* start studying." How many times has a student caught herself saying that as the homework piles up and the hours tick by? I myself am a chronic homework procrastinator. I simply will do anything rather than sit down and do homework assignments. But sometimes it is not my fault. It seems that whenever I get serious about sitting down to study, I get distracted.

One of the reasons why I get distracted is food, or simply wanting to eat. The minute I sit down to read my English textbook, the thought suddenly pops into my head, "Wouldn't a piece of Mom's apple pie be great to eat before I start reading this?" Or if I happen to make the mistake of passing through the kitchen on the way to the den to begin studying and even glance at the refrigerator, I take a detour and concentrate on satisfying my taste buds. Food is my greatest distraction when trying to study.

Another thing that I have found distracting when trying to study is the incessant ringing of the telephone. More times than I care to remember, I will be in the middle of studying for a vocabulary test, and the telephone rings. "Hey, it's for you." Naturally, one cannot be rude and decline to speak to the person, and so thirty minutes or more of studying time are used up. This can be very frustrating when I receive four or more phone calls a day.

A third reason why I get distracted when attempting to study is the allure of radio and television. Before sitting down to study, I will out of habit turn on the television set or radio, depending on whichever I am closer to at the time. If the "Richard Simmons Show" is on or "Days of Our Lives," I simply cannot move until I learn that new exercise for the hips or find out what is happening between Jessica and Don Craig. The same principle can be applied to the radio. All of the Top Forty rock-and-roll hits are my favorites, and chances are that if I turn the radio on, one of these songs will be playing. So naturally I must hear it in its entirety, and perhaps the one after that, and the one after that, and so on, until an hour or more has passed with no studying done.

The above are the main distractions that I encounter when trying to study. But just these few are enough to detain me for hours. So after I have "pigged out" on food, chatted to my friends, and listened to my favorite songs, I must get serious about studying. Unless I just happen to peek into the cookie jar and think, "Just one more cookie and then I *will* start studying."

DISCUSSION QUESTIONS

1. What clever device does the writer use to create an overall sense of unity and completeness in this essay?
2. What device does the writer use to link the discussions of her three main distractions together?
3. What is the effect of mentioning the names of particular television programs, together with the names of characters from one of them, rather than simply mentioning exercise shows and soap operas?

STUDENT WORK

Why Students Leave College

There seem to be six basic reasons why some of our classmates will not be with us when graduation day arrives in four years. The first to leave are the dissatisfied, such as my high school friend who could not adjust to being away from home and among so many strangers. Next to leave are those who get sick or have bad accidents. This happened to a girl down the hall in my dormitory, but she plans to be back after Christmas. Another reason to leave is marriage, either "shotgun" style or being unable to wait until summer or graduation. Also, after the first year or two, some students transfer, either for the reasons that might also make them drop out (get closer to home, marry, money problems) or to earn a degree only offered elsewhere. I, for instance, have been thinking about changing to an engineering major, and I would have to transfer to N.C. State after my sophomore year to finish up. There are two final reasons that cause dropouts: money problems and bad grades. College students everywhere are always short on funds, as seen by such signs as "Dad, Send $. Chip" held up on televised college games; there always seems to be something else to buy—and not just snacks and beer, either. (I know my checkbook balance stays sick, and I've had one emergency loan from home already.) Sometimes even with a part-time job the financial drain cannot be plugged, and students must drop out to work full-time for a while. Finally, some students cannot handle the academic part of college life. For many reasons, from too much partying to weak high school preparation, they flunk out of school. In fact, after looking back over this list, it will be surprising if anyone sitting in this class will be left to graduate in four years.

DISCUSSION QUESTIONS

1. What transitional phrases does the writer use to list the six reasons for leaving school mentioned in the topic sentence?

2. What is the purpose of the sentence that begins, "Also, after the first year or two . . ."? Does this sentence provide a new reason for leaving school? If so, what? If not, why is it in the paragraph?
3. What other expository strategy is abundantly evident in this paragraph?

Robert Redford Moves to Lenoir

Lenoir is a small town where almost everyone knows everyone else, or at least who their parents were and who they married. Life is very calm and peaceful, with people enjoying their homes, families, and friends. Nothing of national importance or deserving national attention happens there; a few politicians have campaigned and caused a tremendous momentary stir in the community, but life soon returned to normal. Yet I sometimes wonder what would happen if a movie star like Robert Redford moved to Lenoir.

First, the moving van would appear, and neighbors, especially the women, would start looking out their windows, inspecting the furniture and speculating about the newcomer's bank account, life-style, and job. Women all over town would know within twenty-four hours about the new residents.

After a week of minor excitement the neighborhood would get back to normal. The movers, painters, carpet servicemen, and various other people will have finished their work, and the only thing lacking will be the arrival of the new neighbors. Then one afternoon a car pulls up in front of the house, and simultaneously women peek out between sheer curtains in bedrooms and living rooms. A tall, beautiful blonde woman steps out of the car, and children pile out behind her, running for the house, excited at the prospect of moving into a new home. Now all spying eyes center on the next person getting out of the car. A tall, rugged blond man with sunglasses on steps out and looks around. As he begins strolling easily toward the house, it is easy to imagine the resulting telephone conversations of the neighborhood women. They are struck nearly dumb by the realization that the man of their dreams is moving into their neighborhood. Robert Redford! It is simply too good to be true!

By nightfall, every woman and teen-aged girl in Lenoir knows 4
of the luck which has befallen them. Some nonbelievers actually
ride by the home, hoping for a glimpse of their idol. The men,
though, scoff at this excitement and at the way women are acting
over this "ordinary" man. Secretly, they are half-jealous and
half-curious; so during the following week at the houses near the
Redfords' the grass gets cut more often, or the garbage is carried
out promptly, or fathers decide that their sons need extra softball
practice in the backyard, or friends—even mere acquaintances—
drop by for a variety of reasons, mostly contrived. Everyone in
town finds something to do in that special neighborhood. In
some cases, even old grudges are buried in order to get closer to
the house and, for a lucky few, to see its inhabitants.

It is impossible, of course, for small-town people, such as 5
those in Lenoir, to try to act normally when Mrs. Redford walks
into a store to buy a dress. Salespeople all but run over one
another to wait on her, anticipating a large sale, and also to see
if their hero has a wife worthy of him. In the end she smiles
graciously and asks to see something a little less expensive,
saying the dress is nice, but costs a bit more than she wants to
spend. By nightfall the news is out—Mrs. Redford is a sale nut, a
bargain hunter!

Meanwhile, the neighborhood is buzzing with still another 6
news item—Robert Redford carries out his own garbage! And his
wife was actually overheard asking him to please cut the grass
that day. That afternoon when the usual crowd of high-school
girls takes the new route home through the Redford neighborhood, they nearly swoon when they spot *him* cutting grass,
wearing shorts and no shirt. After that the traffic is terrible in the
afternoons.

Men and boys laugh at the women for the crazy way they are 7
acting. But motorcycle sales have nearly tripled since Robert
Redford was seen riding one. And after a teen-aged boy discovered that Robert Redford sends his wife a single red rose every
day, the sale of roses has also skyrocketed. Jogging has also
become the chic exercise since the glamorous couple were seen
jogging after dinner in matching sweat suits.

Certainly if Robert Redford ever did move to Lenoir, it would 8
be by far the biggest thing ever to happen, and it would be
discussed by generations to come.

DISCUSSION QUESTIONS

1. Perhaps Robert Redford will never move to Lenoir, or to your hometown, but if he did, how would the effects differ from those described in the student essay?
2. How many effects are listed? Are they in the best order?
3. What different results might occur if the new resident were a female movie star?

The Downfall of Downtown

Almost every average-sized American town or city has seen   1
its downtown business decrease considerably since the early
1970's. This drop in business is the result of the construction of
huge, modern shopping malls. Until these new creations became
popular, most downtown stores were not experiencing any serious financial difficulties.

Then, as the 1970's began, the idea of constructing shopping   2
malls just outside the city limits spread like wildfire. Plans were
made; convenient sites were selected; contracts were signed; and
then construction began. The idea of a mall being located in their
hometown always excited the local residents, and they anxiously
awaited the grand opening.

The location of the mall is in itself a great contributing factor   3
to its success. The shopper is not confronted with countless
stoplights and parking meters as he is on Main Street. Instead,
his trip to the mall on a freeway or bypass is quick and convenient, and parking in the vast lots is free.

The new mall is also always a sight to behold. In the new,   4
spacious stores, the customer is swept away by the pleasing
surroundings, which include tasteful displays, modern furnishings, modish young salespersons, and other agreeable features
that lure buyers. Not only are the stores themselves pleasing to
the customer, but the enclosed areas connecting them are an
important element that always brings him back to the mall.
Unlike the downtown stores where one must go outside on the
street and expose himself to all kinds of inclement weather in
order to go from one store to another, the hallways in shopping
malls are always kept at a desirable temperature and humidity.
There are no passing cars to splash water on shoppers' clothes,
no icy winds to blow away hats and chill cheeks and ears, no hills

to climb. Instead, there is a pleasant, restful atmosphere, with a variety of plants, a multitude of bubbling fountains, a scattering of comfortable benches, plus several effort-saving escalators. Is it any wonder that consumers abandoned the downtown stores and their inconveniences?

Shortly after the malls are completed, the finer stores move 5 from their old buildings on Main Street to the new mall. Only the small shops, owned by those who cannot afford to lease a space in the mall, are left in the downtown section. Of course, fewer and fewer customers will venture onto Main Street to shop in small, dark, seemingly ancient buildings run by old men and women who crouch in tiny back rooms, sipping coffee between spells of coughing. FOR SALE OR LEASE signs appear on increasing numbers of vacant downtown buildings, so that soon a walk down Main Street is much like a walk down a street in a ghost town.

Thus, because of the success of the malls, downtown busi- 6 ness across the nation has been reduced terribly, leading city governments to attempt a variety of rescue efforts, intended to revive that business and bring customers back (and, incidentally, to preserve an important part of the tax base). Such promotions as sidewalk sales and downtown festivals have been tried, mostly vain attempts to boost slow sales. Officials have even tried removing parking meters in order to regain customers.

Generally, however, all such attempts are failures. The malls 7 become increasingly successful, while downtown conditions become even worse. Soon there is nothing left but a few privately owned shops and stores, the chain operations having long since fled to the mall. Many of these remaining stores have no place in a mall even if the owners could afford the rent. For example, one does not expect to see a used clothing store or a paperback book shop in a modern shopping mall, not to speak of a pawn shop or an adult book and novelty store. Other downtown businesses include department stores, often dilapidated. Their operators are usually elderly persons who do not remodel their premises because they question whether or not they will live to see the completion of the project, or else are so set in their ways that they stubbornly refuse to modernize.

It is therefore clear that the downtown areas of most Ameri- 8 can cities will deteriorate more and more, just as city apartments and homes are also becoming decrepit and unsightly as residents flee to suburban housing developments, often to be nearer the new shopping malls.

DISCUSSION QUESTIONS

1. In this essay, does the writer concentrate on the causes for the downfall of downtown or on the effects, or both?
2. What is the purpose of paragraphs 1–5? Of paragraphs 6–8? How do you account for the natural break that occurs between paragraphs 5 and 6?
3. What technique that you studied earlier does the writer use with particular effectiveness in paragraphs 4 and 7?

PARAGRAPHS

W-a-t-e-r

HELEN KELLER

We walked down the path to the wellhouse, attracted by the fragrance of the honeysuckle with which it was covered. Someone was drawing water and my teacher placed my hand under the spout. As the cool stream gushed over one hand, she spelled into the other the word *water*, first slowly, then rapidly. I stood still, my whole attention fixed upon the motions of her fingers. Suddenly I felt a misty consciousness as of something forgotten—a thrill of returning thought; and somehow the mystery of language was revealed to me. I knew then that "w-a-t-e-r" meant the wonderful cool something that was flowing over my hand. That living word awakened my soul, gave it light, hope, joy, set it free! There were barriers still, it is true, but barriers that could in time be swept away.

DISCUSSION QUESTIONS

1. This paragraph is probably the most important one in Helen Keller's autobiography, *The Story of My Life*. Perhaps you have read that book, or know something of Keller's life from the play or the movie (*The Miracle Worker*) based on it. A child of seven, she was blind, deaf, and mute, and her teacher, Anne Sullivan,

had been frustrated in all attempts to break through that barrier of darkness and silence. This episode marks the first breach in the barrier. Yet even in the single paragraph there are suggestions, through word choice and figurative language, about the crucial nature of this experience. Identify those key words and figures of speech.

2. The fact that this paragraph is a small part of a biography also recalls something else: the connection between process, cause and effect, and narration. What event in your life could you relate that integrates these three modes?

Little Lost Appetite

ANDREW WARD

I was sitting at an inn with Kelly Susan, my ten-year-old niece, when she was handed the children's menu. It was printed in gay pastels on construction paper and gave her a choice of a Ferdinand Burger, a Freddie the Fish Stick, or a Porky Pig Sandwich. Like most children's menus, it first anthropomorphized the ingredients and then killed them off. As Kelly read it her eyes grew large, and in them I could see gentle Ferdinand being led away to the stockyard, Freddie gasping at the end of a hook, Porky stuttering his entreaties as the ax descended. Kelly Susan, alone in her family, is a resolute vegetarian and has already faced up to the dread that whispers to us as we slice our steaks. She wound up ordering a cheese sandwich, but the children's menu had ruined her appetite, and she spent the meal picking at her food.

DISCUSSION QUESTIONS

1. What is the exact cause of Kelly Susan's lost appetite?
2. Although the movement of this paragraph is from cause to effect, the paragraph itself is illustrative of other methods of development you have studied earlier. What methods are those?
3. Look up *personification* in the Glossary. Besides pointing out the anthropomorphizing of the three animals on the menu, Ward uses a more subtle personification. Where is it?

Smells and Our Memories

DIANE ACKERMAN

Nothing is more memorable than a smell. One scent can be unexpected, momentary, and fleeting, yet conjure up a childhood summer beside a lake in the Poconos, when wild blueberry bushes teemed with succulent fruit and the opposite sex was as mysterious as space travel; another, hours of passion on a moon-lit beach in Florida, while the night-blooming cereus drenched the air with thick curds of perfume and huge sphinx moths visited the cereus in a loud purr of wings; a third, a family dinner of pot roast, noodle pudding, and sweet potatoes, during a myr-tle-mad August in a midwestern town, when both of one's parents were alive. Smells detonate softly in our memory like poignant land mines, hidden under the weedy mass of many years and experiences. Hit a tripwire of smell, and memories explode all at once. A complex vision leaps out of the under-growth.

DISCUSSION QUESTIONS

1. Ackerman announces her thesis in the topic sentence that begins her paragraph. How many supporting examples does she provide? Which is the most specific?
2. Mark the qualities, details, and comparisons in the last three sentences. What image or mental picture unifies those sentences? Is the emphasis there on causes or effects?
3. Try to recall your own experiences by substituting memories and their smells from your past for those in Ackerman's second sentence. Try to be more detailed and concrete than she is in the first two segments of that sentence.

Pain Is Not the Ultimate Enemy

NORMAN COUSINS

Professional athletes are sometimes severely disadvantaged by trainers whose job it is to keep them in action. The more famous the athlete, the greater the risk that he or she may be subjected to extreme medical measures when injury strikes. The star baseball pitcher whose arm is sore because of a torn muscle or tissue damage may need sustained rest more than anything else. But his team is battling for a place in the World Series; so the trainer or team doctor, called upon to work his magic, reaches for a strong dose of butazolidine or other powerful pain suppressants. Presto, the pain disappears! That could be the last game, however, in which he is able to throw a ball with full strength. The drugs didn't repair the torn muscle or cause the damaged tissue to heal. What they did was to mask the pain, enabling the pitcher to throw hard, further damaging the torn muscle. Little wonder that so many star athletes are cut down in their prime, more the victims of overzealous treatment of their injuries than of the injuries themselves.

DISCUSSION QUESTIONS

1. Just how much pressure is actually exerted on athletes to perform in spite of injury? Are you an athlete, or are you acquainted with one who has had such problems? Share this information with your class.
2. What does your grammar handbook suggest regarding the punctuation of the sentence beginning, "But his team is battling for a place . . ."? Why does Cousins use a semicolon? Could he have just as well have used a comma? Why, or why not?
3. Why do you suppose Cousins has suddenly put a four-word sentence into a paragraph whose other sentences are generally rather lengthy ones?

ESSAYS

The Arctic Forest

BARRY LOPEZ

Barry Holstun Lopez (b. 1945) is an award-winning nonfiction writer whose works frequently deal with the environment. His

most significant books include Desert Notes: Reflections in the
Eye of a Raven *(1976);* Giving Birth to Thunder, Sleeping with
His Daughter: Coyote Builds North America *(1977);* Of Wolves
and Men *(1978);* River Notes: The Dance of Herons *(1979); and*
Crossing Open Ground *(1988). The following selection is from*
Arctic Dreams *(1986).*

The growth of trees in the Arctic is constrained by several   1
factors. Lack of light for photosynthesis of course is one; but
warmth is another. A tree, like an animal, needs heat to carry on
its life processes. Solar radiation provides this warmth, but in the
Arctic there is a strong correlation between this warmth and
closeness to the ground. In summer there may be a difference of
as much as 15°F in the first foot or so of air, because of the cooling
effect of the wind above and the ability of dark soils to intensify
solar radiation. To balance their heat budgets for growth and
survival, trees must hug the ground—so they are short. Willows,
a resourceful family to begin with, sometimes grow tall, but it is
only where some feature of the land stills the drying and cooling
wind.

Lack of water is another factor constraining the development   2
of trees. No more moisture falls on the arctic tundra in a year
than falls on the Mojave Desert; and it is available to arctic plants
in the single form in which they can use it—liquid water—only
during the summer.

Permafrost, the permanently frozen soil that underlies the   3
tundra, presents arctic trees with still other difficulties. Though
they can penetrate this rocklike substance with their roots, deep
roots, which let trees stand tall in a windy landscape, and which
can draw water from deep aquifers, serve no purpose in the
Arctic. It's too cold to stand tall, and liquid water is to be found
only in the first few inches of soil, for only this upper layer of the
ground melts in the summer. (Ironically, since the permafrost
beneath remains impervious, in those few weeks when water *is*
available to them, arctic trees must sometimes cope with boglike
conditions.)

Trees in the Arctic have an aura of implacable endurance   4
about them. A cross-section of the bole of a Richardson willow
no thicker than your finger may reveal 200 annual growth rings
beneath the magnifying glass. Much of the tundra, of course,
appears to be treeless when, in many places, it is actually covered

with trees—a thick matting of short, ancient willows and birches. You realize suddenly that you are wandering around on *top* of a forest.

DISCUSSION: CONTENT

1. What four factors, according to Lopez, constrain the growth of trees in the Arctic?
2. Why is air so much warmer near the ground in the Arctic during the summer?
3. What effect does the permafrost have on arctic forests?
4. In the final paragraph, Lopez suggests that a view of the arctic tundra is misleading in at least two ways. What ways are these?

DISCUSSION: FORM

1. What is the central thesis of this essay?
2. Is this thesis best stated as a cause or as an effect?
3. Why does Lopez present his four "constraints" in the order that he does? How might he have varied the order?
4. How does the concluding paragraph differ from the preceding ones?

Revenge of the Atari Warriors

BARBARA EBERLY

Barbara Walter Eberly (b. 1944) is a free-lance writer who also operates her own computer business in Cullowhee, North Carolina. The author of numerous poems, short stories, and essays, she is also the editor of The Author, *the newsletter of the Writers' Guild of Western North Carolina.*

As we evaluate the success of Desert Storm, we need to look at one aspect of the war which has received little attention. 1

Military training used to begin with boot camp. But the new age of computers has changed all that. These days, anyone can begin flight training as soon as he can hold a joystick—not the one in the airplane but the one on the computer or video game. 2

Whether we realize it or not, the soldiers we sent to the   3
Middle East began training the day they shoved the first quarter
into an arcade game or walked into a discount store and went
home with an Atari 2600.

The games were primitive by today's standards and parents   4
lamented the time and money wasted on the newfangled inventions which were rapidly replacing the good old-fashioned pinball
machines. But the way was paved for the brave new warrior.

The early Atari games might as well have been prepared by   5
the Defense Department. Consider the way the games were designed: you had to score a direct hit in order to make points, you
were usually under attack by enemy forces while you tried to hit
your targets, you had to take evasive action, and success in one
mission merely led you to a more difficult mission.

The first video of the strikes in Iraq looked a lot like those   6
old video games. But don't let the old-fashioned look of those
pictures fool you. We have created weapons so advanced that
most adults can't begin to understand them. What is even more
amazing is that we have also produced a generation of soldiers
not only physically but mentally capable of handling them.

So far as I can tell, the only flaw in the psychological prepa-   7
ration is the concept of being allowed two or three lives per game.
Of course, a soldier who subconsciously thinks he can play again
even if he dies is probably unbeatable—so perhaps that wasn't a
flaw from a military point of view.

We have come a long way since those simplistic beginnings.   8
The pilots operating the stealth bombers have had much more
sophisticated training. But they probably still relax with Nintendo and Sega.

Saddam Hussein realized quickly that he couldn't compete in   9
an air war. It must have been frustrating to watch the children of
a society he holds in contempt flying circles around him.

While he spent his money on weapons and kept the people of   10
his country at a subsistence level, we produced a "decadent
society" which practically guarantees every seven-year-old a
Nintendo or Sega—or both. Slightly more affluent homes have
computers—and the best selling game for years has been "Flight
Simulator."

By the time push came to shove and a ground war was   11
inevitable, Hussein had realized that he had gravely miscalcu-
lated. He had spent years playing war games by the old rules. He

presumed that because he was willing to sacrifice thousands of his troops, that he could win a ground war. He bragged at great length about how he would win because the American public was too soft to accept the casualties expected in a ground war. He would win because he would outlast us.

But about a week before the beginning of the ground war, he   12
obviously started having second thoughts. I wonder if someone finally told him what came with the Atari 2600. It was a game called "Combat." In case you don't know, it's a tank battle.

Whatever the reason, the results speak for themselves. The   13
Atari-Nintendo-Sega connection may or may not be the primary reason we won the war, but it doesn't hurt to have virtually every child in the country preparing to use the sophisticated military equipment we have designed.

In fact, according to reports in the computer industry, not   14
only will the next generation be even more prepared for the real thing with such new technology as Virtual Reality, but by the turn of the century, anyone with access to computer data bases will be able to plan his or her own strategy with the use of current satellite maps and programs capable of predicting nearly instant multiple possibilities.

The reverse side of the coin is that dictators concerned with   15
keeping their people in subservient poverty will probably never be able to produce an army capable of competing in modern warfare.

So, remember, the hours and quarters our children spend   16
brushing up on "eye-hand coordination" may well be our first line of defense. But we would do well to provide a solid education in reading and math. They will need to be able to read the instruction manuals if they get to play with the real thing.

DISCUSSION: CONTENT

1. Modern military training, according to Eberly, begins prior to boot camp. When does she suggest that it starts? Of what sort of training does it consist?
2. What is the only possible flaw that Eberly sees in this peculiar kind of pre-military training? Is it really a flaw?
3. What games does she believe were especially useful in the training of aviators for Operation Desert Storm? For training ground combatants?

DISCUSSION: FORM

1. Eberly claims that the hours devoted to computer games have produced one significant *immediate effect* on American youngsters. What is it? How does the development of this immediate effect produce desirable *ultimate effects?*
2. The behavior of dictators such as Saddam Hussein guarantees their vulnerability to the Western military, according to Eberly. Exactly what behavior is she alluding to, and what effect produced by that cause is thereby guaranteed?
3. What tactic common to many essays' concluding paragraphs does Eberly employ in the first sentence of her conclusion?

Where Are the Female Einsteins?

DONNA KAMINSKI

Donna Kaminski has been associate professor of computer science at Western Michigan University, Kalamazoo since 1983. This essay first appeared in Schools and Society: A Reader in Education and Sociology, *ed. Jeanne H. Ballentine (1985).*

The majority of "working" women (i.e., working for pay outside the home) are clustered in a very limited range of occupations, primarily teaching, nursing, social work, and clerical jobs. These are all fields made up of a very high proportion of women—and are relatively poorly paid. On the other hand, the math/science/engineering/computer/technical areas are some of the more highly paid occupations today and have considerably greater employment and mobility potential. But women make up less than 10 percent of these workers.

Indeed, across all occupations, women are less likely to be working in math-related areas—e.g., the high school science teacher, the sociologist specializing in quantitative research, the accountant or economist in business. One can notice a similar underrepresentation of women (and other minorities) majoring in these fields in college. In fact, this pattern is apparent as early as high school, where two to three times as many males as females take physics, chemistry, and advanced math.

Is this a problem? If so, for whom? Women? Society? Can   3
something be done about it? Why are there so few women in the
sciences? Is it because they aren't able to, aren't allowed to, or
don't want to achieve in sciences?

Many questions center on biological differences and whether   4
these affect abilities. Do the different sex hormones facilitate
different intellectual skills? Are males' and females' brains different? (Do they show left/right brain differences?) Is the observed discrepancy due to different rates of early physiological
development? A noted psychologist has done an extensive review
of the studies on this topic. Sherman (1976) concludes from this
review that there does not appear to be a natural ability difference between females and males that could explain much (if any)
of the observed difference in areas such as math behavior.

Looking further, one begins to note other evidence contra-   5
dicting a "biological difference" explanation. For example, most
studies find that girls and boys do about equally well on
math/science ability tests up through junior high school; only
then do girls seem to fall behind, at a time when gender roles and
gender-appropriate behavior suddenly become increasingly important to students. And if one examines actual academic performance, girls consistently earn better grades than boys all
through the school years—including math and science marks.
Studies today have also begun to take into account the important
variable "number of previous math courses taken" when comparing overall male and female test scores. Most of the differences
in scores disappear when similarly prepared students are compared. Also, some females do successfully study and enter careers
in the sciences, and their numbers are growing. These may eventually match the proportions of women scientists found in Eastern European countries, where females and males are much more
equally represented.

The evidence makes it difficult to assume an innate sex   6
difference; instead it suggests an examination of social, cultural,
and educational causes. Researchers have done considerable
study in this area since the early 1970s. A major focus has been
on trying to explain why there is such a gender gap in the number
of students studying math and science in high school. This factor, more than ability or performance differences, appears to be
the critical filter differentiating men's and women's career options.

But why do so many fewer young women than men take   7
elective math, science, mechanical drawing, and computer
courses in high school? Given our culture's current definitions of
sex roles, young women are likely to lack both the pushes and
the pulls to science areas. Consider gender socialization. Studies
show that girls get less experience and encouragement to be
independent, curious, active experimenters and manipulators of
the physical and abstract world by being socialized into the
traditional female role. For example, families are less likely to
give girls chemistry or erector sets, telescopes and microscopes,
science books and math puzzles. Teachers are less likely to ask
girls to run machinery (i.e., movie projectors), demonstrate science experiments, or to fix broken things. The peer group gives
girls fewer opportunities to play computer games, which not only
develop certain skills, but also foster favorable attitudes toward
space and computers (as well as conquering and aggression!).
Children also see relatively few role models of women as scientists or as competent in math. Consider images in children's
science textbooks, toy packaging, TV advertising of science-re-
lated toys and games, books on famous scientists, and children's
books showing adult occupations. Other questions arise: Are
parents likely to help with math homework or a science project?
What are the high school science teacher's attitudes toward female students? Studies show that even by junior high school,
attitudes, interests, and career plans toward or away from the
sciences are being formed.

Commonly held gender stereotypes about women and girls   8
hold that they aren't logical; aren't good with figures; can't think
abstractly; don't do well in math; don't like computers; aren't
inventors, experimenters, tinkerers, constructors, adventurers,
or puzzle solvers—all skills related to being a scientist. Studies
show that comedians think so, textbook publishers seem to
think so (there are three to four times as many pictures of boys
as girls in science books), toy manufacturers appear to believe it
(note the advertising and packaging of chemistry sets, erector
sets, computer games), elementary school teachers expect it (expectations are that girls will like spelling and reading, boys will
like math and science), high school counselors give advice on
courses and careers based on the stereotypes, parents are likely
to accept the idea that daughters are more likely than sons to be
"forgiven" for doing poorly in math and science—even females
themselves believe it.

Is this ideology based on fact? Statistics do support this to an   9
extent. As mentioned, males are much more likely to choose
courses and careers in the sciences. Boys use more books, toys,
and games related to computers and science. Boys are more likely
to be involved in programs for the mathematically gifted. Men
also score higher than women on the math section of the SAT,
Graduate Record Examination, civil service tests, and various
math/science ability tests.

This lack of support for girls is manifested directly in math   10
and science schoolwork. Teachers hold lower expectations for
girls' performance in these areas, parents are more likely to allow
girls to do poorly in math and opt out when it becomes elective
("Oh, your mother was never good in math, either"), counselors
are less likely to push girls toward taking optional advanced
courses ("What will you ever use it for?" or "Physics will only
hurt your good GPA"), and peers don't provide much support to
young women for being a "brain" or taking "male subjects." All
this feedback operates to lower girls' self-confidence in their
math/science/technical abilities and becomes a self-fulfilling
prophecy. By early high school, girls are already much more
likely than boys to rate their math/science ability as "just average," as opposed to "above average" or "among the best"—in
spite of their earning better grades in these subjects. Young
women are likewise much more likely to develop mathophobia—
a fear of math.

Another important obstacle to women's entry into science-   11
related courses and careers is our cultural stereotypes of science
and the scientist—some perhaps accurate, some not so. First of
all, science is seen as largely a male endeavor—as embodied in
famous scientists; high school and college teachers; the majority
of students taking advanced math and science courses in high
school; math/science/computer/engineering majors in college;
students participating in science fairs, accelerated programs, and
computer workshops; and so on. Thus females making a commitment to such a field are seen as deviant and may lack peer
reinforcment. Some young women obviously do overcome this
label barrier—and as more and more do so, the field will become
less restricted. For example, studies of all-female high schools
show young women's course taking and ability in math and
science are much higher than for those in mixed-sex schools.

A second important stereotype of science and the scientist   12
that inhibits women's (and perhaps some men's) entry into the

science field is the negative picture of what scientists and their jobs are like. High school women perceive the scientist to be quiet, unpopular, unsociable, not good looking, head in the clouds, not "with it"; the woman scientist is a large, manly, rumpled old spinster. The job is seen to involve extra time and hard work in training, working all alone in a laboratory, putting in long hours, working on something impersonal which has little direct relevance to humans. These characteristics are especially at odds with the traditional female role, particularly as it is defined by adolescents. Young women are more likely to want a job working with people rather than things, to be concerned with positive physical, psychological, and social characteristics and to deal more directly with human concerns. Given the realities of women's continued responsibility for home and family, women are less likely to look toward careers rather than jobs, the extra years of schooling in preparation, or the long work hours. And whether or not these stereotypes are accurate, students' (especially females') perceptions contribute to their decision to close off these career options in mid-adolescence.

This leads to a final important barrier—young women's per- 13
ceptions of the lack of future usefulness of math, science, and computer courses. As adolescents, young women are less concerned with occupational plans; many still view wife/mother/ homemaker as the major female role. Many also see their job or career as supplemental, temporary, combined with with raising a family, and secondary to their husband's career. So why take hard courses if they're not seen as necessary for adult life? Studies show that high school students rate physics, chemistry, and advanced math as the hardest in high school. Why prepare for a career in science when another occupation may take less schooling, work, and commitment? Why be concerned with the pay and long-term employment potential of a field when your job is supplemental? Isn't it better to be able to choose something you like, working with people, as a tradeoff for pay, security, and advancement? These are the views of many adolescent women, but not exactly an accurate picture of many adult women's lives today.

The majority of women work many years of their lives; many 14
have preschool children. Nearly half the labor force is women, and increasing with the rapidly rising divorce rate; many women are the sole support of themselves and their families. On the average, female college graduates earn less than male high school

dropouts. This is in part due to the different fields women and men choose to enter—decisions influenced by courses taken or not taken in high school. Unlike fields such as psychology, elementary education, or social work where students may postpone commitment decisions until mid-college, the math and science areas generally require adequate foundations in high school coursework. Thus, not studying chemistry in high school virtually closes off the chemistry career option by mid-adolescence.

The potential benefits from an emphasis on greater involve- 15 ment by women in science can be viewed from several value perspectives. Economic, political, and family institutions must alter to bring about meaningful change. It would certainly seem to be in the interest of society as a whole to increase the number of possible scientists and the potential for scientific contributions to society. The value of greater involvement for women seems particularly important as it could increase women's career options, open up higher paying, higher status jobs to women, and counteract current gender-based occupational segregation and its many consequences. Besides improving and enlarging the future potential pool of scientists, increasing the number of young women taking elective science courses has the potential for contributing to a more knowledgeable and scientifically aware future adult population of nonscientists. For example, in dealing with issues such as energy conservation and environmental pollution, in maintaining technological conveniences, in dealing with an increasingly computerized society, a more scientifically informed citizenry seems desirable. Women stand to benefit from improved investigative, mechanical, analytic, and problem-solving skills (in which they have traditionally been weak) by increasing their training in science and laboratory work.

One could also argue for greater math preparation because of 16 its benefits to nonmath-related jobs. For example, screening tests for entry into college, graduate school, and civil service jobs as well as many job aptitude tests include a significant portion covering math-related skills. Also, many fields today such as education, sociology, business, and psychology are requiring greater quantitative, computer, and experimental skills. Largely female occupations—clerical jobs, library work, teaching—are moving in this direction as computers are incorporated into their everyday work worlds. And in spite of a current overall surplus of teachers, there is a shortage of qualified science and math teachers; the entry of more women into these fields might help solve this problem if women continue to choose the teaching profession and can provide role models for young women.

And lastly, our society should try to eliminate the barrier to 17 females' entry into science because of its potential intrinsic interests for women—as great as for men. Must sex role stereotypes and the accompanying socialization discourage the next generation from choosing a field they might find interesting, challenging, and rewarding?

DISCUSSION: CONTENT

1. Kaminski says that gender socialization discourages girls from becoming interested in science. What evidence does she present to support this statement?
2. What are some gender stereotypes about girls and science? Is there evidence that people actually put much faith in these stereotypes? What about stereotypes about scientists? What effects do these have on young girls?
3. What school experiences serve to produce science and math phobias for girls?

DISCUSSION: FORM

1. Where does Kaminski state her thesis?
2. Paragraph 3 sets up three alternative answers to the question posed in the title of this essay, thus serving to divide the paper into three parts. Locate those parts. What paragraphs are devoted to each? What transitional devices are used to introduce each of these segments?
3. Does Kaminski deal exclusively with causes in this essay, or with effects?

Crime and Criminals

CLARENCE DARROW

Clarence Darrow (1857–1938) was the most famous criminal lawyer of his time, his two most notable trials being the defense of the child-murderers Leopold and Loeb (he won them life sentences instead of the death penalty) and of John Scopes

*in the so-called Monkey Trial (Scopes was convicted and fined
for teaching the doctrine of evolution in a public school,
though impartial observers considered Darrow to have bested
his equally famous legal opponent, William Jennings Bryan).
Among Darrow's publications are two books,* Crime: Its Cause
and Treatment *(1922) and* The Story of My Life *(1932). The
following selection, however, originated as a speech made by
Darrow in 1902 to prisoners in the Cook County (Chicago),
Illinois, jail.*

If I looked at jails and crimes and prisoners in the way the   1
ordinary person does, I should not speak on this subject to you.
The reason I talk to you on the question of crime, its cause and
cure, is because I really do not in the least believe in crime. There
is no such thing as a crime as the word is generally understood.
I do not believe there is any sort of distinction between the real
moral condition of the people in and out of jail. One is just as
good as the other. The people here can no more help being here
than the people outside can avoid being outside. I do not believe
that people are in jail because they deserve to be. They are in jail
simply because they can not avoid it on account of circumstances which are entirely beyond their control and for which
they are in no way responsible.

I suppose a great many people on the outside would say I was   2
doing you harm if they should hear what I say to you this
afternoon, but you can not be hurt a great deal anyway, so it will
not matter. Good people outside would say that I was really
teaching you things that were calculated to injure society, but it's
worthwhile now and then to hear something different from what
you ordinarily get from preachers and the like. These will tell
you that you should be good and then you get rich and be happy.
Of course we know that people do not get rich by being good, and
that is the reason why so many of you people try to get rich some
other way, only you do not understand how to do it quite as well
as the fellow outside.

There are people who think that everything in this world is   3
an accident. But really there is no such thing as an accident. A
great many folk admit that many of the people in jail ought not
to be there, and many who are outside ought to be in. I think
none of them ought to be here. There ought to be no jails, and if
it were not for the fact that the people on the outside are so

grasping and heartless in their dealings with the people on the inside, there would be no such institution as jails.

I do not want you to believe that I think all you people here   4
are angels. I do not think that. You are people of all kinds, all of you doing the best you can, and that is evidently not very well— you are people of all kinds and conditions and under all circumstances. In one sense everybody is equally good and equally bad. We all do the best we can under the circumstances. But as to the exact things for which you are sent here, some of you are guilty and did the particular act because you needed the money. Some of you did it because you are in the habit of doing it, and some of you because you are born to it, and it comes as natural as it does, for instance, for me to be good.

Most of you probably have nothing against me, and most of   5
you would treat me the same as any other person would; probably better than some of the people on the outside would treat me, because you think I believe in you and they know I do not believe in them. While you would not have the least thing against me in the world, you might pick my pockets. I do not think all of you would, but I think some of you would. You would not have anything against me, but that's your profession, a few of you. Some of the rest of you, if my doors were unlocked, might come in if you saw anything you wanted—not out of any malice to me, but because that is your trade. There is no doubt there are quite a number of people in this jail who would pick my pockets. And still I know this, that when I get outside pretty nearly everybody picks my pocket. There may be some of you who would hold up a man on the street, if you did not happen to have something else to do, and needed the money; but when I want to light my house or my office the gas company holds me up. They charge me one dollar for something that is worth twenty-five cents, and still all these people are good people; they are pillars of society and support the churches, and they are respectable.

When I ride on the streetcars, I am held up—I pay five cents   6
for a ride that is worth two-and-a-half cents, simply because a body of men have bribed the city council and legislature, so that all the rest of us have to pay tribute to them.

If I do not want to fall into the clutches of the gas trust and   7
choose to burn oil instead of gas, then good Mr. Rockefeller holds me up, and he uses a certain portion of his money to build universities and support churches which are engaged in telling us how to be good.

Some of you are here for obtaining property under false pre- 8
tenses—yet I pick up a great Sunday paper and read the advertisements of a merchant prince—"Shirtwaists for 39¢, marked down
from $3."

When I read the advertisements in the paper I see they are all 9
lies. When I want to get out and find a place to stand anywhere
on the face of the earth, I find that it has all been taken up long
ago before I came here, and before you came here, and somebody
says, "Get off, swim into the lake, fly into the air; go anywhere,
but get off." That is because these people have the police and
they have the jails and the judges and the lawyers and the soldiers
and all the rest of them to take care of the earth and drive
everybody off that comes in their way.

A great many people will tell you that all this is true, but that 10
it does not excuse you. These facts do not excuse some fellow
who reaches into my pocket and takes out a five-dollar bill; the
fact that the gas company bribes the members of the legislature
from year to year, and fixes the law, so that all you people are
compelled to be "fleeced" whenever you deal with them; the fact
that the streetcar companies and the gas companies have control
of the streets and the fact that the landlords own all the earth,
they say, has nothing to do with you.

Let us see whether there is any connection between the 11
crimes of the respectable classes and your presence in jail. Many
of you people are in jail because you have really committed
burglary. Many of you, because you have stolen something: in the
meaning of the law, you have taken some other person's property.
Some of you have entered a store and carried off a pair of shoes
because you did not have the price. Possibly some of you have
committed murder. I can not tell what all of you did. There are
a great many people here who have done some of these things
who really do not know themselves why they did them. I think
I know why you did them—every one of you; you did these things
because you were bound to do them. It looked to you at the time
as if you had a chance to do them or not, as you saw fit, but still
after all you had no choice. There may be people here who had
some money in their pockets and who still went out and got
some more money in a way society forbids. Now you may not
yourselves see exactly why it was you did this thing, but if you
look at the question deeply enough and carefully enough you
would see that there were circumstances that drove you to do
exactly the thing which you did. You could not help it any more

than we outside can help taking the positions that we take. The reformers who tell you to be good and you will be happy, and the people on the outside who have property to protect—they think that the only way to do it is by building jails and locking you up in cells on weekdays and praying for you Sundays.

I think that all of this has nothing whatever to do with right   12
conduct. I think it is very easily seen what has to do with right conduct. Some so-called criminals—and I will use this word because it is handy, it means nothing to me—I speak of the criminals who get caught as distinguished from the criminals who catch them—some of these so-called criminals are in jail for first offenses, but nine-tenths of you are in jail because you did not have a good lawyer and of course you did not have a good lawyer because you did not have enough money to pay a good lawyer. There is no very great danger of a rich man going to jail.

Some of you may be here for the first time. If we would open   13
the doors and let you out, and leave the laws as they are today, some of you would be back tomorrow. This is about as good a place as you can get anyway. There are many people here who are so in the habit of coming that they would not know where else to go. There are people who are born with the tendency to break into jail every chance they get, and they can not avoid it. You can not figure out your life and see why it was, but still there is a reason for it, and if we were all wise and knew all the facts we could figure it out.

In the first place, there are a good many more people who go   14
to jail in the winter time than in the summer. Why is this? Is it because people are more wicked in winter? No, it is because the coal trust begins to get in its grip in the winter. A few gentlemen take possession of the coal, and unless the people will pay $7 or $8 a ton for something that is worth $3, they will have to freeze. Then there is nothing to do but to break into jail, and so there are many more in jail in the winter than in summer. It costs more for gas in the winter because the nights are longer, and people go to jail to save gas bills. The jails are electric-lighted. You may not know it, but these economic laws are working all the time, whether we know it or do not know it.

There are more people who go to jail in hard times than in   15
good times—few people comparatively go to jail except when they are hard up. They go to jail because they have no other place to go. They may not know why, but it is true all the same. People are not more wicked in hard times. That is not the reason. The

fact is true all over the world that in hard times more people go to jail than in good times, and in winter more people go to jail than in summer. Of course it is pretty hard times for people who go to jail at any time. The people who go to jail are almost always poor people—people who have no other place to live first and last. When times are hard then you find large numbers of people who go to jail who would not otherwise be in jail.

Long ago, Mr. Buckle, who was a great philosopher and his-   16
torian, collected facts and he showed that the number of people who are arrested increased just as the price of food increased. When they put up the price of gas ten cents a thousand I do not know who will go to jail, but I do know that a certain number of people will go. When the meat combine raises the price of beef I do not know who is going to jail, but I know that a large number of people are bound to go. Whenever the Standard Oil Company raises the price of oil, I know that a certain number of girls who arc seamstresses, and who work night after night long hours for somebody else, will be compelled to go out on the streets and ply another trade, and I know that Mr. Rockefeller and his associates are responsible and not the poor girls in the jails.

First and last, people are sent to jail because they are poor.   17
Sometimes, as I say, you may not need money at the particular time, but you wish to have thrifty forehanded habits, and do not always wait until you are in absolute want. Some of you people are perhaps plying the trade, the profession, which is called burglary. No man in his right senses will go into a strange house in the dead of night and prowl around with a dark lantern through unfamiliar rooms and take chances of his life if he has plenty of good things of the world in his own home. You would not take any such chances as that. If a man had clothes in his clothes-press and beefsteak in his pantry, and money in the bank, he would not navigate around nights in houses where he knows nothing about the premises whatever. It always requires experience and education for this profession, and people who fit themselves for it are no more to blame than I am for being a lawyer. A man would not hold up another man on the street if he had plenty of money in his own pocket. He might do it if he had one dollar or two dollars, but he wouldn't if he had as much money as Mr. Rockefeller has. Mr. Rockefeller has a great deal better holdup game than that.

The more that is taken from the poor by the rich, who have   18
the chance to take it, the more poor people there are who are

compelled to resort to these means for a livelihood. They may
not understand it, they may not think so at once, but after all
they are driven into that line of employment.

There is a bill before the Legislature of this State to punish   19
kidnaping children with death. We have wise members of the
Legislature. They know the gas trust when they see it and they
always see it—they can furnish light enough to be seen, and this
Legislature thinks it is going to stop kidnaping children by making a law punishing kidnapers of children with death. I don't
believe in kidnaping children, but the Legislature is all wrong.
Kidnaping children is not a crime, it is a profession. It has been
developed with the times. It has been developed with our modern
industrial conditions. There are many ways of making money—
many new ways that our ancestors knew nothing about. Our
ancestors knew nothing about a billion-dollar trust; and here
comes some poor fellow who has no other trade and he discovers
the profession of kidnaping children.

This crime is born, not because people are bad; people don't   20
kidnap other people's children because they want the children or
because they are devilish, but because they see a chance to get
some money out of it. You cannot cure this crime by passing a
law punishing by death kidnapers of children. There is only one
way to cure it. There is one way to cure all the offenses, and that
is to give the people a chance to live. There is no other way, and
there never was any other way since the world began, and the
world is so blind and stupid that it will not see. If every man and
woman and child in the world had a chance to make a decent,
fair, honest living, there would be no jails, and no lawyers and no
courts. There might be some persons here or there with some
peculiar formation of their brain, like Rockefeller, who would do
these things simply to be doing them; but they would be very,
very few, and those should be sent to a hospital and treated, and
not sent to jail; and they would entirely disappear in the second
generation, or at least in the third generation.

I am not talking pure theory. I will just give you two or three   21
illustrations.

The English people once punished criminals by sending them   22
away. They would load them on a ship and export them to
Australia. England was owned by lords and nobles and rich people. They owned the whole earth over there, and the other people
had to stay in the streets. They could not get a decent living.
They used to take their criminals and send them to Australia—I

mean the class of criminals who got caught. When these criminals got over there, and nobody else had come, they had the whole continent to run over, and so they could raise sheep and furnish their own meat, which is easier than stealing it; these criminals then became decent, respectable people because they had a chance to live. They did not commit any crimes. They were just like the English people who sent them there, only better. And in the second generation the descendants of those criminals were as good and respectable a class of people as there were on the face of the earth, and then they began building churches and jails themselves.

A portion of this country was settled in the same way, landing prisoners down on the southern coast; but when they got here and had a whole continent to run over and plenty of chances to make a living, they became respectable citizens, making their own living just like any other citizen in the world; but finally these descendants of the English aristocracy, who sent the people over to Australia, found out they were getting rich, and so they went over to get possession of the earth as they always do, and they organized land syndicates and got control of the land and ores, and then they had just as many criminals in Australia as they did in England. It was not because the world had grown bad; it was because the earth had been taken away from the people. 23

Some of you people have lived in the country. It's prettier than it is here. And if you have ever lived on a farm you understand that if you put a lot of cattle in a field, when the pasture is short they will jump over the fence; but put them in a good field where there is plenty of pasture, and they will be law-abiding cattle to the end of time. The human animal is just like the rest of the animals, only a little more so. The same thing that governs in the one governs in the other. 24

Everybody makes his living along the lines of least resistance. A wise man who comes into a country early sees a great undeveloped land. For instance, our rich men twenty-five years ago saw that Chicago was small and knew a lot of people would come here and settle, and they readily saw that if they had all the land around here it would be worth a good deal, so they grabbed the land. You cannot be a landlord because somebody has got it all. You must find some other calling. In England and Ireland and Scotland less than 5 percent own all the land there is, and the people are bound to stay there on any kind of terms the landlords 25 give. They must live the best they can, so they develop all these various professions—burglary, picking pockets and the like.

Again, people find all sorts of ways of getting rich. These are   26
diseases like everything else. You look at people getting rich, organizing trusts, and making a million dollars, and somebody gets the disease and he starts out. He catches it just as a man catches the mumps or the measles; he is not to blame, it is in the air. You will find men speculating beyond their means, because the mania of money-getting is taking possession of them. It is simply a disease; nothing more, nothing less. You can not avoid catching it; but the fellows who have control of the earth have the advantage of you. See what the law is; when these men get control of things, they make the laws. They do not make the laws to protect anybody; courts are not instruments of justice; when your case gets into court it will make little difference whether you are guilty or innocent; but it's better if you have a smart lawyer. And you can not have a smart lawyer unless you have money. First and last it's a question of money. Those men who own the earth make the laws to protect what they have. They fix up a sort of fence or pen around what they have, and they fix the law so the fellow on the outside can not get in. The laws are really organized for the protection of the men who rule the world. They were never organized or enforced to do justice. We have no system for doing justice, not the slightest in the world.

Let me illustrate: Take the poorest person in this room. If the   27
community had provided a system of doing justice the poorest person in this room would have as good a lawyer as the richest, would he not? When you went into court you would have just as long a trial, and just as fair a trial as the richest person in Chicago. Your case would not be tried in fifteen or twenty minutes, whereas it would take fifteen days to get through with a rich man's case.

Then if you were rich and were beaten, your case would be   28
taken to the Appellate Court. A poor man can not take his case to the Appellate Court; he has not the price; and then to the Supreme Court, and if he were beaten there he might perhaps go to the United States Supreme Court. And he might die of old age before he got into jail. If you are poor, it's a quick job. You are almost known to be guilty, else you would not be there. Why would any one be in the criminal court if he were not guilty? He would not be there if he could be anywhere else. The officials

have no time to look after all these cases. The people who are on the outside, who are running banks and building churches and making jails, they have no time to examine six hundred or seven hundred prisoners each year to see whether they are guilty or innocent. If the courts were organized to promote justice the people would elect somebody to defend all these criminals, somebody as smart as the prosecutor—and give him as many detectives and as many assistants to help, and pay as much money to defend you as to prosecute you. We have a very able man for State's Attorney, and he has many assistants, detectives and policemen without end, and judges to hear the cases—everything handy.

Most of all our criminal code consists in offenses against 29 property. People are sent to jail because they have committed a crime against property. It is of very little consequence whether one hundred people more or less go to jail who ought not to go—you must protect property, because in this world property is of more importance than anything else.

How is it done? These people who have property fix it so they 30 can protect what they have. When somebody commits a crime it does not follow that he has done something that is morally wrong. The man on the outside who has committed no crime may have done something. For instance: to take all the coal in the United States and raise the price two dollars or three dollars when there is no need of it, and thus kill thousands of babies and send thousands of people to the poor-house and tens of thousands to jail, as is done every year in the United States—this is a greater crime than all the people in our jails ever committed, but the law does not punish it. Why? Because the fellows who control the earth make the laws. If you and I had the making of the laws, the first thing we would do would be to punish the fellow who gets control of the earth. Nature put this coal in the ground for me as well as for them, and nature made the prairies up here to raise wheat for me as well as for them, and then the great railroad companies came along and fenced it up.

Most of all, the crimes for which we are punished are prop- 31 erty crimes. There are a few personal crimes, like murder—but they are very few. The crimes committed are mostly those against property. If this punishment is right the criminals must have a lot of property. How much money is there in this crowd? And yet you are all here for crimes against property. The people

up and down the Lake Shore have not committed crimes, still
they have so much property they don't know what to do with it.
It is perfectly plain why those people have not committed crimes
against property; they make the laws and therefore do not need
to break them. And in order for you to get some property you are
obliged to break the rules of the game. I don't know but what
some of you may have had a very nice chance to get rich by
carrying the hod for one dollar a day, twelve hours. Instead of
taking that nice, easy profession, you are a burglar. If you had
been given a chance to be a banker you would rather follow that.
Some of you may have had a chance to work as a switchman on
a railroad where you know, according to statistics, that you can
not live and keep all your limbs more than seven years, and you
can get fifty dollars or seventy-five dollars a month for taking
your lives in your hands, and instead of taking that lucrative
position you choose to be a sneak thief, or something like that.
Some of you made that sort of choice. I don't know which I would
take if I was reduced to this choice. I have an easier choice.

I will guarantee to take from this jail, or any jail in the world,   32
five hundred men who have been the worst criminals and law-
breakers who ever got into jail, and I will go down to our lowest
streets and take five hundred of the most abandoned prostitutes,
and go out somewhere where there is plenty of land, and will give
them a chance to make a living, and they will be as good as the
average in the community.

There is a remedy for the sort of condition we see here. The   33
world never finds it out, or when it does find out it does not
enforce it. You may pass a law punishing every person with death
for burglary, and it will make no difference. Men will commit it
just the same. In England there was a time when one hundred
offenses were punishable with death, and it made no difference.
The English people strangely found out that so fast as they
repealed the severe penalties and so fast as they did away with
punishing men by death, crime decreased instead of increased;
that the smaller the penalty the fewer the crimes.

Hanging men in our county jails does not prevent murder. It   34
makes murderers.

And this has been the history of the world. It's easy to see   35
how to do away with what we call crime. It is not so easy to do
it. I will tell you how to do it. It can be done by giving the people
a chance to live—by destroying special privileges. So long as big

criminals can get the coal fields, so long as the big criminals have control of the city council and get the public streets for streetcars and gas rights, this is bound to send thousands of poor people to jail. So long as men are allowed to monopolize all the earth, and compel others to live on such terms as these men see fit to make, then you are bound to get into jail.

The only way in the world to abolish crime and criminals is   36
to abolish the big ones and the little ones together. Make fair conditions of life. Give men a chance to live. Abolish the right of private ownership of land, abolish monopoly, make the world partners in production, partners in the good things of life. Nobody would steal if he could get something of his own some easier way. Nobody will commit burglary when he has a house full. No girl will go out on the streets when she has a comfortable place at home. The man who owns a sweatshop or a department store may not be to blame himself for the condition of his girls, but when he pays them five dollars, three dollars, and two dollars a week, I wonder where he thinks they will get the rest of their money to live. The only way to cure these conditions is by equality. There should be no jails. They do not accomplish what they pretend to accomplish. If you would wipe them out there would be no more criminals than now. They terrorize nobody. They are a blot upon any civilization, and a jail is an evidence of the lack of charity of the people on the outside who make the jails and fill them with the victims of their greed.

DISCUSSION: CONTENT

1. What is Darrow's thesis? State it as briefly as possible.
2. What, according to Darrow, is the basic reason for the existence of prisons and prisoners?
3. In what season of the year does Darrow believe more people go to jail? Why? Do you agree, or not?
4. Some of Darrow's examples are outdated, or at least show their age. Which ones are? What would you put in their places? Which examples are still appropriate, indicating that the problem Darrow sees is a continuing one?
5. How is the history of the settlement and development of Australia important in Darrow's discussion?
6. How feasible is Darrow's solution for the problem or effect that he discusses?

DISCUSSION: FORM

1. We have learned that exposition seeks to inform, while argumentation seeks to change minds. Darrow's thesis is contrary to run-of-the-mill opinion. Yet we have placed it with exposition rather than argumentation. Can you determine why?
2. In addition to cause and effect, Darrow uses comparison; what are some of the important comparisons that he makes?
3. He also uses examples or illustrations to support his assertions. Locate at least six of these, including one extended example. Comment on their effectiveness.
4. What is Darrow's **tone?** How does he achieve it? Why does he adopt it?
5. Where does Darrow announce his solution to the problem or effect that he discusses? Was it wise to put it there? Why, or why not?

11

Definition

Definition is a fundamental expository device. Because no two people share exactly the same vocabulary, sooner or later you will use a word or expression unknown to or misunderstood by your reader. Unless you pause to define the unknown term, your reader will fail to understand you. Most definitions are very brief and unpretentious: we seldom notice them at all. Look at the following sentence:

> Chaucer wrote a treatise on *the astrolabe, a medieval inven-* *tion that enabled navigators to steer by the stars.*

Tucked away in a paragraph, such a sentence would hardly call undue attention to itself. Nevertheless, it contains an excellent example of a definition, one that contains every element that is essential to a satisfactory definition. In short, it follows a simple formula for defining terms: x is a y that is z.

Let us look more closely. The x in our formula is simply the thing to be defined, here an astrolabe. The y is a larger, more general class to which x belongs: the astrolabe belongs to the more general class of *medieval inventions*. The z is that information which serves to differentiate x from all other members of y. In our definition, z is the information that restricts the domain of medieval inventions to just the one that enabled navigators to steer by the stars, effectively ruling out such other medieval inventions as arquebuses, culverins, chastity belts, and plenary indulgences. Here are more definitions, with the essential elements marked for you:

$$x \qquad\qquad y \qquad\qquad z$$
<u>*Pornography*</u> is <u>*an attempt*</u> <u>*to insult sex.*</u> (D. H. Lawrence)

$$x \qquad\quad y \qquad\qquad z$$
<u>*A noun*</u> is <u>*the name*</u> <u>*of a person, place, or thing.*</u>

$$x \qquad\quad y \qquad z$$
<u>*A touchdown*</u> is <u>*a score*</u> <u>*in football.*</u>

In most cases the statement of elements *x* and *y* is fairly simple. But the formulation of *z* may be more difficult. Generally speaking, there are two ways to differentiate a member from a larger class: one is to tell what it is not, and the other is to tell what it is, or what makes it unique. The majority of definitions will be of phrase or clause length, as were the examples above. Some particularly troublesome ones may be expanded to a paragraph. Occasionally, a writer may even use the technique of definition as the controlling pattern for an entire essay. When this happens, the writer is usually trying to define an abstract term, such as *love* or *patriotism*, or an unfamiliar or elusive one, such as *quasar*. Most of the space will be devoted to the *z* element of the definition formula, and very often the writer will be obliged to use several modes of development to differentiate *x* from *y*. The writer may give examples, classify, describe, show causes, even tell a story, all in an attempt to establish the uniqueness of the object or concept being defined. Such longer explanations of a word or expression are known as *extended definitions*.

Stipulative definitions are another type of explanation of a word or an expression. In such cases the writer wants to use a word, often a common or familiar one, but in a special or unexpected sense, and consequently must make clear that special use to readers. A brief look at a few pages of a dictionary will remind you that many English words have several meanings, making stipulative definition an occasional necessity. For instance, if you were going to use the word *gig,* and the word's context did not make clear which of five very different meanings you were using, you would have to explain, perhaps simply in parentheses, perhaps at more length, that you meant a pronged spear for fishing, rather than a boat, a two-wheeled carriage, a military demerit, or a musician's job.

In the following pages you will find model definitions of all three sorts for you to study and learn to use—the typical short ones as well as extended and stipulative definitions. As the fore-going discussion suggests, it is important that you notice and understand definitions in your reading, and that you use them effectively in your writing. Particularly on examinations, you'll be asked to define special terms for a field of study. You'll want to do so accurately and efficiently, following the x is a y that is z formula. Likewise, in research papers and reports, especially in your major field, you will often need to define key terms. Later on, in your working career, particularly if your profession is law-related in any fashion (criminal justice, social work, environmental protection, and so on), you will find defining a variety of special terms to be a vital part of your job. So what follows is of real value to you as a reader and as a writer.

Commentary on Student Work

When the method of developing definitions was first intro-duced in class, the instructor encouraged students to list things that might deserve a good definition: things and people in and around the campus that were familiar to students and locals but would need some defining if these things and people were to be recognizable and understood by out-of-towners. They experi-mented with the formula x is a y that is z, singling out some campus landmarks, customs, and persons for definition. Some of the definitions were trivial, some were quite accurately and care-fully drawn, some were whimsical, but all provided excellent practice in freewriting, a warm-up for a larger, more serious exercise in defining. Several of the better efforts appear later in "Some Campus Definitions" (p. 279).

The next step was to turn attention to extended definition. After reading Simpson's definition of dyslexia, they were ready to try a few such definitions of their own. Kristi wrote in her journal a number of formulaic entries, among them these:

"A snob is a person who doesn't like me."
"A liberal is a voter who cares about other people."
"A conservative is a voter who cares about himself."
"A president is a politician who tries to fool all the people all the time."
"A feminist is a woman who has gotten fed up."

During the next class meeting when Kristi shared these definitions with her reading/writing group, some cheered her views, but others criticized her cynicism; all agreed that the last definition was perhaps the most worthy of pursuing in an extended definition format. They quizzed Kristi about the *z* term in her definition, and she responded with the following list of things that feminists had become fed up with:

1. Men become doctors while women become nurses.
2. Men become priests while women become nuns.
3. Men go into politics and leave women out.
4. Men get high-paying jobs while women get bypassed for hiring, raises, and promotions.

At the following class meeting, Kristi brought in an essay that was fairly close to the one that follows. She had incorporated each of the examples in support of her *z* term into separate paragraphs. The first was dedicated to education, the second to religion, the third to politics, and the last to American society, thereby providing labels for each of the institutions represented by her examples. She had placed her initial statement in an opening paragraph. All that was lacking at this point was some polishing of grammar, usage, and style, and a good conclusion. Several members of the group agreed that the best, most forceful way to yoke the paragraphs together was the repetition that begins each of the supporting paragraphs. Another member recommended the concluding idea, which connects the idea of the possibility of women being drafted with the passage of the Equal Rights Amendment (at the time of Kristi's composition still a live issue).

Here is Kristi's final product.

Feminist

The best definition of a feminist that I know of is a woman   1
who has gotten fed up. What has she gotten fed up with? There
are a number of things.

She is fed up with education as it is usually practiced. The   2
girls are made to believe that they can't do math and are taught
to make biscuits instead. They are encouraged to become nurses

instead of doctors, secretaries instead of engineers, and wives and mothers before everything else. And even in high school sports it's more prestigious to be head cheerleader for the football team or homecoming queen than to be the leading scorer on the girls' basketball team.

A feminist is fed up with organized religion—not with religion, but with the way that it's usually organized. Girls are encouraged to become nuns but never priests. They don't lead Sunday school lessons; they prepare the pot-luck buffets and decorate the altars. 3

A feminist is fed up with politics and politicians. The general sentiment is that this game is too rough and too sordid for women, who are too naive to know what is going on, even though the League of Women Voters is still the only source of unbiased information on the candidates and the issues at election time. 4

A feminist is fed up with American society. She likes to have doors opened for her and chairs pulled back, but not at the expense of a couple of thousand dollars less a year in her paychecks. She is sickened by reports of Mrs. X being the *only* woman electrician, board member, representative, judge, etc. She is incensed at the feeling of inadequacy which makes a woman on a quiz program admit that she is "just a housewife." (Whoever heard a man admit that he was "just a lawyer"?) She is fed up with ladies' auxiliaries, where there are no men's auxiliaries. She is fed up with being a second-class citizen in the land of the free and the home of male hypocrites. 5

And now that they are suggesting that she register for the draft, she just may be angry enough to refuse—until they pass the Equal Rights Amendment for her. 6

DISCUSSION QUESTIONS

1. The writer of "Feminist" takes the *x* is a *y* that is *z* formula quite seriously and introduces the definition in its barest terms. What is it?
2. What sort of transitional device does the writer use to signal that paragraphs 2 through 5 have a similar purpose, i.e., to support or expand the *z* portion of the definition?
3. How does the writer support the contentions made in each of the paragraphs 2 through 5?

STUDENT WORK

Laughter

What is laughter? A bizarre action that is solely a trait of the human race—I think. If you take a closer look, you will realize that people laugh at unconscious, painful situations concerning themselves, friends, or world events. We laugh at cartoons full of violence, such as *Tom and Jerry*, where the mice beat up the cat. We giggle at jokes that portray the weaker side of people. We chuckle at the monkeys in the zoo when the big one picks on the little one. We laugh at our friends or even at strangers when they say something stupid or have a minor accident, such as dropping a lunch tray in the middle of the cafeteria. All of these associations between pain and laughter are too numerous to be overlooked, yet they are mysterious. The only unraveling clue that has shed some light on this strange association is the occurrence of a substance called endomorphine—a natural pain killer that is released in small quantities by our brains every time we laugh. This means that laughter is in reality one of our body's mechanisms for coping with pain—perhaps even its most important one.

DISCUSSION QUESTIONS

1. Does the student apply the formulaic statement in composing this definition?
2. What rhetorical devices does the student use to support the definition?

Women

Women are a source of vitality upon which men draw for a meaningful life. They are suppliers of man's spiritual needs: comfort, inspiration, and charm. Women comfort frustrated husbands by giving receptive ears to their grumblings when they are misunderstood by good friends or discouraged by not getting deserved promotions. Women provide such profound inspiration that many of the greatest works of literature, painting, sculpture, and music have been inspired by their smiles, tears, raptures, and agonies. So irresistible is their charm that men have fought for and given up kingdoms and empires to win their favors. Any man, be he commoner or king, who has been exposed to these unique characteristics will find his life more worth living.

DISCUSSION QUESTIONS

1. This student's definition of "women" is clearly not the sort one will find in a dictionary. How does it differ and what might be a reason for its differing?
2. What role does sentence 2 play in the organization of the rest of the paragraph?
3. As we said in the introduction to this section on definition, the writer of an extended definition may rely on various writing strategies to clarify a term. What two expository techniques are important to this definition?

BRIEF EXAMPLES

Some Campus Definitions

Pre-registration is a formality which students must endure in order to find out what courses they won't get next term. 1

A Campus Rock Concert is a social event where the normal behavior is anti-social; the featured group, which had its hit record three years ago, starts playing two hours late, if at all. 2

A Campus Cop is a man, usually retired from a real job, who puts parking tickets on student cars when not drinking coffee or misdirecting traffic. 3

The University Center is a place to watch T.V., play pool and video games, Foosball and cards, and flunk out of school. 4

The Cafeteria is a center for gastronomical torture built to test the intestinal fortitude of students. 5

The Gymnasium is a haven for aspiring athletes and a good place to pick up new towels. 6

A Campus Snob is a person who doesn't like me. 7

DISCUSSION QUESTIONS

1. Do each of these student definitions conform rigidly to the definition formula?
2. How is humor achieved in these definitions? What part of the formula is the chief source of the humor?
3. You will probably find it an interesting exercise to create some definitions for objects or phenomena peculiar to your own campus. Assume your audience to be persons unfamiliar with your surroundings; then try to formulate some campus definitions similar to the preceding ones to share in class.

Eight Definitions of Religion

Religion, after trying to see as best I could what various religions and religious people had in common, I felt impelled to define as the reaction of the personality as a whole to its experience of the Universe as a whole. (Sir Julian Huxley)

Religion is that voice of the deepest human experience. (Matthew Arnold)

Religion is the belief in spiritual things. (E. B. Taylor)

Religion is a daughter of Hope and Fear, explaining to Ignorance the nature of the Unknowable. (Ambrose Bierce)

Religion is the opium of the people. (Karl Marx)

Religion is the propitiation or conciliation of powers superior to man which are believed to direct or control the course of nature and of human life. (Sir James Frazer)

Being religious means asking passionately the question of the meaning of our existence and being willing to receive answers, even if the answers hurt. (Paul Tillich)

Pure religion and undefiled before God is this, to visit the fatherless and widows in their affliction, and to keep oneself unspotted from the world. (Saint James)

DISCUSSION QUESTIONS

1. Demonstrate how each of these definitions of religion employs the formula x is a y that is z.
2. How might you adjust those definitions that do not rigidly conform to the formula?

Some Definitions from The Devil's Dictionary

AMBROSE BIERCE

Ambrose Bierce (1842–1914?) was an American journalist, humorist, and satirist, most famous for The Cynic's Word Book *(now known as* The Devil's Dictionary, *1906, 1911). A Civil War hero, a self-educated and itinerant journalist, and a constant traveler, Bierce disappeared for good at the age of 72 when he crossed into Mexico during the revolution, perhaps joining the rebel forces of Pancho Villa.*

[Editor's note: One of the definition's numerous functions is to amuse.]

ACQUAINTANCE, *n.* A person whom we know well enough to 1 borrow from, but not well enough to lend to. A degree of friendship called slight when its object is poor or obscure, and intimate when he is rich or famous.

BAROMETER, *n.* A ingenious instrument which indicates what 2 kind of weather we are having.

BRAIN, *n.* An apparatus with which we think that we think. 3 That which distinguishes the man who is content to *be* something from the man who wishes to *do* something. A man of great wealth, or one who has been pitchforked into high station, has commonly such a headful of brain that his neighbors cannot keep their hats on. In our civilization, and under our republican form of government, brain is so highly honored that it is rewarded by exemption from the cares of office.

CONNOISSEUR, *n.* A specialist who knows everything about 4 something and nothing about anything else. An old wine-bibber having been smashed in a railway collision, some wine was poured upon his lips to revive him. "Pauillac, 1873," he murmured and died.

FIDDLE, *n.* An instrument to tickle human ears by friction of 5 a horse's tail on the entrails of a cat.

HAPPINESS, *n.* An agreeable sensation arising from contemplating the misery of another. 6

HASH, *x.* There is no definition for this word—nobody knows 7 what hash is.

HISTORY, *n.* An account mostly false, of events mostly unim- 8
portant, which are brought about by rulers mostly knaves, and
soldiers mostly fools.

IDIOT, *n.* A member of a large and powerful tribe whose 9
influence in human affairs has always been dominant and controlling. The Idiot's activity is not confined to any special field of
thought or action, but "pervades and regulates the whole." He
has the last word in everything; his decision is unappealable. He
sets the fashions of opinion and taste, dictates the limitations of
speech, and circumscribes conduct with a deadline.

LAUGHTER, *n.* An interior convulsion, producing a distortion 10
of the features and accompanied by inarticulate noises. It is
infectious and, though intermittent, incurable. Liability to attacks of laughter is one of the characteristics distinguishing man
from the animals—these being not only inaccessible to the
provocation of his example, but impregnable to the microbes
having original jurisdiction in bestowal of the disease. Whether
laughter could be imparted to animals by inoculation from the
human patient is a question that has not been answered by
experimentation.

LEAD, *n.* A heavy blue-gray metal much used in giving sta- 11
bility to light lovers—particularly to those who love not wisely
but other men's wives. Lead is also of great service as a counter-
poise to an argument of such weight that it turns the scale of
debate the wrong way. An interesting fact in the chemistry of
international controversy is that at the point of contact of two
patriotisms lead is precipitated in great quantities.

MIRACLE, *n.* An act or event out of the order of nature and 12
unaccountable, as beating a normal hand of four kings and an ace
with four aces and a king.

OPTIMISM, *n.* The doctrine, or belief, that everything is 13
beautiful, including what is ugly, everything good, especially
the bad, and everything right that is wrong. It is held with
greatest tenacity by those most accustomed to the mischance
of falling into adversity, and is most acceptably expounded
with the grin that apes a smile. Being a blind faith, it is
inaccessible to the light of disproof—an intellectual disorder,
yielding to no treatment but death. It is hereditary, but fortu-
nately not contagious.

REVOLUTION, *n.* In politics, an abrupt change in the form of 14
misgovernment. Specifically, in American history, the substitu-

tion of the rule of an Administration for that of a Ministry, whereby the welfare and happiness of the people were advanced a full half-inch. Revolutions are usually accompanied by a considerable effusion of blood, but are accounted worth it—this appraisement being made by beneficiaries whose blood had not the mischance to be shed.

TURKEY, *n.* A large bird whose flesh when eaten on certain   15 religious anniversaries has the peculiar property of attesting piety and gratitude. Incidentally, it is pretty good eating.

WHEAT, *n.* A cereal from which a tolerably good whiskey can   16 with some difficulty be made, and which is used also for bread. The French are said to eat more bread *per capita* of population than any other people, which is natural, for only they know how to make the stuff palatable.

ZENITH, *n.* A point in the heavens directly overhead to a   17 standing man or a growing cabbage. A man in bed or a cabbage in the pot is not considered as having a zenith, though from this view of the matter there was once a considerable dissent among the learned, some holding that the posture of the body was immaterial. These were called Horizontalists; their opponents, Verticalists. The Horizontalist heresy was finally extinguished by Xanobus, the philosopher-king of Abara, a zealous Verticalist. Entering an assembly of philosophers who were debating the matter, he cast a severed human head at the feet of his opponents and asked them to determine its zenith, explaining that its body was hanging by the heels outside. Observing that it was the head of their leader, the Horizontalists hastened to profess themselves converted to whatever opinion the Crown might be pleased to hold, and Horizontalism took its place among *fides defuncti.*

DISCUSSION QUESTIONS

1. Bierce adheres strictly to the formula for definitions, but occasionally he embellishes his initial statements with additional comments. What rhetorical mode do these comments usually represent? What is their purpose?
2. How exactly does Bierce inject humor into his definitions? What parts of the definition formula does he take liberties with most frequently?

PARAGRAPHS

Love
LIZ CARPENTER

Love is a moment and a lifetime. It is looking at him across a room and feeling that if I don't spend the rest of my life with him, I'll have missed the boat. Love is working together, laughing together, growing together. It is respect for each other and the people each cares about, however difficult it is sometimes to like his kinfolk or his friends. Love is wanting to shout from the rooftops the successes, little and big, of one another. Love is wanting to wipe away the tears when failure comes. Love is liking the feel of each other. It is wanting to have children together because they are the exclamation point of love. Love is laughter, especially in the middle of a quarrel.

DISCUSSION QUESTIONS

1. How many times does Carpenter use the *x* is a *y* that is *z* formula in her paragraph? What is the effect of that repetition?
2. Where and how does she use contrast in her paragraph to express the complexity of love?
3. Choose the defining sentence that you think best conveys the essence of love and explain the basis of your choice in a paragraph of your own.

Euphemism
NEIL POSTMAN

A euphemism is commonly defined as an auspicious or exalted term (like "sanitation engineer") that is used in place of a more down-to-earth term (like "garbage man"). People who are partial to euphemisms stand accused of being "phony" or of trying to hide what it is they are really talking about. And there is no doubt that in some situations the accusation is entirely proper. For example, one of the more detestable euphemisms I have come across in recent years is the term "Operation Sunshine," which is the name the U.S. Government gave to some experiments it conducted with the hydrogen bomb in the South Pacific. It is obvious that the government, in choosing this name, was trying to expunge the hideous imagery that the bomb evokes and in so doing committed, as I see it, an immoral act. This sort of process—giving pretty names to essentially ugly realities—is what has given euphemizing such a bad name.

DISCUSSION QUESTIONS

1. Postman actually defines euphemism in two ways in this paragraph. What is the difference between the term as defined in the first sentence and as defined in the last one?
2. Postman provides the example of sanitation engineer/garbage man to illustrate the sorts of contrasting substitutions common to the first sort of euphemism. What other examples of this sort of euphemism can you recall from your own experiences?
3. Look up **connotation** in the Glossary. What part does that aspect of word meaning play in euphemisms and in the words and realities that they either exalt or mask?

Abstractitis

H. W. FOWLER

abstractitis. The effect of this disease, now endemic on both sides of the Atlantic, is to make the patient write such sentences as *Participation by the men in the control of the industry is non-existent* instead of *The men have no part in the control of the industry; Early expectation of a vacancy is indicated by the firm* instead of *The firm say they expect to have a vacancy soon; The availability of this material is diminishing* instead of *This material is getting scarcer; A cessation of dredging has taken place* instead of *Dredging has stopped; Was this the realization of an anticipated liability?* instead of *Did you expect you would have to do this?* And so on, with an abstract word always in command as the subject of the sentence. Persons and what they do, things and what is done to them, are put in the background, and we can only peer at them through a glass darkly. It may no doubt be said that in these examples the meaning is clear enough; but the danger is that, once the disease gets a hold, it sets up a chain reaction. A writer uses abstract words because his thoughts are cloudy; the habit of using them clouds his thoughts still further; he may end by concealing his meaning not only from his readers but also from himself, and writing such sentences as *The actualization of the motivation of the forces must to a great extent be a matter of personal angularity.*

DISCUSSION QUESTIONS

1. Because Fowler's classic book, *Modern English Usage,* follows a dictionary format, his definitions do not necessarily follow the pattern that we have described. Can you recast the first sentence of this paragraph into the *x* is a *y* that is *z* pattern?
2. Can you restate the definition in less concrete terms?
3. What, according to Fowler, is the danger of abstractitis?

Good

W. NELSON FRANCIS

Applied to language, the adjective *good* can have two meanings: (1) "effective, adequate for the purpose to which it is put" and (2) "acceptable, conforming to approved usage." The first of these is truly a value judgment of the language itself. In this sense the language of Shakespeare, for example, is "good English" because it serves as a highly effective vehicle for his material. On the other hand, the language of a poorer writer, which does not meet adequately the demands put upon it, might be called "bad English." The second meaning of good is not really a judgment of the language itself but a social appraisal of the persons who use it. An expression like *I ain't got time for youse* may be most effective in the situation in which it is used, and hence "good English" in the first sense. But most people, including those who naturally speak this way, will call it "bad English" because grammatical features like *ain't, youse,* and the double negative construction belong to a variety of English commonly used by people with little education and low social and economic status.

DISCUSSION QUESTIONS

1. To ensure that readers of his book, *The English Language: An Introduction,* will understand the meaning of the common adjective *good* when it is put to special uses—to describe language—the linguist W. Nelson Francis states precisely what he means by the word. How is this one-paragraph definition organized?
2. Francis makes clear that *good* may be used to judge the language itself; what is the other language-related use of *good* that he names?
3. Is it possible for an expression to be *good* in one sense and not in the other?
4. How is it possible for grammatically correct English ever to be wrong, as Francis implies?

ESSAYS

November in the Hills

JOHN PARRIS

During World War II, John Parris (b. 1914) was a reporter and diplomatic correspondent for two American wire services—the Associated Press and the United Press International. After the war he returned to his native Appalachian mountains, where he serves today as associate editor of the Asheville Citizen-Times *and writes a regular column, "Roaming the Mountains". His first book, a collection of his columns that borrowed the name of his series, appeared in 1955. Others have followed:* My Mountains, My People *(1957),* Mountain Bred *(1967), and* These Storied Mountains *(1972), from which the following essay is taken.*

Out in the country, where folks live close to the soil, November is a time to rest and be thankful.　　1

The corn's in the crib, the fodder's in the shock. 2

The hay's in the mow, the tobacco's in the barn. 3

The picklin's done, the cider's jugged. 4

The firewood's cut, the sorghum's made. 5

The hasty time is at an end. 6

October has slipped away on feet of thistledown, and November now comes rustling down the mountain. 7

The birds are on the wing, and the leaves are footloose and eager for a breeze. 8

The fox stalks the rabbit, and the rabbit is free and whimsical as the wind. 9

Woodchucks and coons raid the cornfields. 10

Gray squirrels rattle the leaves in the hickories and the cricket chirps in the corner of the fireplace. 11

The walnuts fall and there is the day-tang of walnut hulls. 12

The autumn color ebbs, and the season turns from gold to gray. 13

It is November in the hills. 14

And November is many things. . . . 15

It is a time for sitting around the hearthfire and a time for walking down a country road in the starlight. 16

It's a breath of apple cider, a gleam from a possum-hunter's lantern, the belling of fox-hounds in the midwatches of the night. 17

It's a season of wind and rain, frost and rime, and sometimes snow. 18

It's willows going from green to golden bronze. 19

It's pumpkin in the pie and thoughts turning to mincemeat. 20

It's a time for pulling up a rocking chair before the fire and a time for cracking nuts on the hearth. 21

It's a time when the blue smell of woodsmoke haunts the air and a time when violet twilight casts shadows over the cove. 22

It's Indian Summer sighing in the trees and snowy breath on every breeze. 23

It's a cow-bell tinkling as the herd comes home and the lonesome, lonely crow of a rooster. 24

It's grouse exploding underfoot and rocketing into a thicket. 25

It's a wild turkey gobbling in the brush on a high hill. 26

It's a squirrel with bushy tail and shoebutton eyes standing on the trunk of an oak like a carved stone. 27

It's a rabbit hippety-hopping through the sere grass. 28

It's the wind running its fingers through a field of broom-   29
sedge.

It's holly and mountain ash, berry-bright and firelight gay.   30

It's apples in the cellar, dried fruit in the pantry.   31

It's a jug of molasses, a jar of sourwood honey, a crock of   32
homemade kraut.

It's a bouquet of dried onions above the kitchen stove, strings   33
of red peppers, pods of okra, strips of dried pumpkin.

It's a harvest of striped gourds and rainbow-colored ears of   34
Indian corn.

It's a candyroaster and green polka-dotted squash.   35

It's pickled beans and pickled peaches, pickled beets and   36
pickled onions.

It's liver-and-lights, backbones-and-ribs, livermush and   37
sousemeat.

It's pumpkin whiskey and persimmon brandy, apple cider and   38
fox-grape wine.

It's the smell of frost-ripened maypops and gingerbread fresh   39
from the oven.

It's parched corn with butter and salt.   40

It's apple butter and pumpkin butter.   41

November is naked woods and meadows brown and sere.   42

It's gray rain falling from a gray sky upon gray leaves.   43

It's frosty knuckles rapping at the door.   44

It's a groundhog sniffing the wind and scurrying back to his   45
den to sleep until spring.

It's bears fattening on mast for the long winter sleep.   46

It's the creek whispering and the hemlock crooning.   47

It's a fiddle tune and a homespun ballad.   48

It's corncob tales around a stove at the country store.   49

But most of all, November out in the country is a time to rest   50
and be thankful.

DISCUSSION: CONTENT

1. Some of Parris's vocabulary probably strikes you as peculiar. Mark the unfamiliar words and try to make some sense out of them. How many of the apparently unusual words refer to items of Appalachian culture?

2. Why, according to this essay, is November especially a time to rest and be thankful?

DISCUSSION: FORM

1. This piece is organized into three parts. What device signals those parts? What seems to be the subject matter of each part?
2. Parris originally wrote this piece as a newspaper article. Given the journalist's penchant for short paragraphs, the arrangement here is understandable. Would Parris's purpose have been better served if he had chosen to gather his major groups into paragraphs when he anthologized the essay? Why, or why not?
3. How does this piece conform to the definition formula: *x* is a *y* that is *z*?

The Blue Book

DENISE GRAVELINE

Denise Graveline is a free-lance writer who has published articles in a number of nationally distributed magazines, including Ms. *and* McCall's. *She is coauthor with Jamie Quackenbush of* When Your Pet Dies: How to Cope with Your Feelings *(1989). This essay originally appeared in* Campus Voice.

When put to the test, great minds have always had a worthy   1
substance to write their answers on. Moses had his tablets, Rosetta her stone. But you, exam-breath, got stuck with the blue book. Compared to the sturdy surfaces that have held recorded thought for centuries (marble, say, or bathroom walls), blue books just don't stack up. They're the Handi-Wipes of academe: striped, all-purpose, and utterly disposable.

Let me be blunt. Like handguns, blue books are plentiful   2
because they're cheap. Take the paper: it's made from the same trees that supply college dormitories with toilet paper (minus the bark). Worse, these trees are specially grown in Florida swampland, a water-logged environment that produces pulp so absorbent that in blue-book form, it soaks up all the ink from your only pen.

Then there are the staples that are supposed to hold this   3
sodden mess together. Sigh heavily and watch the little buggers unhinge themselves. Turn the page and see them rip through

your answer. Take one that's fallen out and try to commit hara-kiri; watch it crumble on impact with your flesh.

But ignore the paper and staples. Focus on the bright blue 4 lines that guide your shaky handwriting until they begin to waver, fade in and out, and then disappear. No, you're not going blind. It's just one more pothole on the road to understanding how the hell you're supposed to use this thing, anyway.

The blue book looks harmless and simple, but so did Jimmy 5 Carter. Most people can cope with the cover, because teaching assistants are posted at three-foot intervals throughout the test site shouting, "Name, date, course number, section number, ID number!"

But once you've opened the book to the first page, too many 6 choices confront you. There's only one margin; should you use only one margin? What if you write big! Then it looks like a third-grade penmanship workbook. Maybe you shouldn't print. Maybe you should write cursive but double space. If you double-space, maybe you shouldn't use just one side of the page. Maybe you should take the F and go out for a drink.

Resist that last yearning. While you've been sitting there 7 stunned by the logistics, the student next to you—a speedwriter planted by a TA—has already filled her third blue book with precise, phone book-size print. You've got to move. Look at the question. There's 50 percent of your grade, summed up in three-word sentences: Discuss Shakespeare's works. Describe noncor-relative thought. Explain modern socialism. Faced with six blank pages, 12 sides, you know it's a doomed operation. Quash the urge to find out just how doomed it is. The TA will only respond with "Write until you answer the question, then quit." Transla-tion: "Die, sucker."

Try to relax instead. Think of those great minds. Their writ- 8 ing was set down on material appropriate to their thoughts. That's why sailors have MOM tattooed over their hearts, love letters are written on burnable paper, and your checks are printed on rubber. Get the message? You have to lower the level of your essay answer to fit the quality of what it's written on—pulp filler from swamp trees.

When those blue lines start to fade, write about how in our 9 political and economic system, the lines of demarcation between free, white males and minority groups first blurred and then vanished. When your neighbor nudges you for another pen to feed to his absorbent paper, scribble economic theory from Hamlet:

"Neither a borrower nor a lender be." An unhinged staple can inspire long narratives about the flexible nature of democracy—firm when it must defend freedom, but bendable enough to let dissenting forces speak freely as well. A ripped page should get you going on the fabric of everyday life, torn in two by the demise of the nuclear family and the threat of nuclear war. The possibilities—unfortunately—are endless.

Thankfully, the blue book will fall apart before you do. In 10 fact, by the time you finish, you'll wish you'd taken noncredit *origami* courses just so you could weave what's left of your book into one piece. But pull yourself together and forget it all. Crying will only blot what's left of your answer. You do want at least partial credit, don't you? Just get up, crawl past the industrious neighbor who's now on her fifth blue book, and toss your tattered effort on the pile. Once you're out of the classroom, you can run to the nearest bar, where there surely must be a drink with your name, course number, section number, ID number, and the date on it.

DISCUSSION: CONTENT

1. What important features of college blue books does Graveline focus on in this essay? For what purpose?
2. What sorts of examinations typically require the use of blue books? Which disciplines are mentioned in this essay?
3. How many of Graveline's observations about blue books struck you as apt because such thoughts have occurred to you, at one time or another, as you tried to ready your response to an examination question? What does that suggest to you about the way Graveline may have brainstormed prior to writing this essay?

DISCUSSION: FORM

1. This essay furnishes a definition of a blue book, but it also does more. What other methods of development does Graveline employ? Cite examples.
2. What is the tone of this essay? That is, what is Graveline's attitude toward her subject matter? Toward you, the reader? How does she convey each attitude?

Liberation

ROBERT FULGHUM

Robert Fulghum (b. 1937) lives on a houseboat in Seattle. He is a Unitarian clergyman, but he has worked in a number of other occupations, including IBM salesman, cowboy, and bartender. In 1988 his essay collection All I Really Need to Know I Learned in Kindergarten *soared to the top of the national best-seller lists and remained there until it was joined (in the number two position) a year later by his second collection,* It Was on Fire When I Lay Down on It. *Fulghum is the only author ever to enjoy such sales success. His third collection,* Uh-oh: Some Observations from Both Sides of the Refrigerator Door, *appeared in 1991. Fulghum pronounces his name as "ful-jum."*

Folks across the street are really with-it types. They jog and scarf bean sprouts and recycle everything but the air they breathe. Liberation is a big thing with them, too. Both men's and women's. They aren't married—they have a "contract"—and lead independent lives. Their consciousness is so raised they float. Nice folks. Give the neighborhood a progressive tone. Well, so.

They bought themselves an 18-speed mountain bicycle. Tandem. On the grounds of economy and efficiency. They've been riding it every day. In matching cycle suits and leather helmets, with jugs of go-juice and everything. He always rides in front, I notice. He always steers. Always. Not very libby, really.

Conversations with each of them separately reveal the age-old truth. Privately, he thinks he's stronger and has a better sense of direction. She lets him. Because she gets to look around and enjoy the scenery; because she can stop pedaling and he doesn't notice; and if they crash, he's good padding.

The everlasting tandem. Men in front, women to the rear. It's probably true that men are stronger. But women are smarter—at least this one is. Liberation, I guess, is everybody getting what they want, without knowing the whole truth. Or in other words, liberation finally amounts to being free from things we don't like in order to be enslaved by things we approve of. Here's to the eternal tandem.

DISCUSSION: CONTENT

1. The liberated couple Fulghum describes always ride their tandem bicycle the same way: man in front, woman behind. Why?
2. What conclusion does Fulghum draw on the couple's behavior?
3. Besides their bicycling activities, what else signals this couple's liberation?

DISCUSSION: FORM

1. Where does Fulghum actually state his definition of *liberation* in its barest terms? What was he doing before that?
2. What is your attitude toward Fulghum's use of sentence fragments? What sort of tone does it establish? In other words, how does their use help to reveal Fulghum's attitude toward his audience?
3. How does the couple's behavior on their bicycle serve to illustrate Fulghum's definition of *liberation?*

Dyslexia

EILEEN SIMPSON

Eileen B. Simpson, despite her own history of dyslexia, is a published author of fiction and nonfiction works. The selection that follows is from her 1979 book, Reversals: A Personal Account of Victory over Dyslexia. *In it she discusses her personal trials with this reading disorder from fourth grade through her adult career as an author and practicing psychotherapist, against a background of factual data, famous fellow sufferers, and case studies.*

Dyslexia (from the Greek, *dys,* faulty, + *lexis,* speech, cognate 1
with the Latin *legere,* to read), developmental or specific dyslexia as it's technically called, the disorder I suffered from, is the inability of otherwise normal children to read. Children whose intelligence is below average, whose vision or hearing is defective, who have not had proper schooling, or who are too emotionally disturbed or brain-damaged to profit from it belong in other diagnostic categories. They, too, may be unable to learn to read, but they cannot properly be called dyslexics.

For more than seventy years the essential nature of the afflic- 2
tion has been hotly disputed by psychologists, neurologists, and
educators. It is generally agreed, however, that it is the result of
a neurophysiological flaw in the brain's ability to process language. It is probably inherited, although some experts are reluctant to say this because they fear people will equate "inherited"
with "untreatable." Treatable it certainly is: not a disease to be
cured, but a malfunction that requires retraining.

Reading is the most complex skill a child entering school is 3
asked to develop. What makes it complex, in part, is that letters
are less constant than objects. A car seen from a distance, close
to, from above, or below, or in a mirror still looks like a car even
though the optical image changes. The letters of the alphabet are
more whimsical. Take the letter *b*. Turned upside down it becomes a *p*. Looked at in a mirror, it becomes a *d*. Capitalized, it
becomes something quite different, a *B*. The *M* upside down is a
W. The *E* flipped over becomes Ǝ. This reversed *E* is familiar to
mothers of normal children who have just begun to go to school.
The earliest examples of art work they bring home often have I
LOVƎ YOU written on them.

Dyslexics differ from other children in that they read, spell, 4
and write letters upside down and turned around far more frequently and for a much longer time. In what seems like a capri-
cious manner, they also add letters, syllables, and words, or, just
as capriciously, delete them. With pallindromic words (was-saw,
on-no), it is the order of the letters rather than the orientation
they change. The new word makes sense, but not the sense
intended. Then there are other words where the changed order—
"sorty" for story—does not make sense at all.

The inability to recognize that g, *g*, and G are the same letter, 5
the inability to maintain the orientation of the letters, to retain
the order in which they appear, and to follow a line of text
without jumping above or below it—all the results of the flaw—
can make of an orderly page of words a dish of alphabet soup.

Also essential for reading is the ability to store words in 6
memory and to retrieve them. This very particular kind of memory dyslexics lack. So, too, do they lack the ability to hear what
the eye sees, and to see what they hear. If the eye sees "off,"' the
ear must hear "off" and not "of," or "for." If the ear hears "saw,"
the eye must see that it looks like "saw" on the page and not
"was." Lacking these skills, a sentence or paragraph becomes a
coded message to which the dyslexic can't find the key.

It is only a slight exaggeration to say that those who learned   7
to read without difficulty can best understand the labor reading
is for a dyslexic by turning a page of text upside down and trying
to decipher it.

While the literature is replete with illustrations of the way   8
these children write and spell, there are surprisingly few examples of how they read. One, used for propaganda purposes to alert
the public to the vulnerability of dyslexics in a literate society,
is a sign warning that behind it are guard dogs trained to kill. The
dyslexic reads:

> Wurring
> Guard God
> Patoly

for

> Warning
> Guard Dog
> Patrol

and, of course, remains ignorant of the danger.

Looking for a more commonplace example, and hoping to   9
recapture the way I must have read in fourth grade, I recently
observed dyslexic children at the Educational Therapy Clinic in
Princeton, through the courtesy of Elizabeth Travers, the director. The first child I saw, eight-year-old Anna (whose red hair and
brown eyes reminded me of myself at that age), had just come to
the Clinic and was learning the alphabet. Given the story of
"Little Red Riding Hood," which is at the second grade level, she
began confidently enough, repeating the title from memory, then
came to a dead stop. With much coaxing throughout, she read as
follows:

> Grandma you a top. Grandma [looks over at picture of Red
> Riding Hood]. Red Riding Hood (long pause, presses index finger
> into the paper. Looks at me for help. I urge: Go ahead] the a
> [puts head close to the page, nose almost touching] on Grandma
>
> for
>
> Once upon a time there was a little girl who had a red coat with
> a red hood. Etc.

"Grandma" was obviously a memory from having heard the story read aloud. Had I needed a reminder of how maddening my silences must have been to Miss Henderson, and how much patience is required to teach these children, Anna, who took almost ten minutes to read these few lines, furnished it. The main difference between Anna and me at that age is that Anna clearly felt no need to invent. She was perplexed, but not anxious, and seemed to have infinite tolerance for her long silences. 10

Toby, a nine-year-old boy with superior intelligence, had a year of tutoring behind him and could have managed "Little Red Riding Hood" with ease. His text was taken from the *Reader's Digest's Reading Skill Builder,* Grade IV. He read: 11

A kangaroo likes as if he had but truck together warm. His saw neck and head do not . . . [Here Toby sighed with fatigue] seem to feel happy back. They and tried and so every a tiger likes Moses and shoots from lonesome day and shouts and long shore animals. And each farm play with five friends . . .

He broke off with the complaint, "This is too hard. Do I have to read any more?" 12

His text was: 13

A kangaroo looks as if he had been put together wrong. His small neck and head do not seem to fit with his heavy back legs and thick tail. Soft eyes, a twinkly little nose and short front legs seem strange on such a large strong animal. And each front paw has five fingers, like a man's hand.

An English expert gives the following bizarre example of an adult dyslexic's performance: 14

An the bee-what in the tel mother of the biothodoodoo to the majoram or that emidrate eni eni Krastrei, mestriet to Ketra lotombreidi to ra from treido as that.

His text, taken from a college catalogue the examiner happened to have close at hand, was: 15

It shall be in the power of the college to examine or not every licentiate, previous to his admission to the fellowship, as they shall think fit.

That evening when I read aloud to Auntie for the first time,   16
I probably began as Toby did, my memory of the classroom lesson
keeping me close to the text. When memory ran out, and Auntie
did not correct my errors, I began to invent. When she still didn't
stop me, I may well have begun to improvise in the manner of
this patient—anything to keep going and keep up the myth that
I was reading—until Auntie brought the "gibberish" to a halt.

DISCUSSION: CONTENT

1. What groups of children who also have trouble reading cannot be
   properly classed as dyslexics?
2. What is thought to be the basic cause of dyslexia?
3. Why are letters of the alphabet harder to comprehend than many
   other physical objects, such as cars?
4. What does Simpson suggest a person who reads without difficulty
   should do with a printed page to understand better the challenge
   dyslexics face when reading?
5. What example does Simpson provide of the sort of danger dyslexics must contend with as a result of their reading disorder?

DISCUSSION: FORM

1. Beyond using the formula x is a y that is z, what other means does
   Simpson use to define dyslexia in paragraph 1?
2. How do paragraphs 3–6, discussing the complex skill of reading,
   contribute to the definition of dyslexia?
3. What part do examples of the sorts of reading errors made by
   dyslexics play in Simpson's definition of the disorder?
4. Why do you suppose Simpson compares Anna and Toby to herself
   as a child?
5. How much knowledge of dyslexia does Simpson seem to assume
   her audience holds?

PART THREE

<hr>

Persuasive Writing

Persuasive or argumentative writing differs from expository writing in a number of ways, but the foremost differences involve the writer's purpose and attitude toward the audience. In exposition you wish to inform or educate your readers; that is, your basic purpose is to provide some information that your audience presumably lacks. However, when you write persuasively, your intention is different. You assume that your readers are already informed about the subject, at least to some extent. Hence, your objective is both different and more difficult. Your goal is no longer to inform your readers so much as it is to change their minds.

Most people—unless they are hopelessly stubborn, unreasonable, or unfeeling—will yield to two forms of persuasion: logical appeals and emotional appeals. They may also need to be shown that the reasoning that led them to their original opinions was defective in some way. Accordingly, the following chapter contains four sections, each dealing with a different persuasive strategy. The first two sections treat two traditional kinds of logical appeals: the inductive argument and the deductive argument. The third section introduces methods of refutation or rebuttal, that is, methods for showing how the opposing opinion is faulty or wrong. The final section introduces emotional appeals (attempts to win the audience's sympathy by means other than logic or reason).

In order to persuade audiences, you will need to develop some new writing skills, but the ones you have already studied and started to master will still prove very useful. You will still need to describe, to narrate, and to explain; you will also need to illustrate by examples; analyze, classify, and divide; delineate processes; make comparisons and analogies; discover probable causes and effects; and define terms. You cannot realistically hope to argue satisfactorily until you have some control over these skills. Now you should be ready to put some—or all—of them to work.

The Roman statesman and orator Cicero (106–43 B.C.) once listed the six parts of an argument:

1. Introduction
2. Background
3. Partition, or statement of propositions
4. Confirmation, or proof of propositions
5. Refutation
6. Conclusion, or appeal to sympathy.

Cicero was not prescribing that all attempts at persuasion should contain each of these steps in exactly this order; he was merely observing that most arguments that he had witnessed—and he had witnessed a lot of them—did in fact contain these elements. Consequently, it is worthwhile to discuss, at least briefly, the parts of Cicero's classical argument, so that you will recognize them in the arguments you encounter and so that you will develop the special vocabulary needed to discuss arguments knowledgeably.

The introduction and background segments of the argument are often expository. The **introduction,** as its name implies, introduces the topic, either directly or obliquely, and states that there are differences of opinion about it. The *background* portion sketches the history of events leading up to the present confrontation—facts that your readers will need to know in order to understand the argument. Since disagreements often arise because people are poorly informed, the background component of the argument takes on a key role. Getting readers to change their minds is sometimes simply a matter of providing them with additional information on which to base their conclusions.

The third step, the *partition,* narrows the scope of the argument to just those issues (or perhaps even a single issue) over which there is disagreement. Usually you will try to search out and describe points of agreement with your audience. Such concessions help to establish good will and encourage an open-minded response by the audience. They also serve to pare away everything that is not essential in the statement of the disputed proposition or propositions.

Here it is necessary to define very carefully what is meant by the term **proposition.** According to classical rhetoric, a proposition is a statement that can be either affirmed or denied; that is, it is a statement that you as a writer wish to affirm as true and whose truth you may expect your audience to deny. In its barest form a proposition will look very much like a definition: for example, *John Smith is an honest man* or *John Smith is a man who can be trusted.* In actual practice, propositions may frequently he disguised, in sentences like *You can trust John Smith* or *Who can be more trustworthy than John Smith?* In the final analysis, though, it is John Smith's honesty that is being debated—either he is honest or he is not. These expressions qualify as propositions because each is capable of being reduced to a simple statement that can be affirmed or denied. While *Vote for lower taxes* is not a proposition in a strict sense, it is acceptable in a broad sense because it can be reduced to this: *The lowering of taxes is something that deserves your vote.*

To better understand how the first three parts of an argument work, look at the following paragraphs, taken from a 1915 argument favoring women's right to vote.

The men of three eastern States—Massachusetts, New York, and New Jersey—will have an opportunity this fall to put themselves on record for or against woman suffrage. In each State a constitutional amendment extending the suffrage to women is to be submitted to the voters at the polls. What will the men of Massachusetts, New York, and New Jersey do with the opportunity? Will they follow the enlightened example of the men of Wyoming, Colorado, Idaho, Utah, Washington, California, Arizona, Kansas, Oregon, Alaska, Illinois, Montana, and Nevada? Or will they choose to keep their States awhile longer groping in the mists of reaction?

Women should vote for four good and sufficient reasons:

It will be good for the women.
It will be good for the men.
It will be good for the family.
It will be good for the State.

The first paragraph functions as both introduction and background. Its first sentence introduces the topic of women's suffrage and announces that three states are about to vote on the constitutional amendment needed to achieve that goal. It then brings the reader up-to-date on the progress of ratification: thirteen legislatures have already voted favorably. The second paragraph states the propositions to be proved in a quite unmistakable way.

Not all introductions, backgrounds, and partitions will be quite so straightforward, but it is worth pointing out that your success in sifting the facts to focus on the actual areas of disagreement will go a long way toward winning your case. In the following letter, notice how clearly and succinctly Abraham Lincoln stated the areas of disagreement. Although cast as a question, each could be reduced to a proposition.

Executive Mansion, Washington, February 3, 1862

Major-General McClellan:

My dear Sir: You and I have distinct and different plans for a movement of the Army of the Potomac—yours to be down the Chesapeake, up the Rappahannock to Urbana, and across land to the terminus of the railroad on the York River; mine to move directly to a point on the railroad southwest of Manassas.

If you will give satisfactory answers to the following questions, I shall gladly yield my plan to yours.

First. Does your plan involve a greatly larger expenditure of time and money than mine?

Second. Wherein is a victory more certain by your plan than mine?

Third. Wherein is a victory more valuable by your plan than mine?

Fourth. In fact, would it not be less valuable in this, that it would break no great line of the enemy's communications, while mine would?

Fifth. In case of disaster, would not a retreat be more difficult by your plan than mine?

> Yours truly,
> Abraham Lincoln

Lincoln did not go on to prove each of his propositions, but presumably he could have. This brings us to the fourth of Cicero's parts of an argument: *confirmation* or proof of the propositions. We stated earlier that a writer may use both logical and emotional appeals in order to change the reader's mind. But customarily in the confirmation section only logical proofs can be admitted. We shall examine two traditional sorts of logical proofs—**induction** and **deduction**—momentarily. After that, we shall take up Cicero's fifth part of the argument, **refutation**—the disproof of competing arguments (i.e., opposing propositions). Finally, we shall take up emotional appeals, which Cicero reserved for the **conclusion** section of the classic argument.

It is worth repeating that each of the six parts of the classic argument need not always be present in every piece of persuasive writing that you encounter or that you create yourself. The writer who fashions a logical proof of a proposition may not feel obliged to refute the opposite claim, and may or may not desire to arouse the reader's sympathy. On the other hand, the author of an emotional appeal may abandon logical argumentation altogether. It is, however, always to your advantage to be able to recognize each of these devices (inductive proofs, deductive proofs, refutations, and emotional appeals) when you see them and to be able to use them in your own writing.

After all, others often try to change our minds (think of political speeches, editorials, advertisements), just as we often want or need to change the minds of others. You will have occasion—at school, at work, and as a private citizen—to employ your persuasive skills, especially when you must communicate with persons in power or when you achieve a position of power yourself. The occupational need for such skills in a lawyer or politician or journalist is obvious, but it also exists for people in other vocations: business (especially marketing and management), education, science, and technology. To convince yourself of the wide variety of situations that call for persuasive writing, you need only to glance through the selections that follow, asking yourself in each case: "What prompted this argument?"

12

Argumentation Techniques

Inductive Proofs

In Chapter 5, "Examples," in the "Expository Writing" part, we stated that development by examples is one of the most frequently used methods of exposition. Here we must add that it is also the basis for one of the most frequently used methods of argumentation, namely **induction.**

What is the difference? When is development by examples exposition, and when is it argumentation? The main difference lies in the reader's attitude. Recall that in Chapter 5 we suggested that the following thesis statements could be developed by offering examples:

1. Studying differential equations can be a terrifying experience.
2. Ellen Brown is clever as well as attractive.
3. Basketball is now a popular sport in many countries around the world.
4. Neanderthal man practiced a rudimentary form of democracy.

In calling these sentences thesis statements, we assumed that readers did not know very much, if anything, about differential equations, Ellen Brown, basketball's popularity, or Neanderthal life. Our purpose in each case was to explain by providing information.

But notice now that each of these sentences could be viewed differently. Each could be a **proposition**: a statement that can be either affirmed or denied. All that is needed is to adjust the reader's expected attitude. For instance, if the reader is familiar with differential equations and thinks that they are easy, or if the reader knows Ellen Brown and thinks that she is not clever, but a little dumb, then the writer's problem is more difficult. In the first case, the writer would be wise to qualify the proposition by stating that differential equations are terrifying for a great many people, a step that would exclude the mathematical wizards who might object; then the forthcoming examples could paint the grim picture. In the case of Ellen Brown, the writer must hope that the examples seeking to present her favorably will outweigh or outnumber those that can be supplied by her detractors.

In inductive proofs the writer purports to have examined all available information and to have come to a conclusion on the basis of that examination. But since it is never realistically possible to examine all of the possible information, the writer must settle for something less than a perfect induction. In other words, the best that a writer could hope to show would be that there tend to be more people who find differential equations difficult than otherwise and that Ellen Brown has more redeeming qualities than faults. Thus, it is more correct to say that, rather than proving a proposition, induction establishes a probability that the proposition is true, in much the same way that Gallup polls establish the probability that a particular candidate will win an election.

Certainly, an inductive proof may be overthrown by the appearance of sufficient contradictory support, just as Truman defeated Dewey for President in 1948, despite what public opinion polls had forecast. But what is common to all inductions is the notion of accumulating evidence that outweighs or outnumbers the contradictory evidence. Since induction is based on this accumulation of evidence, one piece of evidence is never enough, and the more relevant evidence you can supply, the better your induction.

Another type of inductive proof is based on comparison and contrast. Take the proposition that the sport of basketball is gaining popularity around the world. You could argue that the number of countries fielding basketball teams in the most recent Olympic Games exceeded by six the number competing in the preceding Olympiad, which in turn had shown an increase of ten national teams over those competing in the preceding games four years earlier. This comparison clearly demonstrates a trend toward greater popularity for basketball as an international sport. Similarly, if archaeologists can show that the accumulated artifacts of Neanderthal society closely parallel those that can be found today among the primitive tribes of the Amazon basin (who also find a democratic social structure crucial to their survival) then it is reasonable to suppose that the Neanderthals might also have practiced democracy. In neither of these cases is the conclusion a certainty, but the data point to a probability.

Finally, the inductive examination of evidence can also be used to establish probable causes. If, for example, we wished to discover why a great many sophomore math majors shifted their major to accounting during the second semester each year, we might poll them for their reasons, and this would clearly be an inductive approach. Alternatively, we might examine the math curriculum. There are ten sophomore-level math courses, ranging from modern algebra to vector analysis, but of these ten the only one that is an absolute requirement for the second-semester sophomore is differential equations. On this evidence you might claim that it is this course in differential equations that is separating the pure mathematicians from the applied ones.

Deductive Proofs

Suppose you were to be stopped for speeding and were to tell the highway patrol officer, "You shouldn't give me a ticket. The speed limit is not clearly marked." You would not be arguing inductively. Admittedly you would have to produce some evidence (namely, the speed limit sign) to show that, for instance, it was missing, knocked down, obscured, or defaced. But there is more to the argument than that.

In effect, what you are doing is appealing to a much more basic assumption, something that modern logicians call a **warrant**. A warrant is a shared belief, in this case something about which you hope that you and the officer can agree: you should not be held accountable for things you were not told. The case in point is this faulty sign, which did not adequately inform you of the legal speed limit. The conclusion is quite obvious: you shouldn't be held accountable in this situation.

The patrol officer, of course, has his own argument, and it is structured very much like yours. "State Law 76352-81," he says, "prescribes that persons who exceed the posted speed limit shall

be fined fifty dollars. You have exceeded the posted limit; therefore, you shall be fined fifty dollars."

What you and the patrol officer have been doing is engaging
in deductive argumentation. Each of you has used a **syllogism:** a
statement consisting of three propositions. These propositions
are so interrelated that if your audience will admit that the first
two are true, then they *must* admit that the last is true. To show
how the relationship works, let's begin with the argument you
used on the patrol officer. You began by stating your warrant: "I
shouldn't be held accountable for things I'm not informed of."
Let's convert that to a proposition. *People who have not been
informed about certain things are people who should not be held
accountable for those things.* You might draw a diagram, like
Figure 12.1, to illustrate the proposition.

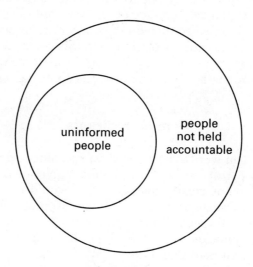

FIGURE 12.1

The diagram shows that the uninformed people are part of a
larger group of persons who are not held accountable. The remainder of those not held accountable might consist of mentally
incompetent persons and relatives of the sheriff, for example,
people who would not be held accountable even though they had
been informed.

The second proposition in your syllogism states: "I was not
informed about this thing." A diagram of this proposition, like
Figure 12.2, will place you inside the inner circle in the first

diagram, specifying you as a member of the group of uninformed people.

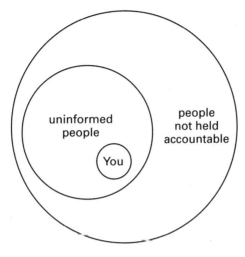

FIGURE 12.2

If you are inside the inner circle, you must be inside the larger circle, which you remember represented the group of people who were not to be held accountable. Your conclusion is unchallengeable: "I should not be held accountable."

Of course, we could also diagram the patrol officer's argument as in Figure 12.3.

FIGURE 12.3

And this argument also is unchallengeable; according to it, you now owe $50. Remember, however, that deductive arguments work only if the opponent admits the truth of the first two propositions. You might question the patrol officer's propositions. The first one, that speeders forfeit $50, is a law; the patrol officer has quoted a competent authority, and you will have to admit that he is right. The officer will prove his second proposition by offering inductive proof—a freshly calibrated radar set, which clocked you at 53 miles per hour—clearly in excess of the posted limit of 45. Thus, he says, you owe the fine.

You can't challenge the first proposition, and you can't challenge the conclusion, but you can challenge the second proposition—and that is what you have done with your argument. You have argued that the limit you exceeded was not posted. As you said in your second proposition, you were not informed. In order to prove your case, you would have to go back along the road you traveled and point out the absence or illegibility of the speed limit signs, again an inductive proof. If our officer accepts this demonstration and agrees with your first proposition that people should not be held accountable for things they don't know about (which seems reasonable enough even though you have offered no proof), then he will accept your conclusion and tear up your ticket.

The basic features of deductive arguments can be summed up as follows:

1. Deductive proofs consist of statements called "syllogisms"; these syllogisms are made up of propositions so related that if the first and second are true, the third must logically be true.
2. The first two propositions of a syllogism must be acceptable to your opponent because:
   a. they are warrants; that is, they are intuitively true. (People should not be held accountable for things they don't know about.)
   b. they are supported by authority. (Speeders will be fined $50: State Law 76352-81.)
   c. they are proved inductively. (I was not informed; the signs were torn down vs. You were speeding; I clocked you at 53 m.p.h.)

3. To challenge a deductive proof, you may not attack the conclusion, but you can attack one or both of the first two propositions. If either of them is unsound, the argument collapses.

4. Very few syllogisms are ever stated as nakedly as those we have examined here. More often they look like your initial statement: "You shouldn't give me this ticket; the speed limit isn't clearly marked." This statement contains only your second proposition and the conclusion, leaving unsaid your first proposition (I shouldn't be held accountable for things I don't know about). Syllogisms with missing but understood propositions are called **enthymemes,** and you should become familiar with them.

Remember that most deductive proofs appear in the form of enthymemes. Here are some additional examples:

1. I wouldn't trust her; she's a politician.
   (Politicians aren't to be trusted.)
   She's a politician.
   Therefore, she's not to be trusted.
2. As long as he gossips that way, he won't be a friend of mine.
   (None of my friends are gossips.)
   He is a gossip.
   Therefore, he is not one of my friends.
3. I wouldn't be surprised if she flunks; she cuts class at least once a week.
   (People who cut class frequently will flunk out.)
   She cuts class frequently.
   Therefore, she will flunk out.
4. If cutting classes causes people to flunk out, he's a goner for sure.
   People who cut class frequently will flunk out.
   (He cuts class frequently.)
   Therefore, he will flunk out.

For additional background information concerning deductive proofs, study the Appendix, "A Short Guide to Material and Formal Fallacies," which begins on p. 377.

Refutation

Sports commentators tell us that the best defense is a strong offense, and the same thing is true in persuasive writing. If you fashion your own arguments soundly and forcefully, then you needn't always be concerned about refuting your opponent's arguments. Nevertheless, knowing how to prepare a refutation is still a good idea, since you can't always be on the offensive. Sometimes you have to counterattack.

First, it is necessary to study your opponent's argument to determine whether the approach is an inductive or deductive one. Your strategies will vary accordingly. If, for example, your opponent argues inductively, offering examples to illustrate that a certain proposition is true (or at least is likely to be true) then you may counter the argument by claiming that your opponent's conclusion was made too hastily, that it was based on too little evidence. You would support your claim by supplying examples that tend to weaken the opponent's claim or perhaps even prove the opposite claim.

To cite a specific example, suppose your opponent argues that high schools are doing a poorer job each year in preparing students for college. The evidence offered is the steadily declining college board scores over the past fifteen years. These figures seem to be fairly convincing. Nevertheless, you might point out that with more and more students wanting to attend college, the number taking the tests during each of the past fifteen years has also grown. Now the declining scores—representing the work of a growing portion of each senior class, not just the top third—do not seem quite so devastating, and you have correctly pointed out that your opponent has not examined all the evidence.

Similarly, your opponent might argue from comparison, drawing the analogy that this year's football team is likely to win the conference title because it has at least six things in common with the last conference champion, the team of 1992. Your response might well be that the analogy is a faulty one since there are some significant differences that your opponent has overlooked between this team and the 1992 champions. Or suppose your opponent argues from cause, claiming that many majors abandon math for accounting at the end of the sophomore year because of their terrifying experiences in the required course in differential equations. You might respond that your opponent has not discovered the correct cause at all but has assumed that since many students drop out of math *after* taking differential equations, they have done so *because of* differential equations. The more convincing reason for the shift in majors is that it is among sophomore math majors that the accounting department does its most strenuous recruiting, luring them away from the pursuit of pure mathematics by tantalizing them with promises of financial rewards in the business world.

When you refute arguments by showing that your opponent has made a *hasty generalization*, a *faulty analogy*, or has proposed a *false cause*, you are pointing out some logical fallacies that entrap a great many writers. Other logical fallacies exist besides these three, and the most common are defined for you in the Appendix.

Deductive arguments, like inductive ones, may also prove to be faulty and subject to refutation. You have already seen one way to refute a deductive argument, in which you attack one or the other of the first two propositions, showing it to be untrue, unsupported, fallacious, or otherwise indefensible. If one of the first two propositions fails, the conclusion is unacceptable. Recall the example of the contested speeding ticket:

Those who exceed the posted speed limit will pay $50.
You exceeded the posted speed limit.
Therefore, you will pay $50.

Your chance of avoiding the fine depended on your success at refuting the second proposition by showing that the speed limit had not been properly posted—proving, in other words, that the proposition was not completely true.

Besides showing that one of the propositions of a syllogism is untrue, you may perhaps wish to claim that the reasoning itself is faulty and that the conclusion is therefore invalid. For example, a person might argue that since those who spare the rod spoil their children and since Mr. Smith's children are all spoiled rotten, then he is certainly not a believer in corporal punishment. This syllogism is not valid, as Figure 12.4 shows.

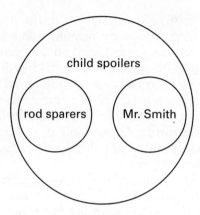

FIGURE 12.4

The diagram shows that although we have asserted that rod sparers are child spoilers and that Mr. Smith is a child spoiler, we do not necessarily have to agree that Mr. Smith is a rod sparer. The person who argues in this way is guilty of a formal fallacy (that is, one that violates the proper form of a syllogism). Formal fallacies are discussed in detail on pp. 387–392 of the Appendix.

There is still another way to refute an argument, and that is to agree with it, or at least to pretend to agree. For instance, you might *pretend* to agree with your opponent who has proposed the dropping of freshman composition from the curriculum. Your purpose, you say, is merely to point out some additional reasons that had been overlooked. Then you state your reasons for abolishing freshman composition: (1) it robs students of valuable time they could otherwise use to watch television and to attend various campus activities, such as concerts and ball games; (2) it discriminates against students who are illiterate; and (3) it demands that students spend precious hours in grim places like libraries. By reducing the opponent's argument to an absurdity, this type of ironic approach attempts to induce the audience to laugh at the opponent's claim. Even some apparently sound arguments are vulnerable to this kind of treatment, so it is very wise to examine your arguments carefully. Recall once again the seemingly airtight argument that you used on the highway patrol officer:

People should not be held accountable for laws they don't know about.

I was not informed about this law (the speed limit).

Therefore, I should not be held accountable for it.

You fully expected the officer to accept your first proposition as being intuitively sound. But suppose he or she had responded with a smirk, "And I guess the next thing you'll tell me will be that babies who don't know about the law of gravity will never fall out of their cribs." It's clear that to prevent this kind of reduction to absurdity, you'll need to tighten the language of your first proposition.*

Emotional Appeals

By now you may already have read "A Short Guide to Material and Formal Fallacies," which begins on p. 377 of the Appendix. If you have not, now is an excellent time to do so. The discussions of such fallacies as *appeal to pity* and *appeal to the people* are likely to convince you that there is an inherent weakness in arguments that play on people's sympathies and prejudices. After all, we have pointed out these fallacies and in the preceding section we showed how some of them could be used in refuting arguments. That was the purpose of discussing fallacies, wasn't it?

The answer to that question is a guarded "yes." We do like to believe that the best arguments are free from both formal and informal fallacies and appeal to our reason rather than to our emotions. This is true because we are logical, reasoning beings. But we also cry at movies, we like to be flattered, and we want

---

*If you have been guilty of *dicto simpliciter* (see p. 381) in the construction of your proposition, the officer is also guilty of *equivocation* (see p. 381) in deliberately confusing physical laws with traffic laws, but the remark does hint at the way your proposition should be amended; that is, your argument gains force rather than loses it, if you tighten the first proposition to read: "People should not be held accountable for *traffic laws* that they haven't been *informed of.*"

to feel good. And these very natural, human tendencies are in many cases very likely to overrule our reason.

It is because of this likelihood that emotional appeals prove to be so effective. We are bored by television commercials that seek to prove through tedious induction that one pain reliever is more effective than another—that it contains more "active ingredients" or that it provides more "hours of long-lasting relief." We may silently resolve that the next time acid indigestion strikes, we will get the fizzy remedy that in some way or another always contrives to make us laugh at our excesses instead of the one that shows us in sickening color how much stomach acid it can absorb.

We also suspect that pretty girls in seductive apparel and employing the fallacy of *transfer* (see p. 386) have sold more automobiles than serious gentlemen in business suits, convincingly armed with fuel consumption statistics.

Among the paragraphs and essays that appear in the following pages, there will be included some whose appeal is unabashedly emotional, and we make no apology for that. We strongly suggest, however, that the best approach to persuasion is one that appeals both to reason and to emotions. And that is not just our recommendation but Cicero's too. Remember that in his model argument, Cicero demanded that the propositions were to be proved rationally, but he reserved the concluding, and hence the most climactic, portion for emotional appeals.

Commentary on Student Work

At first, Gary was not at all comfortable with the idea of syllogisms when he encountered them in the classroom discussion. But he did finally see the underlying propositions in "The Declaration of Independence," once they had been pointed out to him, and he understood that Jefferson was appealing to a universally accepted warrant when he asserted that certain truths were "self-evident" and that one of these self-evident truths was that tyrannies ought to be overthrown. He then saw clearly that all Jefferson needed to do was demonstrate through a series of inductive examples that the state of affairs in the American colonies in the 1770s constituted a tyranny.

Gary also liked the way that Steinbeck appealed to a similar universal warrant in "How to Cuss," claiming that rare and precious things ought to be preserved. Everyone could agree with that. Then all Steinbeck needed to do was show that truly shocking words were rare and precious.

Consequently, when he met with his reading/writing group to do a bit of brainstorming for the upcoming argumentation paper, Gary felt fairly confident. He even had the germ of an idea, something that had been wandering around in his brain for the last several weeks, born in a late evening bull-session—the notion that students who had A averages going into the final examination period should not be obliged to take a comprehensive final exam.

Gary shared his idea with the group, and together they discussed the ways in which the plan might be presented. Universal warrants were not mentioned at first; rather, the discussion concentrated first on the benefits that would result from the proposal: cramming would be reduced; hard work and diligence would be rewarded. The group even contributed some examples of tangible rewards: getting the jump on Christmas or summer jobs by being able to leave school a week early, removing the risk of losing a top grade, receiving recognition for diligence, and giving faculty a chance to award something of value—beyond a grade—for excellent work.

Once he had jotted all of these ideas down in his journal, Gary began to analyze them. There was something of a universal warrant at stake here, perhaps even more. Cramming was bad—something that should be discouraged. Correspondingly, hard work was good, something that should be rewarded. This plan curbed the bad and rewarded the good. Who could be against that? The trick was to make the readers see it in just those terms.

His initial effort consisted of four paragraphs, very close to the essay that appears here, but lacking the second paragraph. The reading group approved of the direction that the argument was taking. Gary had managed to incorporate all the suggestions that the group had made, neatly fitting them to his general scheme. One student did raise a legitimate objection, however: "Do you know of any colleges where this kind of thing is already done? You could make a stronger case if you did."

The truth was that Gary did not know of any such college. What was he to do? He could ignore the objection, which didn't seem such a good idea, or he could confront it—but how? Then he recalled that *concessions* had been discussed in class. One way to make the reader lean in your direction is to anticipate some possible objections and to admit that they exist. Perhaps Gary could use such an approach to turn this apparent setback to his advantage. The group discussed this possibility, and one member added the crowning touch by noting that if no other colleges had such a plan, then Gary's plan had the additional virtue of being original. Gary wrote that down and added it as a part of his concession. The final revision of his essay follows.

No Finals for A-Students

(Deduction)

The Student Government Association is debating a plan that would allow students with an average of A in a course to skip the final exam. I think the plan should be adopted, not only by the Student Government but also by the Faculty Senate. 1

It would be nice if I could cite examples from colleges where such plans have been adopted and proved successful. But the fact that I don't know of any shouldn't be used as an argument against my position. Surely the students and faculty will not discard a proposal simply because it's original. 2

Just imagine how it would be if this plan were put into effect. Cramming would not be nearly as widespread during exam week as it is now. Students who wanted to make A's would study consistently throughout the semester, because that would be the surest way of getting an A. Poor students would still have to cram, but it would no longer be the kind of thing good students would feel they had to do. 3

Not only would the plan serve to promote good study habits; it would provide a very real reward for them. A-students would have the luxury of going home during finals, and, beyond that, they could get the jump on their classmates in securing the better summer jobs. 4

Perhaps best of all, this plan would give the faculty and university administration a way of rewarding excellence in scholarship. All that the good students see nowadays are awards going to actors, band members, debates, fraternity fund raisers, 5 and athletes. This plan would be an outstanding way to give an overlooked but deserving group of students (perhaps even the most deserving group) a well-earned tribute.

DISCUSSION QUESTIONS

1. The last three paragraphs of this essay can be reduced to syllogisms. The one in paragraph 3 might be stated this way:

   Anything that reduces cramming is a good idea.
   This plan reduces cramming.
   Therefore, this plan is a good idea.

   Here is a partial formulation for the remaining syllogisms. Fill in the missing premises.

   Anything that rewards good study habits is a good idea.

   _____

   Therefore, this plan is a good idea.

   _____

   This plan rewards deserving students.
   Therefore, this plan is a good plan.

2. How are the missing premises in the above syllogisms supported?
3. At one point the writer appears to have toyed with the idea of arguing inductively but dismissed the notion. Where do you get this impression?

STUDENT WORK

Let's Drive Fifty-five

(Induction)

Tom punched the accelerator, and the orange Corvette raced   1
down the interstate. The speedometer rose steadily from 55 to
65, 75, 80, and on up to 85 miles per hour. "There is no danger,"

Tom thought. "It's just road for miles." Even as Tom was thinking this, a dark form darted across the road in front of him. Automatically Tom swerved, but at the great speed he was going, he lost control, and the Corvette bounded across the median, crashing into a bank as Tom lost consciousness.

This is an example of the accidents that can occur due to   2
excessive speeds on the highways. The *North Carolina Blue Book of Traffic Safety* says that no one should drive a vehicle at a speed "greater than is reasonable or prudent under existing conditions." At the present time the speed limit is fifty-five miles per hour for interstate driving. Should this be the maximum speed for highways that are specifically designed for higher speeds? There are three good reasons why the speed limit should not be raised on interstate highways.

First of all, raising the speed limit on interstates would be bad   3
economically. "Punching it" on the interstate and driving at excessive speeds waste gasoline. Raising the speed limit nationwide would eventually result in greater dependence on foreign imports of oil.

Second, personal expenses would be higher if our present   4
speed limit were raised. The car maintenance required is greater when driving at speeds exceeding fifty-five miles per hour. Also, last year an estimated twenty-five billion dollars was spent due to drivers' exceeding the speed limit. This total includes insurance, property damage, and hospital costs due to accidents.

Lastly, speed kills. It is the number-one reason for death on   5
our highways. Last year over 48,000 people were killed in the United States due to speeding. Over three million people were injured last year, and 290,000 of these injured were unable to work.

What are your chances of being killed in relation to speed?   6
The North Carolina Highway Safety Division determines that speed makes accidents and death more likely. At twenty-five miles per hour your chances of being killed are estimated at twelve percent. At fifty-five miles per hour the chances of being killed are 300 percent greater as compared with twenty-five miles per hour, and 600 percent greater when traveling at sixty-five miles per hour.

When properly enforced, the fifty-five miles-per-hour speed   7
limit on interstate highways is safer, cuts down on personal expenses, and is smart economically. But more important, it

could save a life. Few people want to become another statistic, like Tom, or have that happen to a loved one.

DISCUSSION QUESTIONS

1. This essay cites a number of reasons for keeping the speed limit at fifty-five. Are these reasons, strictly speaking, an inductive proof?
2. Examine paragraphs 5 and 6. They contain a separate inductive argument. What is the proposition, and what is the evidence?
3. Look up "due to" in a reference grammar like Fowler's *Modern English Usage*, or ask your instructor about the construction. Are the uses of that phrase in paragraphs 2, 4, and 5 consistent with accepted usage?
4. What effective rhetorical devices does the writer use in the paper's conclusion?

The Right to Pray in School

(Deduction)

Ever since the days of William Penn, Roger Williams, and the Toleration Act of 1649, religious freedom has been one of the uppermost concerns of the citizens of this country. Religious freedom is one of the things guaranteed to each citizen of the United States by our Constitution and its Bill of Rights. The right to worship as one pleases certainly includes the right to pray as one pleases—either privately or publicly. And yet this precious right is being challenged today by those who would limit the places where citizens may pray, denying children the right to pray in school. This blatant obstruction of guaranteed citizen rights has got to end.

DISCUSSION QUESTIONS

1. Who were William Penn and Roger Williams, and why are their names useful in this argument? How about the Toleration Act?

2. How might you state the syllogism that is embedded in this paragraph? Its conclusion is clearly this: "Public prayer is a right guaranteed by the Constitution."
3. The syllogism is valid. Is it materially sound?

Against Public Prayer in the Schools

(Refutation)

Those who favor prayer in the public schools usually do so because of deeply felt religious convictions. They say that it is not enough for students to pray silently but that they should be allowed to express openly and publicly the feelings they hold in the privacy of their hearts. They feel that in denying students this right the government is overstepping itself and denying them a promised freedom, one insured by our Constitution, namely, freedom of religion.

Since the overwhelming majority of those who protest this denial of religious freedom are Christians, I am quite sure that they would be surprised to learn that in finding a right to public prayer in the Constitution they are appealing to a false authority, for Jesus Himself denied His followers such a privilege when He said in the Sermon on the Mount: "And when thou prayest, thou shalt not be as the hypocrites are: for they love to pray standing in the synagogues and in the corners of the streets, that they may be seen of men. Verily I say unto you, they have their reward. But when thou prayest enter into thy closet, and when thou hast shut thy door, pray to thy Father which is in secret; and thy Father which is in secret shall reward thee openly."

Regardless of how we might interpret our Constitution, Jesus—it seems—has come down on the side of those who oppose public prayer in the schools.

DISCUSSION QUESTIONS

1. The first paragraph anticipates a deductive argument in favor of public prayer in the schools. State that argument in its barest form.
2. In what way does the student attack that syllogism?

Guns for Self-Defense

(Emotional Appeal)

Of all the reasons why an American's right to own guns should never be challenged, there is a very personal one that for me outweighs all the rest. I want to protect my home. My home, my family, and our possessions mean more to me than all the constitutional and humanitarian claims of the gun controllers put together. Their arguments look good on paper, and they sound good when you hear them. But you can bet your next paycheck that they would each like to have a .38 in a drawer by their bed the next time they hear the tinkle of breaking glass and know that somewhere in their home there is a thief, a rapist, or a murderer.

DISCUSSION QUESTIONS

1. A contrast is the basis of the argument in "Guns for Self-Defense." What is the contrast between?
2. What specific factors of the writer's stance or tone, word choice, and organization make the last sentence of this paragraph so emotionally appealing?
3. Does this paragraph's argument have any basis in logic, or is it totally emotional? How might this argument be refuted, if at all?

Guns Aren't for Everyone

(Refutation)

People who argue for unlimited ownership of firearms seem to have it all going their way. Their case is hardly open to rebuttal. The Constitution insures all citizens the right to bear arms. They are citizens of this country; therefore, they have the right to bear arms. What could be simpler?

Their logic is unassailable. Their citizenship cannot be chal-   2
lenged, nor can the Constitution unless we choose to amend it.
But wait a moment. Does the Constitution really guarantee to all
the right to own firearms? Is that part of their argument as solid
as they would have us believe?

Let's look at what the Constitution actually says: "A well   3
regulated Militia, being necessary to the security of a free State,
the right of the people to keep and bear Arms, shall not be
infringed."

Now to me that statement seems to stop short of insuring   4
every citizen the right to keep and bear arms. It insures citizens
that right just as long as they are willing to take up the responsibility to protect the security of this free state by serving in the
militia or national guard. I think we have been misreading the
Constitution for a long time in allowing anyone with enough
money to buy a gun. The fathers of our country clearly intended
that the right to bear arms should carry with it the responsibility
to use that weapon to defend the country.

Well, those who favor free access to guns usually make all   5
kinds of claims about protecting their homes from all sorts of
enemies, ranging from burglars to invading Russians. You would
think they wouldn't mind my interpretation of the Constitution.
But just mention registration of firearms and they go berserk.
Nevertheless, it seems quite clear that the fathers of our country
intended that too. For here is another argument as sound and as
logical as theirs. A governor must know how to locate all the
members of his militia. And all gun owners are constitutionally
obligated to be members of the militia. Therefore, the governor
must know how to locate all gun owners.

Let them argue their way out of that one.   6

DISCUSSION QUESTIONS

1. The syllogism to be refuted is stated in the opening paragraph.
   What is it?
2. How does the writer refute this argument?
3. The rebuttal turns into an argument in favor of gun registration,
   one that is also based on a syllogism. How can that syllogism be
   stated?

Let Women Fight

(Induction)

I can see but one reason why women shouldn't be drafted into 1
combat, but there are several good reasons why they should be.

Women are good fighters. Other countries have not shrunk 2
from using women fighters. Russian women were valiant in the
defense of Stalingrad, hiding in shell craters and pulling the pin
on a hand grenade as a Nazi tank rolled over. Israeli women have
fought alongside their men in their recent wars, and the women
of the Viet Cong could whittle pungi sticks just as well as the
men.

It's worth remembering also that the Russians, the Israelis, 3
and the Viet Cong were winners.

It is also worth remembering that the primary thing that 4
makes men fight isn't patriotism or discipline. It's that they're
ashamed not to—afraid their comrades-in-arms would think
them cowards. Can you imagine how much fiercer the average
male soldier would be if his comrade-in-arms were a woman?

Those are the reasons for letting the women fight. The only 5
reason why they shouldn't is that they should simply refuse—until the Constitution guarantees them equal rights.

DISCUSSION QUESTIONS

1. Would you characterize this writer as being politically moderate,
   right of center, or left of center?
2. The writer asserts at the outset that there are a number of reasons
   why women should be drafted. How many are actually stated?
3. The clearest use of induction in this essay seems to occur in the
   second paragraph. What exactly is the evidence that is examined,
   and what is the unstated generalization arising from it?
4. Would you be surprised to learn that this student writer also
   wrote the definition essay "Feminist" on p. 276? What do the
   essays have in common?
5. Look up the term *a fortiori* in a dictionary. How is this term
   applicable to paragraph 4?

All Reasons but One

(Emotional Appeal)

I agree that rape victims should have the right to abortions on demand. And I also agree that victims of incest should have the same right. I am even sympathetic with the mother who cannot afford to raise another unplanned child. And I do not think that the high school or college girl should have to be the victim of a tragic sexual accident, one that the male partner can walk away from uninjured. I can find abortion acceptable in a good many situations which do not endanger the mother's life. All but one. I'm glad my mother didn't have one.

DISCUSSION QUESTIONS

1. What is the purpose of the first five sentences in this paragraph? What sort of emotional rapport do they establish with the audience?
2. What additional reasons for supporting abortion has the writer neglected to mention?
3. What is grammatically wrong with the next to last sentence? How would you correct that flaw? Or if you were the student writer, what might you say in defense of your original choice?
4. Why is the last sentence so effective?

PARAGRAPHS

Strike Out Little League

(Induction)

ROBIN ROBERTS

I still don't know what those three gentlemen in Williamsport had in mind when they organized Little League baseball.

I'm sure they didn't want parents arguing with their children about kids' games. I'm sure they didn't want to have family meals disrupted for three months every year. I'm sure they didn't want young athletes hurting their arms pitching under pressure at such a young age. I'm sure they didn't want young boys who don't have much athletic ability made to feel that something is wrong with them because they can't play baseball. I'm sure they didn't want a group of coaches drafting the players each year for different teams. I'm sure they didn't want unqualified men working with the young players. I'm sure they didn't realize how normal it is for an eight-year-old boy to be scared of a thrown or batted baseball. For the life of me, I can't figure out what they had in mind.

DISCUSSION QUESTIONS

1. How many elements are there to Roberts' induction? That is, how many pieces of evidence does he cite to support his contention that Little League baseball should be done away with?
2. What is peculiar about the way Roberts introduces each piece of evidence? Is that method of presentation effective?
3. If you do not already know who he is, look up Robin Roberts in a baseball history or reference book. How does knowledge of his great major-league career affect your reaction to what he has written here?

Laws We Need Not Obey

(Deduction)

MARTIN LUTHER KING, JR.

You express a great deal of anxiety over our willingness to   1
break laws. This is certainly a legitimate concern. Since we so diligently urge people to obey the Supreme Court's decision of 1954 outlawing segregation in public schools, at first glance it may seem rather paradoxical for us consciously to break laws.

One may well ask: "How can you advocate breaking some laws and obeying others?" The answer lies in the fact that there are two types of laws: just and unjust. I would be the first to advocate obeying just laws. Conversely, one has a moral responsibility to disobey unjust laws. I would agree with St. Augustine that "An unjust law is no law at all."

Now, what is the difference between the two? How does one   2 determine whether a law is just or unjust? A just law is a manmade code that squares with the moral law or the law of God. An unjust law is a code that is out of harmony with the moral law. To put it in the terms of St. Thomas Aquinas: An unjust law is a human law that is not rooted in eternal law and natural law. Any law that uplifts human personality is just. Any law that degrades human personality is unjust. All segregation statutes are unjust because segregation distorts the soul and damages the personality. It gives the segregator a false sense of superiority and the segregated a false sense of inferiority. Segregation, to use the terminology of the Jewish philosopher Martin Buber, substitutes an "I-it" relationship for an "I-thou" relationship and ends up relegating persons to the status of things. Hence segregation is not only politically, economically, and sociologically unsound, it is morally wrong and sinful. Paul Tillich has said that sin is separation. Is not segregation an existential expression of man's tragic separation, his awful estrangement, his terrible sinfulness? Thus it is that I can urge men to obey the 1954 decision of the Supreme Court, for it is morally right; and I can urge them to disobey segregation ordinances, for they are morally wrong.

DISCUSSION QUESTIONS

1. We might state the first proposition of King's syllogism this way: All laws that degrade human personality are laws that we have no moral responsibility to obey. Supply his next proposition and the conclusion.
2. Does King support the first two propositions in his syllogism? If so, how?
3. The argument is taken from King's 1963 "Letter from Birmingham Jail," addressed to the clergy who had suggested he be more patient in his quest for civil rights. What is there about King's argument that has a special appeal for this audience?

Where's the Help for Our Home Front?

(Refutation)

MARIAN WRIGHT EDELMAN

In response to a distant tyrant, we sent hundreds of thousands of American mothers and fathers, sons and daughters, husbands and wives, sisters and brothers to the Persian Gulf. According to Secretary of State James Baker, the Gulf War was fought to protect our "life style" and standard of living and the rights of the Kuwaiti people. No deficit or recession was allowed to stand in the way. How, then, can we reconcile our failure to engage equally the enemies of poverty and violence and family disintegration within our own nation? When are we going to mobilize and send troops to fight for the "life style" of the 100,000 American children who are homeless each night, to fight for the standard of living of thousands of young families whose earning capacity is eroding and who are struggling to buy homes, pay off college loans, and find and afford child care? Where are the leaders coming to the rescue of millions of poor working- and middle-class families fighting to hold together their fragile households on declining wages and jobs? Why are they not acting to help the one in six families with children headed by a single mother—29 percent of whom are poor? Isn't it time to tell our leaders to bail out our young families with the same zeal as they bailed out failed thrift and banking institutions to the tune of an estimated $115 billion by 1992?

DISCUSSION QUESTIONS

1. Where does Edelman present the basic proposition she is refuting? What is that proposition?
2. In her paragraph's first sentence, rather than just writing "Hundreds of thousands of American troops," Edelman instead lists eight kinds of American family members who were sent to the Persian Gulf for 1991s Operation Desert Storm. What does her refutation seem to gain by this tactic?
3. How does Edelman use comparison/contrast to organize and to strengthen her refutation?

4. What part do *rhetorical questions* (see Glossary) play in Edelman's refutation?
5. How is the unity of her paragraph affected by its final sentence?

Shame

(Emotional Appeal)

MALCOLM X

As long as the white man sent you to Korea, you bled. He sent you to Germany, you bled. He sent you to the South Pacific to fight the Japanese, you bled. You bleed for white people, but when it comes to seeing your own church being bombed and little black girls murdered, you haven't got any blood. You bleed when the white man says bleed; you bite when the white man says bite; and you bark when the white man says bark.

DISCUSSION QUESTIONS

1. Malcolm X mentions a bombed church and murdered girls. What event is he probably referring to?
2. What is the effect of the repetitions Malcolm uses in his delivery?
3. What device does Malcolm use in the last sentence to heighten the feeling of shame that he wishes to instill in his audience?

ESSAYS

To Err Is Wrong

(Induction)

ROGER VON OECH

Roger Von Oech holds the only Ph.D. in the History of Ideas ever granted by Stanford University, a degree he designed for himself. After completing that degree in 1975, he founded a business consulting firm named Creative Think, in Menlo

Park, California. His major writings include A Kick in the Seat
of the Pants *(1986) and* A Whack on the Side of the Head *(1983),
from which this essay is taken.*

In the summer of 1979, Boston Red Sox first baseman Carl   1
Yastrzemski became the fifteenth player in baseball history to
reach the three thousand hit plateau. This event drew a lot of
media attention, and for about a week prior to the attainment of
this goal, hundreds of reports covered Yaz's every move. Finally,
one reporter asked, "Hey Yaz, aren't you afraid all of this attention will go to your head?" Yastrzemski replied, "I look at it this
way: in my career I've been up to bat over ten thousand times.
That means I've been unsuccessful at the plate over seven thousand times. That fact alone keeps me from getting a swollen
head.

Most people consider success and failure as opposites, but   2
they are actually both products of the same process. As Yaz
suggests, an activity which produces a hit may also produce a
miss. It is the same with creative thinking; the same energy
which generates good creative ideas also produces errors.

Many people, however, are not comfortable with errors. Our   3
educational system, based on "the right answer" belief, culti-
vates our thinking in another, more conservative way. From an
early age, we are taught that right answers are good and incorrect
answers are bad. This value is deeply embedded in the incentive
system used in most schools:

Right over 90% of the time = "A"
Right over 80% of the time = "B"
Right over 70% of the time = "C"
Right over 60% of the time = "D"
Less than 60% correct, you fail.

From this we learn to be right as often as possible and to keep
our mistakes to a minimum. We learn, in other words, that "to
err is wrong."

Playing It Safe

With this kind of attitude, you aren't going to be taking too   4
many chances. If you learn that failing even a little penalizes you
(e.g., being wrong only 15% of the time garners you only a "B"

performance), you learn not to make mistakes. And more important, you learn not to put yourself in situations where you might fail. This leads to conservative thought patterns designed to avoid the stigma our society puts on "failure."

I have a friend who recently graduated from college with a Master's degree in Journalism. For the last six months, she has been trying to find a job, but to no avail. I talked with her about her situation, and realized that her problem is that she doesn't know how to fail. She went through eighteen years of schooling without ever failing an examination, a paper, a midterm, a pop-quiz, or a final. Now, she is reluctant to try any approaches where she might fail. She has been conditioned to believe that failure is bad in and of itself, rather than a potential stepping stone to new ideas.

Look around. How many middle managers, housewives, administrators, teachers, and other people do you see who are afraid to try anything new because of this fear of failure? Most of us have learned not to make mistakes in public. As a result, we remove ourselves from many learning experiences except for those occurring in the most private of circumstances.

A Different Logic

From a practical point of view, "to err is wrong" makes sense. Our survival in the everyday world requires us to perform thousands of small tasks without failure. Think about it: you wouldn't last very long if you were to step out in front of traffic or stick your hand into a pot of boiling water. In addition, engineers whose bridges collapse, stock brokers who lose money for their clients and copywriters whose ad campaigns decrease sales won't keep their jobs very long.

Nevertheless, too great an adherence to the belief "to err is wrong" can greatly undermine your attempts to generate new ides. If you're more concerned with producing right answers than generating original ideas, you'll probably make uncritical use of the rules, formulae, and procedures used to obtain these right answers. By doing this, you'll by-pass the germinal phase of the creative process, and thus spend little time testing assumptions, challenging the rules, asking what-if questions, or just playing around with the problem. All of these techniques will produce some correct answers, but in the germinal phase errors are viewed as a necessary by-product of creative thinking. As Yaz would put it, "If you want the hits, be prepared for the misses." That's the way the game of life goes.

Errors as Stepping Stones

Whenever an error pops up, the usual response is "Jeez, an-   9
other screwup, what went wrong this time?" The creative thinker, on the other hand, will realize the potential value of errors, and perhaps say something like, "Would you look at that! Where can it lead our thinking?" And then he or she will go on to use the error as a stepping stone to a new idea. As a matter of fact, the whole history of discovery is filled with people who used erroneous assumptions and failed ideas as stepping stones to new ideas. Columbus thought he was finding a shorter route to India. Johannes Kepler stumbled on to the idea of interplanetary gravity because of assumptions which were right for the wrong reasons. And, Thomas Edison knew 1800 ways *not* to build a light bulb.

The following story about the automotive genius Charles   10
Kettering exemplifies the spirit of working through erroneous assumption to good ideas. In 1912, when the automobile industry was just beginning to grow, Kettering was interested in improving gasoline-engine efficiency. The problem he faced was "knock," the phenomenon in which gasoline takes too long to burn in the cylinder—thereby reducing efficiency.

Kettering began searching for ways to eliminate the "knock."   11
He thought to himself, "How can I get the gasoline to combust in the cylinder at an earlier time?" The key concept here is "early." Searching for analagous situations, he looked around for models of "things that happen early." He thought of historical models, physical models, and biological models. Finally, he remembered a particular plant, the trailing arbutus, which "happens early," i.e., it blooms in the snow ("earlier" than other plants). One of this plant's chief characteristics is its red leaves which help the plant retain light at certain wavelengths. Kettering figured that it must be the color red which made the trailing arbutus bloom earlier.

Now came the critical step in Kettering's chain of thought.   12
He asked himself, "How can I make the gasoline red? Perhaps I'll

put red dye in the gasoline—maybe that'll make it combust earlier." He looked around his workshop, and found that he didn't have any red dye. But he did have some iodine—perhaps that would do. He added the iodine to the gasoline and, lo and behold, the engine didn't "knock."

Several days later, Kettering wanted to make sure that it was   13
the redness of the iodine which had in fact solved his problem. He got some red dye and added it to the gasoline. Nothing happened! Kettering then realized that it wasn't the "redness" which had solved the "knock" problem, but certain other properties of iodine. In this case, an error had proven to be a stepping stone to a better idea. Had he known that "redness" alone was not the solution, he may not have found his way to the additives in iodine.

Negative Feedback

Errors serve another useful purpose: they tell us when to   14
change direction. When things are going smoothly, we generally don't think about them. To a great extent, this is because we function according to the principle of negative feedback. Often it is only when things or people fail to do their job that they get our attention. For example, you are probably not thinking about your kneecaps right now; that's because everything is fine with them. The same goes for your elbows: they are also performing their function—no problem at all. But if you were to break a leg, you would immediately notice all of the things you could no longer do, but which you used to take for granted.

Negative feedback means that the current approach is not   15
working, and it is up to you to figure out a new one. We learn by trial and error, not by trial and rightness. If we did things correctly every time, we would never have to change direction— we'd just continue the current course and end up with more of the same.

For example, after the supertanker *Amoco Cadiz* broke up off   16
the coast of Brittany in the spring of 1978, thereby polluting the coast with hundreds of thousands of tons of oil, the oil industry rethought many of its safety standards regarding petroleum transport. The same thing happened after the accident at Three Mile Island nuclear reactor in 1979—many procedures and safety standards were changed.

Neil Goldschmidt, former Secretary of Transportation, had   17
this to say about the Bay Area Rapid Transit (BART):

> It's gotten too fashionable around the country to beat up on
> BART and not give credit to the vision that put this system in
> place. We have learned from BART around the country. The
> lessons were put to use in Washington, in Atlanta, in Buffalo,
> and other cities where we are building mass transit systems.
> One of the lessons is not to build a system like BART.

We learn by our failures. A person's errors are the whacks that
lead him to think something different.

Trying New Things

Your error rate in any activity is a function of your familiarity   18
with that activity. If you are doing things that are routine and
have a high likelihood of correctness, then you will probably
make very few errors. But if you are doing things that have no
precedence in your experience or are trying different approaches,
then you will be making your share of mistakes. Innovators may
not bat a thousand—far from it—but they do get new ideas.

The creative director of an advertising agency told me that he   19
isn't happy unless he is failing at least half of the time. As he puts
it, "If you are going to be original, you are going to be wrong a
lot."

One of my clients, the president of a fast-growing computer   20
company, tells his people: "We're innovators. We're doing things
nobody has ever done before. Therefore, we are going to be making mistakes. My advice to you: make your mistakes, but make
them in a hurry."

Another client, a division manager of a high-technology com-   21
pany, asked his vice president of engineering what percentage of
their new products should be successful in the marketplace. The
answer he received was "about 50%." The division manager
replied, "That's too high. 30% is a better target; otherwise we'll
be too conservative in our planning."

Along similar lines, in the banking industry, it is said that if   22
the credit manager never has to default any of his loans, it's a sure
sign he's not being aggressive enough in the marketplace.

Thomas J. Watson, the founder of IBM, has similar words: 23
"The way to succeed is to double your failure rate."

Thus, errors, at the very least, are a sign that we are diverging 24
from the main road and trying different approaches.

Nature's Errors

Nature serves as a good example of how trial and error can be 25
used to make changes. Every now and then genetic mutations
occur—errors in gene reproduction. Most of the time, these mutations have a deleterious effect on the species, and they drop out
of the gene pool. But occasionally, a mutation provides the species with something beneficial, and that change will be passed on
to future generations. The rich variety of all species is due to this
trial and error process. If there had never been any mutations
from the first amoeba, where would we be now?

Summary

There are places where errors are inappropriate, but the ger- 26
minal phase of the creative process isn't one of them. Errors are
a sign that you are diverging from the well-traveled path. If you're
not failing every now and then, it's a sign that you're not being
very innovative.

Tip #1:
If you make an error, use it as a stepping stone to a new idea
you might not have otherwise discovered.

Tip #2:
Differentiate between errors of "commission" and those of
"omission." The latter can be more costly than the former. If
you're not making any errors, you might ask yourself, "How
many opportunities am I missing by not being more aggressive?"

Tip #3:
Strengthen your "risk muscle." Everyone has one, but you have
to exercise it or else it will atrophy. Make it a point to take at
least one risk every twenty-four hours.

Tip #4:
Remember these two benefits of failure. First, if you do fail, you
learn what doesn't work; and second, the failure gives you an
opportunity to try a new approach.

DISCUSSION: CONTENT

1. If you have read the essay in Chapter 8, "How Asian Teachers Polish Each Lesson to Perfection," compare the attitude that the authors of that essay exhibit toward errors and the attitude that von Oech expresses here.
2. What, according to von Oech, is the general attitude of America's educational establishment toward error? What effect does that have on students, particularly on their ability to think creatively?
3. The author supplies several examples of flawed thinking, or errors, that led to insight and success. What are they?
4. What does von Oech mean by "negative feedback"? What examples does he supply to explain the term?
5. Truly creative thinkers, according to von Oech, expect a large number of errors. How does he support that claim?

DISCUSSION: FORM

1. The first two paragraphs of this essay serve as its introduction. What method of development is von Oech using there? How does that method serve to introduce his thesis?
2. The inductive method of argumentation is used most obviously in the section of the essay bearing the subhead "Errors as Stepping Stones." Describe how that induction is organized. Induction occurs again in another section as well. Which one? How is it arranged there?
3. How would you describe the author's tone, that is, his attitude toward the subject matter and his attitude toward his audience? What clues signal that attitude?

Sexism in English: A Feminist View

(Induction)

ALLEEN PACE NILSEN

Alleen Pace Nilsen (b. 1936), who is professor of English and assistant vice-president for academic personnel at Arizona State University, has published a number of essays and books on the topic she treats in this essay, the most notable being

Sexism and Language *(1977). Her most recent book is* Literature for Today's Young Adults, *3d ed. (1989).*

Does culture shape language? Or does language shape culture? This is as difficult a question as the old puzzler of which came first, the chicken or the egg, because there's no clear separation between language and culture.   1

A well-accepted linguistic principle is that as culture changes   2
so will the language. The reverse of this—as a language changes so will the culture—is not so readily accepted. This is why some linguists smile (or even scoff) at feminist attempts to replace *Mrs.* and *Miss* with *Ms.* and to find replacements for those all-inclusive words which specify masculinity, e.g., *chairman, mankind, brotherhood, freshman,* etc.

Perhaps they are amused for the same reason that it is the   3
doctor at a cocktail party who laughs the loudest at the joke about the man who couldn't afford an operation so he offered the doctor a little something to touch up the X-ray. A person working constantly with language is likely to be more aware of how really deep-seated sexism is in our communication system.

Last winter I took a standard desk dictionary and gave it a   4
place of honor on my night table. Every night that I didn't have anything more interesting to do, I read myself to sleep making a card for each entry that seemed to tell something about male and female. By spring I had a rather dog-eared dictionary, but I also had a collection of note cards filling two shoe boxes. The cards tell some rather interesting things about American English.

First, in our culture it is a woman's body which is considered   5
important while it is a man's mind or his activities which are valued. A woman is sexy. A man is successful.

I made a card for all the words which came into modern   6
English from somebody's name. I have a two-and-one-half-inch stack of cards which are men's names now used as everyday words. The women's stack is less than a half inch high and most of them came from Greek mythology. Words coming from the names of famous American men include *lynch, sousaphone, sideburns, Pullman, rickettsia, Shick test, Winchester rifle, Franklin stove, Bartlett pear, teddy bear,* and *boysenberry.* The only really common words coming from the names of American women are *bloomers* (after Amelia Jenks Bloomer) and *Mae West*

jacket. Both of these words are related in some way to a woman's physical anatomy, while the male words (except for *sideburns* after General Burnsides) have nothing to do with the namesake's body.

This reminded me of an earlier observation that my husband and I made about geographical names. A few years ago we became interested in what we called "Topless Topography" when we learned that the Grand Tetons used to be simply called *The Tetons* by French explorers and *The Teats* by American frontiersmen. We wrote letters to several map makers and found the following listings: *Nippletop* and *Little Nippletop* near Mt. Marcy in the Adirondacks, *Nipple Mountain* in Archuleta County, Colorado, *Nipple Peak* in Coke County, Texas, *Nipple Butte* in Pennington, South Dakota, *Squaw Peak* in Placer County, California (and many other places), *Maiden's Peak* and *Squaw Tit* (they're the same mountain) in the Cascade Range in Oregon, *Jane Russell Peaks* near Stark, New Hampshire, and *Mary's Nipple* near Salt Lake City, Utah.

We might compare these names to Jackson Hole, Wyoming, or Pikes Peak, Colorado. I'm sure we would get all kinds of protests from the Jackson and Pike descendants if we tried to say that these typographical features were named because they in some way resembled the bodies of Jackson and Pike, respectively.

This preoccupation with women's breasts is neither new nor strictly American. I was amused to read the derivation of the word *Amazon.* According to Greek folk etymology, the *a* means "without" as in *atypical* or *amoral* while *mazon* comes from *mazos* meaning "breast." According to the legend, these women cut off one breast so that they could better shoot their bows. Perhaps the feeling was that the women had to trade in part of their femininity in exchange for their active masculine role.

There are certain pairs of words which illustrate the way in which sexual connotations are given to feminine words while the masculine words retain a serious, businesslike aura. For example, being a *callboy* is perfectly respectable. It simply refers to a person who calls actors when it is time for them to go on stage, but being a *call girl* is being a prostitute.

Also we might compare *sir* and *madam. Sir* is a term of respect while *madam* has acquired the meaning of a brothel manager. The same thing has happened to the formerly cognate terms, *master* and *mistress.* Because of its acquired sexual connotations, *mistress* is now carefully avoided in certain contexts.

For example, the Boy Scouts have *scoutmasters* but certainly not *scoutmistresses*. And in a dog show the female owner of a dog is never referred to as the *dog's mistress*, but rather as the *dog's master*.

Master appears in such terms as *master plan, concert master, schoolmaster, mixmaster, master charge, master craftsman*, etc. But *mistress* appears in very few compounds. This is the way it is with dozens of words which have male and female counterparts. I found two hundred such terms, e.g., *usher-usherette, heir-heiress, hero-heroine*, etc. In nearly all cases it is the masculine word which is the base with a feminine suffix being added for the alternate version. The masculine word also travels into compounds while the feminine word is a dead end; e.g., from *king-queen* comes kingdom but not *queendom*, from *sportsman-sportslady* comes *sportsmanship* but not *sportsladyship*, etc. There is one—and only one—semantic area in which the masculine word is not the base or more powerful word. This is in the area dealing with sex and marriage. Here it is the feminine word which is dominant. *Prostitute* is the base word with *male prostitute* being the derived term. *Bride* appears in *bridal shower, bridal gown, bridal attendant, bridesmaid*, and even in *bridegroom*, while *groom* in the sense of *bridegroom* does not appear in any compounds, not even to name the groom's attendants or his prenuptial party. 12

At the end of a marriage, this same emphasis is on the female. If it ends in divorce, the woman gets the title of *divorcée* while the man is usually described with a statement, such as, "He's divorced." When the marriage ends in death, the woman is a *widow* and the -*er* suffix which seems to connote masculine (probably because it is an agentive or actor type suffix) is added to make *widower*. *Widower* doesn't appear in any compounds (except for *grass widower*, which is another companion term), but *widow* appears in several compounds and in addition has some acquired meanings, such as the extra hand dealt to the table in certain card games and an undesirable leftover line of type in printing. 13

If I were an anthropological linguist making observations about a strange and primitive tribe, I would duly note on my tape recorder that I had found linguistic evidence to show that in the area of sex and marriage the female appears to be more important than the male, but in all other areas of the culture, it seems that the reverse is true. 14

But since I am not an anthropological linguist, I will simply   15
go on to my second observation, which is that women are expected to play a passive role while men play an active one.

One indication of women's passive role is the fact that they   16
are often identified as something to eat. What's more passive
than a plate of food? Last spring I saw an announcement advertising the Indiana University English Department picnic. It read
"Good Food! Delicious Women!" The publicity committee was
probably jumped on by local feminists, but it's nothing new to
look on women as "delectable morsels." Even women compliment each other with "You look good enough to eat," or "You
have a peaches and cream complexion." Modern slang constantly
comes up with new terms, but some of the old standbys for
women are: *cute tomato, dish, peach, sharp cookie, cheese cake,
honey, sugar, and sweetie-pie.* A man may occasionally be addressed as *honey,* or described as a *hunk of meat,* but certainly
men are not laid out on a buffet and labeled as women are.

Women's passivity is also shown in the comparisons made to   17
plants. For example, to *deflower* a woman is to take away her
virginity. A girl can be described as a *clinging vine,* a *shrinking
violet,* or a *wall flower.* On the other hand, men are too active to
be thought of as plants. The only time we make the comparison
is when insulting a man we say he is like a woman by calling him
a *pansy.*

We also see the active-passive contrast in the animal terms   18
used with males and females. Men are referred to as *studs, bucks,*
and *wolves,* and they go *tomcatting* around. These are all aggressive roles, but women have such pet names as *kitten, bunny,
beaver, bird, chick, lamb,* and *fox.* The idea of being a pet seems
much more closely related to females than to males. For instance, little girls grow up wearing *pigtails* and *ponytails* and
they dress in *halters* and *dog collars.*

The active-passive contrast is also seen in the proper names   19
given to boy babies and girl babies. Girls are much more likely
to be given names like *Ivy, Rose, Ruby, Jewel, Pearl, Flora, Joy,*
etc., while boys are given names describing active roles such as
Martin (warlike), *Leo* (lion), *William* (protector), *Ernest* (resolute
fighter), and so on.

Another way that women play a passive role is that they are   20
defined in relationship to someone else. This is what feminists
are protesting when they ask to be identified as *Ms.* rather than
as *Mrs.* or *Miss.* It is a constant source of irritation to women's

organizations that when they turn in items to newspapers under their own names, that is, Susan Glascoe, Jeanette Jones, and so forth, the editors consistently rewrite the item so that the names read Mrs. John Glascoe, Mrs. Robert E. Jones.

In the dictionary I found what appears to be an attitude on the part of editors that it is almost indecent to let a respectable woman's name march unaccompanied across the pages of a dictionary. A woman's name must somehow be escorted by a male's name regardless of whether or not the male contributed to the woman's reason for being in the dictionary, or in his own right, was as famous as the woman. For example, Charlotte Brontë is identified as Mrs. Arthur B. Nicholls, Amelia Earhart is identified as Mrs. George Palmer Putnam, Helen Hayes is identified as Mrs. Charles MacArthur, Zona Gale is identified as Mrs. William Llewelyn Breese, and Jenny Lind is identified as Mme. Otto Goldschmidt. 21

Although most of the women are identified as Mrs. ___ or as the wife of ___ , other women are listed with brothers, fathers, or lovers. Cornelia Otis Skinner is identified as the daughter of Otis, Harriet Beecher Stowe is identified as the sister of Henry Ward Beecher, Edith Sitwell is identified as the sister of Osbert and Sacheverell, Nell Gwyn is identified as the mistress of Charles II, and Madame Pompadour is identified as the mistress of Louis XV. 22

The women who did get into the dictionary without the benefit of a masculine escort are a group sort of on the fringes of respectability. They are the rebels and the crusaders: temperance leaders Frances Elizabeth Caroline Willard and Carry Nation, women's rights leaders Carrie Chapman Catt and Elizabeth Cady Stanton, birth control educator Margaret Sanger, religious leader Mary Baker Eddy, and slaves Harriet Tubman and Phillis Wheatley. 23

I would estimate that far more than fifty percent of the women listed in the dictionary were identified as someone's wife. But of all the men—and there are are probably ten times as many men as women—only one was identified as "the husband of. . . ." This was the unusual case of Frederic Joliot, who took the last name of Joliot-Curie and was identified as "husband of Irene." Apparently Irene, the daughter of Pierre and Marie Curie, did not want to give up her maiden name when she married and so the couple took the hyphenated last name. 24

There are several pairs of words which also illustrate the more powerful role of the male and the relational role of the 25 female. For example a *count* is a high political officer with a *countess* being simply the wife of a count. The same is true for a *duke* and a *duchess* and a *king* and a *queen*. The fact that a king is usually more powerful than a queen might be the reason that Queen Elizabeth's husband is given the title of *prince* rather than *king*. Since *king* is a stronger word than *queen*, it is reserved for a true heir to the throne because if it were given to someone coming into the royal family by marriage, then the subjects might forget where the true power lies. With the weaker word of *queen*, this would not be a problem; so a woman marrying a ruling monarch is given the title without question.

My third observation is that there are many positive connotations connected with the concept of masculine, while there are either trivial or negative connotations connected with the corresponding feminine concept.   26

Conditioning toward the superiority of the masculine role   27 starts very early in life. Child psychologists point out that the only area in which a girl has more freedom than a boy is in experimenting with an appropriate sex role. She is much freer to be a *tomboy* than is her brother to be a *sissy*. The proper names given to children reflect this same attitude. It's perfectly all right for a girl to have a boy's name, but not the other way around. As girls are given more and more of the boys' names, parents shy away from using boy names that might be mistaken for girl names, so the number of available masculine names is constantly shrinking. Fifty years ago *Hazel, Beverly, Marion, Frances* and *Shirley* were all perfectly acceptable boys' names. Today few parents give these names to baby boys and adult men who are stuck with them self-consciously go by their initials or by abbreviated forms such as *Haze* or *Shirl*. But parents of little girls keep crowding the masculine set and currently popular girls' names include *Jo, Kelly, Teri, Cris, Pat, Shawn, Toni,* and *Sam*.

When the mother of one of these little girls tells her to *be a*   28 *lady*, she means for her to sit with her knees together. But when the father of a little boy tells him to *be a man*, he means for him to be noble, strong, and virtuous. The whole concept of manliness has such positive connotations that it is a compliment to call a male a *he-man*, a *manly man*, or a *virile man* (*virile* comes from the Indo-European *vir*, meaning "man"). In each of these three terms, we are implying that someone is doubly good because he is doubly a man.

Compare *chef* with *cook, tailor* and *seamstress,* and *poet*   29
with *poetess.* In each case, the masculine form carries with it an
added degree of excellence. In comparing the masculine *governor*
with the feminine *governess* and the masculine *major* with the
feminine *majorette,* the added feature is power.

The difference between positive male and negative female   30
connotations can be seen in several pairs of words which differ
denotatively only in the matter of sex. For instance compare
bachelor with the terms *spinster* and *old maid. Bachelor* has
such positive connotations that modern girls have tried to borrow the feeling in the term *bachelor-girl. Bachelor* appears in
glamorous terms such as *bachelor pad, bachelor party,* and
bachelor button. But *old maid* has such strong negative feelings
that it has been adopted into other areas, taking with it the
feeling of undesirability. It has the metaphorical meaning of
shriveled and unwanted kernels of pop corn, and it's the name of
the last unwanted card in a popular game for children.

Patron and *matron* (Middle English for *father* and *mother*) are   31
another set where women have tried to borrow the positive
masculine connotations, this time through the word *patroness,*
which literally means "female father." Such a peculiar term
came about because of the high prestige attached to the word
patron in such phrases as "a patron of the arts" or "a patron
saint." *Matron* is more apt to be used in talking about a woman
who is in charge of a jail or a public rest room.

Even *lord* and *lady* have different levels of connotation. *Our*   32
Lord is used as a title for deity, while the corresponding *Our Lady*
is a relational title for Mary, the mortal mother of Jesus. *Land-*
lord has more dignity than *landlady* probably because the landlord is more likely to be thought of as the owner while the
landlady is the person who collects the rent and enforces the
rules. *Lady* is used in many insignificant places where the corresponding *lord* would never be used, for example, *ladies' room,*
ladies' sizes, ladies' aid society, ladybug, etc.

This overuse of *lady* might be compared to the overuse of   33
queen, which is rapidly losing its prestige as compared to *king.*
Hundreds of beauty queens are crowned each year and nearly
every community in the United States has its *Dairy Queen* or its
Freezer Queen, etc. Male homosexuals have adopted the terms to
identify the "feminine" partner. And advertisers who are constantly on the lookout for euphemisms to make unpleasant
sounding products salable have recently dealt what might be a

death blow to the prestige of the word *queen*. They have begun to use it as an indication of size. For example, *queen-size* panty hose are panty hose for fat women. The meaning comes through a comparison with *king-size,* meaning big. However, there's a subtle difference in that our culture considers it desirable for males to be big because size is an indication of power, but we prefer that females be small and petite. So using *king-size* as a term to indicate bigness partially enhances the prestige of *king,* but using *queen-size* to indicate bigness brings unpleasant associations to the word *queen.*

Another set that might be compared are *brave* and *squaw.* 34 The word *brave* carries with it the connotations of youth, vigor, and courage, while *squaw* implies almost opposite characteristics. With the set *wizard* and *witch,* the main difference is that *wizard* implies skill and wisdom combined with magic, while *witch* implies evil intentions combined with magic. Part of the unattractiveness of both *squaw* and *witch* is that they suggest old age, which in women is particularly undesirable. When I lived in Afghanistan (1967–1969), I was horrified to hear a proverb stating that when you see an old man you should sit down and take a lesson, but when you see an old woman you should throw a stone. I was equally startled when I went to compare the connotations of our two phrases *grandfatherly advice* and *old wives' tales.* Certainly it isn't expressed with the same force as in the Afghan proverb, but the implication is similar.

In some of the animal terms used for women the extreme 35 undesirability of female old age is also seen. For instance consider the unattractiveness of *old nag* as compared to *filly,* of *old crow* or *old bat* as compared to *bird,* and of being *catty* as compared to being *kittenish.* The chicken metaphor tells the whole story of a girl's life. In her youth she is a *chick,* then she marries and begins feeling *cooped up,* so she goes to *hen parties* where she *cackles* with her friends. Then she has her *brood* and begins to *henpeck* her husband. Finally she turns into *an old biddy.*

DISCUSSION: CONTENT

1. How did Nilsen secure the evidence that she presents in this essay to prove that there is sexism in our language?

2. According to Nilsen, the English language reveals that men and
   women are not valued for the same reasons. What are women
   valued for? And men?
3. What does she mean by "Topless Topography"?
4. Nilsen claims that in English masculine words form more compounds than do feminine words—except in what area?
5. Passivity of women in American society is illustrated by what
   facts of language, according to Nilsen?
6. List five examples of masculine words that have more positive
   connotations than their female counterparts.

DISCUSSION: FORM

1. An inductive argument follows the scientific method of investigation, gathering evidence and then making generalizations based
   on the evidence accumulated. Explain how Nilsen's argument
   follows this pattern.
2. In what paragraph does Nilsen state the proposition to be proved
   in its most general terms? After that initial statement she organ-
   izes her evidence into three parts to support three distinct and
   more concrete propositions, each subordinate to the general one,
   In what paragraphs does she introduce these three concrete
   propositions? What are they?
3. The evidence that Nilsen presents to support each of these propositions is very clearly examples—and a great many of them. What
   differentiates this presentation of examples in support of a thesis
   from those that appear in the exposition section of this text?

The Declaration of Independence

(Deduction and Induction)

THOMAS JEFFERSON

*Thomas Jefferson (1743–1826), lawyer, scientist, inventor, and
statesman, served his state, Virginia, and his country in numerous capacities, most notably as the author of* The Declaration of Independence *and as the third President of the United
States.*

When in the course of human events, it becomes necessary 1
for one people to dissolve the political bands which have connected them with another, and to assume among the Powers of
the earth, the separate and equal station to which the Laws of
Nature and of Nature's God entitle them, a decent respect to the
opinions of mankind requires that they should declare the causes
which impel them to the separation.

We hold these truths to be self-evident, that all men are 2
created equal, that they are endowed by their Creator with certain unalienable Rights, that among these are Life, Liberty and
the pursuit of Happiness. That to secure these rights, Governments are instituted among Men, deriving their just powers from
the consent of the governed. That whenever any Form of Government becomes destructive of these ends, it is the Right of the
People to alter or to abolish it and to institute new Government,
laying its foundation on such principles and organizing its powers in such form, as to them shall seem most likely to effect their
Safety and Happiness. Prudence, indeed, will dictate that Governments long established should not be changed for light and
transient causes; and accordingly all experience hath shown, that
mankind are more disposed to suffer, while evils are sufferable,
than to right themselves by abolishing the forms to which they
are accustomed. But when a long train of abuses and usurpations
pursuing invariably the same Object evinces a design to reduce
them under absolute Despotism, it is their right, it is their duty,
to throw off such government, and to provide new Guards for
their future security. Such has been the patient sufferance of
these Colonies; and such is now the necessity which constrains
them to alter their former Systems of Government. The history
of the present King of Great Britain is a history of repeated
injuries and usurpations, all having in direct object the establishment of an absolute Tyranny over these States. To prove this,
let Facts be submitted to a candid world.

He has refused his Assent to Laws, the most wholesome and 3
necessary for the public good.

He has forbidden his Governors to pass Laws of immediate 4
and pressing importance, unless suspended in their operation till
his Assent should be obtained; and when so suspended, he has
utterly neglected to attend to them.

He has refused to pass other Laws for the accommodations of 5
large districts of people, unless those people would relinquish the

right of Representation in the Legislature, a right inestimable to
them and formidable to tyrants only.

He has called together legislative bodies at places unusual,   6
uncomfortable, and distant from the depository of their Public
Records, for the sole purpose of fatiguing them into compliance
with his measures.

He has dissolved Representative Houses repeatedly, for op-   7
posing with manly firmness his invasions on the rights of the
people.

He has refused for a long time, after such dissolutions, to   8
cause others to be elected; whereby the Legislative Powers, incapable of Annihilation, have returned to the People at large for
their exercise, the State remaining in the mean time exposed to
all the dangers of invasion from without, and convulsions
within.

He has endeavoured to prevent the population of these   9
States; for that purpose obstructing the Laws for Naturalization
of Foreigners, refusing to pass others to encourage their migra-
tions hither, and raising the conditions of new Appropriations of
Lands.

He has obstructed the Administration of Justice, by refusing   10
his Assent to Laws for establishing Judiciary Powers.

He has made Judges dependent on his Will alone, for the   11
tenure of their offices, and the amount and payment of their
salaries.

He has erected a multitude of New Offices, and sent hither   12
swarms of Officers to harass our People, and eat out their substance.

He has kept among us, in times of peace, Standing Armies   13
without the Consent of our Legislature.

He has affected to render the Military independent of and   14
superior to the Civil Power.

He has combined with others to subject us to jurisdiction   15
foreign to our constitution, and unacknowledged by our laws;
giving his Assent to their acts of pretended Legislation:

For quartering large bodies of armed troops among us: 16

For protecting them, by a mock Trial, from Punishment for   17
any murders which they should commit on the Inhabitants of
these States:

For cutting off our Trade with all parts of the world: 18

For imposing Taxes on us without our Consent: 19

For depriving us in many cases, of the benefits of Trial by Jury: 20

For transporting us beyond Seas to be tried for pretended offences: 21

For abolishing the free System of English Laws in a Neighbouring Province, establishing therein an Arbitrary government, and enlarging its boundaries so as to render it at once an example and fit instrument for introducing the same absolute rule into these Colonies: 22

For taking away our Charters, abolishing our most valuable Laws, and altering fundamentally the Forms of our Governments: 23

For suspending our own Legislatures, and declaring themselves invested with Power to legislate for us in all cases whatsoever. 24

He has abdicated Government here, by declaring us out of his Protection and waging War against us. 25

He has plundered our seas, ravaged our Coasts, burnt our towns, and destroyed the Lives of our people. 26

He is at this time transporting large Armies of foreign Mercenaries to compleat the works of death, desolation and tyranny, already begun with circumstances of Cruelty and perfidy scarcely paralleled in the most barbarous ages, and totally unworthy the Head of a civilized nation. 27

He has constrained our fellow Citizens taken Captive on the high Seas to bear Arms against their Country, to become the executioners of their friends and Brethren, or to fall themselves by their Hands. 28

He has excited domestic insurrections amongst us, and has endeavoured to bring on the inhabitants of our frontiers, the merciless Indian Savages, whose known rule of warfare is an undistinguished destruction of all ages, sexes and conditions. 29

In every stage of these Oppressions we have Petitioned for Redress in the most humble terms: Our repeated petitions have been answered only by repeated injury. A Prince, whose character is thus marked by every act which may define a Tyrant, is unfit to be the ruler of a free People. 30

Nor have we been wanting in attention to our British brethren. We have warned them from time to time of attempts by their legislature to extend an unwarrantable jurisdiction over us. We have reminded them of the circumstances of our emigration and 31 settlement here. We have appealed to their native justice and magnanimity and we have conjured them by the ties of our common kindred to disavow these usurpations, which would inevitably interrupt our connections and correspondence. They too have been deaf to the voice of justice and of consanguinity. We must, therefore acquiesce in the necessity, which denounces our Separation, and hold them, as we hold the rest of mankind, Enemies in War, in Peace, Friends.

We, therefore, the Representatives of the United States of 32 America, in General Congress, Assembled, appealing to the Supreme Judge of the world for the rectitude of our intentions, do, in the Name, and by Authority of the good People of these Colonies, solemnly publish and declare, That these United Colonies, are, and of Right ought to be Free and Independent States; that they are Absolved from all Allegiance to the British Crown, and that all political connection between them and the State of Great Britain, is and ought to be totally dissolved; and that as Free and Independent States, they have full power to levy War, conclude Peace, contract Alliances, establish Commerce, and to do all other Acts and Things which Independent States may of right do. And for the support of this Declaration, with a firm reliance on the protection of Divine Providence, we mutually pledge to each other our lives, our fortunes and our sacred Honor.

DISCUSSION: CONTENT

1. Most readers of the Declaration of Independence pass rapidly over paragraph 1, but Jefferson, a brilliant lawyer and statesman, included it. What is its subject? Does it seem necessary to you? Why, or why not?
2. According to paragraph 2, why are oppressed people naturally reluctant to overthrow long-established governments?
3. Can you group the "injuries and usurpations" listed in paragraphs 3–29 into a limited number of classes? What problems do you encounter? What overlap or repetition do you notice?
4. Look at the U.S. Constitution and the original Bill of Rights. Which injuries and usurpations are corrected by them?
5. Condense the long first sentence of paragraph 32 into a shorter sentence of your own composition while retaining the basic thought of the original.

DISCUSSION: FORM

1. What is Jefferson's syllogism in the Declaration of Independence? State it in its barest terms.
2. What support does he offer for his major premise?
3. What support does he offer for his minor premise?
4. Why do you suppose that Jefferson puts each piece of support for his minor premise in a separate paragraph?
5. Which of his examples could be more specific?
6. Comment on the emotional appeal of the final sentence.

What Employees Need Most

(Deduction)

PETER DRUCKER

Peter Ferdinand Drucker (b. 1909) was born in Vienna, but he has lived in the United States since 1937. An internationally known management consultant, educator, and writer, he has been a professor at Bennington College, New York University, and the Claremont Graduate School, California. He has been awarded over 15 honorary degrees in the United States and five foreign countries. He has published over 25 books. Some of the most influential of them have been Concept of the Corporation *(1944);* Practice of Management *(1954);* Managing for Results *(1962);* The Effective Executive *(1967);* Technology, Management and Society *(1970);* Management: Tasks, Responsibilities, Practices *(1974);* People and Performance *(1977);* Managing in Turbulent Times *(1980);* The Changing World of the Executive *(1982);* Innovation and Entrepreneurship *(1985); and* Managing the Non-Profit Organization *(1990). The following essay was originally presented as a college commencement address.*

Most of you . . . will be employees all your working life, working for somebody else and for a pay check. And so will most, if not all, of the thousands of other young Americans . . . in all the other schools and colleges across the country. 1

Ours has become a society of employees. A hundred years or so ago only one out of every five Americans at work was em- 2 ployed, i.e., worked for somebody else. Today only one out of five is not employed but working for himself. And where fifty years ago "being employed" meant working as a factory laborer or as a farmhand, the employee of today is increasingly a middle-class person with a substantial formal education, holding a professional or management job requiring intellectual and technical skills. Indeed, two things have characterized American society during these last fifty years: the middle and upper classes have become employees; and middle-class and upper-class employees have been the fastest-growing groups in our working population—growing so fast that the industrial worker, that oldest child of the Industrial Revolution, has been losing in numerical importance despite the expansion of industrial production.

This is one of the most profound social changes any country   3 has ever undergone. It is, however, a perhaps even greater change for the individual young person about to start. Whatever he does, in all likelihood he will do it as an employee; wherever he aims, he will have to try to reach it through being an employee.

Yet you will find little if anything written on what it is to be   4 an employee. You can find a great deal of very dubious advice on how to get a job or how to get a promotion. You can also find a good deal on work in a chosen field, whether it be metallurgy or salesmanship, the machinist's trade or bookkeeping. Every one of these trades requires different skills, sets different standards, and requires a different preparation. Yet they all have employeeship in common. And increasingly, especially in the large business or in government, employeeship is more important to success than the special professional knowledge or skill. Certainly more people fail because they do not know the requirements of being an employee than because they do not adequately possess the skills of their trade; the higher you climb the ladder, the more you get into administrative or executive work, the greater the emphasis on ability to work within the organization rather than on technical competence or professional knowledge.

Being an employee is thus the one common characteristic of   5 most careers today. The special profession or skill is visible and clearly defined; and a well-laid-out sequence of courses, degrees, and jobs leads into it. But being an employee is the foundation. And it is much more difficult to prepare for it. Yet there is no recorded information on the art of being an employee.

The first question we might ask is: what can you learn in   6 college that will help you in being an employee? The schools teach a great many things of value to the future accountant, the future doctor, or the future electrician. Do they also teach anything of value to the future employee? The answer is: "Yes—they teach the one thing that it is perhaps most valuable for the future employee to know. But very few students bother to learn it."

This one basic skill is the ability to organize and express 7 ideas in writing and in speaking.

As an employee you work with and through other people. 8 This means that your success as an employee—and I am talking of much more here than getting promoted—will depend on your ability to communicate with people and to present your own thoughts and ideas to them so they will both understand what you are driving at and be persuaded. The letter, the report or memorandum, the ten-minute spoken "presentation" to a committee are basic tools of the employee.

Of course . . . if you work on a machine your ability to ex- 9 press yourself will be of little importance. But as soon as you move one step up from the bottom, your effectiveness depends on your ability to reach others through the spoken or the written word. And the further away your job is from manual work, the larger the organization of which you are an employee, the more important it will be that you know how to convey your thoughts in writing or speaking. In the very large organization, whether it is the government, the large business corporation, or the military, this ability to express oneself is perhaps the most important of all the skills a [person] can possess.

Of course, skill in expression is not enough by itself. You 10 must have something to say in the first place. The popular picture of the engineer, for instance, is that of a man who works with a slide rule, T square, and compass. And engineering students reflect this picture in their attitude toward the written word as something quite irrelevant to their jobs. But the effectiveness of the engineer—and with it his usefulness—depends as much on his ability to make other people understand his work as it does on the quality of the work itself.

Expressing one's thoughts is one skill that the school can 11 really teach, especially to people born without natural writing or speaking talent. Many other skills can be learned later—in this country there are literally thousands of places that offer training to adult people at work. But the foundations for skill in expression have to be laid early: an interest in and an ear for language; experience in organizing ideas and data, in brushing aside the irrelevant, in wedding outward form and inner content into one structure; and above all, the habit of verbal expression. If you do not lay these foundations during your school years, you may never have an opportunity again.

If you were to ask me what strictly vocational courses there   12
are in the typical college curriculum, my answer—now that the good old habit of the "theme a day" has virtually disappeared— would be: the writing of poetry and the writing of short stories. Not that I expect many of you to become poets or short-story writers—far from it. But these two courses offer the easiest way to obtain some skill in expression. They force one to be economical with language. They force one to organize thought. They demand of one that he give meaning to every word. They train the ear for language, its meaning, its precision, its overtones— and its pitfalls. Above all they force one to write.

I know very well that the typical employer does not under-   13
stand this as yet, and that he may look with suspicion on a young college graduate who has majored, let us say, in short-story writing. But the same employer will complain—and with good reason—that the young [people] whom he hires when they get out of college do not know how to write a simple report, do not know how to tell a simple story, and are in fact virtually illiterate. And he will conclude—rightly—that the young [people] are not really effective, and certainly not employees who are likely to go very far.

DISCUSSION: CONTENT

1. What does Drucker say is the ratio of employees to employers in America? How does this differ from the situation a hundred years ago? Does Drucker assign any reasons for the change?
2. What one characteristic, according to Drucker, do all the professions taught in universities have in common?
3. What is the one basic skill in which Drucker claims all employees should strive to achieve proficiency?
4. List three vocations in which "ability to organize and express ideas in writing and speaking" is important. Is your chosen vocation among them, or could it be?
5. What particular courses does Drucker recommend for students to make them more proficient in written and spoken communication? Why?

DISCUSSION: FORM

1. Drucker's argument rests on a syllogism. The initial proposition could be stated: An employee's most-needed skill is the ability to speak and write. How might you complete this syllogism, providing the second, more specific proposition and the conclusion?
2. How does Drucker support his first proposition?
3. What is Drucker trying to accomplish in paragraphs 1–3?
4. Why is paragraph 7 so brief?
5. Who is probably Drucker's audience for this argument?

Bad Grammar Seen as Unsafe

(Deduction)

VIRGINIA HALL

Virginia Hall (b. 1943) a native of Texas, was educated at the University of Kansas, where she taught freshman English for two years while completing her master's degree. After two more years of teaching English, at a private school in Kansas City, Hall joined the editorial staff of The Kansas City Star and Times in 1969. Also a published poet, Hall in 1972 began writing a weekly column, "Random Views," for the Star and, in 1976, for the Times. The following essay, which reflects her experiences and concerns as a teacher, citizen, and writer, appeared November 3, 1979, in the Times.

One of the most literally radical explanations of the frightful turn of events at Three Mile Island last spring was understandably not acknowledged by the presidential commission investigating that episode. A quite longer probe than six months would be required to come up with a root cause consisting of split infinitives, poor spelling, faulty punctuation and meandering tenses.

Richard Mitchell, instructor of English at Glassboro State College, New Jersey, and publisher of *The Underground Grammarian,* apparently has been long at the tap waiting for just such an occurrence as the nuclear power plant dysfunction at Harrisburg, Pa. Immediate causes of the near disaster are generally thought to have been a combination of human and mechanical failures pyramiding to the point of huge confusion, but, as Governor Bruce Babbit of Arizona, a member of the commission, put it recently, "The Three Mile Island accident was *preeminently* a case of operator error."

It is clear, according to the governor, that "the operators erred   3 because they had not been adequately trained. . . . The manufacturer of the nuclear system blames the utility for exercising improper control over its employees. The utility points its finger at the manufacturer for failing to provide adequate technical guidance. Nearly everyone blames the Nuclear Regulatory Commission for failing to ride herd on the industry."

Mr. Mitchell, in turn, sees the whole thing as the conse-   4 quence of deliberate meltdown in the American educational system in general and blames the National Council of Teachers of English in particular.

A linguistic stickler who crusades against language abuse,   5 especially abuse by educators, Mitchell believes the Three Mile Island incident and subsequent panic might have been avoided if the mechanics of writing, spelling and punctuation were not so blithely passed over by permissive pedagogues favoring "holistic" composition. Students who are permitted—indeed, encouraged—to skip the fundamentals of English usage, he asserts, "learn that the mastery of skills is of little importance. . . . They learn to be shoddy workers in any endeavor, comforting themselves, as their teachers did, by fantasies of holistic excellence unfettered by precision in small details, or 'emphasis on trivia.' Then they take jobs with power companies . . . where machines and toxic substances, unmindful of 'holistic ratings,' take heed only—and always, always—of the little things, the valves and the switches, the trivia."

If language does, as many linguists contend, shape as well as   6 reflect the user's worldview, Mitchell could be striking at the core of ideological matters as troublesome as Three Mile Island. Critics of public school spending like to point out that the more money local, state and federal governments commit to education the lower students score on standard tests, costly "frills" apparently diverting educators from their primary purpose of communicating basic skills. (Pennsylvania is among the top ten states in the nation in per-pupil spending.) Cadres of functional illiterates are loosed on the job market or sent off to college where standards must be lowered to accommodate them—lowered not slightly, but in some instances to the sixth- or seventh-grade level.

Ask instructors of freshman English at state universities. 7 Those teachers confront classes in which half or more of the students can't spell, are barely able to read and haven't an inkling of how to put a sentence together other than as a string of hip phrases loosely related and connected by the surrogate conjunctive "you-know."

Attempting to teach an eighteen-year-old what should 8 have been absorbed ten or more years earlier is very nearly impossible. Where does the instructor start with a young adult who believes the planet is populated by human "beans"? It is more than a spelling problem; it's a mindset. It makes no difference to the student. Being. Bean. What's the big deal about a few lousy letters, anyway? *Or a few lousy valves and switches and stuff. . . .*

Coming around to Mitchell's viewpoint is scary. Malfunc- 9 tioning machinery can be fixed or shut down, but what is to be done with sloppy mentalities in the work force—on auto assembly lines, at air terminals, behind desks, in board rooms, at hospitals; teaching, operating computers, handling insurance claims, policing the streets, or serving hot soup in your lap?

Might this language deficiency notion about Three Mile Is- 10 land be right? Could it be that lack of discipline and precision in language use is back of very many current problems? Government is bogged up in oceans of turbid memos and regulatory doublespeak. Business communications often are just as bad. Advertising, education, and journalism perpetrate "deliberately deformed jargons," linguist L. E. Sissman has charged. "Writers in these fields," he observes, "shroud themselves in such opaque English that they lose their ability to distinguish right from wrong." There are, of course, no longer any such creatures as "right" and "wrong" in the opinion of psychologists, whose seductive babblegab has infiltrated every area of work and play.

I recently attended a PTA meeting at which a specialist in 11 child psychology spoke of "information processing" when he meant (I think) "talking" to a child and referred to "cognitive-level behavior" for "seeing." Worse, though, was the frequent and obviously calculated use of four-letter words to prove that despite such erudition he was just an ordinary guy. He called to mind a former student whose, uh, *delayed entry* into *the controlled learning environment of higher education* apparently was due to several years devoted to memorization of bureaucratic directives, Roget's *Thesaurus* and gutter comics. Words flowed from him endlessly in elaborate combination as he strove throughout the semester to say something, one thing, meaningful. He never did, and I hope not to have to try to listen to him again in the here and now or ever after. And I don't want him working on my car or carrying soup in my direction either. Heaven help us if he's into energy.

DISCUSSION: CONTENT

1. What, according to Hall, were generally thought to be the "immediate causes" of the Three Mile Island nuclear plant near-disaster in Spring 1979? What do Hall and Richard Mitchell, publisher of *The Underground Grammarian*, believe the real or remote or "root" cause was?
2. Hall believes the "root cause" problem is not confined to the Three Mile Island incident, but affects what other parts of American society?
3. Hall uses *grammar* as a catch-all term for spelling, punctuation, and grammatical usage; in the last two paragraphs she discusses another English language problem. What is it, and why is it as much a problem as bad grammar?

DISCUSSION: FORM

1. Part of Hall's argument rests on deduction. Her key syllogism, minus its major premise, would look something like this:

   Bad grammar is an example of inattention to detail.
   Therefore, bad grammar is dangerous.

   What is her first or major premise? How does she support it?
2. Hall also argues inductively, using an analogy she gets from Mitchell's writings. Mitchell, himself an English teacher, says that students who learn that details of grammar are unimportant then "learn to be shoddy workers in any endeavor." Does this analogy necessarily hold true? Why, or why not?
3. Hall's essay is not clearly organized into a unified whole; this can be seen by removing some of its paragraphs. Which ones can be extracted without really damaging her basic argument?

How to Cuss

(Deduction and Refutation)

JOHN STEINBECK

John Steinbeck (1902–1968) was born in the Salinas valley of California, which furnishes a backdrop for many of his works, including Tortilla Flat *(1935),* Of Mice and Men *(1937),* Grapes of Wrath *(1939), and* East of Eden *(1952). He received the Nobel Prize for Literature in 1963. The following argument appeared in Steinbeck's syndicated newspaper column in 1966.*

In a way I hated to leave America last December. Every day 1
was interesting, some of it dangerous, I suppose, but all of it
fascinating to me. For instance, the student organizations and
picketing and even rioting. It's not so long ago that the biggest
and best smash our college students could manage was a panty
raid on a girls' dormitory. Serious people despaired of them.
Foreign students were politically alive while ours barely managed to swallow goldfish or see how many could get into a
telephone booth.

Well, that's all changed, you must admit. A goodly number 2
of our students are raring to go. It's a relief to see. They'll march
and picket and tip over automobiles with the best students anywhere. I'd back them against the medieval scholars who tore up
the Ile de la Cite in the day of Aucassin. I admire rebellion—any
time and against anything. Besides, it passes the time. And it
takes energy to study and riot at the same time.

The Berkeley students who struck a blow for freedom of 3
speech are particularly to be praised. I hope when they get it
themselves, they will allow it to others. And I think they should
certainly have the right to speak or print four-letter words on the
campus as well as off it.

My only reservation about this doesn't come from a censori- 4
ous impulse, but one of conservation. We don't have many four-
letter words of sturdy quality and, when you use them up, there's
no place to go. Also, overuse milks all the strength out of them.
One of our middle-aged young writers has worn out his stock so
completely that a simple English sentence would shock his readers to death.

No, if you crowd a window with diamonds, they become   5
uninteresting. It is the single jewel centered on black velvet,
alone and glorious, that jars us into appreciation. Obscenities are
too valuable to waste and, if one can combine with another to
explode like a star-spangled sky rocket, that is true art and, like
all true art, rare and precious.

I may tell you that once long ago, when I was working on a   6
ship, a seaman of Irish extraction dawdled his hand into a winch
drum and the steel cable snipped off three of his fingers. For a
moment he looked at the wreck which hadn't yet started to bleed
and then softly, slowly and sweetly he came up with the greatest
curse I have ever heard. It had everything—vulgarity, obscenity,
irreverence and sacrilegiousness, all precisely placed in one short
staccato burst of prose that peeled the paint off the deck machinery and tattooed itself on the deck engineer's chest. I have cher-
ished this oath ever since, even alone. I am saving it for the time
when I need it. But it will have to be an enormous need, a
tomwallager of a need, but I am content that when it comes I am
equipped for it. Imagine the waste if I had piddled it away on
some picayune crisis.

If I am stern about this, it is because I know that overexpo-   7
sure withers the rich bloom of our dear heritage of obscenity.

DISCUSSION: CONTENT

1. Steinbeck makes an allusion to the medieval scholars "who tore
   up the Ile de la Cite in the day of Aucassin." Can you follow the
   argument without knowing the historical fact alluded to? Can
   you appreciate Steinbeck's argument without knowing about the
   Berkeley students he is admonishing in 1966? Who were those
   students, and what were they doing?
2. What is Steinbeck's attitude toward four-letter obscenities?
3. Steinbeck concludes with a story about an Irish seaman. What
   happens in that story, and how is it pertinent to Steinbeck's
   argument?

DISCUSSION: FORM

1. Steinbeck's argument is based on a warrant that both he and the
   radical students of Berkeley can agree on. What is that warrant
   and where exactly does Steinbeck state it?

2. Can you state Steinbeck's argument in terms of a syllogism? Does Steinbeck offer any support for the premises of his syllogism? What is the nature of that support?
3. How might this argument be viewed as a refutation? What notion is Steinbeck refuting?

Life After Death

(Refutation)

CARL SAGAN

Carl Sagan (b. 1934), a native of New York City, received his Ph.D. from the University of Chicago in 1960 and since 1968 has been the Director of the Laboratory for Planetary Studies at Cornell University. A member of NASA and the National Academy of Sciences, Sagan is probably the best-known scientist in America, largely because of his popular public television series, Cosmos, *which he converted into a best-seller in 1980.* Dragons of Eden *won him the Pulitzer Prize in 1978. Among his dozen other books are* Other Worlds *(1975),* Contact *(a novel; 1985), and* Comet *(1985). The following essay is taken from* Broca's Brain *(1979).*

William Wolcott died and went to heaven. Or so it seemed. 1
Before being wheeled to the operating table, he had been reminded that the surgical procedure would entail a certain risk. The operation was a success, but just as the anaesthesia was wearing off his heart went into fibrillation and he died. It seemed to him that he had somehow left his body and was able to look down upon it, withered and pathetic, covered only by a sheet, lying on a hard and unforgiving surface. He was only a little sad, regarded his body one last time—from a great height, it seemed—and continued a kind of upward journey. While his surroundings had been suffused by a strange permeating darkness, he realized that things were now getting brighter—looking up, you might say. And then he was being illuminated from a distance, flooded with light. He entered a kind of radiant kingdom and there, just ahead of him, he could make out in silhouette, magnificently lit from behind, a great godlike figure whom he was now effortlessly approaching. Wolcott strained to make out His face. . . .

And then awoke. In the hospital operating room where the   2
defibrillation machine had been rushed to him, he had been
resuscitated at the last possible moment. Actually, his heart had
stopped, and by some definitions of this poorly understood process, he had died. Wolcott was certain that he *had* died, that he
had been vouchsafed a glimpse of life after death and a confirmation of Judaeo-Christian theology.

Similar experiences, now widely documented by physicians   3
and others, have occurred all over the world. These perithanatic,
or near-death, epiphanies have been experienced not only by
people of conventional Western religiosity but also by Hindus
and Buddhists and skeptics. It seems plausible that many of our
conventional ideas about heaven are derived from such near-
death experiences, which must have been related regularly over
the millennia. No news could have been more interesting or
more hopeful than that of the traveler returned, the report that
there is a voyage and a life after death, that there is a God who
awaits us, and that upon death we feel grateful and uplifted, awed
and overwhelmed.

For all I know, these experiences may be just what they seem   4
and a vindication of the pious faith that has taken such a pum-
meling from science in the past few centuries. Personally, I
would be delighted if there were a life after death—especially if
it permitted me to continue to learn about this world and others,
if it gave me a chance to discover how history turns out. But I am
also a scientist, so I think about what other explanations are
possible. How could it be that people of all ages, cultures and
eschatological predispositions have the *same sort* of near-death
experience?

We know that similar experiences can be induced with fair   5
regularity, cross-culturally, by psychedelic drugs. Out-of-body
experiences are induced by dissociative anaesthetics such as the
ketamines (2-[o-chlorophenyl]-2-[methylamino] cyclohexanones.)
The illusion of flying is induced by atropine and other belladonna
alkaloids, and these molecules, obtained, for example, from
mandrake or jimson weed, have been used regularly by European witches and North American *curanderos* ("healers") to
experience, in the midst of religious ecstasy, soaring and glorious flight. MDA (2,4-methylene-dioxyamphetamine) tends to
induce age regression, an accessing of experiences from youth
and infancy which we had thought entirely forgotten. DMT
(*N,N*-dimethyltryptamine) induces micropsia and macropsia,

the sense of the world shrinking or expanding, respectively—a little like what happens to Alice after she obeys instructions on small containers reading "Eat me" or "Drink me." LSD (lysergic acid diethylamide) induces a sense of union with the universe, as in the identification of Brahman with Atman in Hindu religious belief.

Can it really be that the Hindu mystical experience is   6 prewired into us, requiring only 200 micrograms of LSD to be made manifest? If something like ketamine is released in times of mortal danger or near-death, and people returning from such an experience always provide the same account of heaven and God, then must there not be a sense in which Western as well as Eastern religions are hard-wired in the neuronal architecture of our brains?

It is difficult to see why evolution should have selected   7 brains that are predisposed to such experiences, since no one seems to die or fail to reproduce from a want of mystic fervor. Might these drug-inducible experiences as well as the near-death epiphany be due merely to some evolutionarily neutral wiring defect in the brain which, by accident, occasionally brings forth altered perceptions of the world? That possibility, it seems to me, is extremely implausible, and perhaps no more than a desperate rationalist attempt to avoid a serious encounter with the mystical.

The only alternative, so far as I can see, is that every human   8 being, without exception, has already shared an experience like that of those travelers who return from the land of death: the sensation of flight; the emergence from darkness into light; an experience in which, at least sometimes, a heroic figure can be dimly perceived, bathed in radiance and glory. There is only one common experience that matches this description. It is called birth.

DISCUSSION: CONTENT

1. What two unusual experiences or sensations accompanied William Wolcott's brush with death?
2. Near-death experiences like Wolcott's are frequently cited as evidence for what common belief?
3. What is especially peculiar and intriguing about such near-death experiences, according to Sagan?

4. What does Sagan propose as an alternative explanation for the occurrence of these near-death sensations?
5. Why is it important to Sagan's argument that many of the near-death sensations can be duplicated by taking drugs?

DISCUSSION: FORM

1. Sagan's refutation begins with a brief narrative. What purpose does it serve?
2. Paragraph 4 is a crucial one for this essay. What purpose does it serve?
3. The technique that Sagan uses in his refutation is to point out the material fallacy of *labored hypothesis* (see p. 383 of "A Short Guide to Material and Formal Fallacies"). How does this fallacy apply here?

Let's Keep Christmas Commercial

(Refutation)

APRIL OURSLER ARMSTRONG

April Oursler Armstrong (b. 1926) is an American writer of more than 500 articles and 15 books, mostly on religion, such as The Book of God *(1957),* The Tales Christ Told *(1959),* What's Happening to the Catholic Church *(1966), and* Cry Babel *(1979). She comes by that interest naturally, for her father, Fulton Oursler, wrote* The Greatest Story Ever Told *(1949), a continuing best-seller in the religious field, and after his death she completed* The Greatest Faith Ever Known *(1961) for him. Armstrong's essay demonstrates her skill at discussing religious subjects.*

Every year right after Halloween, the world becomes Christ-   1
mas-conscious—and people begin deploring. If only we could have a *real* Christmas, they say. The good old kind. Quiet, inexpensive, simple, devout. If only we could retrieve the holy day from the hands of vulgar moneygrubbers, they say. They say, with earnest horror, that the price tag has become the liturgical symbol of the season.

As a Christian, I do find facets of the Christmas season   2
ridiculous, offensive or disturbing, but I believe most complaints
about the commercialization of Christmas are unconsciously
hypocritical nonsense. I'm afraid that often the complainers are
kidding themselves, striking spiritual poses. I'm not ashamed to
admit that if I had to spend Christmas somewhere far from the
crowd and the vulgar trappings, I'd hate it. I love the lights, the
exquisite ones in *boutiques,* the joyful ones in village centers,
even the awkward ones strung on drugstores and filling stations.
I love the Santa Clauses, including those on street corners, the
intricately animated windows, the hot bewilderment of the bargain basement, the sequins of the dime store. Cut off from the
whole wild confusion, I'd not be holier. I'd be forlorn. So, I
suspect, would most of us.

What's supposed to be wrong with a commercialized Christ-   3
mas?

For one thing, it's usually said that Christmas has become   4
the time of parties where people drink and eat too much. ("Turning Yuletide into fooltide"—that exact phrase was used to describe the holiday in Merrie Olde England, so those who yearn
for the "good old Christmas" should carefully define their terms.)
Oddly enough, it seems to me that often the people who most
loudly criticize this holiday partying are those folks who acquire
Christmas hangovers and indigestion. And they deplore it as if
no one ever had to avoid hangovers, indigestion or exhaustion at
any other time of the year.

They say that commercialization has made the buying of   5
Christmas presents a rat race. God knows, most of the gifts we
peddle to each other have nothing to do with the infant of
Bethlehem. For my part, I enjoy gawking in the catalogues at
the new luxuries for people who have everything. My imagination romps over items for my private Ostentatious Wastefulness
list: silver-plated golf clubs, hundred-dollar dresses for little girls
to spill ice cream on. Dime and department stores are crammed
with gifts no wise man would bring anyone. Things like stuffed
dinosaurs twelve feet high and replicas of the *Pietà* that glow in
the dark.

With rare exceptions it is foolishly pompous to get scandal-   6
ized and accuse manufacturers, advertisers and vendors of dese-
crating Christmas by trying to sell what you or I may think is
silly junk. Obviously some people like it and buy it, and that's
their business. It's said to be the fault of the commercializers that

parents buy overpriced, unnecessary toys for children. And that's a fancy alibi. If you don't like what's being hawked this Christmas, you don't have to buy it. And if you're a sucker, your problem isn't seasonal.

Christians began giving presents to each other to celebrate Jesus' birthday in imitation of the Wise Men who came to Bethlehem. The basic idea was and is to bring joy, to honor God in others, and to give in His name with love for all. But in our social structure, with or without the blessings of the Internal Revenue Service, Christmas presents serve many purposes. Gift givers are, in practice, often diplomats, almoners, egoists, or investors. A shiny box with gold ribbon may be a guilt assuager, a bribe, a bid for attention, or merely payment for services past or future. And what is in the box must look rightly lavish, conveying subliminal impact while not costing too much. That kind of petty ugliness we all know about. And we know that often, too, gift givers play Santa Claus against their will, badgered by cozy reminders in the parking lot about how the boys wish you Season's Greetings, or by collections taken up in offices, clubs, Sunday schools, Scouts and third grades.

But are extortion, begging, status seeking and advantage taking so unusual among us that they occur only once a year? Isn't it more realistic to admit that whatever is sleazy about Christmas isn't seasonal?

After all, the instinct and art of commercialization are neither good nor bad. People normally, naturally, make a living from every kind of want, aspiration and occasion. We exploit births, weddings, deaths, first communions, bar mitzvahs, the wish to smell nice, the craving for amusement, and the basic desires for housing, clothes, love and food. Is anything more commercialized than food? But no one complains when millions cash in on our need to eat.

Do we assume that eating is so earthy and undignified that commercialization upgrades it, while celebrating Christmas should be so totally ethereal a process that it shouldn't be treated in a human way? If so, we are both pretentious and mistaken. We are creatures who both eat and worship, and God doesn't want us as split personalities. When Christ once raised a little girl from death, the next thing He did was to tell her mother to feed her.

Simony is a sin, the sin of trying to buy or sell what is sacred. But this is not simony or sin, this peddling of manger sets, this pitchman heralding the season. No one can buy or sell Christmas. No one can steal it from us, or ruin it for us, except ourselves. If we become self-seeking, materialistic, harried and ill-willed in this Christmas melee, that's our problem, not the fault of the world in which we live.

Some people are dismayed today in a different way, because 12 they honestly fear Christmas is being de-Christianized, made nonsectarian. They are upset when someone who does not share their faith sets up a tree and exchanges gifts and wishes them "Season's Greetings" instead of naming the holy day. They resent the spelling "Xmas." Others fret over the way Santa Claus and snowmen crowd out the shepherds. Put Christ back into Christmas, these offended people cry.

As far as I know, Christ never left it. He could never be cut 13 out of Christmas, except in the privacy of individual hearts. I don't care if some people designate Xmas as the Time for Eggnog, or Toys. Let them call it the Time to Buy New Appliances, the Time to Use the Phone, or the Time for New Loans. The antics of the rest of the world can't change Christmas. Why on earth should we expect everyone to share our special joy our way?

Actually, what bothers most people who decry the vulgar 14 American Christmas is a matter of taste, not of morals or of religious commitment. Taste is a very personal matter, relative, changing and worldly; we're all a rather tacky lot anyway, religious or not. Some Christians like those new stark liturgical Christmas cards, and some dote on luminous plastic crèches, and I hate both, and the Lord doesn't care a bit. Maybe you can't stand Rudolf, are bored with the same old carols, and cringe at Santa in a helicopter. But don't blame your discomfort on commercialization and become righteous and indignant. After all, if your taste is better than that of most other people, you're probably proud of it, and you should be willing to suffer the consequences in kindly forbearance.

I believe the root of complaints about commercialized 15 Christmas is that we're falling into the dangerous habit of thinking that religion is somehow coarsened by contact with real people. I suspect that unconsciously we're embarrassed at the prospect of trying to live with God here and now. At times we modern Christians seem to have a neurotic refusal to embrace reality in the name of the Lord who was the supreme realist, and maker of the real.

It's always easier, if you're not doing very well religiously, to 16 insist that the secularizing world prevents you from devotion. Christmas is meant to be lived in the noisy arena of the shopping day countdown, amid aluminum trees, neckties and counterfeit French perfume. If all the meditation I get around to is listening to Scrooge and Tiny Tim, or begging heaven for patience to applaud a school pageant, I'm a fool to blame anyone but myself. Census time in Bethlehem was distracting too.

I know a man who confides that he learns more about pa- 17 tience and love of his neighbor in post-office lines than anywhere else. More than one mother has learned that Christmas shopping on a tight budget can be a lesson in mortification, humility, willpower and joy. There's grist for meditation in the reflection of tree lights in a sloshy puddle. Families have their own customs, their private windows on glory. And families that are honest and relaxed find that the commercially generated atmosphere of goodwill hinders them not at all in their celebration. God works in wondrous ways still, even among assemble-it-yourself toys.

Christmas is a parable of the whole Christian venture. The 18 Christian's attitude toward it, his willingness to make it relevant repeatedly in his own time and space, is a symptom of his whole encounter with God. The first Christmas happened, so Christians believe, because God lovingly plunged Himself into human nature to transform it. He is not honored by men and women who want to disown other people's human nature in His name.

Let's not make the mealy-mouthed error of complaining that 19 paganism threatens Christmas today. Christmas has already absorbed and recharged the vestiges of Druid feasts, Norse gods and sun worship. Christmas took the world as it was and built on it, and it's still doing just that.

To those who fear that Christmas is prostituted by the al- 20 mighty dollar, I suggest that it's remarkable and beautiful that Christmas is publicly touted at all. Nor do I make that suggestion, as some might suspect, in a tone of meek appeasement to groups that object to Christmas celebrations in public schools, or crèches in town squares. Realistically, I know that in our society what is important to people and concerns them deeply, whether it's cancer or get-rich-quick schemes, patriotism or religion, is talked about and exploited.

If Christmas becomes for some people primarily a subject for 21 commercials, at least God is getting equal time with toothpaste. If people didn't care about Him, He wouldn't even get that.

In good taste or bad, by your standards or mine, the fact of 22 Christ, the good news of the meeting of heaven and earth, the tidings of love and peace for human nature, are announced everywhere. It is still true that he who has ears to hear will hear.

DISCUSSION: CONTENT

1. In paragraphs 4–8, Armstrong notes that people who deplore the commercialism of Christmas do so because they feel that the real meaning of Christmas has been lost as a result of three kinds of human activity. What are they?
2. In the remainder of the essay Armstrong examines another common objection. What is it?
3. To make her argument succeed, Armstrong must demonstrate not only her knowledge of the development of Christian traditions, but also her religious background. Where in the essay does she demonstrate these?
4. What does Armstrong mean when she says that Christmas is a parable of the whole Christian venture?
5. Why does Armstrong take it as a hopeful sign that Christmas has become commercialized?

DISCUSSION: FORM

1. In refuting the notion that the commercialization of Christmas tempts people to purchase overpriced, unnecessary junk, Armstrong responds that such an argument is a fancy alibi, that if a person is a sucker, the problem isn't seasonal. What fallacy is she pointing out?
2. What about the suggestion that Christmas gifts are a form of extortion, begging, status seeking, or advantage taking? How does Armstrong refute this one?
3. By pointing out that commercialism is found objectionable only during Christmas season, while the commercialism attendant on other occasions—such as births, deaths, and weddings—is judged acceptable, Armstrong is pointing to what fallacy?
4. How is the claim that the commercialization of Christmas is in bad taste an example of the bandwagon fallacy?

5. In paragraph 9, Armstrong begins to construct her final argument. What proposition is she refuting, and how does she go about it?

Black Hawk's Farewell

(Emotional Appeal)

BLACK HAWK

Ma-ka-tai-me-she-kia-kiah (Black Sparrow Hawk) (1767–1838) was a Native American chief of the Sauk tribe in the upper Midwest. Always a valiant foe, he led his first war party against American settlers at age seventeen, and he fought on the British side under Tecumseh against them during the War of 1812. In 1831 and 1832, he led the Sauk in an attempt to recover their traditional village at Rock River, Illinois, but he was driven back both times by United States troops. In 1832, the Black Hawk War began after Illinois militiamen killed two Sauk who were advancing under a flag of truce to parley. The Sauk fled north, finally surrendering in Wisconsin, where Black Hawk delivered the following speech.

You have taken me prisoner with all my warriors. I am much grieved, for I expected, if I did not defeat you, to hold out much longer, and give you more trouble before I surrendered. I tried hard to bring you into ambush, but your last general understands Indian fighting. The first one was not so wise. I determined to rush on you, and fight you face to face. I fought hard. But your guns were well aimed. The bullets flew like birds in the air, and whizzed by our ears like the wind through the trees in the winter. My warriors fell around me; it began to look dismal. I saw my evil day at hand. The sun rose dim on us in the morning, and at night it sunk in a dark cloud, and looked like a ball of fire. That was the last sun that shone on Black Hawk. His heart is dead, and no longer beats quick in his bosom. He is now a prisoner to the white men; they will do with him as they wish. But he can stand torture, and is not afraid of death. He is no coward. Black Hawk is an Indian.

He has done nothing for which an Indian ought to be ashamed. He has fought for his countrymen, the squaws and papooses, against white men, who came, year after year, to cheat them and take their lands. You know the cause of our making war. It is known to all white men. They ought to be ashamed of it. The white men despise the Indians, and drive them from their homes. But the Indians are not deceitful. The white men speak bad of the Indian, and look at him spitefully. But the Indian does not tell lies; Indians do not steal.

An Indian who is as bad as the white men could not live in our nation; he would be put to death, and eaten by the wolves. The white men are bad schoolmasters; they carry false looks, and deal in false actions; they smile in the face of the poor Indian to cheat him; they shake them by the hand to gain their confidence, to make them drunk, to deceive them, and to ruin our wives. We told them to let us alone, and keep away from us; but they followed on, and beset our paths, and they coiled themselves among us, like a snake. They poisoned us by their touch. We were not safe. We lived in danger. We were becoming like them, hypocrites and liars, adulterers, lazy drones, all talkers, and no workers.

We looked up to the Great Spirit. We went to our great father. We were encouraged. His great council gave us fair words and big promises; but we got no satisfaction. Things were growing worse. There were no deer in the forest. The opossum and beaver were fled; the springs were drying up, and our squaws and papooses without victuals to keep them from starving; we called a great council, and built a large fire. The spirit of our fathers arose and spoke to us to avenge our wrongs or die. We set up the war-whoop, and dug up the tomahawk; our knives were ready, and the heart of Black Hawk swelled high in his bosom when he led his warriors to battle. He is satisfied. He will go to the world of spirits contented. He has done his duty. His father will meet him there, and commend him.

Black Hawk is a true Indian, and disdains to cry like a woman. He feels for his wife, his children, and his friends. But he does not care for himself. He cares for his nation and the Indians. They will suffer. He laments their fate. The white men do not scalp the head; but they do worse—they poison the heart; it is not pure with them. His countrymen will not be scalped, but they will, in a few years, become like the white men, so that you can't trust them, and there must be, as in the white settlements, nearly as many officers as men, to take care of them and keep them in order.

Farewell, my nation! Black Hawk tried to save you, and   6
avenge your wrongs. He drank the blood of some of the whites.
He has been taken prisoner, and his plans are stopped. He can do
no more. He is near the end. His sun is setting, and he will rise
no more. Farewell to Black Hawk.

DISCUSSION: CONTENT

1. What does Black Hawk apparently hope to accomplish with this
   speech? What is his purpose? Do you think he achieves his purpose?
2. Late in the nineteenth century, another Native American said,
   "The white man broke every promise he made to us but one; he
   said he would take our land, and he took it." How does Black
   Hawk's speech confirm or refute this statement?
3. Assume you are a white U.S. military officer accepting Black
   Hawk's surrender and listening to his speech; what is your reaction to each of the speech's parts?

DISCUSSION: FORM

1. How is comparison basic to Black Hawk's approach? What does
   he compare? Is the comparison probably accurate and fair, or not?
2. Look for examples of figurative language. In your estimation,
   where is the most effective use?
3. Black Hawk's speech is by no means a formal argument, yet his
   opening paragraph does correspond to which of the six Ciceronian
   parts of an argument (see p. 300)?
4. This speech shows in particular the emotional impact of short
   sentences; cite such instances.

Thanks for Attacking the NEA

(Emotional Appeal)

GARRISON KEILLOR

*Garrison Keillor (b. 1942) is perhaps best known as the creator
and master of ceremonies of the National Public Radio Weekly*

program "Prairie Home Companion," in which he regularly narrated recent events in his fictional hometown, Lake Woebegone. His essays and stories have appeared in The New Yorker, *and his books have been best-sellers:* Happy to Be Here *(1982),* Lake Woebegone Days *(1985),* Leaving Home *(1987), and* WLT: A Radio Romance *(1991). In 1987 Keillor received the Grammy Award for the best non-musical recording of that year. Keillor appeared before a U.S. Senate Committee in 1989 investigating charges that the National Endowment for the Arts had sponsored an exhibition of photographs, some of which were deemed pornography. The text of his comments, which appears here, was first published in the* Congressional Record.

1   It's a pleasure to come down to Washington and speak in support of the National Endowment for the Arts, one of the wisest and happiest pieces of legislation ever to come through Congress. I'm grateful to those who have so ably attacked the Endowment over the past year or so for making it necessary to defend it. I enjoy controversy and I recognize the adversary: they are us.

2   My ancestors were Puritans from England. They arrived here in 1648 in the hope of finding greater restrictions than were permissible under English law at the time. But over the years, we Puritans have learned something about repression, and it's as true today as when my people arrived: man's interest in the forbidden is sharp and constant.

3   If Congress doesn't do something about obscene art, we'll have to build galleries twice as big to hold the people who want to see it. And if Congress does do something about obscene art, the galleries will need to be even bigger than that. We've heard three or four times this morning that of 85,000 works funded by the NEA, only 20 were controversial. I don't know why anyone would cite that as something to be proud of.

4   All governments have given medals to artists when they are old and saintly and successful and almost dead. But 25 years ago, Congress decided to boldly support the creators of art—support the act of creation itself—to encourage artists who are young and vital and unknown, very much alive and therefore dangerous. This courageous legislation has changed American life.

5   Today, in every city and state, when Americans talk up their home town invariably they mention the arts—a local orchestra or theater or museum or all three. It didn't use to be this way.

Forty years ago, if an American meant to have an artistic career, you got on the train to New York. Today, you can be a violinist in North Carolina, a writer in Iowa, a painter in Kansas.

This is a revolution—small and lovely—that the Endowment   6
has helped to bring about. The Endowment has fostered thousands of art works—many of which will outlive you and me—but even more important, the Endowment has changed the way we think about the arts. Today, no American family can be secure against the danger that one of its children may decide to become an artist.

Twice in my life, at crucial times, grants from the Endow-   7
ment made it possible for me to be a writer. The first, in 1969, arrived when I was young, broke, married with a baby, living on very little cash and a big vegetable garden. I was writing for the *The New Yorker* at the time but they weren't aware of it.

I wrote every morning and every night. I often had fantasies   8
of finding a patron. A beggar would appear at my door one day; I'd give him an egg salad sandwich, and suddenly he'd turn into a man in a pinstripe suit, Prince Bob from the Guggenheim Foundation. But instead of him, I got a letter offering me a job for one month in the Poets in the Schools program in Minneapolis, funded by the NEA, directed by Molly LaBerge, which sent young writers into the schools to read and teach. In 1969, there were three such programs: In New York, California and Minnesota. Today, there's at least one in every state.

It was the first time anybody paid me to be a writer. It was   9
the sort of experience a person looks back at and wonders what would have happened if it hadn't.

In 1974, a grant from the NEA enabled me and my colleagues   10
at Minnesota Public Radio to start "A Prairie Home Companion." The help of the Endowment was crucial because the show wasn't that great to begin with.

For our first broadcast, we had a crowd of 12 persons, and   11
then we made the mistake of having an intermission and we lost half of them. The show wasn't obscene, just slow. It took us a few years to figure out how to do a live radio show with folk music and comedy, and stories about my hometown of Lake Wobegon.

By the time the show became popular and Lake Wobegon   12
became so well-known that people thought it was real, the Endowment had vanished from the credits, its job done.

When you're starting out—I think it is true in the arts as in   13
politics—it seems like nobody wants to give you a dime. When
you have a big success and everything you could ever want,
people can't do enough for you. The Endowment is there at the
beginning, and that's the beauty of it. Now my desk is filled with
offers to speak, to write, to endorse, which I've thoroughly enjoyed, but I remember very well when nobody else but my
mother and the Endowment was interested. I'm grateful for this
chance to express my thanks.

When I graduated from college, the degrees were given out in   14
reverse order of merit, so I got mine early and had a chance to
watch the others. I remember the last graduate, the summest
cum laude, a tall shy boy who walked up the stairs to the plat-
form and en route stepped on the hem of his own gown and
walked right up the inside of it.

Like him, the Endowment has succeeded in embarrassing   15
itself from time to time, to the considerable entertainment of us
all, and like him the Endowment keeps on going. It has contributed mightily to the creative genius of America: to art, music,
literature, theater and dance, which to my wife and other foreigners is the most gorgeous aspect of this country. Long may it wave.
I hope it lives another 25 years; I hope we will continue to argue
about it.

DISCUSSION: CONTENT

1. What is the NEA? How do you feel about giving national support
   to artwork that is controversial or whose merit is questionable?
2. In what ways does Keillor claim that the NEA came to his assistance?
3. For what purpose does Keillor relate the story of his graduation
   exercises?

DISCUSSION: FORM

1. What tone does Keillor establish in the initial paragraph? How
   does he sustain that tone through the next two paragraphs?
2. Remember that Keillor's remarks were delivered orally to a Senate committee. In paragraph 5 there are some instances of usage

that are more appropriate to spoken English than to written
English. Which expressions are these? How might you revise
them? Or would you?
3. Paragraphs 2–5 function, in Cicero's terms, as the *background* of
Keillor's argument. What does each paragraph add to his case?
4. What sort of defense does Keillor offer on behalf of the NEA? To
what emotions does he appeal? Where exactly does he make these
appeals?

APPENDIX

A Short Guide To Material and Formal Fallacies

Fallacies are various types of deceptive or erroneous or false reasoning; they cause an argument to be logically flawed, even though that argument may be emotionally persuasive and may appear to be true. A flawed argument may contain one or several fallacies.

The value of being able to recognize fallacies may already be clear, even before you read the brief descriptions that follow. For instance, since all of us are consumers, we are confronted every day with fallacious media advertisements and salespersons' propositions. As citizens, we must often consider explanations from officials, pronouncements from government agencies, and speeches from politicians; any of these may contain fallacies. Finally, we can expect, as employees and employers, to have to contend with fallacies in the public and private communications that help business, industry, and professions operate. Therefore, at home and at work, we need to be alert for and ready to resist conscious or unconscious fallacies, in others' arguments or in our own. After all, fallacies hinder or even prevent honest, rational discussions and the making of correct, logical decisions.

As an aid to understanding, fallacies are often divided into two broad categories: material and formal. *Material fallacies* (sometimes called informal fallacies) result from errors in the content or wording of arguments, and thus could be separated into two groups (although they overlap in places): emotional and language. These sorts of fallacies tend to be present in arguments that we intuitively recognize as wrong but whose flaws we have trouble explaining.

Formal fallacies (sometimes called structural fallacies) result from errors in the form or structure of deductive arguments. Their conclusions are unacceptable because of those flaws in reasoning, and you should be able to learn to pick out those flaws.

You will see in what follows that some fallacies have several names. They may also be best known by their traditional Latin names, dating from an earlier time when fallacies were a familiar part of rhetorical study in schools. You will need to learn the various names and definitions for fallacies in order to read this book's model essays and paragraphs critically and to understand and to participate in class discussions and other course exercises.

Material Fallacies

Material Fallacies result either from: (1) imprecise or improper use of language, or from (2) appeals to emotion rather than to reason. Here are short discussions, with examples, of some of the most common material fallacies.

Appeal to Force. This emotion-based fallacy can cause people to act in inappropriate ways, or not to act in appropriate ways. Either real force or the threat of force is used in an attempt to cause the acceptance of a conclusion. The threat may be veiled and nonphysical, as in a threat to withhold votes from one politician or to deliver them to an opponent, based on government actions that the politician may influence or control. In contrast, an open threat might include beatings, the brandishing of weapons, kidnappings, bombings, or even war. Appeals to force are the staples of gang warfare and revolutions.

This fallacy is very closely related to another emotion-based fallacy, the *appeal to fear*, which plays upon its audience's sense of danger; you may have seen useful but still fallacious examples in anti-drug and anti-drunk driving public service advertisements. The appeal to fear is a particular favorite of insurance companies, which capitalize upon our legitimate worries concerning potential losses of property, health, or even life itself.

Appeal to the People (ad Populum). This fallacy is the "my friends and fellow Americans" (or New Yorkers or teachers or Presbyterians or whatever group is being addressed) approach especially favored by some politicians, who hope to hide the flimsiness of an idea or argument behind a verbal screen that emphasizes attitudes or beliefs that are presumably shared. But emotional language will not suffice as supporting evidence.

Appeal to Pity (ad Misericordiam). This emotional approach tries to arouse the sympathy or pity of a person or group in order to influence a decision. For instance, a defense attorney may put her client's family prominently on display in the courtroom in an attempt to persuade the jury or judge that the future welfare and happiness of that family depends wholly on lenient treatment of the accused. A student might be using a similar approach when, having missed a class—or wanting to miss one— she or he tells an instructor about the illness, accident, or death of a relative or close friend. If the story is false, the student is both lying and appealing to pity; if the student is telling the truth, then this would be an instance of an appeal to pity only if the student was actually unmoved by the other person's misfortune and merely used it as an excuse.

Appeal to Tradition. This rather transparent fallacy is based on the assumption that whatever has existed for a long time, or has been repeated fairly regularly for a number of times, is somehow made legitimate by its history. But historical maltreatment of others, for instance as members of a minority group, certainly cannot justify continuation of that bad behavior; it should be easy enough to think of examples of the appearance of this fallacy in arguments involving civil rights, women's rights, animal rights, and the like. The person proposing to maintain a tradition that is dangerous, oppressive, or cruel should be made to provide reasons or backing, beyond the mere fact of historical precedent, as support for the continuation of that tradition. Just because a person has never worn a seatbelt is not a valid reason for refusing to do so.

Argument ad Hominem (at the Person). This emotional fallacy occurs when someone attacks an adversary's character in the course of an argument. One familiar and open form of the fallacy involves *name calling*, which occurs when a person's ideas are criticized because he or she has some apparent background flaw, such as being a reformed alcohol or drug abuser, or having flunked out of college, or even having served a prison sentence. At other times the fallacy may be more subtle, for instance through the use of familiar psychological labels for neuroses, such as inferiority complex, compulsive behavior, Oedipus complex, and so forth. However, such criticisms, even if true (frequently they are not, or else they are overstated), are generally irrelevant to the points in dispute to which attention must be directed to neutralize this fallacy.

The *genetic* or *stereotypical fallacy* is closely related. In this case, a person's ideas are criticized because of his or her race, sex, religion, nationality, and the like. But even if suspect because of possible self-interest, a feminist's ideas about abortion or a police officer's ideas on capital punishment may be perfectly sound. Certainly in fairness we ought to try to keep the background of a person separate from the ideas she or he supports, and ought to accept or reject those ideas on logical, not emotional, grounds.

A pernicious subvariety of these two fallacies is labeled *poisoning the well*. In this case, an attack is made on a person's background or character, or on a person or group originating an idea, before the argument has actually begun.

Bandwagon. This familiar fallacy is really a variety of the appeal to fear, for it profits from our desire to be part of a group, or "in the parade." Thus, because we don't want to be left out, we "jump on the bandwagon." Accordingly, we are often fallaciously encouraged to buy a product because it is the most popular (or so its commercials claim), or we may be urged to support a candidate who is shown by the polls to be ahead in a political race. Yet we should depend first on logical, not emotional, reasons for the choices we make. The teenager's familiar claim, "Everyone else has one," is not a logical reason; "Everyone else" can be wrong again, just as they have often been before.

Begging the Question (Circular Reasoning). This fallacy might be classed as formal rather than material, for in it the conclusion of a deductive argument is contained among the deductive argument's premises: "Of course cocaine users lack will power. That's why they're cocaine users." This fallacy is very difficult to notice when buried in a lengthy argument or when it is expressed in difficult language, as in this example: "To allow every person unrestricted freedom of speech must always be, on the whole, advantageous to the state; for it is highly conducive to the interests of the society at large when each individual citizen enjoys the liberty, perfectly unlimited, of expressing his or her sentiments." In simpler words: "Free speech is good for the state because it's good for the state when there is free speech." Taking an argument through a full circle does not prove anything.

Dicto Simpliciter (Unqualified Generalization). This fallacy results when an argument is based upon a generalization that is completely inclusive and presented as unequivocally true in all circumstances. "Milk is good for you" is simply not true for everybody; neither is "Alcohol is bad for your health" (physicians sometimes recommend an occasional glass of beer for nursing mothers, to aid their milk flow, and may suggest a daily moderate amount of alcohol for some aged patients).

Either/Or (False Dilemma). This fallacy denies that there is any intermediate possibility between two extremes. Examples include: "Ms. Franklin must be a communist; she won't join the other local business owners in the Chamber of Commerce." "Mary has become an atheist since she went off to college; she hasn't been to church all semester." "Jason wants to become a killer; he just enlisted in the Army." Unfortunately, because such statements too often appeal to our prejudices and ignorance, we sometimes accept them as true without considering any probable alternative explanations.

Equivocation. This language fallacy is produced by accidental or deliberate misuse of two or more meanings of the same word or phrase in a statement. The ambiguous results may be amusing, sometimes in a grim way, as in these sample newspaper headlines: "Mass Murderer Receives Last Rights Before Execution," "Eastern Airlines Drops Union Pilots From Flights," "Doctors to Offer Poor Examinations." Equivocation can also occur in serious contexts, thereby causing critical disagreements. This is particularly so when abstract words such as "right," "guarantee," and "natural" are involved. Consider, for instance, the commonly used phrase "lifetime warranty." Without any qualifying information, how can you tell what either word means? Whose "lifetime"? What is covered by the "warranty"? The best policy in such cases is to be sure that all equivocal words are explained or defined, thus greatly reducing the possibility of misunderstandings that may be personally or financially damaging.

Faulty Analogy. This fallacy results when two subjects are compared, and while the two share certain similarities, their differences may be so important that they negate the value of the comparison; a familiar statement used to point out faulty analogy is "You're comparing apples and oranges." Of course, comparing the current world political situation to one 20, 50, or 100 years back may be interesting and even enlightening. But many factors have changed in the intervening time spans, so any conclusions based on this analogy are liable to be imperfect.

A related fallacy is *faulty metaphor,* which makes a comparison based on a few resemblances (or just one), usually to criticize. The language is sometimes lively and colorful, as in this example: "Knee-jerk milktoast-eating liberals always want to confiscate our guns, leaving us red-blooded American patriots nothing but our teeth and nails as protection for the living treasures of our homes against a host of drug-crazed perverts." But such metaphor-laden statements offer little basis for rational understanding or logical choice.

Hasty (Faulty, Sweeping) Generalization. This fallacy occurs when a proposed inductive conclusion is based on either a too limited sample or number of examples or else is based on unrepresentative examples. For instance, while you and most of your neighbors may prefer a certain presidential candidate or soft drink, that sample is so small and localized that it is of questionable value; neither the candidate nor the soft drink company would be wise to use the results as the basis for important decisions about the success of the candidate's campaign or the likelihood that Pepsi and Coke can be displaced as leading brands.

Hypostatization. This language fallacy results from the failure to differentiate between abstract and concrete words, speaking of abstractions such as *nature, justice, science,* and the like as though they were concrete. Although such abstract words can convey and create emotion, they are not specific enough to convey useful, precise information that will help in reaching a rational decision. "Have you thanked nature today?" is one example of hypostatization, as are "Love conquers all" and "Science puts industry to work."

Hypothesis Contrary to Fact. In this fallacy a hypothesis (a proposition offered as an explanation for the occurrence of some event or phenomenon) that is not true is used as the starting place for a deductive argument. "If Albert Einstein had stayed in Germany, the Nazis would have had an atomic bomb before the United States did" is one such fallacious argument, for Einstein did not stay in Germany, and even if he had, various other factors might well have prevented the Nazis from producing an atomic bomb before the United States did.

Irrelevance (Red Herring). This fallacy results when the argument or discussion deliberately or accidentally strays off the subject and begins to deal with another, even an unrelated, subject, just as dragging smoked (red) herring across a trail will divert hunting dogs from following their prey and lead them off in another direction. Thus, opponents of gun registration may display bumper stickers which read "If guns are outlawed, only outlaws will have guns." This slogan has emotional appeal (its ending assertion uses the *appeal to fear* fallacy), but it has fallaciously changed the point of contention from *registering* guns to *outlawing* them, thus misrepresenting the gun registration supporters' position.

Labored Hypothesis. This fallacy results when a hypothesis drawn from one body of evidence is more complex, unlikely, or unusual than an alternative one, for example, "Dozens of laboratory animals were released from their cages at University Medical Center during the night, and they escaped through an outside door whose lock was broken; there were no witnesses, but Medical Center personnel must have done it in order to get the local animal rights activist group in trouble with the police."

Non Sequitur. This fallacy's Latin phrase means "It does not follow." The conclusion is such an argument lacks a connection to the premises: "I grew up in Miami, therefore I have always wanted to be a movie star." This example is clearly nonsense, but sometimes the argument may go astray in a less obvious way:

"Free enterprise is being undermined by the federal government, which tells all companies how to operate, has taken over management of our farms, and even forces managers to cooperate with union organizers. Democracy is almost extinct in the United States." Perhaps this argument has quite a bit of emotional appeal for you and seems convincing. But you then must not have noticed how the argument shifted, for free enterprise is an economic system, while democracy is a political system; thus there is no connection between the premises and the conclusion.

Post Hoc, Ergo Propter Hoc (False Cause). Latin words that translate as "after this, therefore because of this" commonly identify this fallacy. The problem occurs when a person assumes that a cause and effect relationship exists just because one event follows another. But there must be a demonstrable causal link between the two events before such reasoning can be considered sound. An example familiar to us all is assuming that bad luck will occur if a black cat crosses our path. It's clear that we are being led astray by our superstitious natures, but most of us too often resort to similar fallacious reasoning, assigning our good and bad experiences to some questionably related causes.

Reductio ad Absurdum. This is another fallacy with a Latin name, here meaning "reduction to absurdity." An effective means of refuting another argument, frequently with a satirical effect, this approach, though fallacious, makes an idea or an attitude seem to be irrational by exaggerating or extending its logical consequences, sometimes to the point of ridiculousness. The classic example of this approach is Jonathan Swift's essay, "A Modest Proposal," in which he ironically recommends that, to solve the terrible poverty in eighteenth century Ireland, the poor should sell their children to be used as food. A modern example resulted after former President Reagan, in a speech opposing environmental legislation, asserted that trees gave off greater quantities of deadly pollutants than industrial plants do. At his next public appearance, environmental activists ridiculed his statement by showing up costumed as trees and carrying signs that read: "Stop Me Before I Kill Again!"

Slippery Slope (Domino Theory). This fallacy, like *post hoc, ergo propter hoc,* has its basis in the fallacious linking of causes and effects. A slippery slop argument hypothetically links a series of events, asserting that if the first event takes place, then the other will follow, just as one false step on an icy hill may result in an injured person at the hill's bottom, and just as a row of closely spaced dominoes placed on their ends will topple, one after another, if the end one is pushed over. But often events are not as closely linked as those carefully placed dominoes (a *faulty analogy* is also present here), and therefore bans on automatic weapons and cheap handguns need not lead inevitably to the confiscation of Great Grandpa's hunting rifle that has been passed down in the family for generations. Stopping places usually exist along the way, and pointing those out is one appropriate way to refute such fallacies.

Special Pleading (Card Stacking). This inductive fallacy results when certain evidence, generally numerical or statistical, is emphasized, while other evidence, equally or even more pertinent, is suppressed or minimized. When we are told by the local power company's news release that its coal-burning smokestack has new pollution control devices that have reduced its sulphur dioxide emissions (the key ingredient in acid rain) to one-half of one percent, that may seem commendable, but then we realize we haven't been told what that "percent" is part of. Eventually we learn that the percent is of the total volume of emissions, which amount to 10 tons per day, so that annually the plant is still producing over 18 tons of sulphur dioxide, or enough to form quite a few railroad tank cars of sulphuric acid. Mark Twain indirectly referred to just this fallacy when he said, "There are three kinds of lies: lies, damn lies, and statistics." News media can be guilty of this fallacy in a modified form if they feature the activities of certain political figures or government programs that they favor and ignore or give abbreviated coverage to those that they do not.

Syntactic Ambiguity. This language fallacy is the result of faulty sentence structure. Sometimes parts are misplaced: "Sam cut firewood with his best friend"; "The students couldn't understand why Shakespeare was so well liked in high school"; "The professor explained why plagiarism is wrong on Monday." Sometimes multiple or complex questions are phrased so they are self-incriminating whether answered yes or no: "Have you stopped spending all of your money on beer?" or "Are you still cheating on tests?" Similarly, because pauses and emphasis on words can create different meanings, they can result in deliberate or accidental misunderstandings. If you repeat this short sentence, "She slapped him," three times and emphasize a different word each time, the potential for ambiguity will be obvious.

Transfer (False Authority). This fallacy is based on the principle of favorable association, even though there may be little or no logical connection. In one variety, the subject is identified with some idea or entity that is inherently pleasing or attractive. Any viewer of television or reader of popular magazines is constantly bombarded with advertisements or commercials that use transfer. The association may be with having a good time (see soft drink, alcohol, and cigarette ads) or with pleasant memories (food and telephone) or with looking better (clothing and personal care products, always featuring attractive models).

Another variety of transfer, also favored by advertisers, is related to the use of authority in an argument, except here the prestige or reputation of a respected or admired person or institution is used to support an idea or product. This *false authority* fallacy occurs when the person featured is removed from his area of expertise; thus Ray Charles and Joe Montana are great stars in their respective fields of popular music and professional football, but their claims of value regarding soft drinks are not likely to be any more accurate than the average person's—and furthermore they are being paid considerable sums for their promotional efforts. In a related way, biblical references may be used fallaciously to support political or other ideas. In any case, the association or identifications should certainly be examined for a logical connection; if there is none, the fallacy of transfer or false authority is present.

Tu Quoque. This Latin term for "you also" or "you're another" identifies a fallacy that avoids the subject or deflects questions or accusations by making similar accusations against an opponent. For instance, a person being criticized for eating a second candy bar might reply to the critic, "Well, you're *already* too fat or you'd take a *third* one!" or "If you weren't on a diet, you'd be reaching for a Snickers yourself!" Neither of these responses provides logical reasons for eating a second candy bar, but each instead attempts to divert attention elsewhere.

Formal Fallacies

Formal Fallacies result from the improper construction of syllogisms, which form the frameworks of deductive arguments. Such fallacies are therefore errors of structure or form. In order to understand formal fallacies, you will also need to have a working knowledge of the simple syllogism. A *syllogism* is a series of three statements arranged according to this formula:

All humans are mortal.	(First or major premise)
Jill is a human.	(Second or minor premise)
Therefore, Jill is mortal.	(Conclusion)

The syllogism must meet certain standards of construction and arrangement in order to be *valid,* or logically consistent. First, the syllogism must consist of three two-term statements: two propositions *(premises)* and a *conclusion,* as in the example just given.

Second, it must consist of three different *terms* ("humans," "mortal," and "Jill" in the above example); one term must appear in both premises but not in the conclusion, and each of the other two terms must appear in one premise and in the conclusion. The term that appears in both premises but not in the conclusion ("human") is called the *middle term;* the other terms ("mortal" and "Jill") are called *end terms.*

Third, in order to be valid a syllogism must conform to three simple rules, the first and most important being that the middle term must be *distributed* only once. To be distributed, a term, whether middle or end, must appear *either* as the subject of a universal statement (one that by means of such words as "every," "all," or "no" totally includes or totally excludes all members of a class or group) or as the predicate term of a negative statement. (For our purposes, a predicate term is one that completes either the verb "to be" or some other linking verb—as, for example, "eater of plants" does in this negative statement: "Fido is not an eater of plants.")

A term is *undistributed* if it is the subject of a particular statement or the predicate term of a positive statement. For instance, in this syllogism,

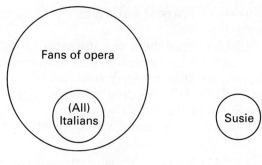

FIGURE A.1

All Italians are fans of opera.	(First or major premise)
Susie is not a fan of opera.	(Second premise)

Susie is not an Italian.	(Conclusion)

the middle term, "fan(s) of opera," is undistributed in the first premise, since it is the predicate term of a positive statement, and distributed in the second premise as the predicate term of a negative statement. The end term "Susie" is undistributed in both of its positions, being the subject of a particular statement, while "Italians" is distributed twice, once as the subject of a universal statement ("*All* Italians . . .") and once as the predicate term of a negative statement (". . . is *not* an Italian").

The case of the end term "Italian" also illustrates rule two: No end term may be distributed only once in a valid syllogism. The third and final rule, as you will see demonstrated later, is that no valid syllogism can have two negative premises.

Either to understand why this last rule is necessary or to determine the validity of any syllogism, you will probably find it useful to draw circles to represent the various classes or groups and individuals named. For example, draw a large circle to represent the class consisting of fans of opera. Then, since all Italians are fans of opera, draw a small circle within the large circle to represent all Italians (you must, of course, leave room for fans of opera from other countries). Now, where does Susie's small individual circle go? Outside both larger circles, of course (see Figure A.1). But what happens if you then give the syllogism two negative premises, like this:

No Italians are fans of opera.
Susie is not a fan of opera.

What can you conclude? By drawing the circles you will see the you cannot really say anything exclusively and positively about Susie's nationality, for you do not know exactly where to place her circle (see Figure A.2). Susie may or may not be an Italian, which is not a useful conclusion. Now you should understand why rule three is important. By using the circles you should also be able to determine why the rest of the standards and rules for validity are important.

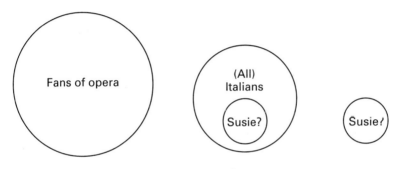

FIGURE A.2

So far we have been concentrating on the question of the *validity* of the deductive syllogism. A quick glance at the sample syllogisms and circles, however, will suggest that the question of *truth* in a deductive syllogism is a separate one, for while it is commonly known that many Italians are indeed fans of opera, we can also be reasonably sure that at least some Italians prefer rock, jazz, or other musical entertainment. However, and this is a point that you must understand about deductive arguments, *if* a syllogism meets the standards of *validity*, and *if* the premises are accepted as true propositions, whether intuitively, inductively, or even deductively as conclusions of other syllogisms, then the conclusion of the syllogism in question is logically and undeniably true. Of course, few of us consciously use deductive syllogisms in the formal sense, although we do use deductive logic daily, often in an abbreviated form called an enthymeme.

An *enthymeme* is a syllogism with one of its three statements missing or unstated, and perhaps with its conclusion preceding its premise(s), as in this case: "Susie's not Italian. She doesn't like opera." Clearly the first premise, "All Italians are fans of opera," is absent, perhaps because the speaker thinks it is too obvious to need mentioning. Yet the speaker's audience, if they are critical thinkers, might realize the problem with the truth of the unstated first premise and reject the speaker's conclusion about Susie's nationality. (They could also reject the conclusion without really knowing exactly why, perhaps on the basis of "common sense.") Similarly, another speaker might state, "Dr. Green probably eats meat, since she is a veterinarian." But this conclusion might also be false, perhaps because the syllogism is invalid:

> Most veterinarians eat meat.
> Dr. Green is a veterinarian.
> _____
> Dr. Green eats meat. X

Here the middle term ("veterinarian") is not distributed, for "most" is not a word that includes or excludes all of a class or group. Or even if in valid form, with "all" substituted for "most," the first premise or proposition could be rejected as inductively false by a person who knows of one or more veterinarians who are vegetarians.

This is not to suggest, though, that all enthymemes are either invalid or false. Instead, you should be aware when they are being used and examine the total syllogism for validity and for true, acceptable propositions before you agree with or reject any deductive conclusions.

The five most common formal fallacies are discussed below. If you care to do so, you can use scratch paper to draw and appropriately label circles for each argument, in order to determine its invalidity.

1. *The four-term argument.*

> All persons who drink to excess are alcoholics.
> Sandra drinks beer.
> _____
> Therefore, Sandra is an alcoholic. X

The four terms here are "persons who drink to excess," "Sandra," "drinkers of beer," and "alcoholics." To make the argument a valid one, it must be shown that Sandra drinks to excess, thus eliminating the fourth term and providing a properly distributed middle term, "persons who drink to excess."

2. *Improperly distributed middle term.* This fallacy results when the middle term of a deductive syllogism is distributed more or less than once. For instance, in this invalid syllogism the middle term, "fans of opera," is not distributed at all:

All Italians are fans of opera.
Wolfgang is a fan of opera.

Wolfgang is an Italian. X

Nothing prevents people of other nationalities from joining the class of fans of opera, since the middle term is not distributed. So Wolfgang may well be of some nationality other than Italian. If the middle term is distributed more than once, this invalid syllogism results:

All Italians are fans of opera.
All Italians are friendly.

?

When the middle term drops out, as it always does in a valid syllogism, we are left with no conclusion at all, for some fans of opera are not Italian and some friendly people are not Italians; we can assert nothing validly or positively about the friendliness of non-Italian fans of opera.

3. *Unequal distribution.* In this fallacy, an end term is distributed only once, as in this example:

All Italians are fans of opera.
No Germans are Italians.

No Germans are fans of opera. X

Here, since the end term "fans of opera" is distributed in the conclusion (as the predicate of a negative statement) yet not distributed in the premise (as the predicate of a universal statement), it violates the basic rule of deduction that no end term may be distributed only once.

4. *Two particular premises.* No valid conclusion may be drawn from two particular premises. Consider this example:

> Some tall persons are awkward.
> Jim is a tall person.

> ---
>
> Therefore, Jim is awkward. X

Maybe he is, and maybe he isn't. No positive or negative conclusion can be reached.

5. *Two negative premises.* This fallacy results because no valid syllogism may have two negative premises, for then no exclusive and no positive conclusion can be drawn. For example,

> No Australians have ever lived in my neighborhood.
> Kathleen has never lived in my neighborhood.

> ---
>
> ?

Kathleen may be an Australian or not. We can't say for sure either way.

You've now finished this short discussion of material and formal fallacies. You'll probably find it useful to turn back now and then to this section and to review it, just to maintain your ability to detect fallacies in arguments created by you and by others.

Glossary

The following list provides brief definitions of key logical, rhetorical, and stylistic terms arranged alphabetically. Italics show that a word or phrase found in a definition also has its own definition in this glossary.

abstract words: Words representing ideas, feelings, or generalities (peace, hate, food) as opposed to *concrete words*, which represent specific and particular objects or things. Since their meanings are sometimes ambiguous and their subjects cannot be readily visualized or otherwise imagined, abstract words are usually less effective than concrete words. However, only abstract words will serve in certain contexts and must be used; in such cases the writer should not assume the *audience* agrees with or even understands the use of abstract words and should make some effort to define such words.

allegory: A kind of *narration* based on an extended *metaphor* or pattern of symbols in which persons, places, and things are associated with meanings in the basic story, but also with another, correlated set of meanings (and perhaps persons, places, or things) which lie outside the original narrative. The characters in an allegory are often personifications of abstract qualities such as virtues or vices; in some allegories, the names of characters make clear the association with the abstract qualities. Familiar varieties of allegory include some parables of Christ and those nursery tales or fables which have animal or machine characters who talk and act like representative human types.

allusion: A brief reference to a person, place, thing, or event, or to a literary work or passage. Sometimes classified as historical, literary, or topical (current events), allusions are comparisons used by writers to expand on or clarify ideas.

analogy: A comparison of two things that are alike in some but not in all respects. Analogy can be an effective aid in communicating in speech or in writing because it helps one's audience understand a strange or difficult concept or thing by reference to one that is familiar and similar. Thus, African wedding customs might be compared to American ones, or the flow of electricity in a wire to the flow of water in a pipe.

anecdote: A brief story that illustrates a concept or idea.

argument: The systematic process of providing proof to support a conclusion; the support for a *claim.*

argumentation: One of the three basic forms of *prose* (sometimes called modes of discourse). Because it often uses one or more of the other forms *(exposition, narration, description),* it may be confused with them, particularly exposition. The key difference is in purpose: the writer of argumentative prose assumes there is more than one side to the subject being discussed, but intends to resolve the conflict by influencing the reader to favor one side. A distinction may be made between *logical argument* and *persuasion* (the former appeals to reason, while the latter appeals to emotions), but their aims are the same and they are often blended.

assertion: A specific declarative statement *(claim, proposition)* expressing a belief or opinion that the writer or speaker must support with *evidence* in order to gain the approval of an *audience.*

assumption: A statement or idea accepted or supposed true without demonstration or substantial proof.

audience: The person(s) for whom a piece of writing is composed. The best writers have a particular audience in mind as they compose their work, taking into account the intended audience's knowledge of the subject, its opinions or biases, and the like. Although the real audience may differ from the intended one, the writer seeking success must select and organize the material, determine *purpose,* and adjust *tone* with his or her perceived audience in mind.

authority: A person or a source of information presumed or known to be reliable. An appeal to authority, made by referring to such a person, or to that person's findings or work, is one way to support a *claim.*

backing: The support for a *warrant* or *assertion.*

bibliography: A list of works, usually on a specific subject or by a specific person or group of persons, normally appearing at the end of a research paper, scholarly article, or book.

cause and effect: An important *method of development* that focuses on results (effects) and the reasons for (causes of) those results.

claim: A statement or *assertion* that the writer of an *argument* must successfully support or prove. These can be classified as one of three types: claims of fact, claims of policy, claims of value.

classification: An important *method of development*, based on the technique of grouping together types or classes of persons, things, or ideas on the basis of shared characteristics.

cliché: A worn-out idea or expression, usually a comparison, that is so familiar that it no longer causes thought or calls to mind a visual image. "Good as gold," "beginner's luck," "happy as a lark" are examples; their use by a writer suggests mental dullness or laxity.

coherence: The integrated whole formed when the various parts of a sample of prose, such as a paragraph or an essay, fit together logically and clearly. Thus, the sentences that compose a given paragraph and the paragraphs that compose an essay should be arranged in logical order and their relationship(s) with one another should be clear. (See also *unity, transition.*)

comparison/contrast: An important *method of development* which uses the similarities and/or differences of two or more members of the same class of things or ideas as the foundation for orderly, logical, and informative analysis.

conclusion: The closing sentence, paragraph, or summary section of a piece of writing. The conclusion should add a sense of unity and finality to the entire composition while directing attention to the main point(s). Practices to avoid include apologizing, rambling, repetition, and stopping in the middle of things. In an *argument*, the specific statement or *assertion* being proven by a line of reasoning.

concrete words: Words that stand for tangible objects or things, ones that can be perceived by the human senses. Due to their sensory appeal, concrete words (in contrast to *abstract words*) help a writer's *audience* to imagine the object or thing, thereby adding clarity of expression while reducing ambiguity.

connotation: The secondary or associational meanings that most words have, due either to their contexts or to their emotional overtones for readers. (Compare to *denotation.*)

deduction: A traditional method of *logical argument* in which a *conclusion* (specific statement or *assertion*) is derived from *premises* (general or inclusive statement or *assertions*). (Compare to *induction.*)

definition: Normally, a synonym for or a statement of the exact meaning(s) of a word, such as can be found in a dictionary. Also a *method of development* used to support a *claim* by clarifying or demonstrating the meaning of a word or concept.

denotation: The literal or dictionary meaning of a word, as opposed to its *connotation.*

description: A form of writing relying mainly on *concrete words* to convey exact sensory impressions of persons, places, and things, and therefore often valuable in supporting a *claim;* frequently used in conjunction with *narration.*

details: Individual parts of an item being described, or of an event being narrated; concrete particulars, such as lead pipe, 6 feet tall, blonde hair, legs crossed.

diction: The selection of words in writing or speaking, with emphasis on accuracy, appropriateness, and *level of usage.* (See also *tone.*)

documentation: The references a writer provides in order to show the source(s) of any borrowed or adapted information. (See also *bibliography.*)

editing: The process of correcting writing problems of *diction,* grammar, or phrasing. (See also *proofreading, revising.*)

enthymeme: A *syllogism* with an unstated or implied *premise.*

essay: A *prose* composition that attempts to explain something, discuss a topic, express an attitude, or persuade an *audience* to accept a *proposition.*

evidence: Facts, statistics, or other data used to support a *claim* or *thesis.*

exemplification: Sometimes called illustration, this is the most important *method of development,* especially useful for supporting a *claim;* it is based on the use of examples to clarify a subject or to support a *thesis.*

exposition: One of the basic *modes of discourse* or forms of *prose,* which are classified according to *purpose.* The writer of exposition attempts to explain a subject, or to inform the intended *audience* about it.

fact: Something accepted as true based on experience or observation, and which all reasonable persons normally will accept as true (wood comes from trees; seat belts save lives; milk contains calcium). A *claim* of fact is usually not debatable. Contrary to fact is *opinion.*

fallacy: Any of various types of deceptive, erroneous, or false reasoning that cause an *argument* to be logically flawed, even though the fallacy may be psychologically persuasive and seem to be true. (A complete discussion is provided in "A Short Guide to Material and Formal Fallacies," beginning on p. 377 in the Appendix.)

figurative language: Writing that includes one or more figures of speech, among which are *allusion, metaphor, simile,* and *personification.* Figures of speech are brief comparisons based on the intentional departure from the ordinary or literal meanings of words in order to achieve such desired results as clarity, freshness, or additional special meanings.

focus: Confining a subject to a single point of view. In order to provide appropriate and steady focus, a writer must especially keep in mind the intended *audience,* the *purpose,* and the *subject.*

free modifier: A modifier that is set off from the main clause by punctuation. Usually such modifiers are nonrestrictive, describing some part of the main clause or the main clause itself. They may be placed before the main clause, after it, or between the subject and predicate: *His hands in his pockets,* the hobo stood beside the lamppost. The hobo stood beside the lamppost, *his hands in his pockets.* The hobo, *his hands in his pockets,* stood beside the lamppost.

hypothesis: A *claim* presented as an explanation for some event or set of phenomena; also the *premise* for an *argument.*

induction: A method of *logical argument* in which a generalization (general statement or conclusion) is reached based on observation of representative things, actions, or other phenomena which serve as evidence. The best and most representative evidence must be sought before a generalization is offered, and even then it can only be tentative: the conclusion that a new neighbor is a physician because she leaves home at irregular hours, carries a beeper and a black bag, and drives a new Cadillac may be true—or she could be a drug dealer.

introduction: The beginning of a piece of writing, varying in length from a single sentence to several pages or even a chapter, depending on the complexity of the subject and approach and on the work's length. An effective introduction identifies the subject, limits the subject, interests the *audience,* and may indicate the work's overall organization.

invalid: Not following the rules of *logical argument,* especially in the case of *deduction.* An invalid *argument* is not in the proper form, so its conclusion does not necessarily follow from its *premises.*

irony: A manner of writing or speaking so as to present one surface meaning while also presenting one or more veiled, contrasting meanings. Sometimes used quite effectively for argumentation, it may employ such specific techniques as exaggeration, sarcasm, or understatement.

level of generality: Any of the points existing between the extremes of abstract and concrete. For example, if we place *abstract words* at one end of a scale and *concrete words* at the other end, we might have a scale that looks like this:

> abstract word: vehicle
> automobile
> Chevrolet
> concrete word: Corvette

Level of generality refers to any point on this scale; *Chevrolet* is at a higher level of generality than *Corvette*; *vehicle* is at the highest level of generality; and *Corvette* is at the lowest level of generality. With modification we can achieve an even lower level of generality: *used Corvette convertible.*

level of usage: The kind of English, especially in terms of word choice and *syntax,* appropriate to one's *audience.* Frequently the levels are separated into four categories: general (consisting of words or phrases listed in dictionaries without special usage labels and suitable for both formal and informal writing); informal (based on words or phrases labeled "informal" or "colloquial" in dictionaries and though widely used by everyone, not always suitable in formal contexts); formal (basically a written form, ordinarily composed for a restricted audience consisting of specially educated or trained readers); nonstandard (words or expressions not part of the preceding categories; primarily spoken, these are labeled in dictionaries as "illiterate," "slang," "vulgar," and so on). It should be obvious that the level of usage in a letter to an ex-roommate might be primarily informal or even nonstandard, while general or even formal would be the choice for a letter to a prospective employer.

logical argument: A kind of *argumentation* which relies on an appeal to reason (in contrast to *persuasion,* which appeals primarily to emotions). The *tone* is often reserved and detached, while *deduction* and *induction* are relied upon to carry the rational force of the argument.

metaphor: A figure of speech that suggests an unstated comparison between one object and another, basically unlike object. Unless a *cliché,* the metaphor can make prose more lively and interesting, as well as increase the clarity of the writing. Example: The farmer's brick red hands rested on the snowy hospital sheet.

method of development: Those organizational techniques used in *paragraphs* or larger pieces of *prose*, especially *argumentation* and *exposition*, with the intent of achieving the best rhetorical effect on the intended *audience*. The most common methods are *cause and effect, classification, comparison/contrast, definition,* and *exemplification;* several or even all of these methods may be used at once in a piece of writing.

modes of discourse: The three *prose* forms, *argumentation, description-narration, exposition,* that may appear separately or in various combinations in a piece of writing.

narration: The process of telling about events, as in story form. Combined with *description,* this is one of the three basic *prose* forms (or *modes of discourse*). Often used for purposes of *argumentation* or *exposition,* it may also exist separately for its own sake.

objective: Expressing opinions or ideas based on detached observation, undistorted by personal feelings. (See also *subjective.*)

opinion: A belief confidently held but not necessarily shared by other reasonable persons (city life is better than rural life; no dessert tastes better than blueberry cheesecake; skydiving is fun). Compare to *fact.*

paradox: A statement that on its face seems self-contradictory or in conflict with general belief, yet nevertheless contains some truth. "No news is good news" is a familiar example.

paragraph: A separate portion of a composition, usually marked by indentation of its first written line, it expresses a thought or point related to the whole work but often is essentially complete by itself. Varying in length from one sentence to many, paragraphs may function as *introduction, conclusion,* and *transition* elements of an *essay;* other paragraphs form the main body of the essay and are used to develop or to present the subject.

paraphrase: Restating another person's words either (1) to make them more understandable or concise, or else (2) to show how those words are understood. In contrast with a *summary,* a paraphrase more closely approximates the length of the original version.

personification: A figure of speech in which nonhuman creatures, objects, or ideas are given human characteristics.

persuasion: A kind of *argumentation* that relies primarily on appeal to the emotions of an *audience* (compare to *logical argument*). Featuring a personal, even a friendly, *tone,* persuasion depends minimally, if at all, on *fact* and other elements of logical argument.

plagiarism: Presenting the words or ideas of another person as one's own, or without proper *documentation.*

premise: The *claim* or *proposition* on which an *argument* is based.

process: An important *method of development* whose parts are organized chronologically, as steps in a sequence.

proofreading: The correcting of a piece of writing for errors of mechanics (spelling, punctuation, capitalization, and the like) and of typing and transcription. (See also *editing, revising.*)

proposition: A statement that is to be affirmed or denied, usually offered near the beginning of an example of *argumentation.* Example: "All men are created equal" in the opening sentences of the Declaration of Independence.

prose: Written (or spoken) language that lacks metrical structure (as opposed to poetry or verse). It appears in three basic forms (or *modes of discourse*): *argumentation, description-narration,* and *exposition.*

purpose: The writer's intended goal. The purpose may be to describe *(description),* to tell a story *(narration),* to explain *(exposition),* to change the *audience*'s opinion *(argumentation),* or some combination of the four. In any case, the most effective writing is usually done when the writer clearly determines the purpose before beginning to write.

qualifier: A word or words used to limit a *claim* or *assertion,* indicating that it may not always be true as stated. Familiar examples of qualifying words include "often," "normally," "in general," "with few exceptions," and the like.

qualities: General or non-specific attributes or characteristics of items being described or of events being narrated; usually adjectives (good, pretty, small) or adverbs (slowly, awkwardly, intensely).

refutation: The process of examining statements, theories, arguments, and the like, and of showing logical reasons for rejecting them.

revising: The major reworking of a piece of writing, including changes in organization, development, approach to the subject, point of view, and the like. (See also *editing* and *proofreading.*)

rhetoric: Written or spoken language consciously composed to influence the thought and conduct of an *audience.*

rhetorical question: A question posed mainly for effect, with either no answer expected or an obvious answer implied. Usually a rhetorical question is presented to gain the assent of the *audience* to something the writer assumes is obvious.

simile: A figure of speech in which a similarity between two things is directly expressed, most often by using *like, as,* or *than* to link the pair. Example: Among the unpainted, tumbledown houses, the neatly kept white house stood, like a sound tooth in a rotting mouth.

slanting: Using *diction* (especially the *connotation* of words) and choosing facts so as to make the writer's argument seem better than it is. This practice may result in a *fallacy.*

style: The distinctive features of a piece of writing, especially as created by the writer's *diction, syntax, tone,* and arrangement of material.

subjective: Expressing opinions or ideas based on personal feelings or interests rather than on detached, disinterested observation. (See also *objective.*)

summary: A concise statement of the major points or ideas of a piece of writing.

support: Anything used to prove a *claim,* including not only *evidence* but also appeals to the values and emotions of the audience.

syllogism: An orderly process of *deduction,* consisting of a major premise (general or inclusive proposition), a minor premise (a specific factual proposition), and a conclusion drawn from terms or parts of each premise. The most famous syllogism is this one:

"All men are mortal." (major premise)
"Socrates is a man. (minor premise)
"Socrates is mortal." (conclusion)

The so-called "middle" term (in this case "men/man") is common to and links both premises; the "major" term becomes the predicate ("is mortal") of the conclusion; the minor term becomes the subject ("Socrates") of the conclusion. While syllogisms in their pure, orderly forms seldom appear in writing, they are used by us in our reasoning, and the student should have some knowledge of the basic process. (See also *enthymeme.*)

symbol: something which has a separate existence yet also represents or suggests something else. A familiar example is the cross, standing for Christianity.

syntax: The arrangement and relationship of words, phrases, and sentences.

thesis: A writer's assumption or specific statement, usually expressed in the *introduction*, that he or she then attempts to validate. A thesis statement or sentence (in a paragraph, called a topic sentence) often reveals the writer's *purpose*.

tone: The apparent attitude of the writer toward both *subject* and *audience*, especially as revealed by *diction*, selection of details and examples, and *syntax*. (See also *style*.)

transition: Any of various means of linking one topic (or aspect of a topic) to another. The most basic means of achieving effective transitions is logical organization, but a writer may also use such tactics as transitional words and phrases, repetition of key words and phrases, and repetition of sentence structure.

unity: The quality found in a piece of writing that is limited to a single idea or topic. In an essay that single idea is usually stated in the introductory paragraph and is called the *thesis*.

valid: Following the rules of *logical argument*. A valid deductive argument adheres to the correct form, and thus its *conclusion* necessarily follows from its *premises*.

warrant: An underlying assumption or general principle that provides a connection between the *claim* and its *support*.

Index of Titles and Authors